Editor-in-Chief
Asa S. Knowles

Chancellor, Northeastern University

THE INTERNATIONAL ENCYCLOPEDIA OF HIGHER EDUCATION

Volume 1

Contents, Contributors
Acronyms, Glossary

Jossey-Bass Publishers

San Francisco • Washington • London • 1978

THE INTERNATIONAL ENCYCLOPEDIA OF HIGHER EDUCATION
Volume 1

Asa S. Knowles, Editor-in-Chief

Copyright © 1977 by: Jossey-Bass, Inc., Publishers
433 California Street
San Francisco, California 94104
&
Jossey-Bass Limited
28 Banner Street
London EC1Y 8QE

Library of Congress Cataloging in Publication Data

Main entry under title:

The international encyclopedia of higher education.

    Includes index.
    1. Education, Higher—Dictionaries.   I. Knowles,
Asa Smallidge, 1909–
LB15.157   378'.003   77-73647
ISBN 0-87589-323-6 (set)
ISBN 0-87589-324-4 (v. 1)

Manufactured in the United States of America
    Composition by Chapman's Phototypesetting
    Printing by Hamilton Printing Company
    Binding by Payne Edition Bindery

COVER DESIGN BY WILLI BAUM
FIRST EDITION
        First printing: December 1977
        Second printing: November 1978

Code 7723

THE
INTERNATIONAL
ENCYCLOPEDIA
OF HIGHER
EDUCATION

Contents

Editorial Advisory Board

Board of Consultants

Encyclopedia Staff

Editor-in-Chief
Asa S. Knowles

Senior Editor
Joy Winkie Viola

Special Editors
Solveig M. Turner—National Systems of Higher Education
Joy Winkie Viola—Topical Essays
Gary E. Kraske—Fields of Study and International Documentation and
Information Centers
Hazel M. Williamson—Educational Associations
Gwen Lindberg Nagel—Fields of Study
Margo Hammond—Centers and Institutes of Higher
Education Research
Barbara L. Fisher—Reports on Higher Education

Associate Editors
Beverly A. Bendekgey—National Systems of Higher Education
Katherine Burnes—Fields of Study
Margo Hammond—Educational Associations
Jonathan C. Moody—National Systems of Higher Education and Reports
on Higher Education
Donna S. Sanzone—Fields of Study
Kathryn A. Wons—National Systems of Higher Education and Reports
on Higher Education

13a

Staff Editors
Margaret E. Casey, Marya E. Dantzer-Rosenthal
Antoinette Frederick, Carol E. Green
Elizabeth G. Labine, Catherine E. Lamb
James T. Murphy, Katharine O. Parker
Merrily D. Sterns, Janet Williams
Lynne E. Yerby

Reference Librarian
Gary E. Kraske

Project Secretary and Coordinator
Katherine Cummings McIntyre

Research Staff
Judith Quarrington DeCelles, Elizabeth H. Holmes
Elizabeth Lewis, Keiko Fujiwara Oh
Nancy E. Sciarappa, Chester A. Storey

Translators
Luis F. Jaramillo, Madeleine W. Weiss

Secretaries, Editorial Assistants, and Staff
Susan M. Killian, Gayle D. Otis
Elizabeth G. Pinson, Evelyn I. Sibelle
Frances M. Slowe, Mary T. Casilli
Robert J. Donovan, Barbara Riley

Clerical and Student Assistants
Robert Bentley, Robert Canavazzi
Patricia M. Conville, Judith Ragnow
Suzanne M. Sack, Beverly Solinger
Pamela Stewart, Elizabeth Swett
David Tilden

Staff Assistant
Michael Fumicello

Foreword

The compilation of an encyclopedia of higher education, even if it were on a state or national scale, is a test of formidable intellectual resourcefulness, discipline, and stamina. The subject is not easily reduced to constant, unqualifiable definitions and neat distinctions. Even for such basic concepts as *college, university, curriculum,* and *faculty,* the points of reference are always shifting. For every example, there is a variation. Moreover, higher education is concerned with colleges and universities not only as places and things but also as institutions that mirror the concerns of humanity and the broad range of knowledge which is at humanity's disposal. The vastness of such concerns and the variety of academic disciplines to which they give rise seem beyond the grasp of even the most able and talented scholars.

When such efforts have an international dimension, not just a local or regional one, the task borders on the impossible. Yet, in these volumes of *The International Encyclopedia of Higher Education,* this nearly impossible task has been accomplished. A labor of five years, it was performed with a thoroughness and integrity that should earn its editors and contributors for many years to come the admiration of all persons seriously concerned with higher education.

Editor-in-Chief Asa S. Knowles explains that this important work was undertaken because of a growing sense of internationalism and interdependency among institutions of higher education throughout the world. In these days of international scholarly conferences and multinational cooperation, the need for clear and consistent information about different higher education systems throughout the world is expanding and such information will have increasing value as a means of facilitating mutual understanding among the participants in such endeavors. For that reason alone, it is good that this *Encyclopedia* has been compiled. But there is an even more fundamental reason: the need to understand the universality of efforts to teach and learn at advanced levels.

As others have pointed out, knowledge itself is not the possession of one person or one nation. The great diversity of institutions and systems of higher education is caused not by differences in the substance of what is sought and taught so much as by differences in the uses of learning and the ways of seeking and teaching. To know about such differences is to understand not only why professors or administrators organize themselves and do things differently in various countries but also to acquire an awareness of alternative ways of doing what persons engaged in higher education do everywhere in the world. To the degree that such alternatives are transportable, knowing about them gives us greater flexibility in adjusting to current problems and future opportunities. The transportability of alternatives is made possible in many cases by the universality of knowledge.

Another universality is that of the people higher education most directly serves. Everywhere, these are predominantly young persons. And in most societies, young people have become almost displaced persons, with ambiguous roles in the world of work, in the life of their communities, and even in their own families. In many societies, higher education is also serving older persons in greater numbers. Some of these older students also have ambiguous places in society due to such factors as obsolescent job skills and new roles and opportunities that are emerging by reason of changes in class, racial, and sexual attitudes. Higher education is providing mechanisms for facilitating the integration of the displaced young and the older persons who are in transition within the general society of many nations. Today, the efforts of colleges and universities only begin to meet the challenges of the situation, but they will surely be called upon to give more attention to these problems in the future. So the more we know about higher education in all countries, the better we will understand its possibilities and limitations in this increasingly important context.

For readers grounded in the European tradition, this *Encyclopedia* may well awaken new interest in higher education in non-European cultures. The articles on higher education in the People's Republic of China and the Arab world, for example, illustrate dramatically how colleges and universities may be shaped by political and religious philosophies that lie outside the traditions of the classical academies or the medieval universities of Europe. By contributing to this more cosmopolitan view of higher education, these volumes greatly enrich our understanding of the relationship between colleges and universities and the societies they serve.

In his preface to these volumes, Asa S. Knowles indicates that *The International Encyclopedia of Higher Education* may have a useful life of a decade or two. If one is concerned only with the currency of the factual information the work provides, that estimate may be optimistic. Everywhere, higher education is so dynamic in its adjustments to social and economic trends that hard, reliable data are quickly out of date. In another sense, however, Dr. Knowles' estimate is undoubtedly too modest. For one thing, it is not likely that such an ambitious undertaking will be attempted, much less completed, within another decade. More importantly, even when the information this work contains is no longer "current," it will surely be used as a valuable record of the development of the world's concerns and achievements in higher education until now and as an overview of the situation in the later half of the 1970s. And these years might prove to be historically significant ones for a long time to come, characterized as they are by soul searching and long-range planning in an era when colleges and universities almost everywhere are faced with uncertainty and adjustment. The conditions and trends recorded here may well mark the beginning of significant developments in the future. One cannot help but think of how much better oriented we might be to the developments of higher education in Europe if an encyclopedia comparable to this one had been available in 1770, or how much more certain of our understanding of American higher education we might be if such a work had been compiled in 1870. I suspect that, far into the future, educators and scholars will be grateful to the compilers of *The International Encyclopedia of Higher Education* for sparing them such regrets about information gaps for the 1970s.

In the past, Asa S. Knowles has provided us with many carefully prepared and widely consulted publications, including two major handbooks, that give the basis for understanding and for policy decisions on many questions in higher education. We are fortunate that he has drawn upon this rich experience as author and compiler, as well as on his skills and wisdom honed by years of practical service as an educator, to give us this important reference work. His achievement will not soon be repeated and certainly not surpassed—it is a monumental achievement impressively executed.

CLARK KERR
September 1977   *Chairman*
Berkeley, California   *Carnegie Council on Policy*
                                  Studies in Higher Education

Preface

In recent years higher education has been increasingly characterized by a growing sense of internationalism and interdependency among colleges and universities of all nations. Concurrent with these trends, colleges, universities, and other postsecondary institutions have assumed important new roles in meeting the needs of a global society. New nations are building, and older and more established nations are consolidating their gains. Those developing nations that are based on oil economies are enjoying the rapid expansion of forms and facilities for postsecondary learning. Educational conferences the world over are assuming multinational, regional, and international themes. In some instances, efforts are being made to internationalize the content and structure of entire educational systems.

These trends have given impetus to a great need for up-to-date global information about all aspects of higher learning. Sensing this need, Jossey-Bass Publishers invited me to serve as Editor-in-Chief of a new reference work offering a perspective on higher education that transcends geographical borders: *The International Encyclopedia of Higher Education*.

The decision to produce the *Encyclopedia* was greatly influenced by the international acceptance of the *Handbook of College and University Administration* (New York: McGraw-Hill, 1971), of which I was privileged to serve as Editor-in-Chief. The substantial overseas sales of the *Handbook,* which was devoted exclusively to the United States and Canadian practices and procedures, emphasized the need for a more comprehensive encyclopedic presentation of the policies and procedures governing higher education around the world.

It has been said that an encyclopedia bears the hallmark of the person who assumes the principal responsibilities for its production, such as the clasic example of the *Encyclopédie* of Diderot. And today, most educators agree that the newest edition of the *Encyclopedia Britannica* reflects the

19a

influence of Robert Hutchins and incorporates many of the structures and philosophies of the highly successful *Great Books of the Western World* and their *Syntopican*. As Editor-in-Chief I must acknowledge that I have been influenced in the organization and structure of the *Encyclopedia* by the reception and proved usefulness of the *Handbook of College and University Administration*. The *Encyclopedia* reflects my belief that administrative practices and procedures, often overlooked by education writers, should be accorded equal space with academic concerns. Administration is an area of concern sorely neglected in the prevailing international literature. Consequently, the most difficult international data to obtain are those for the administrative topics.

A second concern of mine was that the *Encyclopedia* encompass more than that which in various sections of the world is classified as higher education, postsecondary education, or tertiary education. The term *higher education* has been used in the title of the *Encyclopedia* with the thought that it will be most acceptable to all and readily understood. Information presented in the *Encyclopedia,* however, includes a considerable amount on postsecondary learning below the university level.

There is also some confusion about the words *national, international,* and *comparative* when describing global studies of higher education. The International Council for Educational Development (ICED) distinguishes between these various classifications as follows: "*National* studies are those in which the data and analyses tend to be drawn exclusively from one culture or nation; *international* studies are those which include coverage of more than one nation but usually in separate country-by-country chapters, with a minimum of actual comparative treatment; *comparative international* studies are those which draw upon comparative data and offer extended comparative analyses." The *Encyclopedia* includes studies in all three classifications.

Definition of Scope

The word *encyclopedia* in the title was selected because it, above all others, most clearly defines the nature of the contents. By common usage and definition, the titles *encyclopedia, dictionary of education, lexicon,* and *handbook* are all appropriate for a major comprehensive reference work; *The International Encyclopedia of Higher Education* combines the various features of each of these forms of reference material.

Prior to the publication of this *Encyclopedia,* there was no single compendium that served as a reference work on all aspects of higher education throughout the world. In the course of our research, the staff and I found that those people who are specialists in higher education tend to be knowledgeable about only one or more countries or areas of the world. Similarly, international publications about higher education tend to deal with single topics, single nations, or single geographical areas. Thus, *The International Encyclopedia of Higher Education* represents a first attempt to bring together in one publication all major aspects of international higher education. Worldwide contacts and continuing research have made it clear that this *Encyclopedia* will be the first among higher education publications to present in a global perspective national systems; academic fields of study; educational associations; research centers, institutes, and documentation centers; academic and administrative policies and procedures; and current issues and trends in higher education.

Aims and Objectives

The creation of a new encyclopedia suggests that existing works do not meet all the educational reference needs of the times. In an effort to identify and meet those needs it became important, at the very beginning, to define the aims and objectives of this new work.

Generally, there appear to be three primary functions that an encyclopedia is expected to serve: (1) be a storehouse of knowledge to which both the lay person and the specialist may refer, (2) be an educational interagent by which readers may be directed to additional material on a subject, and (3) be an historical record of the state of knowledge in a given field at a particular period in time.

To accomplish the first objective, all entries are presented at a level meaningful to the lay person, whose work may be indirectly associated with the field of postsecondary education, and at the same time presents material of sufficient depth to merit the attention of the specialist as well. All entries are written in such a way that it is possible for everyone to understand the major points being discussed.

No encyclopedia entry on any subject can be so all-inclusive as to serve as a comprehensive source of information to specialists in their own fields. But many experts in a given area have a lay person's knowledge of the status of their special interests in other countries. The international perspective offered by many of the entries will enlarge scholars' understanding of their own specialization. There is also a great need to help specialists better understand the work of their colleagues in related fields. The age of specialization has hindered communication among faculty, administrators, students, government officials, business people, scientists, and others in related policymaking roles. In this sense the *Encyclopedia* follows a horizontal more than a vertical structure, presenting a broad overview of several international aspects of higher education rather than an in-depth probe of a few selected topics. We hope that the *Encyclopedia* will enable readers to gain a comprehensive understanding of postsecondary education as a whole.

To create the educational interagent aspect of the *Encyclopedia*, we took a variety of steps to direct readers to additional source materials and discussions of related topics within the *Encyclopedia* that may further augment their understanding of a subject. The inclusion of information on world-famous libraries and archives is an extension of the interagent purpose of the *Encyclopedia*. On the advice of noted authorities in these areas, we developed a series of regional articles on major national archives of interest to researchers in the academic community. In addition, we compiled a list of libraries that have the world's largest and most accessible collections and sought articles from these institutions detailing their principal resources and availability to scholars.

Finally, although recognizing the role of an encyclopedia as an historical record of its time, it also became necessary for us to provide in some way for the issue of change. Those familiar with the longevity of an encyclopedia estimate the useful life of such a work as approximately fifteen to twenty years. There are some topical discussions that remain valid indefinitely; others are subject to revision with every changing government or fiscal appropriation.

Some educators have voiced the belief that an encyclopedia can do no more than summarize the achievements of an outgoing generation. I do not hold this view. A work such as *The International Encyclopedia of Higher Education*, which both discusses contemporary innovations and records historical accomplishments, will help set the pace on the educational race-tracks of the future every bit as much as it will record the successes and failures of races already run. Educational borrowing, especially on an international level, is a well-entrenched tradition in the academic community; for example, the structure of United States higher education was built on the foundations of the British college and the German research-oriented graduate school. In the 1970s mutual influences are so extensive that innovation and reform in one nation often have a profound impact on the development of other nations. It is important, therefore, that the *Encyclopedia* record major innovative thoughts, whatever their present stage of development, because such innovations may ultimately have worldwide implications.

During the years in which the *Encyclopedia* has been in preparation, the point frequently has been made that this is a work which, to have international acceptance, could be accomplished only if it were independent of any government or political organization. The editorial autonomy of the *Encyclopedia* has been ensured through the cooperation of a private, independent, academic institution—Northeastern University in Boston, Massachusetts, where I have served as President and now serve as Chancellor—and the cooperation of the publisher and a substantial number of individuals and foundations who contributed modestly to the financial underwriting of the project.

Many people suggested that it would take a decade to complete so vast an undertaking as an international encyclopedia of higher education, but the *Encyclopedia* has been only five years in the making. The initial years were spent surveying educational books, journals, monographs, and the educational supplements of prominent newspapers in an effort to determine those subjects having the greatest concern to higher education in all nations. This research continued throughout the five years the *Ency-*

clopedia was in preparation to guarantee the inclusion of current developments and changes in educational thought. During these formative years a concerted effort was made to structure the *Encyclopedia* so that it might supplement, rather than duplicate, established and highly regarded existing references in the field.

At various points during the post–World War II period, international surveys of education at all levels have been published. Some studies present national systems from the primary through the tertiary level; other studies select a single level but place their emphasis on a few significant topics. Still other studies are primarily a source of statistical records. Our goal was to combine these various approaches to produce an up-to-date compendium that would give insight into academic fields, educational agencies, and national systems as independent entities, while at the same time to show policies and procedures common to all.

Organization and Format

We gave considerable thought to the manner in which the *Encyclopedia* could be organized most effectively. The major debate was over alphabetization versus systematization. Initially we attempted a systematic grouping of materials, but eventually we determined that a single alphabetical presentation would be more in keeping with encyclopedic tradition and would be the easiest format for an international readership. Some variations occur, however, where we felt that the grouping of certain materials would reduce duplication of data and give readers easier access to related subjects. We created an extensive system of indexing, including cross references and *See also's*, to refer the reader to nonalphabetical entries. In addition, several names are often used for the same concept when higher education globally is discussed. The reader is urged to consult the indexes, the cross references, and the list of related *Encyclopedia* articles given at the end of many essays as guides to the full range of information available on the subject of concern.

Early in the definitive stages of the work we decided that no biographical information would be included because it would be impossible to determine, on an international basis, the names of those who ought to be recognized. In addition, there were considerable differences of opinion as to whether biographies in an encyclopedia of this sort should include the names of individuals still living. Some people suggested that only those persons of historical significance be included. But this was felt to be an improper criterion, particularly in developing nations, where failure to include living persons among the biographies would make no provision for influential national contemporaries in countries recently emerging from colonial rule.

A further point was that many published biographical collections are available, so the *Encyclopedia* would serve no new purpose by including such information. (Similarly, we decided not to single out any individual college or university for individual treatment because it would be equally difficult to establish international criteria for such a selection.) To other people, or to editors of future editions of this work, is left the awesome task of establishing international criteria for the selection of individuals whose efforts on behalf of national systems of higher education, fields of endeavor within higher education, government programs in support of education, and the newly established concept of international higher education clearly and universally qualify them for such honor.

Thus, having concluded the original plan for the work, our next priority was its execution. Research and consultation with advisers and consultants resulted in the evolution of five thousand individual entries. Over a period of several months these entries were consolidated to form the present listings. For administrative purposes the work was then organized by categories: (1) national systems of higher education, (2) topical essays, (3) fields of study, (4) educational associations, (5) research centers and institutes, (6) reports on higher education, (7) documentation centers, (8) a listing of acronyms, and (9) a glossary of terminology. We then further consolidated within each category by establishing definitive outlines for many of the entries to maintain control over the entire project and to avoid duplication of coverage by those writing about related areas. All manuscripts were prepared exclusively for the *Encyclopedia*. For a variety of reasons, not all the manuscripts originally commissioned were received. Also, some manuscripts were not accepted because it was felt that they did not follow the format or the standards desired. In some instances, last-minute assignments had to be made. In the final analysis, however, all major entries originally planned for the *Encyclopedia* were included.

A survey of the completed contents of the *Encyclopedia* reveals that more than 2000 persons were involved, serving as editorial advisers, consultants, contributing authors, bibliographers, reviewers, and sources of information. The *Encyclopedia* has approximately 1300 entries. The 588 authors, whose names are given in Volume 1 and at the end of articles, are located in 69 countries throughout the world, representing 211 colleges, universities, and academic institutions. Hundreds of other entries have been prepared by associations, organizations, and the *Encyclopedia* staff.

Nature of Contents

As stated above, the *Encyclopedia* contains several types of entries and various categories within those entries.

NATIONAL SYSTEMS OF HIGHER EDUCATION

This category consists of individual articles about the systems of education in 198 countries and territories. There are extensive articles about 136 countries. These articles outline the history of the country's higher education system; major legislation; types of institutions available; the relationship between the three levels of education (primary, secondary, postsecondary); admissions policies; administration and financing procedures; the nature of educational programs and the degrees and other awards offered; student financial aid and access to education; policies and requirements pertaining to teaching staff; research activities; and current educational problems and trends. There are brief descriptions for 62 nations and territories that presently offer limited or no opportunities for postsecondary education.

The information for this section was obtained from questionnaires and letters of inquiry to educational authorities (education officers within embassies, ministries of education, boards of education, and other pertinent governmental agencies) or to the institutions (university presidents, vice-chancellors, rectors, departments of education, or institutes of educational research). A number of articles were prepared by individual authors recommended for their expertise on the system in question by educational authorities, international agencies, or government or university officials working, studying, or on international exchange programs in the United States. In addition, we consulted standard reference works for verification of certain facts.

TOPICAL ESSAYS

There are 282 articles on contemporary topics in higher education, written by educational leaders from every region of the world. Whenever possible, these topical essays have been written from a multinational viewpoint. Some essays are more international than others. For some topics comparative data was available to the authors, but for other articles, such data did not exist. Nevertheless, we made a concerted effort to present articles in as much of an international perspective as possible.

The topical essays included in the *Encyclopedia* discuss economic, political, administrative, social, scientific, historical, and contemporary concerns in higher education. Articles on budget administration, the steady state, economic influences, and manpower planning reflect the economic concerns of the current educational scene. The political concerns are reflected in such topics as academic freedom and political persecution of academics. Some topics, such as accountability, reflect the movement of what was once an economic concern to the status of a political concern.

Administrative concerns are reflected in essays on accounting and financial reporting, governance and control, and the use of computers in higher education. In recognition of the universality of approach and understanding of basic concepts in these fields, we purposely presented articles on many administrative topics in accordance with United States practice. It is generally recognized that the United States has been one of the most progressive and innovative nations in the adaptation of general management principles to college and university administration. The acceptance by educators in the developing nations of the *Handbook of College and University Administration*, which, as mentioned in the opening statements, details United States and Canadian administrative practices, is a further testimony to this fact.

Social concerns are reflected in the topical essays on access to higher education, including access of minorities, women in higher education, and higher education for the handicapped. Articles devoted to science policies, research, and technology transfer reflect the scientific concerns of today. Historical perspectives are presented in several essays, but especially in those concerned with the history of higher education and in the eight articles on influences of major religions on higher education. Contemporary issues are discussed in essays such as those on individualized instruction, the open university, and trends in higher education. Several articles discuss various aspects of cooperative education and off-campus learning in recognition of the growing international interest in such programs.

In addition to topics directly related to the field of education, there are several entries on subjects of indirect importance. These entries include the discussions of national and international manpower planning and national science policies. We have made, however, every effort to discuss these issues in terms of their impact on higher education.

Several topical essays are presented in an "umbrella" fashion, whereby articles that are closely related in content are grouped under a single heading. Examples include Religious Influences in Higher Education, Adult Education, Governance and Control of Higher Education, and International Exchange. In some instances, articles such as the regional analyses have been structured according to geographical considerations. In the discussions of science policies, however, nations are categorized according to economic status. In many instances it was not possible to make a clear distinction between these categories. In Africa, for example, colonial traditions have created diverse educational patterns and economic levels within a single geographic area. Emerging African nationalism dictates, however, that we present our regional analyses of this area on a geographical basis.

Although similar outlines initially were prepared for the presentation of topics under umbrella headings, there are wide variations in the structure of the final essays. These variations are necessary because of cultural, socioeconomic, political, and geographical interactions present in higher education. Despite these variations, the umbrella presentations help the reader understand the similarities and dissimilarities that exist.

Some topical essays include information that will be foreign to the reader's experience. Many of the authors themselves discovered and readily admitted their own provincialism when trying to discuss a topic from a global perspective. The attempt to overcome such provincialism proved to be the greatest challenge, but, when achieved, the greatest reward. It is my hope that the publication of this *Encyclopedia* will serve as a catalyst for further international research in all areas of higher education.

The authors invited to present the topical essays are established men and women in their fields, most of whom have been selected on recommendation of their peers. We included the writings of not only those whose names are well known but also those younger individuals with fresh ideas who are attempting to develop international expertise. We also made every effort to obtain as authors qualified scholars from all regions of the world in order to present a variety of geographical, institutional, and individual points of view.

Upon being invited to contribute, authors were given detailed instructions indicating the nature of the articles they were to prepare. They were told to emphasize contemporary trends and analytical, comparative data. Historical background material was to be included only insofar as it was germane to the understanding of the contemporary scene. We asked all authors to submit outlines for approval in advance of the completed manuscripts. We reviewed these outlines for comprehensiveness, international content, and potential duplication of other entries. In many instances the final manuscripts also were reworked in cooperation with the authors to ensure clarity of presentation and as much international content as possible. We made every effort to avoid individual bias or prejudice on matters where honest differences of opinion occur. There are some topics and sections within topics that are quite controversial—controversy has been included when necessary for an honest portrayal of the topic under discussion. Theoretical discussion essays are a valid part of a pioneering publication of this sort, a function of which is to stimulate worldwide discussion of the materials included herein.

FIELDS OF STUDY

The 142 fields of study entries included in the *Encyclopedia* form perhaps the most complete reference source yet compiled. Each entry describes the nature of the field, provides information on the levels and programs of study available around the world, lists the major national and international organizations in the field, and includes a bibliographic guide to information sources in the field.

We studied four educational classification taxonomies in an effort to establish the *Encyclopedia* fields of study taxonomy: (1) *International Standard Classification of Education (ISCED)* (Paris: UNESCO, 1974; revised 1976); (2) Organisation for Economic Co-operation and Development (OECD), *Development of Higher Education, 1950–1967. Statistical Survey; Analytical Report* (Paris: OECD, 1970); (3) *School System—A Guide* (Strasbourg: Council of Europe, Council for Cultural Cooperation, 1965); and (4) *A Taxonomy of Instructional Programs in Higher Education* (Washington, D.C.: U.S. Department of Health, Education and Welfare, Office of Education, 1970).

The *Encyclopedia* taxonomy was based primarily on the *International Standard Classification of Education*. The *ISCED* was designed by an international committee under the auspices of UNESCO to facilitate the collection and compilation of educational statistics both internationally and within individual countries. As an international classification scheme, it is necessarily abstract in its approach in order to accommodate the many differences in international education. Therefore, its structure, although based on existing patterns of education found in many countries, does not reflect the exact educational situation of any one country, nor does its terminology exactly conform to that found in any one country. The *ISCED* covers higher education at three levels: (1) education, primarily technical and vocational programs, that leads to an award not equivalent to a first university degree or its equivalent (certificate, diploma, associate degree); (2) education that leads to a first university degree (baccalaureate, licence); and (3) education that leads to a postuniversity degree (master's degree, doctorate).

Although *ISCED* is presently the most comprehensive international classification of education, it does not include all significant fields of study, nor does it fully reflect many of the new trends and developments in higher education. Consequently, we added many important fields to the *ISCED* scheme, changed some fields of study descriptions, and made other modifications, based on the educational taxonomies consulted and the advice of experts and professionals in the fields concerned.

Nature of the field of study internationally. Each field of study entry includes an introductory essay that describes the nature of the field from an international perspective. Specifically, each essay consists of a brief definition of the field; branches or divisions of the field; related or allied subjects; history of the field as an academic discipline; recent developments, trends, or innovations; and a brief description of education or training in the field internationally.

Included among the 143 fields of study essays are several broad essays that provide a general overview of such major areas as the humanities, engineering, and the natural sciences. Individual fields within these areas are the subjects of separate essays.

Authors of the fields of study essays are, for the most part, professionals with an international perspective who are affiliated with institutions and organizations in the United States. To verify the information contained in the essays and to augment the international content, we often asked appropriate professional organizations to review completed entries.

Levels and programs of study. In most cases we adopted the levels and programs of study section of the field of study entry from UNESCO's *ISCED* descriptions. With the assistance of our authors and reviewers, we condensed and modified the descriptions; for those fields not listed in the *ISCED* taxonomy, we asked authors to provide comparable information.

Major international and national organizations. Major international and national professional organizations are often one of the best sources for up-to-date information. The *Yearbook of International Organizations*

(15th ed., Brussels: Union of International Associations, 1974) and directories in the various fields were our primary sources of information on international organizations. We tried to be as comprehensive as possible, but in those cases where it is not feasible to list all the major international organizations, we refer the reader to a source that has a more complete listing. In many fields, every major country of the world has at least one, and often several, important national professional organizations. Since in most cases it is not possible to list all the professional organizations, only the most active organizations (in publishing or membership, for example) and organizations able to provide educational information about the field are listed. In addition, there are references to other source materials; these references give the names and addresses of other national organizations in the field.

Principal information sources. We selected five categories of published materials offering basic information on each field: general references; current bibliographies; periodicals; encyclopedias, dictionaries, and handbooks; and directories. These categories are not exclusive because we deemed the type of information a particular source provides more important than the form in which it is presented. Materials included are, for the most part, recent publications considered most useful to an international audience. They were selected on the bases of relevance, importance, and availability. Works published in the world's major languages are included, but English-language sources predominate. In addition, such standard reference sources as A. J. Walford's *Guide to Reference Materials* (2nd ed., 3 vols., London: The Library Association, 1968–70; 3rd ed., 1973–) and Constance M. Winchell's *Guide to Reference books* (8th ed., Chicago: American Library Association, 1967 and supplements) were particularly helpful in the compilation of significant information sources.

General references include comprehensive guides to the literature, a representative sample of the many available introductions and histories available, and recent works providing comparative information on education and training in the field.

Current bibliographies given include major current abstracting and indexing services that provide international coverage of the literature in a given field.

Periodicals listed include a selection of the most important, highly respected, and scholarly publications of broad international value and interest. We included an international sampling of periodicals in the major world languages to portray the global scope of the periodical literature in a field of study. When available, a comprehensive international directory to periodicals is listed.

Only the most comprehensive encyclopedias, multilingual dictionaries, and standard handbooks for a field of study are listed.

Among the directories included are those that list educational facilities, research centers, institutes, and information centers for the field. We excluded directories listing biographical data only. We selected some outstanding research centers, institutes, and information centers for separate listing, but for the most part only directories to such centers are cited.

An information source guide in a general encyclopedia on higher education can offer only a sampling of the published literature; however, we included additional sources of information that will lead the reader more deeply into each field of study. In addition to the problem of making selections from the masses of published literature available, there is a further problem of obsolescence. New reference sources appear continually, as do new organizations. Also, existing organizations may change their names or addresses. Information presented herein was accurate when compiled, and revisions were made continually to keep the material as up to date as possible. In almost all cases the bibliographies were checked for accuracy and thoroughness by appropriate professional organizations or library subject specialists.

EDUCATIONAL ASSOCIATIONS

Some 314 national, international, and regional educational associations, organizations, societies, committees, and commissions of importance in higher education have individual listings in the *Encyclopedia*. (Hundreds of others are covered in articles on fields of study, national systems, and topical essays.) Most of these groups are nongovernmental, with large, broad-based membership. These groups serve as spokespeople for institutions of higher education or special groups of institutions and as legislative or public representatives for higher education or segments of higher education in a country or area.

There are five principal categories of associations and organizations included: associations of colleges and universities, associations of university professors, associations of rectors and vice-chancellors, higher education administrative associations, and student associations. Large interdisciplinary organizations and intergovernmental bodies deeply involved in higher education are also listed.

Consultations with embassy personnel, United Nations officials, research associates and heads of sections at the Library of Congress, Washington, D.C., and university administrators determined the final selection of entries. Numerous reference books, educational journals, and the statutes, statements, and publications of the organizations concerned were also reviewed during the selection process.

CENTERS AND INSTITUTES OF HIGHER EDUCATION RESEARCH

We devoted considerable time to establishing criteria for the selection of 91 centers and institutes to be included in the *Encyclopedia*. We had no desire to duplicate the many volumes on the subject already in existence, but we felt it was important to include centers and institutes that are of major significance in the study of higher education.

We sent a questionnaire to approximately 200 institutions whose purpose is research in higher education per se. Those institutions selected for individual presentation were chosen on the bases of their control and policy determination, sources of funds, activities and services in higher education, nature of educational research, number of permanent staff, and record of publication. (Other institutions are listed or described in articles on fields of study, national systems, and topical essays.)

REPORTS ON HIGHER EDUCATION

Educational reform has led to the publication of a large number of publicly and privately supported reports and recommendations on the future of postsecondary education. Reports that pertain to a single country and do not have international applicability are included when appropriate in the individual national systems essays. Reports of significant international interest are given individual treatment. The selection of the 71 reports so treated was based on an extensive review of the literature and consultation with members of the Editorial Advisory Board, Board of Consultants, and representatives of the major international organizations in higher education.

INTERNATIONAL DIRECTORY OF DOCUMENTATION AND INFORMATION CENTERS

Documentation and information centers refer to services that collect, process, and disseminate recorded knowledge. The *Encyclopedia's* International Directory, a guide to information sources on postsecondary education, obtained its material through a questionnaire mailed to national, regional, and international organizations concerned with higher education. It can be found at the end of Volume 9.

The 201 centers that appear in the directory were chosen because of their involvement in one or more of the following areas: collection of information pertaining to higher education; dissemination of information by mail, publications, exhibitions, or loans; and investigation and research. Also included are addresses of other documentation and information centers suggested by respondents to the questionnaires or listed in directories we consulted during research on the directory.

It is generally understood that documentation and information centers concentrate on data-processing and information-retrieval systems, whereas libraries have as their main province the acquisition and provision of knowledge. There are, however, numerous exceptions, such as libraries that fulfill both functions and organizations that disseminate information but have no libraries. Thus, the directory lists a wide range of institutions with a variety of international, regional, and national information.

The directory generally does not list university, national, or large general or public libraries. In the cases of small and developing countries, university libraries may be the only source of information on higher education and are therefore listed.

ACRONYMS

A list of acronyms designating organizations, associations, and government agencies of higher education throughout the world is included in the *Encyclopedia* as a service to readers.

GLOSSARY

A glossary of terminology is of paramount importance in an international publication of this sort. The *Encyclopedia* glossary was compiled from several sources, such as existing reference works in the field of higher education, including definitive though no longer up-to-date references like the *International Glossary of Academic Terms,* published in Paris in 1939 by the International Federation of University Women. Most terms in the glossary, however, were drawn from original materials prepared for the *Encyclopedia,* with the national systems essays and the topical essays contributing the greatest number.

All non-English terms are briefly defined in the text where they occur, and a uniform definition is used for such terms throughout the *Encyclopedia.* A more extensive definition is in the glossary. In addition, many English-language terms that may not be in common usage in non-English-speaking countries are defined in the glossary.

Summary of Contents

In short, the *Encyclopedia* contains a number of elements. *Descriptive* essays relate the historical development and current status of higher education systems or the status of individual issues within such systems. Examples include essays devoted to national systems of higher education; topical essays on such issues as academic freedom, tenure, or governance of higher education; and the brief description of major national and international educational associations.

There are also *instructional* entries presented in the "how to" style of a handbook. These entries detail contemporary administrative practices fundamental to the day-to-day operations of a college or university. Examples include the articles on building and construction administration, financial affairs, and institutional planning. These essays will be helpful to those trying to establish new institutions or to reassess operations or procedures in existing institutions.

The *definitive* article, a third type of entry, outlines the boundaries of a concept or term without interpreting or passing judgment on the process or policy under review. Examples include the numerous essays devoted to academic fields of study at the postsecondary level and the glossary of terminology.

Finally, there is a fourth category of essays, which is neither definitive, descriptive, nor instructional, but which is of paramount importance in a pioneering publication of this sort. This category consists of the *theo-*

retical discussion essays about selected issues in higher education, written by some of the world's leading educators. Such essays are presented in the hope that they will stimulate discussion among members of the academic community and all other people concerned with the development of an international perspective in postsecondary learning. Examples include the topical essays on accountability, manpower, and institutional research.

Editorial Advisory Board and Board of Consultants

A work such as this *Encyclopedia* could not be accomplished without the cooperation of professional organizations, educational associations, national and international government bodies, business concerns, library reference personnel, and the administration and faculty of the world's academic community. From the ranks of these constituencies we invited outstanding individuals to become members of an Editorial Advisory Board and a Board of Consultants, whose responsibility was to offer guidance on the content, organization, and format of the *Encyclopedia*.

The members of the Advisory Board and Board of Consultants gave generously of their time and expertise in the development of the entire *Encyclopedia* project. Initially these advisers and consultants were asked to pass judgment and offer recommendations on several thousand potential subjects. Once the final list of entries had been determined, we sought further recommendations from the advisers and consultants on specific categories of information, such as the criteria for selecting reports on higher education and major research centers and institutes to be included in the *Encyclopedia*.

Many members of the two boards also were helpful in suggesting and soliciting authors who could write about various subjects from a multi-national perspective. Many advisers graciously served as clearinghouses for other authors who were trying to obtain global data for their articles. Some board members reviewed manuscripts written on subjects of which they, as internationally recognized educational authorities, have special knowledge. Finally, most board members agreed to become authors themselves, preparing manuscripts about subjects of both regional and international significance.

Educators in all parts of the world can learn much from one another, and the *Encyclopedia* will provide an important new mechanism by which this learning can be accomplished. It is my hope, as Editor-in-Chief, that *The International Encyclopedia of Higher Education* will be instrumental in bringing about multinational technology transfer in the field of higher education.

September 1977   ASA S. KNOWLES
                                                             Editor-in-Chief

The Editor-in-Chief

ASA SMALLIDGE KNOWLES was chosen to be Editor-in-Chief of *The International Encyclopedia of Higher Education* because of his leadership and extensive experience in higher education. For nearly thirty years he served as a college or university president in addition to holding a wide variety of positions of responsibility and leadership in such diverse institutions as a land-grant university, an ivy league institution, three newly organized temporary colleges, a municipal university, and a large private university. Membership on two statewide educational planning commissions has involved him in educational planning, and serving as an officer of national and regional accrediting agencies has involved him with the preservation and development of academic standards. He is the principal spokesman for the cooperative plan of education in the United States and is known internationally for his writings in the field of higher education administration.

Asa S. Knowles has been a professor, Head of the Department of Industrial Engineering, and Dean of Business Administration at Northeastern University in Boston; Dean of Business Administration and Director of a new Division of General College Extension at the University of Rhode Island in Kingston; founding president of three temporary colleges in New York State, which were organized to serve veterans returning from World War II; Vice-President of University Development at Cornell University in Ithaca, New York; President of the University of Toledo in Toledo, Ohio; and President and Chancellor of Northeastern University, which has the largest enrollment of any private university in the United States.

Chancellor Knowles has served on numerous boards and commissions related to higher education in the United States. His positions have included the presidency of the New England Association of Schools and Colleges, which is the accrediting agency for all colleges, universities,

35a

and schools in the six New England states; and the chairmanship of the Council of the Federation of Regional Accrediting Commissions of Higher Education, a national organization that established policies and standards for all United States regional accrediting agencies, which accredit colleges and universities in the United States and some in other nations.

In the Commonwealth of Massachusetts, Chancellor Knowles has been Chairman of the Higher Education Facilities Commission, of the Commission on Postsecondary Education, and of the Association of Independent Colleges and Universities of Massachusetts. In addition, he was a member of the Commission on the Survey of Public Education, which planned and recommended the organization and governance of the public higher education system of the Commonwealth of Massachusetts. While he was President of the University of Toledo, he served in a similar capacity as a member of the State of Ohio Commission on Education Beyond High School. As Chairman of the National Commission for Cooperative Education in the United States, he has been active in promoting the widespread adoption of cooperative education in the United States and throughout the world.

In addition to his current position as Chancellor of Northeastern University, Asa S. Knowles is a trustee of Northeastern University and Deree-Pierce Colleges in Athens, Greece.

The Chancellor holds honorary degrees from fourteen colleges and universities, as well as numerous awards and certificates for distinguished service to higher education. These awards include the Bowdoin College Distinguished Educator Award; the Honor Society of Phi Kappa Phi Distinguished Member Award; the Hawaii Pacific College Fellow of the Pacific Award; the American College Public Relations Association Tiffany Glass Flame Award; and the Dean Herman Schneider Award for outstanding contributions to the advancement of the philosophy and practice of cooperative education, presented by the Cooperative Education Association of the United States.

Chancellor Knowles' publications include articles in many professional and educational journals and a textbook on industrial management. He is contributing author and editor-in-chief of the *Handbook of College and University Administration* (McGraw-Hill, 1970) and contributing author and editor-in-chief of the *Handbook of Cooperative Education* (Jossey-Bass, 1971).

The Chancellor is involved in numerous community and civic activities. As such, he is a director of the Shawmut Corporation, a bank holding company; director of the Shawmut Bank of Boston, N.A.; director of the Arkwright-Boston Manufacturers Mutual Insurance Company; and trustee of the Middlesex Mutual Building Trust.

To honor the contributions of Chancellor Knowles to the academic and physical development of Northeastern University and to the field of higher education, the Board of Trustees of the university has named a building and a research professorship for him, designated respectively as the Asa S. Knowles Center for Law and Criminal Justice and the Asa S. Knowles Research Professorship in Cooperative Education.

Recognition as an outstanding American educator has earned the Chancellor international acclaim and has motivated many educators from abroad to seek his counsel. This recognition caused him to become interested in international higher education and influenced his decision to undertake the compilation of *The International Encyclopedia of Higher Education*.

Alphabetical Listing
of Entries

Note from the Editor-in-Chief: I urge readers to use the various reference aids extensively since the contents presented here represent only the broad framework of the *Encyclopedia*—the specific detail of what is covered can be found in the name and subject indexes that contain over 10,000 major entries and approximately 40,000 subentries.

Volume 5

Volume 7

Classification of Entries

French Polynesia   *1771*
French Republic   *1772*

Gabon Republic   *1789*
Gambia, Republic of the   *1796*
German Democratic Republic   *1831*
Germany, Federal Republic of   *1840*
Ghana, Republic of   *1849*
Gibraltar   *1853*
Gilbert Islands   *1854*
Greek Republic   *1929*
Greenland   *1933*
Grenada   *1934*
Guadeloupe   *1934*
Guam   *1935*
Guatemala, Republic of   *1936*
Guinea, Republic of   *1941*
Guinea-Bissau, Republic of   *1945*
Guyana, Cooperative Republic of   *1946*

Haiti, Republic of   *1953*
Honduras, Republic of   *2047*
Hong Kong, Colony of   *2052*
Hungarian People's Republic   *2090*

Iceland, Republic of   *2104*
India, Republic of   *2132*
Indonesia, Republic of   *2143*
Iran   *2310*
Iraq, Republic of   *2318*
Ireland, Republic of   *2323*
Israel, State of   *2330*
Italian Republic   *2341*
Ivory Coast, Republic of   *2347*

Jamaica   *2359*
Japan   *2364*
Jordan, Hashemite Kingdom of   *2375*

Topical Essays
(see discussion, page 25a)

Educational Associations
(see discussion, page 30a)

Centers and Institutes of Higher Education Research
(see discussion, page 30a)

Reports on Higher Education
(see discussion, page 31a)

International Directory of Documentation and Information Centers (see discussion, page 31a)

INTERNATIONAL

NATIONAL

Madagascar, Democratic Republic of:
National Institute of Higher Education Research and Educational
      Development   *4544*

Malawi, Republic of:
University of Malawi Library   *4544*

Malaysia, Federation of:
Ministry of Education, Library   *4545*

Mali, Republic of:
National Pedagogical Institute   *4545*

Malta, Republic of:
Information Center on Equivalence, Department of Information,
      Education Office   *4546*

Mauritius:
Mauritius Institute of Education   *4546*

Mexico, United States of:
Educational Research Center   *4547*
National Center for Educational Documentation and
      Information   *4547*

Nepal, Kingdom of:
Tribhuvan University Central Library   *4548*

Netherlands, Kingdom of the:
Center for Research into Higher Education   *4548*
Center for the Study of Education in Changing Societies
      (CESO)   *4548*
Documentation Division   *4549*
Netherlands Universities Foundation for International Cooperation
      (NUFFIC)   *4549*

New Zealand:
New Zealand Council for Education Research   *4550*

Nicaragua, Republic of:
Nicaraguan Association of Institutions of Higher Education   *4550*

Niger, Republic of the:
University of Niamey   *4551*

Norway, Kingdom of:
Norwegian Education Library, Section of the University Library,
    Oslo   *4551*

Pakistan, Islamic Republic of:
Central Bureau of Education   *4552*
Institute of Education and Research   *4552*

Papua New Guinea:
Office of Higher Education   *4553*

Peru, Republic of:
National Council of Peruvian Universities   *4554*
National Institute of Educational Research and Development,
    Department of Educational Documentation   *4554*

Philippines, Republic of the:
Information and Publication Service, Department of Education and
    Culture   *4555*

Polish People's Republic:
Documentation Center and Library, Research Institute of Science Policy
    and Higher Education   *4556*
Institute of Education   *4556*

Rhodesia, Republic of:
University Library, University of Rhodesia   *4557*

Romania, Socialist Republic of:
Central Library of Education   *4558*
Institute for Pedagogical and Psychological Research   *4558*

Rwanda, Republic of:
National University of Rwanda Library   *4559*

Saudi Arabia, Kingdom of:
Center for Statistical Data and Educational Documentation, Ministry of
    Education   *4560*

Singapore, Republic of:
Institute of Education   *4560*
University of Singapore Library   *4561*

South Africa, Republic of:
Committee of University Principals   *4562*

Human Sciences Research Council (HSRC)   *4562*

Spain:
National Institute of Educational Sciences   *4562*

Sudan, Democratic Republic of:
Documentation and Research Center   *4563*

Sweden, Kingdom of:
National Library for Psychology and Education   *4564*
Office of Universities and Colleges   *4565*

Swiss Confederation:
Swiss School Documentation Center   *4565*

Syrian Arab Republic:
Education Documentation Center   *4566*

Tanzania, United Republic of:
Institute of Education   *4566*
University of Dar es Salaam Library   *4567*

Thailand, Kingdom of:
Office of the National Educational Commission (NEC)   *4567*
Office of State Universities   *4568*

Togo, Republic of:
University of Benin   *4568*

Trinidad and Tobago:
University of the West Indies Library   *4569*

Turkey, Republic of:
Bibliographical Institute at the National Library   *4569*
Gazi Educational Institute Library   *4570*

Union of Soviet Socialist Republics:
K. D. Ushinsky State Scientific Pedagogical Library   *4570*

United Kingdom of Great Britain and Northern Ireland:
Center for the Economics of Education, Library   *4571*
Department of Education and Science Library   *4571*
National Foundation for Educational Research in England and Wales
   (NFER)   *4571*

Venezuela, Republic of:
Center for Information and Documentation in Higher Education, Office
    of University Planning   *4586*

Yugoslavia, Socialist Federal Republic of:
Center for Educational Research, Institute for Social Research,
    University of Zagreb   *4586*

Zaire, Republic of:
Center of Interdisciplinary Research for the Development of
    Education   *4587*

Contributors

Listed below are the names of contributors of signed articles in *The International Encyclopedia of Higher Education,* with their affiliations at the time of publication and, within parentheses, the title(s) of their respective articles.

MALCOLM S. ADISESHIAH, Vice-Chancellor, University of Madras, Triplicane, India (*South Asia: Regional Analysis*)

MUNEER AHMAD, Vice-President, Academic Staff Association, Department of Administrative Science, University of the Punjab, Lahore, Pakistan (*Federation of All-Pakistan Universities Academic Staff Associations*)

MATTA AKRAWI, Department of Education, American University of Beirut, Beirut, Lebanon (*Arab World: Regional Analysis*)

JAMES L. ALDRICH, Threshold, Inc., Washington, D.C. USA (*Environmental Studies—field of study*)

A. OWEN ALDRIDGE, Professor of French and Comparative Literature, Editor *Comparative Literature Studies,* University of Illinois at Urbana-Champaign, Urbana, Illinois USA (*Literature—field of study*)

HAROLD J. ALFORD, Dean, College of Continuing Education, Rochester Institute of Technology, Rochester, New York USA (*Conference Centers in the United States*)

GEORGE C. ALLEN, Professor Emeritus, University of Sussex, Brighton, England (*Interdisciplinary Studies—field of study*)

KEITH R. ALLRED, Associate Dean, College of Agriculture, Associate Director of International Programs, Office of International Programs and Studies, Utah State University, Logan, Utah USA (*Aid to Other Nations: Bilateral Participation in Higher Education*)

PHILIP G. ALTBACH, Professor, Department of Higher Education, State University of New York at Buffalo, Buffalo, New York USA (*University Reform*)

GEORGE ALTOMARE, Teachers College, Columbia University, New York, New York USA (*International Colleges and Universities*)

H. AMBERG, General Secretary, Swiss Federation for Adult Education, Zurich, Switzerland (*Swiss Federation for Adult Education*)

FUJIO ANDO, Secretary General, National Association of Local Government Junior Colleges, Tokyo, Japan (*National Association of Local Government Junior Colleges, Japan*)

MICHAEL ANELLO, Director, Division of Higher Education, Boston College, Chestnut Hill, Massachusetts USA (*Italian Republic—national system*)

IKUO ARAI, Associate Professor of Sociology of Education, Faculty of Engineering, Tokyo Institute of Technology, Tokyo, Japan (*Southeast Asia: Regional Analysis*)

BRUCE W. ARDEN, Professor and Chairman, Department of Electrical Engineering, Princeton University, Princeton, New Jersey USA (*Computers, Role of in Higher Education: Computers in Research*)

W. W. ARMISTEAD, Dean, College of Veterinary Medicine, University of Tennessee, Knoxville, Tennessee USA (*Veterinary Medicine—field of study*)

JUAN B. ARRIEN, Rector, University of Central America, Managua, Nicaragua (*Nicaragua, Republic of—national system*)

JIRO ASANO, Chief, Processing Division, University of Tokyo Library, Tokyo, Japan (*Libraries: University of Tokyo Library, Japan*)

HELEN S. ASTIN, Professor, Department of Education, University of California, Los Angeles, California USA (*Women and Higher Education: Equal Rights and Affirmative Action*)

DAVID J. ATTARD, President, Student Representative Council, Royal University of Malta, Msida, Malta (*Student Representative Council, Malta*)

G. S. AURORA, Administrative Staff College of India, Hyderabad, India (*Science Policies: Asian Countries of the Philippines, Indonesia, Republic of Korea*)

GILBERT R. AUSTIN, Associate Director, Bureau of Educational Research and Field Services, College of Education, University of Maryland, College Park, Maryland USA (*Early Childhood Education—field of study*)

ALEXANDER W. AVTGIS, Head, Department of Electrical and Electronics Engineering Technology, Wentworth Institute and College of Technology, Boston, Massachusetts USA (*Electricity, Industrial and Domestic—field of study*)

GEORGE H. AXINN, Professor of Agricultural Economics, Michigan State University, East Lansing, Michigan USA (*Agriculture in Higher Education: Agricultural Research, Extension Services, and Field Stations*)

S. K. BABALOLA, General Secretary, Nigeria Union of Teachers, Lagos, Nigeria (*Nigeria Union of Teachers*)

ANDREW M. BADER, Research Assistant, Center for Applied Social Research, Northeastern University, Boston, Massachusetts USA (*Unrest, Campus*)

TIMOTHY D. BAKER, Professor of International Health, Johns Hopkins University, Baltimore, Maryland USA (*Public Health—field of study*)

ROBERT BALAY, Head, Reference Department, Yale University Library, New Haven, Connecticut USA (*Libraries: Yale University Library, United States*)

JAGBANS K. BALBIR, Chief, Section of International University Relations, UNESCO, Paris, France (*United Nations: Organization, UNESCO, United Nations University*)

H. KENNETH BARKER, Dean, College of Education, Dean, International Programs, University of Akron, Akron, Ohio USA (*Professional Associations, International Role of*)

PEPE BARRÓN, Executive Director, National Congress of College Affairs, Washington, D.C. USA (*Access of Minorities: Spanish-Speaking Peoples*)

DAVID W. BARTON, JR., President, Barton-Gillet Company, Baltimore, Maryland USA (*Promotional Methods in Higher Education*)

MUNIR BASHSHUR, Associate Professor of Education, American University of Beirut, Beirut, Lebanon (*Lebanon, Republic of—national system*)

MARY ELLEN BASS, Reference Department, Yale University Library, New Haven, Connecticut USA (*Libraries: Yale University Library, United States*)

WERNER A. BAUM, Chancellor, University of Wisconsin-Milwaukee, Milwaukee, Wisconsin USA (*Meteorology—field of study*)

JAMES BAY, Professor and Chairman, Automotive Engineering, General Motors Institute, Flint, Michigan USA (*Automotive Technologies—field of study*)

GEORGE V. BAYLISS, Dean, School of Art, University of Michigan, Ann Arbor, Michigan USA (*Arts, Fine and Applied—field of study*)

M. G. BAYNE, Vice-Admiral, U.S. Navy, President, National Defense University, Washington, D.C. USA (*Military Science—field of study*)

CARL BECK, Executive Director, International Studies Association, University Center for International Studies, University of Pittsburgh, Pittsburgh, Pennsylvania USA (*Research: International Research*)

FRANCIS BECKETT, Press Officer, National Union of Students, London, England (*National Union of Students, United Kingdom*)

HUGH L. BEESLEY, Director, Press and Information Services, Council of Europe, formerly Deputy Director of Education, Culture and Science, Head, Division for Higher Education and Research, Council of Europe, Strasbourg, France (*Diploma Mills*)

MOURAD BELGUEDJ, Doctoral Candidate in International Economic Relations, Fletcher School of Law and Diplomacy, Tufts University, Medford, Massachusetts USA (*Algeria, Democratic and Popular Republic of—national system*)

JOSEPH BEN-DAVID, Professor of Sociology, Eliezer Kaplan School of Economics and Social Sciences, Hebrew University, Jerusalem, Israel (*Research: History, Purpose, and Organization of Academic Research*)

BEVERLY ANN BENDEKGEY, Associate Editor, National Systems, *The International Encyclopedia of Higher Education*, Northeastern University, Boston, Massachusetts USA (*United States of America—national system*)

SHMUEL BENDOR, Consultant, Planning and Grants Committee of the Council for Higher Education, Jerusalem, Israel (*Israel Academy of Sciences and Humanities; Israel, State of—national system*)

ROBERT O. BERDAHL, Professor, Department of Higher Education, State University of New York at Buffalo, Buffalo, New York USA (*Planning, Development, and Coordination: State Planning in United States Higher Education*)

GEORGE Z. F. BEREDAY, Professor of Comparative Education, Teachers College, Columbia University, New York, New York USA (*Mass Higher Education*)

RICHARD BERENDZEN, Provost, American University, Washington, D.C. USA (*Astronomy—field of study*)

WILLIAM H. BERGQUIST, Council for the Advancement of Small Colleges, Washington, D.C. USA (*Evaluation of Administrators*)

JAMES M. BERRINI, Assistant Professor, Bunker Hill Community College, Charlestown, Massachusetts USA (*Cookery—field of study*)

CHESTER A. BERRY, Executive Secretary, Association of College Unions-International, Stanford, California USA (*Extracurricular Activities on Campus; Association of College Unions—International*)

ADLI BISHAY, Head, Materials Engineering, Department of Materials Engineering and Physical Sciences, American University in Cairo, Cairo, Egypt (*Science Policies: Arab World*)

RICHARD W. BISHOP, former Assistant to the President, Northeastern University, Boston, Massachusetts USA (*Military Training and Higher Education*)

EUGENE J. BLACKMAN, Chairman, Department of Drama, Northeastern University, Boston, Massachusetts USA (*Theater Arts—field of study*)

FRANCIS C. BLESSINGTON, Professor, Department of English, Northeastern University, Boston, Massachusetts USA (*Classics—field of study*)

JOHN E. BLEWETT, International Center for Jesuit Education, Rome, Italy (*Religious Influences in Higher Education: Catholicism*)

STUART BLUME, 18 Molyneux Street, London, England (*Graduate and Professional Education: International Survey of Reports*)

MARIO SAMAME BOGGIO, Executive Director, National Council of Peruvian Universities, Lima, Peru (*National Council of Peruvian Universities*)

BYRON L. BONDURANT, Professor, Department of Agricultural Engineering, Ohio State University, Columbus, Ohio USA (*Agricultural Engineering—field of study*)

WILLIAM J. BOWERS, Director of Research, Center for Applied Social Research, Northeastern University, Boston, Massachusetts USA (*Unrest, Campus*)

LALAGE BOWN, Secretary, International Congress of University Adult Education, former Secretary, African Adult Education Association, Professor, Department of Adult Education, University of Lagos, Lagos, Nigeria (*African Adult Education Association*)

ELLIE M. BOYD, Liaison Officer, University of Waikato, Hamilton, New Zealand (*New Zealand—national system*)

STANLEY A. BOZEN, Director, Radiologic Technology, Northeastern University, Boston, Massachusetts USA (*Radiologic Technologies— field of study*)

S. BRANDES, Permanent Secretary, Coordination Committee of Faculty Organizations in the Institutes of Higher Learning in Israel, Technion-Israel Institute of Technology, Haifa, Israel (*Coordination Committee of Faculty Organizations in the Institutes of Higher Learning in Israel*)

MAYNARD BRICHFORD, University Archivist, University of Illinois at Urbana-Champaign, Urbana, Illinois USA (*Archives: Archival Resources, History and Development of*)

WILLIAM W. BRICKMAN, Professor of Educational History and Comparative Education, Graduate School of Education, University of Pennsylvania, Philadelphia, Pennsylvania USA (*Aid to Other Nations: Colonial Policies and Practices; Religious Influences in Higher Education: Judaism*)

ASA BRIGGS, Provost, Worcester College, University of Oxford, Oxford, England (*Interdisciplinarity*)

GRACE M. BRIGGS, Senior Assistant Librarian (Publications), Bodleian Library, University of Oxford, Oxford, England (*Libraries: Bodleian Library, England*)

HARVEY BROOKS, Benjamin Peirce Professor of Technology and Public Policy, Aiken Computation Laboratory, Harvard University, Cambridge, Massachusetts USA (*Research: Fields and Priorities in Academic Research*)

MARY KATHLEEN BROWN, Executive Director, Archaeological Institute of America, New York, New York USA (*Archeology—field of study*)

A. W. BURGER, Professor, Department of Agronomy, University of Illinois at Urbana-Champaign, Urbana, Illinois USA (*Crop Science— field of study*)

BARBARA B. BURN, Director, International Programs, University of Massachusetts, Amherst, Massachusetts USA (*Comparative Higher Education*)

GEORGE BURNET, Anston Marston Distinguished Professor and Head, Chemical Engineering Department, Iowa State University, Ames, Iowa USA (*Chemical Engineering—field of study*)

GERALD P. BURNS, President, Our Lady of the Lake University of San Antonio, San Antonio, Texas USA (*Faculty*)

CECIL T. BUTLER, Assistant Director, Trent Polytechnic, Nottingham, England (*United Kingdom of Great Britain and Northern Ireland—national system*)

LOUIS G. BUTTELL, Director, Public Affairs, American Podiatry Association, Washington, D.C. USA (*Podiatry—field of study*)

PORTER BUTTS, Director Emeritus of the Wisconsin Union, Professor of Social Education, University of Wisconsin-Madison, Madison, Wisconsin USA (*Association of College Unions-International; College Unions*)

CARLOS A. CAAMAÑO, Professor, University of Costa Rica, San Jose, Costa Rica (*Costa Rica, Republic of—national system*)

JAIRO CAICEDO C., Colombian Institute for Student Aid and Technical Studies Abroad, Bogota, Colombia (*Colombia, Republic of—national system*)

CHARLES F. CARTER, Vice-Chancellor, University of Lancaster, Lancaster, England (*Planning, Development, and Coordination: Regional Planning of Higher Education*)

CARLOS ALFARO CASTILLO, Rector, University of El Salvador, San Salvador, El Salvador (*El Salvador, Republic of—national system*)

LADISLAV CERYCH, Director, Institute of Education, European Cultural Foundation, University of Paris–Dauphine, Paris, France (*Education Project of Plan Europe 2000*)

M. M. CHAMBERS, Consultant on Higher Education and Professor of Educational Administration, Illinois State University, Normal, Illinois USA (*Courts and Higher Education*)

MAUD H. CHAPLIN, Assistant Professor of History, Associate Dean and Assistant to the President, Wellesley College, Wellesley, Massachusetts USA (*Philosophies of Higher Education, Historical and Contemporary*)

EARL F. CHEIT, Professor and Dean, School of Business Administration, University of California, Berkeley, California USA (*Research: Foundations in Academic Research*)

CARL S. CHRISTENSEN, Professor and Chairman, Department of Physical Education, Northeastern University, Boston, Massachusetts USA (*Physical Education—field of study*)

PAUL B. J. CHU, Professor and Chairman, Department of Labor Studies, Rutgers, the State University, New Brunswick, New Jersey USA (*Adult Education: Role of Labor and Industry*)

BURTON R. CLARK, Professor, Department of Sociology, Institution for Social and Policy Studies, Yale University, New Haven, Connecticut USA (*Structures of Postsecondary Education*)

DESMOND C. CLARKE, Lecturer in Language Arts, School of Education, University of the West Indies, Bridgetown, Barbados (*Barbados—national system*)

PAUL C. CLAYTON, Professor, Department of Poultry Science, Ohio State

University, Columbus, Ohio USA (*Poultry Science—field of study*)

ROBERT J. CLEMENTS, Chairman, Department of Comparative Literature, Graduate School of Arts and Sciences, New York University, New York, New York USA (*Comparative Literature—field of study*)

LIVINGSTONE N. COAKLEY, Minister of Education, Ministry of Education, Nassau, Bahamas (*Bahamas, Commonwealth of—national system*)

A. E. COHEN, Chairman, Board of Rectors of Dutch Universities, The Hague, the Netherlands (*Board of Rectors of Dutch Universities*)

ALBIN A. COLLINS, 3508 Cummings Lane, Chevy Chase, Maryland USA (*Science Policies: Eastern European Socialist Countries*)

JAMES F. COLLINS, Director, National Council of States on In-Service Education, Assistant Dean, School of Education, Syracuse University, Syracuse, New York USA (*Teacher Education*)

HOWARD CONANT, Professor and Head, Department of Art, University of Arizona, Tucson, Arizona USA (*Drawing and Painting, Sculpture —field of study*)

JOSEPH F. CONCEICAO, Director, Extra Mural Studies Department, University of Singapore, Singapore, Republic of Singapore (*Adult Education: Government Programs*)

DAVID R. COOK, Professor and Program Director, Guidance and School Psychology, Graduate College, University of Wisconsin-Stout, Menomonie, Wisconsin USA (*Counselor Education—field of study*)

MICHAEL COOK, Regional Training Centre for Archivists, Department of Library and Archival Studies, University of Ghana, Accra, Ghana (*Archives: Africa and Asia, National Archives of*)

PAUL A. COOK, Director, Facilitative Services Staff, Bureau of Education and Cultural Affairs, United States Department of State, Washington, D.C. USA (*Exchange, International: Government Regulations Concerning International Exchange*)

LOUIS COOPERSTEIN, Professor and Chairman, Department of Modern Languages, Northeastern University, Boston, Massachusetts USA (*Language as a Catalyst in Higher Education*)

MARY CORCORAN, Professor and Director, Graduate Studies in Higher Education, University of Minnesota, Minneapolis, Minnesota USA (*Access to Higher Education*)

VICENTA CORTÉS, Inspector General of Archives, Ministry of Education and Science, Madrid, Spain (*Archives: Mediterranean, the Vatican, and Latin America, National Archives of*)

DONALD D. COWAN, Associate Dean, Mathematics Graduate Studies, Professor, Department of Computer Science, University of Waterloo, Waterloo, Ontario, Canada (*Computers, Role of in Higher Education: Computers in Instruction*)

L. GRAY COWAN, Dean, Graduate School of Public Affairs, State University of New York at Albany, Albany, New York USA (*Public Administration—field of study*)

FRANCIS D. CRISLEY, Professor, Department of Biology, Northeastern

University, Boston, Massachusetts USA (*Biological Sciences—field of study*)

GEOFFREY CROFTS, Dean, Graduate School of Actuarial Science, Northeastern University, Boston, Massachusetts USA (*Actuarial Science —field of study*)

K. PATRICIA CROSS, Senior Research Psychologist, Educational Testing Service, Berkeley, California and Princeton, New Jersey USA (*Instruction, Individualized*)

DAVID M. CROSSMAN, Director, Communication Center, University of Pittsburgh, Pittsburgh, Pennsylvania USA (*Educational Resources: Learning Resources Centers*)

MARCELINO GARCÍA CUERPO, Mediterranean General Foundation, Madrid, Spain (*Spain—national system*)

WILLIAM K. CUMMINGS, Assistant Professor, Department of Sociology, University of Chicago, Chicago, Illinois USA (*Japan—national system*)

T. J. CUNHA, Dean, School of Agriculture, California State Polytechnic University, Pomona, California USA (*Animal Science—field of study*)

JOHN A. CURRY, Vice-President for University Administration, Northeastern University, Boston, Massachusetts USA (*Admissions: An International Perspective*)

FREDERICK DAINTON, Chairman, University Grants Committee, London, England (*Financing of Higher Education: University Grants Committees*)

ROBERT S. DAVIE, Assistant Director, Swinburne College of Technology, Hawthorn, Australia (*Cooperative Education and Off-Campus Experience: Sandwich Plan in the Commonwealth Nations*)

GENEVIEVE C. DEAN, Science Policy Research Unit, University of Sussex, Brighton, England (*Science Policies: China, People's Republic of*)

DAVID DeCAMP, Senior Program Adviser, Center for Applied Linguistics, Professor of Linguistics, English, and Education, University of Texas, Austin, Texas USA (*Languages—field of study*)

KAREL DE CLERCK, Director, Central Bureau for the Study of University Education, Gent, Belgium (*Belgium, Kingdom of—national system*)

R. A. DE MOOR, Chairman, Commission for the Development of Higher Education, School of Economics, Social Sciences and Law, Tilburg University, Tilburg, the Netherlands (*Western Europe and the United Kingdom: Regional Analysis*)

BREWSTER C. DENNY, Dean, Graduate School of Public Affairs, Chairman, Marine Affairs Board, University of Washington, Seattle, Washington USA (*Science Policies: United States*)

ROLF DEPPELER, Secretary General, Swiss University Conference, Bern, Switzerland (*Swiss Confederation—national system; Swiss University Conference*)

HEITOR GURGULINO DE SOUZA, Member, National Council of Education, Director, National Research Council, Brasilia, Brazil (*Brazil, Federative Republic of—national system*)

L. M. DETMER, Assistant Director, Department of Allied Health Evaluation, American Medical Association, Chicago, Illinois USA (*Physician's Assistants, Programs for—field of study*)

CHARLES M. DEVLIN, Assistant to Vice-President for Finance, Northeastern University, Boston, Massachusetts USA (*Ceremonies*)

JACOB C. DIEMERT, Sherburne, Powers and Needham, Boston and Concord, Massachusetts USA (*Legal Aspects of Higher Education*)

JOHN E. DOLIBOIS, Vice-President for Development and Alumni Affairs, Miami University, Oxford, Ohio USA (*Alumni Affairs; Public Relations*)

LESLIE S. DOMONKOS, Professor, Department of History, Youngstown State University, Youngstown, Ohio USA (*History of Higher Education*)

ANDREW J. DOUGHERTY, Colonel, U.S. Air Force, Director of Research, National Defense University, Fort Lesley J. McNair, Washington, D.C. USA (*Military Science—field of study*)

VICTOR DRAPELA, Professor, College of Education, University of South Florida, Tampa, Florida USA (*Counselor Education—field of study*)

ARTHUR D. DRAYTON, former Dean, Faculty of Arts and General Studies, Department of English, University of the West Indies, Kingston, Jamaica (*Jamaica—national system*)

PAUL L. DRESSEL, Professor of University Research, Michigan State University, East Lansing, Michigan USA (*Evaluation*)

MATTHEW DROSDOFF, Professor of Soil Science, Department of Agronomy, Cornell University, Ithaca, New York USA (*Soil and Water Science and Technology—field of study*)

MICHEL DUCHEIN, Secretary of State for Cultural Affairs, Directorate of National Archives, Paris, France (*Archives: France, National Archives of*)

MARION DUDLEY, Director, Public Relations, Zonta International, Chicago, Illinois USA (*Zonta International*)

DONALD P. DUNCAN, Director, School of Forestry, Fisheries, and Wildlife, University of Missouri, Columbia, Missouri USA (*Forestry—field of study*)

MAURICE R. DUPERRE, Dean, Human Affairs Institute, Brookdale Community College, Lincroft, New Jersey USA (*Short-Cycle Education*)

R. P. O. DZANJALIMONDZI, former Chairman, University of Malawi Students' Union, Chancellor College, Zomba, Malawi (*University of Malawi Students' Union*)

HARRY F. EBERT, President, Association of Physical Plant Administrators of Universities and Colleges, Washington, D.C. USA (*Business Management of Higher Education: Facilities, Physical Plant*)

NORMAN L. EPSTEIN, Judge of the Municipal Court, Los Angeles Judicial District, Los Angeles, California USA (*Attorney, University*)

ARNOLDO ESCOBAR, Dean, Faculty of Humanities, University Rafael Landivar, Guatemala City, Guatemala (*Guatemala, Republic of—national system*)

Ramón Fernández Espinar, President, National Association of University Assistant Professors, Madrid, Spain (*National Association of University Assistant Professors, Spain*)

Simón Espinosa, Director of Planning, Catholic University of Ecuador, Quito, Ecuador (*Ecuador, Republic of—national system*)

E. Evans-Anfom, Chairman, National Council for Higher Education, Accra, Ghana (*Ghana, Republic of—national system*)

A. Babs Fafunwa, Dean, Faculty of Education, University of Ife, Ile-Ife, Nigeria (*Africa, Sub-Saharan: Regional Analysis*)

Peter Faid, former Chairman, International Relations Committee, Association of College Unions–International, University of Manitoba, Winnipeg, Canada (*Extracurricular Activities on Campus*)

Leroy Falling, United States Bureau of Indian Affairs, Washington, D.C. USA (*Access of Minorities: The North American Indian*)

Josephine Riss Fang, Professor of Library Science, Simmons College, Boston, Massachusetts USA (*Library Administration Outside the United States*)

R. W. S. Fargher, General Secretary, Association of Teachers in Technical Institutes, Lower Hutt, New Zealand (*Association of Teachers in Technical Institutes, New Zealand*)

Richard N. Farmer, Professor of International Business, Graduate School of Business, Indiana University, Bloomington, Indiana USA (*Finance—field of study*)

Joseph P. Farrell, Chairman, Department of Educational Planning, Ontario Institute for Studies in Education, Toronto, Ontario, Canada (*Planning, Development, and Coordination: International Educational Planning and Development*)

Paul V. Farrell, Director, Professional Activities, National Association of Purchasing Management, New York, New York USA (*Business Management of Higher Education: Purchasing*)

Vladimir A. Fedorovich, Senior Researcher, Institute of United States and Canadian Studies, Academy of Sciences of the USSR, Moscow, USSR (*Science Policies: Union of Soviet Socialist Republics*)

Barbara L. Feret-Schuman, Librarian, Culinary Institute of America, Hyde Park, New York USA (*Cookery—field of study*)

Gary L. Filerman, President, Association of University Programs in Health Administration, Washington, D.C. USA (*Hospital and Health Services Administration—field of study*)

Liliya Filippova, Senior Researcher, Institute of United States and Canadian Studies, Academy of Sciences of the USSR, Moscow, USSR (*Union of Soviet Socialist Republics—national system*)

CAMERON FINCHER, Professor and Director, Institute of Higher Education, University of Georgia, Athens, Georgia USA (*Higher Education —field of study*)

JANICE FIRESTEIN, Associate Director, National Commission for Cooperative Education, Northeastern University, Boston, Massachusetts USA (*Cooperative Education and Off-Campus Experience: Organization and Administration of Programs*)

P. FISBER, President, Union of Grandes Ecoles, Paris, France (*Union of Grandes Ecoles*)

JÜRGEN FISCHER, Secretary General, West German Rectors Conference, Bonn-Bad Godesberg, Federal Republic of Germany (*West German Rectors Conference*)

PATRICIA FLAHERTY, Staff Associate, American Academy of Arts and Sciences, Boston, Massachusetts USA (*American Academy of Arts and Sciences*)

E. L. FLECKENSTEIN, President, Capitol Institute of Technology, Kensington, Maryland USA (*Electronic Equipment Installation and Servicing—field of study*)

STEVENSON W. FLETCHER, Associate Professor and Head, Department of Hotel, Restaurant and Travel Administration, University of Massachusetts, Amherst, Massachusetts USA (*Hotel/Motel Administration —field of study*)

WALTER FOGG, Department of Philosophy, Northeastern University, Boston, Massachusetts USA (*Philosophy—field of study*)

PIERRE-MICHEL FONTAINE, Visiting Professor, Africana Studies and Research Center, Cornell University, Ithaca, New York USA (*Haiti, Republic of—national system*)

SIDNEY FORMAN, Professor of Education, Teachers College, Columbia University, New York, New York USA (*Periodicals, Higher Education*)

ARTHUR R. FOSTER, Professor of Mechanical Engineering, Northeastern University, Boston, Massachusetts USA (*Mechanical Engineering— field of study*)

J. BRUCE FRANCIS, Associate Professor, Department of Higher Education, State University of New York at Buffalo, Buffalo, New York USA (*Curriculum and Instruction*)

CHARLES A. H. FRANKLYN, Wickham Hall House, Hassocks, England (*Academic Dress, History of*)

STEWART E. FRASER, Professor, Centre for Comparative and International Studies in Education, School of Education, LaTrobe University, Bundoora, Australia (*Northeast Asia: Regional Analysis*)

ANTOINETTE FREDERICK, Independent Professional Research and Editorial Consultants, West Newton, Massachusetts USA (*Academies; North America: Regional Analysis*)

MORRIS FREILICH, Professor, Department of Anthropology and Sociology, Northeastern University, Boston, Massachusetts USA (*Anthropology—field of study*)

KURT FREY, former Secretary General, Standing Conference of the Ministers of Education and Cultural Affairs of the States in the Federal Republic of Germany, Bonn, Federal Republic of Germany (*Standing Conference of the Ministers of Education and Cultural Affairs of the States in the Federal Republic of Germany*)

ARNOLD FRIEDMANN, Professor, Department of Art and Design, University of Massachusetts, Amherst, Massachusetts USA (*Interior Design —field of study*)

VICTORIA FROMKIN, Chairman, Department of Linguistics, University of California, Los Angeles, California USA (*Linguistics—field of study*)

W. TODD FURNISS, Director, Office of Academic Affairs, American Council on Education, Washington, D.C. USA (*Academic Tenure*)

DOROTEA FURTH, Directorate for Social Affairs, Manpower and Education, Organisation for Economic Co-operation and Development, Paris, France (*Organisation for Economic Co-operation and Development*)

PAUL MACDONALD FYE, President and Director, Woods Hole Oceanographic Institution, Woods Hole, Massachusetts USA (*Oceanography—field of study*)

ARTHUR W. GALSTON, Professor of Biology, Yale University, New Haven, Connecticut USA (*Vietnam, Socialist Republic of—national system*)

CATHERINE C. GANNON, Associate Professor of English, Associate Dean, Academic Planning, California State College, San Bernardino, California USA (*Trends in Higher Education*)

JOSEPH W. GARBARINO, Professor of Business Administration, Director, Institute of Business and Economic Research, University of California, Berkeley, California USA (*Faculty Unionism: The United States and Great Britain*)

DAVID E. GARDINIER, Professor of History, Marquette University, Milwaukee, Wisconsin USA (*Congo, People's Republic; Gabon Republic —national systems*)

DAVID C. GARDNER, Chairman, Department of Business and Career Education, School of Education, Boston University, Boston, Massachusetts USA (*Career, Vocational, and Technical Education*)

PAUL GARNER, Dean Emeritus, Graduate School of Business, University of Alabama, University, Alabama USA (*Accountancy—field of study*)

VIVIAN S. GAY, Chief Executive, Association of Polytechnic Teachers, Southsea, England (*Association of Polytechnic Teachers, United Kingdom*)

ANDERS GESTRIN, former Secretary General, Swedish National Union of Students, Stockholm, Sweden (*Swedish National Union of Students*)

SHUKRI GHANEM, Economic Adviser, Box 2605, Tripoli, Libya (*Libyan Arab Republic—national system*)

MINA B. GHATTAS, Associate Professor of Education, Director, Office of Learning Resources, Northeastern University, Boston, Massachusetts USA (*Instructional Technology—field of study*)

ARTHUR GILLETTE, Social Sciences Sector, UNESCO, Paris, France (*Student Volunteer Programs*)

CLIFFORD W. GILPIN, Department of Education, International Bank for Reconstruction and Development, Washington, D.C. USA (*Somali Democratic Republic—national system*)

WILLIAM A. GLASER, Bureau of Applied Social Research, Columbia University, New York, New York USA (*Manpower Planning: Migration of Talent*)

ROY ARTHUR GLASGOW, Department of History, Boston University, Boston, Massachusetts USA (*Guyana, Cooperative Republic of—national system*)

GINO GOLDONI, General Secretary, National Academy of Science, Letters, and Arts, Modena, Italy (*National Academy of Science, Letters, and Arts, Italy*)

ULADISLAO GONZÁLEZ-ANDRADE, Secretary General, Colombian Association of Universities, Bogota, Colombia (*Colombian Association of Universities*)

JAMES D. GOODNOW, Executive Secretary, Academy of International Business, Roosevelt University, Chicago, Illinois USA (*Marketing —field of study*)

CAROL GREEN, Staff Editor, *The International Encyclopedia of Higher Education,* Northeastern University, Boston, Massachusetts USA (*Degrees, Diplomas, and Certificates*)

SAM L. GROGG, JR., Education Director, American Film Institute, John F. Kennedy Center for the Performing Arts, Washington, D.C. USA (*Photography and Cinematography—field of study*)

PHILLIP D. GRUB, Aryamehr Professor of Multinational Management, Special Assistant to the President, School of Government and Business Administration, George Washington University, Washington, D.C. USA (*Aid to Other Nations: Multinational Corporations and Lateral Aid*)

JAIME SANTIBAÑEZ GUARELLO, General Secretary, Council of Rectors of Chilean Universities, Santiago, Chile (*Council of Rectors of Chilean Universities*)

ALFONSO RANGEL GUERRA, Executive Secretary General, National Association of Universities and Institutes of Higher Education, Mexico City, Mexico (*National Association of Universities and Institutes of Higher Education, Mexico*)

S. M. GUMA, Rector, University College of Swaziland, University of Botswana and Swaziland, Kwaluseni, Swaziland (*Swaziland, Kingdom of —national system*)

LUIS GARIBAY GUTIÉRREZ, Rector, Autonomous University of Guadalajara, Guadalajara, Mexico (*Mexico, United States of—national system*)

MARIUS-FRANÇOIS GUYARD, President, Conference of French Rectors, Lyon, France (*Conference of French Rectors*)

SOLOMON N. GWEI, Advanced Teacher Training College, Bambili Annex, Bamenda, United Republic of Cameroon (*Cameroon, United Republic of—national system*)

JOHN W. HALL, Chairman, Japan-United States Friendship Commission, Department of History, Yale University, New Haven, Connecticut USA (*Japan-United States Friendship Commission*)

W. D. HALLS, Department of Educational Studies, University of Oxford, Oxford, England (*Equivalences*)

F. S. HAMBLY, Secretary, Australian Vice-Chancellors' Committee, Canberra City, Australia (*Australian Vice-Chancellors' Committee*)

FREDERIC R. HAMIL, Chairman, Department of Technical Science, National Technical Institute for the Deaf, Rochester Institute of Technology, Rochester, New York USA (*Optical Lens Making—field of study*)

MARIUS HĂNGĂNUT, Professor, Faculty of Electrical Engineering, Polytechnic Institute of Cluj-Napoca, Cluj-Napoca, Romania (*Computer Science; Electrical and Electronics Engineering—fields of study*)

WILLIAM HANNON, Associate Professor and Chairman, Department of Design, Massachusetts College of Art, Boston, Massachusetts USA (*Industrial Design—field of study*)

KENT HANSEN, Professor of Nuclear Engineering, Massachusetts Institute of Technology, Cambridge, Massachusetts USA (*Nuclear Engineering—field of study*)

MAURICE HARARI, Director, International Programs, American Association of State Colleges and Universities, Washington, D.C. USA (*Internationalization of Higher Education*)

CHAUNCY D. HARRIS, Samuel N. Harper Distinguished Service Professor of Geography, University of Chicago, Chicago, Illinois USA (*Geography—field of study*)

CHARLES W. HAVICE, Dean of Chapel Emeritus, Northeastern University, Boston, Massachusetts USA (*Religious Influences in Higher Education: Protestantism*)

WILLIAM E. HAVILAND, Secretary, Economic Council of Canada, Ottawa, Ontario, Canada (*Economic Council of Canada*)

JOHN N. HAWKINS, Assistant Professor in Residence, International and Comparative Education, Graduate School of Education, University of California, Los Angeles, California USA (*China, People's Republic of—national system*)

HOWARD HAYDEN, former Visiting Professor, Macquarie University, Sydney, Australia (*Oceania: Regional Analysis*)

PAUL HEBERT, Vice-President for Development and Research, De La Salle University, Manila, the Philippines (*International Management Education*)

JB LON HEFFERLIN, Director, Special Projects, Jossey-Bass Inc., Publishers, San Francisco, California USA (*Processes of Academic Change*)

JOHN W. HEIN, Director, Forsyth Dental Center, Boston, Massachusetts USA (*Dental Auxiliaries; Dentistry and Dental Specialties—fields of study*)

JOHN S. HELMICK, Vice-President, Office of International Activities, Educational Testing Service, Princeton, New Jersey USA (*Examinations and Tests*)

ROBIN M. HENDRICH, Associate Professor, Department of Music, Northeastern University, Boston, Massachusetts USA (*Music—field of study*)

A. DORIS BANKS HENRIES, Director, Higher Education and Textbook Research, Ministry of Education, Monrovia, Liberia (*Liberia, Republic of—national system*)

SIDNEY HERMAN, Associate Dean, University Administration, Director, Faculty and Staff Relations, Northeastern University, Boston, Massachusetts USA (*Due Process and Grievance Procedures*)

KNUD BENT HEY, Secretary, Council for Higher Education and Research, Copenhagen, Denmark (*Association of Graduates from Institutions for Higher Education*)

HENRY W. HOFSTETTER, Professor, School of Optometry, Indiana University, Bloomington, Indiana USA (*Optometry—field of study*)

JOHN HOLLAND, Department of Educational Planning, Ontario Institute for Studies in Education, Toronto, Ontario, Canada (*Planning, Development, and Coordination: National Planning of Higher Education*)

CHARLES M. HOLLOWAY, Director, Special Projects, College Entrance Examination Board, New York, New York USA (*College Entrance Examination Board*)

H. T. HOOKWAY, Chief Executive, British Library, London, England (*Libraries: British Library, England*)

MORRIS A. HOROWITZ, Professor and Chairman, Department of Economics, Northeastern University, Boston, Massachusetts USA (*Economics—field of study; Manpower Planning: Overview*)

LARRY N. HORTON, Associate Dean, Student Affairs for Residential Education, Stanford University, Stanford, California USA (*Business Management of Higher Education: Student Housing*)

DAVID J. HOUNSELL, Institute for Research and Development in Post-Compulsory Education, University of Lancaster, Lancaster, England (*Planning, Development, and Coordination: Regional Planning of Higher Education; Publications, Higher Education*)

RICHARD D. HUBBARD, Professor and Chairman, Department of Audio-

Visual Communications and Technology, State University College, Oswego, New York USA (*Instructional Technology—field of study*)

EARL STEPHEN HUNT, former Research Associate and Editor, World Peace Through Law Center, Washington, D.C. USA (*International Law—field of study*)

TORSTEN HUSÉN, Institute of International Education, University of Stockholm, Stockholm, Sweden (*Articulation: Europe*)

K. M. HUSSAIN, Professor, Department of Computer Science, New Mexico State University, Las Cruces, New Mexico USA (*Financial Affairs: Cost Analysis*)

ROBERTO IBARQUEN, Professor of History, Federal University of Espírito Santo, Vitoria, Brazil (*Uruguay, Oriental Republic of—national system*)

WELDON E. IHRIG, Assistant Vice-President for Administration, Ohio State University, Columbus, Ohio USA (*Computers, Role of in Higher Education: Computers in Administration*)

SUSAN G. ISLAM, Information Specialist, American Foundation for the Blind, Inc., New York, New York USA (*Blind, Higher Education for the*)

INSTITUTE OF EDUCATION, University of Dar es Salaam, Dar es Salaam, Tanzania (*Tanzania, United Republic of—national system*)

FREDERICK H. JACKSON, Director, Committee on Institutional Cooperation, Evanston, Illinois USA (*Interinstitutional Cooperation*)

HERBERT C. JACKSON, Professor, Department of Religious Studies, Michigan State University, East Lansing, Michigan USA (*Religious Influences in Higher Education: Buddhism, Hinduism*)

SANFORD C. JAMESON, Director, Office of International Education, College Entrance Examination Board, Washington, D.C. and New York, New York USA (*Examinations and Tests*)

FRANCISZEK JANUSZKIEWICZ, Interuniversity Institute for Research on Higher Education, Warsaw, Poland (*Eastern European Socialist Countries: Regional Analysis*)

E. JENGO, Head, Department of Art, Music and Theatre, University of Dar es Salaam, Dar es Salaam, Tanzania (*Tanzania, United Republic of—national system*)

HUGH M. JENKINS, Executive Vice-President, National Association for Foreign Student Affairs, Washington, D.C. USA (*Exchange, International: International Student*)

FRANK W. JESSUP, former Director, Department for External Studies, University of Oxford, Oxford, England (*Conference Centers in Great Britain*)

JOHN K. JESSUP, JR., College Venture Program, Institute for Off-Campus Experience, Northeastern University, Boston, Massachusetts USA (*World Affairs and Higher Education*)

EBERHARD JOBST, Senior Staff Member, Federal-State Commission for Educational Planning and Research Promotion, Bonn, Federal

Republic of Germany *(Federal-State Commission for Educational Planning)*

THYS B. JOHNSON, Head, Department of Mining Engineering, Colorado School of Mines, Golden, Colorado USA *(Mining Engineering—field of study)*

WILLIAM JOHNSTON, Writer and Editor, National Center for Higher Education Management Systems, Boulder, Colorado USA *(National Center for Higher Education Management Systems, United States)*

KURT JONASSOHN, Deputy Executive Secretary, International Sociological Association, Montreal, Quebec, Canada, Professor, Department of Sociology and Anthropology, Concordia University, Montreal, Quebec, Canada *(Sociology—field of study)*

J. OWEN JONES, Director, Commonwealth Bureau of Agricultural Economics, Oxford, England *(Agricultural Economics—field of study)*

WALTER S. JONES, Edward W. Brooke Professor of Political Science and Chairman, Department of Political Science, Northeastern University, Boston, Massachusetts USA *(Political Science–field of study)*

HARALD JØRGENSEN, Director, Provincial Archives, Copenhagen, Denmark *(Archives: Northern Europe, National Archives of)*

MIJAILO JUHAS, Director, Institute for Studies in Education, Belgrade, Yugoslavia *(Yugoslavia, Socialist Federal Republic of—national system)*

FRIEDRICH P. KAHLENBERG, Head Archival Director in the Federal Archives, Koblenz, Federal Republic of Germany *(Archives: Federal Republic of Germany, German Democratic Republic, and Austria, National Archives of)*

ALAN A. KAHLER, Associate Professor, Department of Agricultural Education, Iowa State University, Ames, Iowa USA *(Agriculture in Higher Education: Early History of Agricultural Education)*

FRANZ GEORG KALTWASSER, Director, Bavarian State Library, Munich, Federal Republic of Germany *(Libraries: Bavarian State Library, Federal Republic of Germany)*

MOTOHISA KANEKO, Institute of Developing Economies, Tokyo, Japan *(Southeast Asia: Regional Analysis)*

RICHARD A. KAPLOWITZ, Dean, Division of Continuing Education, Merrimack College, North Andover, Massachusetts USA *(Recruitment, Appointment, Promotion, and Termination of Academic Personnel)*

JOHN KAREFA-SMART, Lecturer, Department of Preventive and Social Medicine, Harvard Medical School, Boston, Massachusetts USA *(Political Persecution of Academics)*

L. R. KAY, Secretary, Universities Central Council on Admissions, Cheltenham, England *(Universities Central Council on Admissions, United Kingdom)*

R. S. KELKAR, Secretary, National Academy of Letters, New Delhi, India *(National Academy of Letters, India)*

ARTHUR KELMAN, L. R. Jones Professor, Department of Plant Pathology,

University of Wisconsin-Madison, Madison, Wisconsin USA (*Plant Pathology—field of study*)

KATHERINE KENDALL, Secretary General, International Association of Schools of Social Work, New York, New York USA (*Social Welfare —field of study*)

ALVIN KENT, Director, Media Resources Center, Iowa State University, Ames, Iowa USA (*Educational Resources: Administration*)

GEORGE M. KESSLER, Associate Professor, Department of Horticulture, Michigan State University, East Lansing, Michigan USA (*Horticulture—field of study*)

NATHAN KEYFITZ, Andelot Professor of Demography and Sociology, Harvard University, Cambridge, Massachusetts USA (*Demography and Population Studies—field of study*)

T. KHACHATUROV, Chairman of the Presidium, Association of Soviet Economic Scientific Institutions, Moscow, USSR (*Economics—field of study*)

HIROSHI KIDA, Secretary General, Japanese National Commission for UNESCO, Tokyo, Japan (*Science Policies: Japan*)

J. ROBY KIDD, Professor, Department of Adult Education, Ontario Institute for Studies in Education, Toronto, Ontario, Canada (*Adult Education: Adult Education in Developing Countries; International Council for Adult Education*)

SUN HO KIM, Professor of Comparative Education, Kyung Hee University, Seoul, Korea (*Korea, Democratic People's Republic of—national system*)

ALEXANDER KING, Chairman, International Federation of Institutes of Advanced Study, Paris, France, former Director General for Scientific Affairs, Organisation for Economic Co-operation and Development, Paris, France (*The Club of Rome*)

RUBY KING, School of Education, University of the West Indies, Kingston, Jamaica (*Jamaica—national system*)

EDWARD T. KIRKPATRICK, President, Wentworth Institute and College of Technology, Boston, Massachusetts USA (*Trade, Craft, and Industrial Programs—field of study*)

EDWIN J. KIRSCHNER, E. J. Kirschner and Associates, Bethesda, Maryland USA (*Transportation—field of study*)

KAZUYUKI KITAMURA, Associate Professor, Research Institute for Higher Education, Hiroshima University, Hiroshima, Japan (*Japan—national system*)

W. EUGENE KLEINBAUER, Professor, Department of Fine Arts, Indiana University, Bloomington, Indiana USA (*Art, History of—field of study*)

EVERETT KLEINJANS, President, East-West Center, University of Hawaii, Honolulu, Hawaii USA (*East-West Center*)

ASA S. KNOWLES, Editor-in-Chief, *The International Encyclopedia of Higher*

Education, Northeastern University, Boston, Massachusetts USA (*Academic Standards and Accreditation: International; Governance and Control of Higher Education: Governance and Administration; Manpower Planning: Higher Education in Manpower Development; Remuneration: Faculty, Staff, and Chief Executive Officers*)

ENDEL-JAKOB KOLDE, Professor, Graduate School of Business Administration, University of Washington, Seattle, Washington USA (*Management Education—field of study*)

MICHAEL KORFF, Assistant to the President, Stockton State College, Pomona, New Jersey USA (*Business Management of Higher Education: Student Housing*)

GARY KRASKE, Editor, Documentation Centers of Higher Education, *The International Encyclopedia of Higher Education,* Northeastern University, Boston, Massachusetts USA (*Documentation and Information Centers in Higher Education*)

BORAH L. KREIMER, Associate Professor of Engineering Graphics, Northeastern University, Boston, Massachusetts USA (*Drafting and Design —field of study*)

P. KREYENBERG, Secretary General, Science Council, Cologne, Federal Republic of Germany (*Science Council, Federal Republic of Germany*)

RICHARD KRZYS, Director, International Library Information Center, Professor, Graduate School of Library and Information Sciences, University of Pittsburgh, Pittsburgh, Pennsylvania USA (*Library Administration in the United States*)

DAW HNIN MYA KYI, Educational Research Bureau, Ministry of Education, Rangoon, Burma (*Burma, Socialist Republic of the Union of— national system*)

LOUISE LaFONTAINE, Professor, Department of Special Education and Rehabilitation, Northeastern University, Boston, Massachusetts USA (*Special Education—field of study*)

PHYLLIS LAKING, Staff Assistant, Woods Hole Oceanographic Institution, Woods Hole, Massachusetts USA (*Oceanography—field of study*)

DONALD McL. LAMBERTON, Professor and Head, Department of Economics, University of Queensland, Brisbane, Australia (*Science Policies: Australia and New Zealand*)

ELIZABETH S. LANDIS, Legal Consultant, Commissioner for Namibia, United Nations, New York, New York, Senior Political Affairs Officer, Office of the United Nations Commissioner for Namibia, New York, New York USA (*Namibia, Territory of*)

KENNETH D. LANGLEY, Associate Professor, Department of Textile Sciences, Southeastern Massachusetts University, North Dartmouth, Massachusetts USA (*Textile Technology—field of study*)

PAULA LANNING, Information Officer, National Association of Teachers in Further and Higher Education, London, England (*National Association of Teachers in Further and Higher Education, United Kingdom*)

PHILIP LaTORRE, Director, Environmental Health and Safety, Northeastern University, Boston, Massachusetts USA (*Health, Safety, and Environmental Control in Higher Education Institutions*)

ROBERT S. LAUBACH, President, Laubach Literacy International, Syracuse, New York USA (*Illiteracy of Adults*)

P. J. LAVAKARE, Special Assistant to Chairman, Electronics Commission, Government of India, New Delhi, India (*Science Policies: India*)

ROMANO LAZZERONI, National President, National Association of University Professors, University of Pisa, Pisa, Italy (*National Association of University Professors, Italy*)

LYMAN H. LEGTERS, Professor, Institute for Comparative and Foreign Area Studies, University of Washington, Seattle, Washington USA (*Area Studies—field of study*)

WALTER J. LEONARD, President, Fisk University, Nashville, Tennessee USA, former Special Assistant to the President, Harvard University, Cambridge, Massachusetts USA (*Affirmative Action*)

GEORGES LeRIDER, General Administrator, Bibliothèque Nationale, Paris, France [*Libraries: National Library of France (Bibliothèque Nationale), France*]

LARRY L. LESLIE, Professor of Higher Education, University of Arizona, Tucson, Arizona USA (*Steady State*)

MARY C. LETHBRIDGE, Information Officer, Library of Congress, Washington, D.C. USA (*Libraries: Library of Congress, United States*)

IOAN ALFRED LETIA, Professor, Faculty of Electrical Engineering, Polytechnic Institute of Cluj-Napoca, Cluj-Napoca, Romania (*Computer Science; Electrical and Electronics Engineering—fields of study*)

LIONEL S. LEWIS, Professor of Sociology and Adjunct Professor of Higher Education, Department of Sociology, State University of New York at Buffalo, Buffalo, New York USA (*Sociology of Higher Education*)

MILTON LIPSON, Professor, Center for Safety, New York University, New York, New York USA (*Security, Private or Civil—field of study*)

CHI-PING LIU, Director, National Library of Peking, Peking, People's Republic of China (*Libraries: National Library of Peking, People's Republic of China*)

DOMINGO A. POLETTI LIUZZI, Thermal Engineering, Sao Paulo, Brazil (*Paraguay, Republic of—national system*)

THEODORE E. LOBMAN, Institute of Business and Economic Research, University of California, Berkeley, California USA (*Foundations in Academic Research*)

J. DAVID LOCKARD, Director, International Clearinghouse on Science and Mathematics Curricular Developments, University of Maryland, College Park, Maryland USA (*Natural Sciences—field of study*)

G. LOCKWOOD, Registrar and Secretary, University of Sussex, Brighton, England (*Planning, Development, and Coordination: Institutional Planning*)

MARTIN LOEFFLER, Executive Chairman, International Association for the Promotion of the World University, Stuttgart, Federal Republic of Germany (*International Association for the Promotion of the World University*)

RODNEY C. LOEHR, Professor Emeritus, Department of History, University of Minnesota, Minneapolis, Minnesota USA (*Military Training and Higher Education*)

JUANITA OUTLAW LONG, Dean, College of Nursing, Northeastern University, Boston, Massachusetts USA (*Nursing—field of study*)

CHARLES R. LONGSWORTH, President, Hampshire College, Amherst, Massachusetts USA (*Participatory Democracy*)

HELENE A. LOUX, former Associate Dean, Department of Allied Health, Northeastern University, Boston, Massachusetts USA (*Medical Technologies—field of study*)

HANS LÖWBEER, Chancellor, Swedish Universities, Stockholm, Sweden (*Internationalization of Higher Education—Sweden: A Case Study*)

JOHN LOWE, Directorate for Social Affairs, Manpower and Education, Organisation for Economic Co-operation and Development, Paris, France (*Adult Education: Overview—A Global Perspective*)

ROBERT A. LUKE, Director, Project on Utilization of Inservice Education Research and Development Outcomes, National Education Association, Washington, D.C. USA (*Adult Education, Teacher Training for—field of study*)

D. KEITH LUPTON, Director, Off-Campus Term Program, University of South Florida, Tampa, Florida USA (*Cooperative Education and Off-Campus Experience: Experiential Education in the United States*)

DONLYN LYNDON, President, Association of Collegiate Schools of Architecture, Professor, Department of Architecture, Massachusetts Institute of Technology, Cambridge, Massachusetts USA (*Architecture—field of study*)

CHARLES H. LYONS, Director, Overseas Liaison, American Council on Education, Washington, D.C. USA (*Access of Minorities: Blacks in the United States*)

A. W. MABBS, Deputy Keeper of Public Records, Public Record Office, London, England (*Archives: Public Record Office, London*)

FORBES M. MADZONGWE, Post Doctoral Research Fellow, Graduate School of Education, Harvard University, Cambridge, Massachusetts USA (*Angola; Madagascar, Democratic Republic of; Mozambique, People's Republic of; Rwanda, Republic of—national systems*)

RICHARD A. MALONEY, Bookstore Manager, Northeastern University, Boston, Massachusetts USA (*Business Management of Higher Education: Bookstores*)

WILLIAM F. MALONEY, Tufts University, Medford, Massachusetts USA (*Health Fields—field of study*)

GUY A. MARCO, Dean, School of Library Science, Kent State University,

Kent, Ohio USA (*Library and Information Science—field of study*)

RENÉE MARCOUSÉ, The Old Cottage, Long Crendon, England (*Museums in Higher Education Institutions*)

MELVIN MARK, Dean, College of Engineering, Northeastern University, Boston, Massachusetts USA (*Engineering—field of study*)

FRANK E. MARSH, JR., Dean of Education, Northeastern University, Boston, Massachusetts USA (*Education Science and Teacher Training—field of study*)

BEN MATOGO, Secretary, Makerere University Academic Staff Association, Makerere University, Kampala, Uganda (*Makerere University Academic Staff Association, Uganda*)

LEWIS B. MAYHEW, Professor of Education, Stanford University, Stanford, California USA (*Graduate and Professional Education: General History and Contemporary Survey*)

ROGER J. MAYHEW, Principal Assistant, Personnel Division, University College, University of London, London, England (*Nonacademic Personnel Administration*)

SYLVIA G. McCOLLUM, Education Administrator, United States Department of Justice, Bureau of Prisons, Washington, D.C. USA (*Prisoners, Postsecondary Education Programs for*)

NANCY McCORMACK, Associate Director, Division of International Education, University of Tennessee, Knoxville, Tennessee USA (*Financial Aid: Scholarships and Fellowships, International*)

JAMES J. McCORMICK, Assistant Vice-President and Director of Training, Arkwright-Boston Manufacturers Mutual Insurance Company, Waltham, Massachusetts USA (*Business Management of Higher Education: Insurance and Risk Management*)

NOEL F. McGINN, Graduate School of Education, Harvard University, Cambridge, Massachusetts USA (*Chile, Republic of—national system*)

KYRAN M. McGRATH, Plymouth, Vermont USA (*Museum Administration, College and University*)

ELIZABETH P. McINTOSH, Public Affairs Department, Smithsonian Institution, Washington, D.C. USA (*Smithsonian Institution*)

LAWRENCE McKIBBIN, Dean, College of Business Administration, University of Oklahoma, Norman, Oklahoma USA (*Commerce and Business Administration—field of study*)

PAUL D. McMANUS, Assistant Director, Veterans Affairs, Northeastern University, Boston, Massachusetts USA (*Veterans Education Benefits*)

EDGAR C. McVOY, Director, International Manpower Institute, United States Department of Labor, Employment and Training Administration, Washington, D.C. USA (*Manpower Planning: Role of International Agencies*)

JEROME MEDALIE, Partner, Widett, Widett, Slater and Goldman, Boston, Massachusetts USA (*Legal Status of Faculty Unionization in the United States*)

CHARLES W. MEINERT, Associate in Higher Education, Division of Academic Program Review, The University of the State of New York, State Education Department, Albany, New York USA (*Articulation: United States*)

RICHARD S. MELTZER, Director, Graduate Medical Education, Project HOPE, Washington, D.C. USA (*Health Services, Worldwide University*)

CHARLES MERCIECA, Secretary General, International Association of Educators for World Peace, Huntsville, Alabama USA (*International Association of Educators for World Peace*)

JOSEPH A. MERCURIO, Assistant to the Dean, School of Education, Syracuse University, Syracuse, New York USA (*Teacher Education*)

R. P. MERRIDEW, International Secretary, Kiwanis International, Chicago, Illinois USA (*Kiwanis International*)

EDWARD C. MERRILL, JR., President, Gallaudet College, Washington, D.C. USA (*Deaf, Higher Education for the*)

ROBERT L. MESERVE, Associate Professor, Department of Civil Engineering, Northeastern University, Boston, Massachusetts USA (*Civil Engineering; Surveying—fields of study*)

EMILIO FERMÍN MIGNONE, former Rector, National University of Lujan, Buenos Aires, Argentina (*Argentine Republic—national system*)

GORDON W. MILLER, Centre for Advanced Studies and Research, Institute of Education, University of London, London, England (*Attrition: Wastage in Higher Education*)

HOWARD F. MILLER, JR., Department of Higher Education, State of New Jersey, Trenton, New Jersey USA (*Steady State*)

JERRY W. MILLER, Director, Office on Educational Credit, American Council on Education, Washington, D.C. USA (*Credit, Assessment of Learning for Postsecondary Education*)

RENE HARCOURT MILLER, H. N. Slater Professor of Flight Transportation, Head, Department of Aeronautics and Astronautics, Massachusetts Institute of Technology, Cambridge, Massachusetts USA (*Aeronautical and Astronautical Engineering—field of study*)

JOHN D. MILLETT, Senior Vice-President and Director, Management Division, Academy for Educational Development, Inc., Washington, D.C. USA (*General Administration, Organization for*)

WALTER MILNE, Special Assistant to the President, Massachusetts Institute of Technology, Cambridge, Massachusetts USA (*Town-Gown Relations*)

SHIGEO MINOWA, Director, United Nations University Press, Tokyo, Japan (*Presses, College and University*)

FRANCIS MOLONEY, Assistant Director, Boston Public Library, Boston, Massachusetts USA (*Libraries: Boston Public Library, United States*)

LUIS MONREAL, Secretary General, International Council of Museums, Paris, France (*Museum Studies—field of study*)

WALDO H. MOORE, Chief, Reference Division, Copyright Office, Library of Congress, Washington, D.C. USA (*Copyrights*)

R. PETER MOOZ, Director, Museum of Art, Senior Lecturer, Department of Art, Bowdoin College Museum of Art, Brunswick, Maine USA (*Art Collections, College and University*)

JOHN H. MORIARTY, Senior Project Director, Food and Agribusiness Section, Arthur D. Little, Inc., Cambridge, Massachusetts USA (*Food Science and Technology—field of study*)

MARGARET MORTIMER, former Director of Education, Sliema, Malta (*Malta, Republic of—national system*)

WANDA B. MOSBACKER, Director and Associate Dean Emeritus, Professional Development, Career Dynamics Center, University of Cincinnati, Cincinnati, Ohio USA (*Cooperative Education and Off-Campus Experience: Cooperative Education Worldwide*)

DONALD C. MOULTON, Assistant Vice-President for Community Affairs, Harvard University, Cambridge, Massachusetts USA (*Town-Gown Relations*)

EZEKIEL MPHAHLELE, Professor, Department of English, University of Pennsylvania, Philadelphia, Pennsylvania USA (*South Africa, Republic of—national system*)

SHARIF AL MUJAHID, Professor, Department of Journalism, University of Karachi, Karachi, Pakistan (*Illiteracy of Adults*)

EDMUND J. MULLEN, Dean, University Registrar, Northeastern University, Boston, Massachusetts USA (*Registrar*)

MULUGETA WODAJO, Department of Education, International Bank for Reconstruction and Development, Washington, D.C. USA, former Vice-President, Academic Affairs, Addis Ababa University, Addis Ababa, Ethiopia (*Ethiopia—national system*)

DAVID C. MUNROE, former Director, Institute of Education, McGill University, Montreal, Quebec, Canada (*Canada, Dominion of—national system*)

H. MUCHEMWA MURERWA, Doctoral Candidate, Graduate School of Education, Harvard University, Cambridge, Massachusetts USA (*Rhodesia—national system*)

K. SATCHIDANANDA MURTY, Vice-Chancellor, Sri Venkateswara University, Tirupati, India (*India, Republic of—national system*)

MOSES MUSONDA, Pro-Vice-Chancellor, University of Zambia, Lusaka, Zambia (*Zambia, Republic of—national system*)

ALEJANDRO NADAL, Researcher, College of Mexico, Mexico City, Mexico (*Science Policies: Argentina, Brazil, and Mexico*)

MINORU NAKAHARA, Executive Director, Association of Private Junior Colleges in Japan, Tokyo, Japan (*Association of Private Junior Colleges in Japan*)

SHIGERU NAKAYAMA, 3-7-11 Chuo, Nakano, Tokyo, Japan (*Religious Influences in Higher Education: Confucianism*)

MEHDI NAKOSTEEN, Professor Emeritus, School of Education, University of Colorado, Boulder, Colorado USA (*Religious Influences in Higher Education: Islam*)

GERALDO NASCIMENTO, Office of Statistics, UNESCO, Paris, France (*Statistics in Higher Education*)

WILLIAM Z. NASRI, Associate Professor, Graduate School of Library and Information Science, University of Pittsburgh, Pittsburgh, Pennsylvania USA (*Library Administration in the United States*)

LEE NEHRT, R. P. Clinton Professor of International Management, Wichita State University, Wichita, Kansas USA (*International Business—field of study*)

VALERIE NELSON, Faculty Member, Kennedy School of Government, Harvard University, Associate, University Consultants, Inc., Cambridge, Massachusetts USA (*Proprietary Schools*)

BARBARA W. NEWELL, President, Wellesley College, Wellesley, Massachusetts USA (*Women and Higher Education: Overview*)

W. ROY NIBLETT, Professor Emeritus of Higher Education, Institute of Education, University of London, London, England (*Innovation; Society for Research into Higher Education, United Kingdom*)

DAVIDSON S. H. W. NICOL, Under-Secretary General, United Nations, Executive Director, United Nations Institute for Training and Research, New York, New York USA (*Sierra Leone, Republic of—national system*)

RICHARD L. NOBLE, Associate Professor, Department of Wildlife and Fisheries Sciences, Texas Agricultural and Mechanical University, College Station, Texas USA (*Fisheries Science—field of study*)

GEORGE J. NOLFI, President, University Consultants, Inc., Cambridge, Massachusetts USA (*Proprietary Schools*)

LOUVAN E. NOLTING, 918 G. Street SE, Washington, D.C. USA (*Science Policies: Eastern European Socialist Countries*)

ANWAR AL-NOURI, Secretary General, Kuwait University, Kuwait (*Kuwait, State of—national system*)

J. C. T. OATES, Reader in Historical Bibliography, Cambridge University Library, Cambridge, England (*Libraries: Cambridge University Library, England*)

YVONNE ODDON, I.C.O.M. Training Unit, Paris, France (*Museum Studies—field of study*)

I. OGBUE, Secretary, Committee of Vice-Chancellors of Nigerian Universities, Lagos, Nigeria (*Committee of Vice-Chancellors of Nigerian Universities*)

GLENN A. OLDS, President, Kent State University, Kent, Ohio USA (*Aid to Other Nations: International Cooperation—Overview*)

HENRY OLELA, Atlanta University, Atlanta, Georgia USA (*Kenya, Republic of—national system*)

LOYD C. OLESON, Registrar, Doane College, Crete, Nebraska USA (*Calendars, Academic*)

LINDA OLSHEIM, Assistant to the Director, College and Community Relations, Fashion Institute of Technology, New York, New York USA (*Fashion Design—field of study*)

VICTOR G. ONUSHKIN, Professor, Leningrad State University, Leningrad, USSR (*Adult Education: Postexperience Education*)

W. J. OOSTERMEYER, Office of Higher Education, Konedobu, Papua New Guinea (*Papua New Guinea—national system*)

ENRIQUE OTEIZA, Member, Board of Directors, Latin American Social Science Council, Buenos Aires, Argentina (*Latin American Social Science Council*)

KRISTIAN OTTOSEN, Student Welfare Organization in Oslo, Oslo, Norway (*Business Management of Higher Education: Student Housing: Norwegian Case Study*)

COSTAS PAPAPANOS, former Director General of Higher Education, Athens, Greece (*Greek Republic—national system*)

KATHARINE O. PARKER, Free-lance Editor, Cambridge, Massachusetts USA (*Libraries: National Library of Peking, People's Republic of China*)

MOSES PASSER, Head, Department of Educational Activities, American Chemical Society, Washington, D.C. USA (*American Chemical Society*)

FRANKLIN PATTERSON, Frank L. Boyden Professor of the University, University of Massachusetts, Amherst, Massachusetts USA (*Consortia in the United States; Students, Student Services, and Student Organizations*)

JAMES C. N. PAUL, Director of Research, International Legal Center, New York, New York USA, Professor of Law, Rutgers, the State University, Newark, New Jersey USA (*Law and Jurisprudence—field of study*)

F. ROBERT PAULSEN, Dean, College of Education, University of Arizona, Tucson, Arizona USA (*Educational Administration—field of study*)

ROLLAND G. PAULSTON, Professor, Program in International and Development Education, School of Education, University of Pittsburgh, Pittsburgh, Pennsylvania USA (*Cuba, Republic of—national system*)

KEITH PAVITT, Senior Fellow, Science Policy Research Unit, University of Sussex, Brighton, England (*Science Policies: Western Europe*)

LELAND PEARSON, Captain, USMS, United States Merchant Marine Academy, Kings Point, New York USA (*Nautical Science—field of study*)

ELHANAN PELLES, President, Association of Engineers and Architects in Israel, Engineer's Institute, Tel-Aviv, Israel (*Association of Engineers and Architects in Israel*)

JAMES A. PERKINS, Chairman, International Council for Educational Development, New York, New York USA (*Autonomy*)

WALTER PERRY, Vice-Chancellor, Open University, Milton Keynes, England (*Open University*)

A. D. C. PETERSON, Director General, International Baccalaureate Office, Geneva, Switzerland and London, England (*International Baccalaureate*)

R. A. Peura, Associate Professor of Biomedical and Electrical Engineering, Acting Director, Biomedical Engineering Program, Worcester Polytechnic Institute, Site Director, St. Vincent Hospital Internship Center, Worcester, Massachusetts USA (*Bioengineering—field of study*)

James M. Phillips, Staff Associate, Council on Postsecondary Accreditation,Washington, D.C. USA (*Academic Standards and Accreditation: United States*)

Stephen Pickles, Library, Institute of Education, University of London, London, England (*Literature of Higher Education, Sources of and Access to*)

James Platt, Director, Central Bureau for Educational Visits and Exchanges, London, England (*Exchange, International: Student Exchange Programs*)

Donald G. Porter, Director of Development, Northeastern University, Boston, Massachusetts USA (*Foundations and Philanthropy*)

T. L. Postremova, former Scientific Secretary, V. I. Lenin State Library of the USSR, Moscow, USSR (*Libraries: Lenin State Library, Soviet Union*)

John W. Powell, President, John W. Powell Consultants, Inc., Hamden, Connecticut USA (*Security, Campus*)

Henry Poydar, Professor and Head, Department of Civil Engineering Technology, Wentworth Institute and College of Technology, Boston, Massachusetts USA (*Construction and Building Technology—field of study*)

Bogoda Premaratne, President, National Education Society of Sri Lanka, Faculty of Education, University of Sri Lanka, Colombo, Sri Lanka (*National Education Society of Sri Lanka*)

David C. Pritchard, Adjunct Professor, Center on Aging, School of Social Work, San Diego State University, San Diego, California USA (*Adult Education: Elderly, Programs for the*)

Gordon E. Pruett, Associate Professor, Department of Philosophy and Religion, Northeastern University, Boston, Massachusetts USA (*Religion and Theology—field of study*)

George Psacharopoulos, Department of Economics, London School of Economics and Political Science, University of London, London, England (*Economics of Higher Education*)

Pedro Moreno Quevedo, Head, Division of General Services, National Council of Higher Education, La Paz, Bolivia (*Bolivia, Republic of—national system*)

Tapio Rajavuori, Secretary to the Minister of Education, Ministry of Education, Helsinki, Finland (*Finland, Republic of—national system*)

Karen Eide Rawling, Associate Director, International Studies Association, University of Pittsburgh, Pittsburgh, Pennsylvania USA (*Research: International Research*)

Howard A. Reed, Professor of History, University of Connecticut, Storrs,

Connecticut USA (*Turkey, Republic of—national system*)

RICHARD R. RENNER, Professor of Education, University of Florida, Gainesville, Florida USA (*South America: Regional Analysis*)

EUGENE M. REPPUCCI, JR., Vice-President for Development, Northeastern University, Boston, Massachusetts USA (*Development, College and University*)

RESEARCH DIVISION, Rector's Office, Tribhuvan University, Kathmandu, Nepal (*Nepal, Kingdom of—national system*)

JAMES B. RHOADS, Archivist of the United States, National Archives and Records Service, Washington, D.C. USA (*Archives: United States, National Archives of*)

MODESTO G. RICO, General Secretary, Association of Christian Schools and Colleges, Manila, the Philippines (*Association of Christian Schools and Colleges, the Philippines*)

ALLAN RIX, Canadian Bureau for International Education, Ottawa, Canada (*Exchange, International: Travel Abroad*)

DANIEL J. ROBERTS, Vice-President for Business, Northeastern University, Boston, Massachusetts USA (*Financial Affairs: Accounting and Financial Reporting, Budgeting, Investments*)

ERIC E. ROBINSON, Principal, Bradford College, Bradford, England (*Mergers in Higher Education*)

FRANK M. ROBINSON, JR., Associate Professor of Recreation Education, Northeastern University, Boston, Massachusetts USA (*Handicapped, Higher Education for the Physically*)

JOHN ROBSON, Editor, *Baird's Manual of American College Fraternities*, Menasha, Wisconsin USA (*Fraternities*)

HAROLD P. RODES, former President, General Motors Institute, Flint, Michigan USA (*Automotive Technologies—field of study*)

KENNETH W. RODGERS, Senior Staff, Arthur D. Little, Inc., Cambridge, Massachusetts USA (*General Administration, Organization for*)

GERARDO R. ROSARIO, Director, Management Services Division, Catholic Educational Association of the Philippines, Manila, the Philippines (*Catholic Educational Association of the Philippines*)

SHERMAN ROSS, Graduate Professor of Psychology, Howard University, Washington, D.C. USA (*Psychology—field of study*)

PATRICIA A. ROWE, Professor and Chairman, Department of Dance and Dance Education, New York University, New York, New York USA (*Dance—field of study*)

CHALMER J. ROY, Dean Emeritus, Department of Earth Science, Iowa State University, Ames, Iowa USA (*Geological Sciences—field of study*)

ROBERT A. RUPEN, Professor, Department of Political Science, University of North Carolina, Chapel Hill, North Carolina USA (*Mongolian People's Republic—national system*)

PHILIP J. RUSCHE, Associate Dean and Director, Graduate School of Education, Northeastern University, Boston, Massachusetts USA (*Sciences and Education*)

NICHOLAS O. SADNYTZKY, Department of Higher and Adult Education, Teachers College, Columbia University, New York, New York USA (*Mass Higher Education*)

FRANCISCO R. SAGASTI, Field Coordinator, Science and Technology Policy Instruments Project, Lima, Peru (*Science Policies: Andean Common Market Countries*)

PETER SAMMARTINO, Chancellor, Fairleigh Dickinson University, Rutherford, New Jersey USA (*Branch Campuses*)

IRENE SANDVOLD, Chairperson, Committee on Publicity and Public Relations, American College of Nurse-Midwives, Washington, D.C. USA (*Midwifery—field of study*)

LAURIE SAPPER, General Secretary, Association of University Teachers, London, England (*Association of University Teachers, United Kingdom*)

JOSEPH SATIN, Dean, School of Humanities, California State University, Fresno, California USA (*Humanities—field of study*)

DAVID J. SAUL, Permanent Secretary for Education, Ministry of Education, Hamilton, Bermuda (*Bermuda, Colony of—national system*)

CLAYTON A. SAWYER, Coordinator of Teacher Training, Professor of Methodology of Teaching, Higher Normal School of Mexico, Mexico City, Mexico (*Worldwide Languages of Instruction*)

HANS-DIETER SCHAEFER, Professor of Comparative Education, Institute for Higher Education at the Humboldt-University of Berlin, Berlin, German Democratic Republic (*German Democratic Republic—national system*)

PHYLLIS M. SCHAEN, Assistant to Vice-President for Administration, Northeastern University, Boston, Massachusetts USA (*Admissions: An International Perspective*)

EVERT SCHLINGER, Chairman, Division of Entomology and Parasitology, University of California, Berkeley, California USA (*Entomology—field of study*)

JURGEN SCHMANDT, Professor, Lyndon B. Johnson School of Public Affairs, University of Texas, Austin, Texas USA (*Research: Financing and Control of Research*)

JAMES L. SCHOFIELD, Director, Library Management Research Unit, University of Technology, Loughborough, England (*Library Administration Outside the United States*)

WAYNE E. SCHROEDER, Specialist—International, Center for Vocational Education, Ohio State University, Columbus, Ohio USA (*Agricultural Education, Teacher Training for—field of study*)

BRIGITTE SCHROEDER-GUDEHUS, Professor, Institute of History and the Sociopolitics of the Sciences, University of Montreal, Montreal, Quebec, Canada (*Science Policies: Canada*)

JOSEPH J. SCHWAB, Associate, Center for the Study of Democratic Institutions, Fund for the Republic, Inc., Santa Barbara, California USA (*Scholarship, Classification of in the Curriculum*)

RONALD E. SCOTT, University Professor, School of Engineering, College of Petroleum and Minerals, Dhahran, Saudi Arabia (*Petroleum Engineering—field of study*)

JOHN SCUPHAM, 26 Crabtree Lane, Harpenden, England (*Educational Resources: Radio and Television as Instructional Media*)

C. M. SEAH, Sub-Dean, Faculty of Arts and Social Sciences, Past President, Academic Association of the University of Singapore, Singapore, Republic of Singapore (*Academic Association of the University of Singapore*)

A. N. SEITHLEKO, Ministry of Education, Maseru, Lesotho (*Lesotho, Kingdom of—national system*)

N. O. H. SETIDISHO, Rector, University College of Botswana and Swaziland, Gaborone, Botswana (*Botswana, Republic of—national system*)

BOYD C. SHAFER, Professor Emeritus, University of Arizona, Tucson, Arizona USA (*History—field of study*)

ZAKI SHALOM, former Secretary of Foreign Affairs, National Union of Israel Students, Jerusalem, Israel (*National Union of Israel Students*)

MARVIN SHAPIRO, Past President, American Podiatry Association, Toledo, Ohio USA (*Podiatry—field of study*)

BERNARD S. SHEEHAN, Director, Office of Institutional Research, University of Calgary, Calgary, Alberta, Canada (*Institutional Research*)

PHILIP SHERLOCK, Secretary General, Association of Caribbean Universities and Research Institutes, Kingston, Jamaica (*Caribbean: Regional Analysis*)

MARGARET E. SHERMAN, Publications Editor, Council on International Educational Exchange, New York, New York USA (*Council on International Educational Exchange, United States*)

MICHIYA SHIMBORI, Professor, School of Education, Hiroshima University, Hiroshima, Japan (*Change, Social*)

ZOHER E. SHIPCHANDLER, Associate Professor, Division of Business and Economics, Indiana University-Purdue University, Fort Wayne, Indiana USA (*Business and Office Technologies—field of study*)

M. MOBIN SHORISH, Associate Professor, Comparative Education, College of Education, University of Illinois at Urbana-Champaign, Urbana, Illinois USA (*Access of Minorities: Soviet Union, People's Republic of China, and Islamic Nations*)

MILTON L. SHUCH, Chairman, Department of Management, Simmons College, Boston, Massachusetts USA (*Retailing—field of study*)

SIDNEY N. SHURCLIFF, Shurcliff and Merrill, Landscape Architects, Cambridge, Massachusetts USA (*Landscape Architecture—field of study*)

W. M. SIBLEY, Academic Vice-President, Mount Allison University, Sackville, New Brunswick, Canada (*Accountability*)

JON SIGURDSON, Scandinavian Institute of Asian Studies, Copenhagen, Denmark, Research Policy Program, University of Lund, Lund, Sweden (*Aid to Other Nations: Technology Transfer*)

DAVID L. SILLS, Executive Associate, Social Science Research Council, New York, New York USA (*Social and Behavioral Sciences—field of study*)

HRIDAYA NARAYAN SINGH, Founder Secretary General, All-India Federation of University and College Teachers' Organizations, Jaunpur, India (*All-India Federation of University and College Teachers' Organizations*)

HELVI SIPILÄ, Assistant Secretary General, Social Development and Humanitarian Affairs, United Nations, New York, New York USA (*Women and Higher Education: International Agents of Change*)

EUGENE B. SKOLNIKOFF, Professor and Director of Political Science, Center for International Studies, Massachusetts Institute of Technology, Cambridge, Massachusetts USA (*Science Policies: Overview*)

GERALD SMITH, Associate Dean, School of Engineering, Hatfield Polytechnic, Hatfield, England (*Exchange, International: Student Employment Abroad; Industrial Engineering—field of study*)

HUGH H. SMITH, Professor of Commerce, Rhodes University, Grahamstown, South Africa (*Academic Dress and Insignia*)

MERVIN G. SMITH, Assistant Dean, College of Agriculture, Home Economics and Natural Resources, Ohio State University, Columbus, Ohio USA (*Agriculture, Forestry, and Fisheries—field of study*)

D. MCCORMACK SMYTH, Professor of Administration, Atkinson College, York University, Toronto, Ontario, Canada (*Governance and Control of Higher Education: Academic Decision Making*)

ARCHIE N. SOLBERG, Executive Director, Honor Society of Phi Kappa Phi, Ann Arbor, Michigan USA (*Honor Societies*)

ALBERT H. SOLOWAY, Dean, College of Pharmacy, Ohio State University, Columbus, Ohio USA (*Pharmacy—field of study*)

A. H. SOROUR, Professor, Medical Adviser, Ministry of Health, Abu Dhabi, United Arab Emirates, former Deputy Director, Higher Studies and Research Affairs, University of Cairo, Cairo, Egypt (*Egypt, Arab Republic of—national system*)

HUGH W. SPRINGER, Secretary General, Association of Commonwealth Universities, London, England (*Association of Commonwealth Universities*)

ROBERT M. SPRINKLE, Executive Director, International Association for the Exchange of Students for Technical Experience, Columbia, Maryland USA (*International Association for the Exchange of Students for Technical Experience*)

GEOFFREY SQUIRES, Research Fellow, Group for Research and Innovation on Higher Education, Nuffield Foundation, London, England (*Interdisciplinary Studies—field of study*)

E. PERCIL STANFORD, Director, Center on Aging, School of Social Work, San Diego State University, San Diego, California USA (*Adult Education: Elderly, Programs for the*)

PHILIP JOHN STEAD, Professor of Comparative Police Science, Department of Law, Police Science, and Criminal Justice Administration, John Jay College of Criminal Justice, New York, New York USA (*Police and Law Enforcement Training—field of study*)

JOHN STEEVES, Head, Department of Manufacturing Processes, Wentworth Institute and College of Technology, Boston, Massachusetts USA (*Metal Trades and Mechanical Repair Trades—field of study*)

T. STEGER, Associate Professor, School of the Art Institute of Chicago, Chicago, Illinois USA (*Printmaking—field of study*)

N. G. E. STENT, former President, National Union of South African Students, Cape Town, South Africa (*National Union of South African Students*)

BRANCH K. STERNAL, Assistant Professor of International Business, College of Business Administration, Northeastern University, Boston, Massachusetts USA (*Consultants, Use of*)

CLIFFORD T. STEWART, Dean, Academic Affairs, Adelphi University, Garden City, New York USA (*Trends in Higher Education*)

W. A. CAMPBELL STEWART, Vice-Chancellor, University of Keele, Keele, England (*Further Education*)

STEPHEN STIGLER, Professor, Department of Statistics, University of Wisconsin-Madison, Madison, Wisconsin USA (*Statistics—field of study*)

RALPH D. STOAKS, Assistant Executive Secretary, Coordinator of Research, Council on Chiropractic Education, Des Moines, Iowa USA (*Chiropractic—field of study*)

ARTHUR K. STOCK, Director, National Institute of Adult Education, Leicester, England (*Adult Education: Administration*)

MARSHALL H. STONE, Professor, Department of Mathematics, University of Massachusetts, Amherst, Massachusetts USA, Professor Emeritus, University of Chicago, Chicago, Illinois USA (*Mathematics—field of study*)

WILLIAM B. STRONG, Dean, proposed New England College of Osteopathic Medicine, Biddeford, Maine USA (*Osteopathic Medicine—field of study*)

GEORGE B. STROTHER, Professor of Management, Graduate School of Business, University of Wisconsin-Madison, Madison, Wisconsin USA (*Public Service Role of Higher Education*)

HELEN STROW, Consultant, Home Economics, International Extension Service, United States Department of Agriculture, Washington, D.C. USA (*Home Economics—field of study*)

ELIZABETH W. SUCHAR, Director, Financial Aid Services, College Entrance Examination Board, New York, New York USA (*Financial Aid: Financial Aid to Students—United States*)

Lawrence Susskind, Professor, Department of Urban Studies and Planning, Massachusetts Institute of Technology, Cambridge, Massachusetts USA (*City and Regional Planning—field of study*)

Denis Szabo, Director, International Centre for Comparative Criminology, University of Montreal, Montreal, Quebec, Canada (*Criminology—field of study*)

Henryk Szarras, Member, Executive Committee of the Section of Scientific Workers of the Polish Teachers Union, Warsaw, Poland (*Polish Teachers Union—Section of Scientific Workers*)

P. Tabatoni, Delegate, Delegation of International University Relations, University State Secretary, Paris, France (*Delegation of International University Relations, France*)

L. S. Taiaroa, Deputy Secretary, New Zealand Vice-Chancellors' Committee, Victoria University of Wellington, Wellington, New Zealand (*New Zealand Vice-Chancellors' Committee*)

Nancy H. Talbot, Chairman, Department of Occupational Therapy, Sargent College of Allied Health Professions, Boston University, Boston, Massachusetts USA (*Occupational Therapy—field of study*)

B. H. Taylor, Executive Secretary, Committee of Vice-Chancellors and Principals of the Universities of the United Kingdom, London, England (*Committee of Vice-Chancellors and Principals of the Universities of the United Kingdom*)

Carl E. Taylor, Professor and Chairman, Department of International Health, Johns Hopkins University, Baltimore, Maryland USA (*Public Health—field of study*)

Mary Louise Taylor, Office of Planning and Analysis, Institute of International Education, New York, New York USA (*Exchange, International: Study Abroad*)

James G. Teer, Head, Department of Wildlife and Fisheries Sciences, Texas Agricultural and Mechanical University, College Station, Texas USA (*Wildlife Ecology and Management—field of study*)

Gerrit J. Ten Brink, Vice-President, Council for the Advancement of Small Colleges, Washington, D.C. USA (*Evaluation of Administrators*)

Guy Terny, Professor, Ecole Nationale d'Administration, Paris, France (*Financial Affairs: Cost Analysis*)

Robert C. Tetro, 12012 Aintree Lane, Reston, Virginia USA (*International Cooperation in Agriculture*)

Inge Theierl-Hall, Gent, Belgium (*Women and Higher Education: Day Care Centers*)

John I. Thomas, Professor, Department of Elementary and Secondary Education, New Mexico State University, Las Cruces, New Mexico USA (*Albania, People's Socialist Republic of—national system*)

Kenneth W. Thompson, Commmonwealth Professor of Government and Foreign Affairs, University of Virginia, Charlottesville, Virginia USA (*International Development, Role of Higher Education*)

MELVYN C. THORNE, Assistant Professor, Department of International Health, Johns Hopkins University, Baltimore, Maryland USA (*Public Health—field of study*)

M. ELIZABETH TIDBALL, Professor of Physiology, George Washington University Medical Center, Washington, D.C. USA (*Access of Women Students to Higher Education; Women and Higher Education: Women's Colleges*)

JAMES F. TIERNEY, former Vice-President, Institute of International Education, International Councils on Higher Education, New York, New York USA (*Exchange, International: Overview*)

ROYAL L. TINSLEY, JR., Associate Professor of German, University of Arizona, Tucson, Arizona, President, American Translators Association, Croton-Hudson, New York USA (*Translators' and Interpretors' Programs—field of study*)

SHEILA TOBIAS, Associate Provost, Wesleyan University, Middletown, Connecticut USA (*Women and Higher Education: Women's Studies and Curricular Modification*)

ERNESTO TORO, Graduate School of Education, Harvard University, Cambridge, Massachusetts USA (*Chile, Republic of—national system*)

LOIS E. TORRENCE, Director, Office of Institutional Research, University of Connecticut, Storrs, Connecticut USA (*Institutional Research*)

ROGER TRANCIK, Associate Professor, Urban Design Program, Graduate School of Design, Harvard University, Cambridge, Massachusetts USA (*Urban Design—field of study*)

FRANK A. TREDINNICK, JR., Association of Independent Colleges and Universities in Massachusetts, Boston, Massachusetts USA (*Academic Freedom*)

OLAV M. TROVIK, Secretary General, Conference of Rectors of Universities and Colleges in Norway, Director, University of Oslo, Oslo, Norway (*Conference of Rectors of Universities and Colleges in Norway*)

CARLOS TÜNNERMANN B., former Rector, National Autonomous University of Nicaragua, Leon, Nicaragua (*Central America: Regional Analysis; Guatemala, Republic of—national system*)

KENNETH L. TURK, Professor Emeritus, Department of Animal Science, New York State College of Agriculture and Life Sciences, Cornell University, Ithaca, New York USA (*Dairy Science—field of study*)

SOLVEIG M. TURNER, Editor, National Systems of Higher Education, *The International Encyclopedia of Higher Education*, Assistant Director, Center for International Higher Education Documentation, Northeastern University, Boston, Massachusetts USA (*Financial Aid: Financial Aid to Students—A Global Perspective*)

LEWIS A. TYLER, Assistant Director, Latin American Scholarship Program of American Universities, Harvard University, Cambridge, Massachusetts USA (*Peru, Republic of—national system*)

RALPH W. TYLER, Director Emeritus, Center for Advanced Study in the Behavioral Sciences, Stanford, California USA (*Planning, Development, and Coordination: Overview*)

PREMADASA UDAGAMA, Secretary, Ministry of Education, Colombo, Sri Lanka (*Sri Lanka, Republic of—national system*)

VICTOR L. URGUIDI, President, College of Mexico, Mexico City, Mexico (*Science Policies: Argentina, Brazil, and Mexico*)

EUGENE I. VAN ANTWERP, Staff Associate, Council on Postsecondary Accreditation, Washington, D.C. USA (*Academic Standards and Accreditation: United States*)

MAURICE L. VAN VLIET, President, XI Commonwealth Games Canada (1978) Foundation, Edmonton, Alberta, Canada (*Sport, Interuniversity*)

HENRY VAN ZILE HYDE, Executive Director, World Federation for Medical Education, Bethesda, Maryland USA (*Medicine and Medical Specialties—field of study*)

HARVEY VETSTEIN, Dean, Office of Student Affairs, Northeastern University, Boston, Massachusetts USA (*Student Publications*)

BERNARD VEYRET, Research Fellow, Department of Chemistry, Northeastern University, Boston, Massachusetts USA (*French Republic—national system*)

MILICA VINTER, Counsellor, Institute for Development of Education, Belgrade, Yugoslavia (*Yugoslavia, Socialist Federal Republic of—national system*)

JOY WINKIE VIOLA, Senior Editor, *The International Encyclopedia of Higher Education*, Director, Center for International Higher Education Documentation, Northeastern University, Boston, Massachusetts USA (*Academic Standards and Accreditation: International; Exchange, International: Campus International Offices; United States of America—national system*)

RALPH H. VOGEL, Staff Director, Board of Foreign Scholarships, United States Department of State, Washington, D.C. USA (*Exchange, International: Teaching and Research Exchange*)

LOUIS VRETTOS, Chancellor, Deree-Pierce Colleges, Athens, Greece (*Greek Republic—national system*)

NORMAN WADHAM, Assistant to the Librarian, Teachers College, Columbia University, New York, New York USA (*Periodicals, Higher Education*)

GEORGE R. WAGGONER, Associate Vice-Chancellor, Academic Affairs—International Programs, University of Kansas, Lawrence, Kansas USA (*Venezuela, Republic of—national system*)

WALTER D. WAGONER, Senior Minister, Asylum Hill Congregational Church, Hartford, Connecticut USA (*Religious Influences in Higher Education: Protestantism*)

W. SHERIDAN WARRICK, Executive Director, International House at the University of California, Berkeley, California USA (*Exchange, International: International Houses and Centers*)

SETH H. WASHBURN, Executive Director, Technical Employment, Education, and Salary Administration Division, Bell Laboratories, Murray Hill, New Jersey USA (*Manpower Planning: Role of Industry*)

NANCY T. WATTS, Assistant Director, Educational Planning, Massachusetts General Hospital, Boston, Massachusetts USA (*Physical Therapy—field of study*)

ROBERT K. WEATHERALL, Director, Career Planning and Placement, Massachusetts Institute of Technology, Cambridge, Massachusetts USA (*Graduate and Professional Education: Postdoctoral Education*)

GEORGE B. WEATHERSBY, Associate Professor, Graduate School of Education, Harvard University, Cambridge, Massachusetts USA (*Financing of Higher Education: Financing Institutions and Systems*)

CHARLES A. WEDEMEYER, William H. Lighty Professor of Education, University of Wisconsin-Madison, Madison, Wisconsin USA (*Independent Study*)

BERNARD WEILBRENNER, Assistant Dominion Archivist, Public Archives, Canada, Ottawa, Ontario, Canada (*Archives: Canada, Public Archives of*)

PETER WEINRICH, Executive Director, Canadian Crafts Council, Ottawa, Ontario, Canada (*Crafts—field of study*)

ROY WEINSTEIN, Chairman, Department of Physics, Northeastern University, Boston, Massachusetts USA (*Physics—field of study*)

KARL WEISS, Chairman, Department of Chemistry, Northeastern University, Boston, Massachusetts USA (*Chemistry—field of study*)

WILHELM WENGLER, Professor, Institute for International, Foreign and Comparative Law, Free University of Berlin, Berlin, Federal Republic of Germany (*Governance and Control of Higher Education: University Legislation*)

CHARLES A. WERT, Head, Department of Metallurgy and Mining Engineering, University of Illinois at Urbana-Champaign, Urbana, Illinois USA (*Metallurgical Engineering and Materials Sciences—field of study*)

ROY A. WHITEKER, Dean, University of the Pacific, Stockton, California USA (*Council for International Exchange of Scholars*)

I. J. WHYLE, President, New Zealand Teachers Colleges Association, Wellington, New Zealand (*New Zealand Teachers Colleges Association*)

JOHN WICKLEIN, Dean, School of Public Communication, Boston University, Boston, Massachusetts USA (*Mass Communication—field of study*)

JAMES W. WILSON, Asa S. Knowles Professor of Cooperative Education,

Director, Cooperative Education Research Center, Northeastern University, Boston, Massachusetts USA (*Cooperative Education and Off-Campus Experience: Cooperative Education in the United States*)

LEONARD M. WILSON, Faculty Member, Arthur D. Little Management Education Institute, Cambridge, Massachusetts USA, President, Agribusiness Associates, Inc., Wellesley Hills, Massachusetts USA (*Agriculture in Higher Education: Agribusiness and Agribusiness Education*)

PAMELA L. WILSON, Head, Public Relations, Institute of International Education, New York, New York USA (*Institute of International Education*)

ROBIN S. WILSON, Associate Director, Committee on Institutional Cooperation, Evanston, Illinois USA (*Interinstitutional Cooperation*)

MARY B. WINE, Director of Professional Relations, Association of Independent Colleges and Schools, Washington, D.C. USA (*Association of Independent Colleges and Schools*)

MICHEL WOITRIN, Professor and General Administrator, Catholic University of Louvain, Louvain-La-Neuve, Belgium (*Towns, University*)

DAEL WOLFLE, Graduate School of Public Affairs, University of Washington, Seattle, Washington USA (*Manpower Planning: Role of Government*)

EDWARD G. WOLFMAN, Staff Writer, Public Relations, Credit Union National Association, Inc. Madison, Wisconsin USA (*Credit Union, College and University*)

FREDERIC C. WOOD, Director, Wood and Tower, Inc., Princeton, New Jersey USA (*Building and Construction Administration*)

ROBERT WOOD, President, University of Massachusetts, Amherst, Massachusetts USA (*Urban University*)

RAYMOND J. WOODROW, Assistant for Special Studies, University Research Board, Princeton University, Princeton, New Jersey USA (*Research: Administration of Academic Research*)

ROY L. WOOLDRIDGE, Vice-President for Cooperative Education, Northeastern University, Boston, Massachusetts USA (*Cooperative Education and Off-Campus Experience: Organization and Administration of Programs*)

DAVID C. YU, Professor of History of Religion, Colorado Women's College, Denver, Colorado USA (*Religious Influences in Higher Education: Taoism*)

HAROLD E. YUKER, Provost and Dean of Faculties, Hofstra University, Hempstead, New York USA (*Workloads of Academic Personnel*)

S. J. LUYIMBAZI ZAKE, Professor of Cultural Anthropology, Governors State University, Park Forest South, Illinois USA (*Uganda, Republic of—national system*)

AMI ZUSMAN, Doctoral Candidate, Program in Higher Education, University of California, Berkeley, California USA (*Planning, Devel-*

opment, and Coordination: State Planning in United States Higher Education)

J. L. ZWINGLE, former President, Association of Governing Boards of Universities and Colleges, Washington, D.C. USA (*Governance and Control of Higher Education: Charters—Collegiate Authority*)

Acknowledgments

The work of the Editor-in-Chief and the editorial staff in organizing and developing this *Encyclopedia* has been made possible, in large part, by the generosity of Northeastern University and several individuals and foundations.

Robert H. Willis, Chairman of the Northeastern University Board of Trustees, encouraged the Editor-in-Chief to undertake this project, and made available space, equipment, staff, and a substantial portion of the funds needed to defray salaries of the editorial staff, secretarial and clerical staff, and others who have served as consultants or provided special services. In addition, generous financial contributions for this project were made by David Cogan, Joseph Riesman, and the late Eli Jacobson, members of the Northeastern University Board of Trustees, who demonstrated great interest in the *Encyclopedia* and encouraged the work of the Editor-in-Chief.

Funds were also received from The Braitmayer Foundation, Marion, Massachusetts; the General Service Foundation, St. Paul, Minnesota; and The Henry P. Kendall Foundation, Boston, Massachusetts.

In recognition of the contributions of Northeastern University, individuals, and foundations, the Editor-in-Chief decided that he could not, in good conscience, accept payment of royalties for his work as Editor-in-Chief, responsible for the organization and the preparation of the *Encyclopedia*. The Editor-in-Chief has therefore designated that royalties due him for his work shall be paid directly to Northeastern University in order to reimburse the University for out-of-pocket expenditures.

In further recognition of Northeastern's contributions to this project, the Editor-in-Chief has made available to the University the collection of books, research materials, including many booklets and pamphlets gathered from throughout the world, as well as all correspondence and special documents that have been developed as a result of research in preparing *Encyclopedia* materials. These materials form the nucleus of a special library collection designated as the Center for International Higher Education Documentation. It is hoped that this unique collection, combined with holdings of the Northeastern University Library and additions to be acquired in future years, will be an important source of information on international higher education for scholars interested in conducting research and obtaining information on all aspects of higher education throughout the world.

The preparation of an encyclopedia demands advice and contributions from a great many persons who have expert knowledge to offer. Members of the Editorial Advisory Board and Board of Consultants made substantial contributions to the preparation of the contents of this *Encyclopedia* and helped establish the priorities relative to the appropriateness of certain materials to be included. In addition, the boards suggested names of contributors, authors, and other persons capable of giving advice to help ensure an *Encyclopedia* of high quality and of maximum value to potential users. They also prepared specific articles for inclusion in the *Encyclopedia*. The advice, encouragement, and contributions of the members of the Editorial Advisory Board and Board of Consultants are appreciated.

The Editor-in-Chief has been privileged to have the advice and counsel of many distinguished educators. Special thanks are due to a number of individuals who significantly contributed to the preparation of the *Encyclopedia*. Their names, listed alphabetically, are:

PIERRE AIGRAIN, General Technical Director, Thomson-CSF, Paris, for assistance with the outlines of certain science policy articles

DEBORRAH ARRINDELL, former Program Assistant, American Association of State Colleges and Universities, for assistance in connection with the article on programs for the elderly

MAYNARD BRICHFORD, for assistance in determining the contents pertaining to archives in various nations and for suggesting names of authorities to serve as contributing authors or advisers

THELMA BRISTOW, Comparative Education Librarian, University of London, for assistance in supplying information regarding library administration

HARRISON BROWN, President, International Council of Scientific Unions, Paris, for assistance in advising on science policy outlines, authors, and definitions of groupings of science policy articles

DOUGLAS W. BRYANT, Director, Harvard University Libraries, and EDWIN E. WILLIAMS, Associate University Librarian, for advice on the selection of libraries to be described in the *Encyclopedia* and directing the preparation of the article describing the Harvard University Libraries

J. DOUGLAS CONNER, Executive Secretary, American Association of Collegiate Registrars and Admissions Officers, for assistance in connection with the article on the registrar

THOMAS CRAIG, Assistant Secretary General, Association of Commonwealth Universities, London, for recommending names of contributing authors and sources of materials

BREWSTER C. DENNY, Dean, Graduate School of Public Affairs, University of Washington, for reviewing the articles on science policy

ANN M. DUNCAN-GLASGOW, Associate Dean and Director, Affirmative Action, Northeastern University, for assistance in reviewing and preparing the article on Affirmative Action

EDWIN D. DURYEA, Professor, State University of New York at Buffalo, for assistance on several topical essays

SHIRLEY FISCHER, former Director, Overseas Liaison Committee, American Council on Education, for assistance with the essays on fields of study and national systems

DOROTEA FURTH, Directorate for Social Affairs, Manpower and Education, Organisation for Economic Co-operation and Development, Paris, for advice on the preparation of materials pertaining to social affairs, manpower, and education and for recommending names of contributing authors for the *Encyclopedia*

ROSE HAYDEN, International Education Project, American Council on Education, for recommending contributing authors

SANFORD C. JAMESON, Director, International Education, College Entrance Examination Board, for assistance in defining contents of articles and reviewing outlines on educational exchange

PETER KAPLAN, Associate Vice-President, Management and Business Affairs, University of Massachusetts, for providing information on the determination of remuneration in public postsecondary institutions of the United States

H. M. R. KEYES, Secretary General, International Association of Universities, for recommending sources of information

CHARLES V. KIDD, Executive Secretary, Association of American Universities, for assistance in the definition of articles on science policy

J. ROBY KIDD, Secretary General, International Council for Adult Education, for recommending contributing authors for articles on adult education

THERESA KLEINDIENST, General Secretary, Bibliothèque Nationale, Paris, for cooperation in providing information on library administration

REYNALDO FLORES MACIAS, Chicano Studies Center, University of California, Los Angeles, for advising on Chicano studies and helping define the Chicano minority education issues

LAWRENCE MITCHELL, Staff Director, USSR Eastern European Exchanges, National Academy of Science, for helping define articles on science policies and recommending contributing authors

AKIO MORISHIMA, Professor of Law, Nagoya University Law Faculty, Japan, and Visiting Professor at East Asia Studies Center, Harvard University, for his assistance in supplying information on remuneration and faculty personnel policies of Japanese higher education

BRADFORD MORSE, former Under-Secretary General for Political and General Assembly Affairs of the United Nations, and now Administrator of the United Nations Development Program, for encouragement in the preparation of the *Encyclopedia* and for making it possible for the Editor-in-Chief to meet with those officials of the United Nations and UNESCO whose assistance was sought in the preparation of the *Encyclopedia*

BARBARA NEWELL, President, Wellesley College, for recommending authors and defining contents for the articles on women in higher education

BONIFACE OBICHERE, Director, African Studies Center, University of California, Los Angeles, for suggesting names of African authors

VICTOR RABINOWITCH, Staff Director, Board on Science and Technology for International Development, National Academy of Science, for advice on the contents of science policy articles and recommending authors

STANLAKE SAMKANGE, Professor of African-American Studies, Northeastern University, for his special help in suggesting authors and advising on and reviewing special articles pertaining to African nations

DAVID L. SILLS, Executive Associate, Social Science Research Council, and Editor-in-Chief, *Social Science Encyclopedia*, for his advice concerning the preparation and editing of an encyclopedia

JOHN SPEIGEL, Assistant Professor of Modern Languages, Northeastern University, for assistance in verifying Russian language text materials

LILY VON KLEMPERER, Consultant in International Education, for advice on potential authors and articles pertaining to international exchange, study abroad, and employment abroad

CICELY WATSON, Ontario Institute for Studies in Education, Toronto, for suggesting names of contributing authors to prepare articles on planning

C. A. WILLIAMS, former Deputy Director, Extension Service, United States Department of Agriculture, for assistance in defining the topics pertaining to agricultural higher education

DAEL WOLFLE, Graduate School of Public Affairs, University of Washington, for reviewing articles on science policies

Particular thanks are also due the librarians and staff of numerous libraries for their continuous assistance to the editorial staff during the five-year preparation period of the *Encyclopedia*. Libraries throughout the world furnished, on request, specialized materials and information for use in the preparation of the *Encyclopedia*.

Among those libraries whose staffs have been most helpful are the Harvard University Libraries, the Massachusetts Institute of Technology Library, the Boston Public Library, and in particular, the staff members of the Northeastern University Library and the Library of Congress.

The names of those who have been most helpful to the Editor-in-Chief, as well as to the editorial staff of the *Encyclopedia*, are:

Northeastern University Library Personnel, Boston, Massachusetts USA:
ROLAND H. MOODY, Dean of Libraries and Learning Resources
KRISTINE JO ANDERSON, Assistant Reference Librarian
CHARLES R. AYER, Assistant Reference Librarian
SHARON C. BONK, Periodicals Librarian
LOUISE K. DENNETT, Inter-Library Loan-Orientation Librarian
ALBERT M. DONLEY, JR., Associate Director, University Library
JOYCE E. LUNDE, Assistant Librarian Reference Services
ROXANNE B. PALMATIER, Documents Microforms Librarian
DEIDRE SOCKBESON, former Inter-Library Loan Librarian

Library of Congress Personnel, Washington, D.C. USA:
ROBERT V. ALLEN, Area Specialist, USSR, Slavic and Central European Division
GEORGE T. ATIYEH, Chief, Near East Section
JOHN A. FEULNER, Head, Referral Services Section, National Referral Center, Science and Technology Division
SAM IFTIKHAR, Southern Asia Division
MARY KAHLER, Chief, Latin American Section
THOMAS KANG, Specialist, Korea, Orientalia Division
JOHN KIMBALL, Assistant Head, Union Catalog and International Organizations Reference Section
ANDREW Y. KURODA, Head, Japanese Section, Orientalia Division
ANITA R. NAVON, Area Specialist, Czechoslovakia and East Europe, Slavic and Central European Division
GEORGE E. PERRY, Area Specialist, Greece, Slavic and Central European Division
ARNOLD H. PRICE, Area Specialist, Central Europe, Slavic and Central European Division
A. KOHAR RONY, Area Specialist, Southeast Asia Division
ROBERT W. SCHAAF, Head, Union Catalog and International Organizations, Reference Section
CHI WANG, Head, Chinese and Korean Section
JULIAN W. WITHERILL, Head, African Division

The Editor-in-Chief also wishes to acknowledge the many contributions made by staff members of embassies of all foreign governments accredited to the United States, all embassies accredited to the United Nations, all national commissions for UNESCO, and all ministries of education of nations of the world for assistance to the Editor-in-Chief in the preparation of the *Encyclopedia*.

A special word of thanks is also due to the staff of the Center for International Visitors of Greater Boston, who directed to Northeastern University, and particularly to the Office of the Editor-in-Chief, many visitors from other nations. The conversations with these visitors were productive and considerably valuable in defining the contents of the *Encyclopedia*.

The preparation of the bibliographies required special knowledge and expertise. The following individuals are due thanks for their important assistance in preparing and checking bibliographies for articles, topics, and fields of study contained within this *Encyclopedia*:

NANCY ALLEN, Librarian, Boston Museum of Fine Arts, Boston, Massachusetts USA

KRISTINE JO ANDERSON, Assistant Reference Librarian, Dodge Library, Northeastern University, Boston, Massachusetts USA

KATHY L. BERG, Librarian, Boston Museum of Fine Arts, Boston, Massachusetts USA

ELIZABETH BURDICK, Director of Library, International Theatre Institute of the United States, New York, New York USA

TERRY CARLSON, Library Assistant, Harvard College Library, Cambridge, Massachusetts USA

MARY VAN A. CHATFIELD, Associate Librarian, Baker Library, Harvard Business School, Boston, Massachusetts USA

BARBARA COFFEY, Associate Librarian, Wentworth Institute and College of Technology, Boston, Massachusetts USA

HEATHER COLE, Reference Librarian, Widener Library, Harvard College Library, Cambridge, Massachusetts USA

NANCY COTTRILL, Cambridge, Massachusetts USA

ELEANOR DRUCKMAN, Librarian, Center for the Analysis of Health Practices, Harvard School of Public Health, Boston Massachusetts USA

GERALD FITZMAURICE, Reference Librarian, Lamont Library, Harvard College Library, Cambridge, Massachusetts USA

DEBORAH GARSON, Cataloger, Monroe C. Gutman Library, Graduate School of Education, Harvard University, Cambridge, Massachusetts USA

MALCOLM HAMILTON, Acquisitions Librarian, Monroe C. Gutman Library, Graduate School of Education, Harvard University, Cambridge, Massachusetts USA

SUSAN JOHNSEN HARMON, Cambridge, Massachusetts USA

BEN HOPKINS, Librarian, Massachusetts College of Art, Boston, Massachusetts USA

ARLYNE A. JACKSON, Reference Librarian, Baker Library, Harvard Business School, Boston, Massachusetts USA

JANET KATZ, Charlestown, Massachusetts USA

WINIFRED KISTLER, Public Services Librarian, Health Sciences Library, University of California, Davis, California USA

LAWRENCE KLEIN, Director, Sordoni-Burich Library, National College of Chiropractic, Lombard, Illinois USA

PAULA KLINE, Reference Intern, Baker Library, Harvard Business School, Boston, Massachusetts USA

MARIE LANNON, Senior Reference Librarian, Monroe C. Gutman Library, Graduate School of Education, Harvard University, Cambridge, Massashusetts USA

MARION HOLENA LEVINE, Reference Librarian, Countway Medical Library, Harvard University, Boston, Massachusetts USA

MOLLY McG. LINDNER, Library Cataloger, Boston Museum of Fine Arts, Boston, Massachusetts USA

ANN S. LONGFELLOW, Reference Librarian, Rotch Library, School of Architecture and Planning, Massachusetts Institute of Technology, Cambridge, Massachusetts USA

MARA BREWSTER MUNROE, Information Specialist, Raytheon Service Company, under contract to the U.S. Department of Transportation, Transportation Systems Center, Cambridge, Massachusetts USA

MARGARET MORRIS, Head, Technical Services, Monroe C. Gutman Library, Graduate School of Education, Harvard University, Cambridge, Massachusetts USA

CAROL A. POULLIOTTE, Instructional Materials Specialist, Office of Learning Resources, Northeastern University, Boston, Massachusetts USA

LYNN ROBINSON, Librarian, Wentworth Institute and College of Technology, Boston, Massachusetts USA

ANTONIO RODRIGUEZ-BUCKINGHAM, Librarian, Tozzer Library, Peabody Museum, Harvard University, Cambridge, Massachusetts USA

JANE SANCHEZ, Reference Librarian, Monroe C. Gutman Library, Graduate School of Education, Harvard University, Cambridge, Massachusetts USA

NATALIE SCHATZ, Reference Librarian, Littauer Library, Harvard University, Cambridge, Massachusetts USA

ANDREA SCHULMAN, Reference Librarian, Widener Library, Harvard College Library, Cambridge, Massachusetts USA

JAN STEPAN, Foreign and International Law Librarian, Harvard Law School, Cambridge, Massachusetts USA

DEBORAH TOBIN, Medical Librarian, Medical Library, St. Elizabeth's Hospital of Boston, Brighton, Massachusetts USA

LIBBY TRUDELL, Research Analyst, New England Library Network, Wellesley, Massachusetts USA

PAUL VAIGINAS, Librarian, Medical Library, Lemuel Shattuck Hospital, Jamaica Plain, Massachusetts USA

FAYE KAREN ZUCKER, Medical Information Librarian, Lassiter and Company, Inc., Chicago, Illinois USA

For valuable assistance on the glossary, special thanks is extended to ELIZABETH TEN HOUTEN, Librarian/Archivist, American Association of University Women Educational Foundation, Inc., Washington, D.C.

Other people who assisted in the preparation of the *Encyclopedia* by suggesting names of potential contributors; locating resource material; reviewing manuscripts and articles; conducting special research; and providing books, pamphlets, unpublished papers, and reports are:

BUSHRA MOHAMED ABDALLA, former Registrar, Faculty of Engineering and Architecture, University of Khartoum, Khartoum, Sudan

C. JOSHUA ABEND, Vice-President, Industrial Design, SCM Corporation, Syracuse, New York, USA

TOUFIC ABOUCHAER, Information Officer, Embassy of the Syrian Arab Republic, Washington, D.C. USA

FLOR DE BETHANIA ABREU, Secretary General, Dominican National Commission for UNESCO, Santo Domingo, Dominican Republic

AFGHAN NATIONAL COMMISSION FOR UNESCO, Kabul, Afghanistan

ALAN C. AIMONE, Military History Librarian, United States Military Academy Library, West Point, New York USA

ALEX OLU AJAYI, Registrar, University of Ife, Ile-Ife, Nigeria

YASHUSHI AKASHI, Senior Officer, Offices of the Secretary General, United Nations Secretariat, New York, New York USA

PAUL YAO AKOTO, Minister of National Education, Abidjan, Ivory Coast

HUGO ALBORNOZ, Director, Department of Educational Affairs, Organization of American States, Washington, D.C. USA

T. G. ALEXANDER, Vice-President, Deree-Pierce Colleges, Athens, Greece

JACK ALSIP, Graduate Assistant, Northeastern University, Boston, Massachusetts USA

AMERICAN BAR ASSOCIATION, Chicago, Illinois, USA

AMERICAN CULINARY INSTITUTE, Hyde Park, New York USA

AMERICAN DENTAL ASSOCIATION, Chicago, Illinois USA

AMERICAN SOCIETY OF ACTUARIES, Chicago, Illinois USA

F. ARDALAN, Secretary General, Iranian National Commission for UNESCO, Tehran, Iran

JALIL E. ARRAYED, Under-Secretary, Ministry of Education, Manama, Bahrain

ARTS COUNCIL OF GREAT BRITAIN, London, England

RAGNHILD ASPAAS, Information Officer, University of Tromsø, Tromsø, Norway

CHARLES AUSTIN, Dean, Graduate School, Trinity Unviersity, San Antonio, Texas, USA

S. F. BAILEY, Secretary, University and Polytechnic Grants Committee, Hong Kong

M. A. BAKPESSI, Secretary General, University of Benin, Lomé, Togo

BAKR ABDULLA BAKR, Dean of the College, University of Petroleum and Minerals, Dhahran, Saudi Arabia

NABIBAKHSHKHAN ALIMUHAMMADKHAN BALOCH, Vice-Chancellor, University of Sind, Sind, Pakistan

GABRIEL BARAKANA, Rector, University of Burundi, Bujumbura, Burundi

ELIZABETH E. BARTON, Public Health Nurse and Midwife, Department of Family Health, World Health Organization, Geneva, Switzerland

BAUSCH AND LOMB, Optics Center, Rochester, New York USA

MOURAD BENACHENHOU, Director of Higher Education, Ministry of Higher Education and Scientific Research, Algiers, Algeria

KATHY L. BERG, Librarian, Boston Museum of Fine Arts, Boston, Massachusetts USA

GEORGE BLACK, Science Librarian, Southern Illinois University, Carbondale, Illinois USA

H. BLAKEMORE, Secretary, Institute of Latin American Studies, University of London, London, England

DON BLANDIN, Staff Director, National Association of Schools of Public Affairs and Administration, Washington, D.C. USA

JEAN BLANPAIN, Leuven University of Public Health, Secretary, European Association of Training Programmes in Hospital and Health Services Administration, London, England

C. BONDARENKO, Vice-Rectorate, Administrative Division, Inspectorate of the Academy, Noumea, New Caledonia

PAUL BRENIKOV, Professor, Department of Town and Country Planning, University of Newcastle Upon Tyne, Newcastle Upon Tyne, England

PETER BRINSON, Director, Calouste Gulbenkian Foundation, United Kingdom and Commonwealth Branch, London, England

OSCAR G. BROCKETT, President, American Theatre Association, Professor, Department of Theatre and Drama, Indiana University, Bloomington, Indiana USA

JOHN BROOKS, President, Holy Cross College, Worcester, Massachusetts USA

FABIAN BRUSKEWITZ, Reverend, Sacred Congregation for Catholic Education, Villa Stritch, Rome, Italy

HEINZ BÜHRING, Sworn Interpreter, Ministry of Education, International Office, Copenhagen, Denmark

N. AL-BUKHARI, UNESCO, Paris, France

Lucius Butler, Associate Professor of Education, University of Hawaii, Honolulu, Hawaii USA

Jean Cabot, former Rector, University of Chad, N'Djamena, Chad

G. Canu, Professor, University of the Sorbonne-Nouvelle, Paris, France

Richard I. Carter, Director, Computation Center, Northeastern University, Boston, Massachusetts USA

James E. Caskey, Jr., American Meteorological Society, Boston, Massachusetts USA

T. L. Chang, President, Ming-Chi Institute of Technology, Taishan, Taipei, Hsien, Taiwan

Mary Van A. Chatfield, Associate Librarian, Baker Library, Harvard Business School, Boston, Massachusetts USA

Jack Christensen, Associate Administrator, International Society for Clinical Laboratory Technology, St. Louis, Missouri USA

Raymond Ciszek, American Association of Health, Physical Education and Recreation, Washington, D.C. USA

Jeff R. Clark, Associate Director of College and University Programs, Joint Council on Economic Education, New York, New York USA

David Clarke, Association of Collegiate Schools of Architecture, Washington, D.C. USA

Jerry M. Cohen, Vice-President and Manager, Meidinger and Associates, Inc., Actuaries and Employee Benefit Consultants, Columbia, Maryland, USA

College Art Association of America, New York, New York USA

W. Leighton Collins, Consultant, Engineering Education, Executive Director Emeritus, American Society for Engineering Education, Washington, D.C. USA

Committee on Continuing Education, World Confederation of Organizations of the Teaching Profession, Morges, Switzerland

Commonwealth Bureau of Agricultural Economics, Dartington House, Oxford, England

B. F. Cooling, U.S. Army Military Research Collection, U.S. Army War College, Carlisle Barracks, Pennsylvania USA

Council for Exceptional Children, Reston, Virginia USA

Keith K. Cox, Professor of Marketing, Vice-President, Marketing Education, American Marketing Association, University of Houston, Houston, Texas USA

Edward P. Crowell, Executive Director, American Osteopathic Association, Chicago, Illinois USA

Jack Cullerton, Executive Director, University Council for Educational Administration, Columbus, Ohio USA

Edmund A. Cykler, Professor Emeritus, University of Oregon, Eugene, Oregon USA

Amos Dambe, former Ambassador, Embassy of Botswana, Washington, D.C. USA

HENG DAOVANNARY, Research and Planning Office, Ministry of National Education, Vientiane, Laos

RUSSELL T. DAWE, Assistant Registrar, Swinburne College of Technology, Hawthorn, Australia

A. N. J. DEN HOLLANDER, President, European Association for American Studies, American Institute, University of Amsterdam, Amsterdam, the Netherlands

LISELOTT DIEM, Professor, International Association of Physical Education and Sports for Girls and Women, Cologne, Federal Republic of Germany

HENRI DIEUZEIDE, Director, Division of Educational Methods, Materials and Techniques, UNESCO, Paris, France

GEORGETTE M. DORN, Specialist, Hispanic Culture, Latin American, Portuguese, and Spanish Division, Library of Congress, Washington, D.C. USA

L. DOVI, Minister, Ministry of Education, Youth and Sport, Suva, Fiji

KRYSTYNA D. DOWNEY, Secretary, National Commission for UNESCO, Department of Education, Wellington, New Zealand

MARTHA DUKAS, Middle East Library, Middle Eastern Department, Harvard College Library, Cambridge, Massachusetts USA

J. F. DUKES, Secretary, Higher Education Authority, Dublin, Ireland

MURRAY EDELSTEIN, President, New York College of Podiatric Medicine, New York, New York USA

WALLACE B. EDGERTON, President, Institute of International Education, New York, New York USA

WILLIAM T. EDGETT, Assistant Dean, Director of Counseling, Northeastern University, Boston, Massachusetts USA

ELEANOR T. ELEQUIN, Professor IV and Director, Research and Development, College of Education, University of the Philippines, Quezon City, the Philippines

EDWIN EMERY, President, Association for Education in Journalism, School of Journalism and Mass Communications, Universityof Minnesota, Minneapolis, Minnesota USA

JOHN W. ENELL, Vice-President for Research, American Management Associations, New York, New York USA

MAGNUS ENGSTRÖM, Secretary, Swedish National Commission for UNESCO, International Secretariat, Ministry of Education, Stockholm, Sweden

ALICE J. EPPINK, Librarian, Center for Applied Linguistics, Arlington, Virginia, USA

JULIETTE ERNST, International Federation of the Societies of Classical Studies, Paris, France

IRENE FAIRLEY, Professor of English, Northeastern University, Boston, Massachusetts USA

MARTIN T. FARRIS, Professor of Transportation, Department of Marketing, Arizona State University, Tempe, Arizona USA

Luc Fauvel, Secretary General, International Economic Association, Paris, France

Leonard E. Fay, Executive Vice-President, National College of Chiropractic, Lombard, Illinois USA

Fédération internationale pharmaceutique (International Pharmaceutical Federation), The Hague, the Netherlands

Fédération internationale pour l'économie familiale (International Federation for Home Economics), Boulogne, France

Douwe W. Fokkema, Secretary, International Comparative Literature Association, Institute of Comparative Literature, University of Utrecht, Utrecht, the Netherlands

George R. Foster, Director of Field Services, Institute of Food Technologists, Chicago, Illinois USA

Foundation for Interior Design Education Research, New York, New York USA

John J. Frantz, President, International Electronics Association, Frankfurt/Main, Federal Republic of Germany

Alfred Frazer, Department of Art and Archaeology, Columbia University, New York, New York USA

Donald D. French, Professor, Department of Continuing Education, Northeastern University, Boston, Massachusetts USA

Otto Frostman, International Mathematical Union, Stockholm, Sweden

André Gadaud, Cultural Council, Permanent Representative of the French Universities, Embassy of the French Republic, New York, New York USA

John C. Gaillard, Director, Urban and Housing Programs, American Institute of Architects, Washington, D.C. USA

James J. Garibaldi, Executive Director, American Occupational Therapy Association, Rockville, Maryland USA

Winfried E. Gass, Federal School for Advertising Techniques, Lahr, Federal Republic of Germany

Frédéric Gaussen, Editor-in-Chief, *Le Monde de l'éducation*, Paris, France

M. Orcena Gervais, Commercial Counselor, Embassy of Haiti, Washington, D.C. USA

Roger Gilmore, Director, Commission on Accreditation and Membership, National Association of Schools of Art, Reston, Virginia, USA

Charles C. Glasgow, Executive Director, American Society of Traffic and Transportation, Chicago, Illinois USA

Herbert Goldstein, Director, Curriculum Research and Development Center in Mental Retardation, Graduate School of Humanities and Social Science, Yeshiva University, New York, New York USA

Luis E. Gonzalez-Vales, former Executive Secretary, Council on Higher Education, University of Puerto Rico, Rio Piedràs, Puerto Rico

Earl Goodwin, American Society for Interior Designers, New York,

New York, USA

HOPETON GORDON, Assistant Professor, Faculty of Education, Brandon University, Brandon, Manitoba, Canada

WILLIAM F. GRADY, Professor, Department of Educational Media, Temple University, Philadelphia, Pennsylvania USA, President, Association for Educational Communications and Technology, Washington, D.C. USA

BJARNI GUNNARSSON, Administrative Assistant, Department of Higher Education, Ministry of Culture and Education, Reykjavik, Iceland

C.E. HADJISTEPHANOU, Head, Department for Higher and Secondary Education, Ministry of Education, Nicosia, Cyprus

R. HAESERYN, International Federation of Translators, Sint-Amandsburg, Belgium

CHARLES HALBOWER, Education Management Section Head, Arthur D. Little, Inc., Cambridge, Massachusetts USA

ALICE HALL, Assistant Science Librarian, Massachusetts Institute of Technology Science Library, Cambridge, Massachusetts USA

SUSAN R. HAMMERMAN, Assistant Secretary General, Rehabilitation International, New York, New York USA

F. MARGARET HARDY, Executive Secretary, International Confederation of Midwives, London, England

B. HARRINGTON, Librarian, Institute of Latin American Studies, University of London, London, England

WILLY HAUGLI, Director, University of Tromsø, Tromsø, Norway

SAMUEL L. HAYDEN, former Director, International and Governmental Affairs, American Assembly of Collegiate Schools of Business, New York, New York USA

GWEE YEE HEAN, Senior Lecturer in History, Nanyang University, Singapore, Republic of Singapore

CYNTHIA G. HEILAND, New England Foundation for Osteopathic Medicine, Boston, Massachusetts USA

GLORIA COSPÍN DE HERNÁNDEZ, Guatemala City, Guatemala

CHARLES M. HERSH, Director, Academic Affairs, U.S. Army War College, Carlisle Barracks, Pennsylvania USA

WAYNE HOLTZMAN, Secretary General, International Union of Psychological Science, Hogg Foundation for Mental Health, University of Texas, Austin, Texas USA

SAMUEL HOPE, Executive Director, National Association of Schools of Music, Reston, Virginia USA

PAUL L. HORECKY, Chief, Slavic and Central European Division, Library of Congress, Washington, D.C. USA

ELEANOR HORWITZ, Free-lance Writer, Editor, and Consultant, Concord, Massachusetts USA

ALAN R. HOWES, Instructor, Australian Administrative Staff College, Victoria, Australia

STEPHAN HSU, former Commissioner of Education, Taiwan Provincial

Government, Wufeng, Taiwan

MATS HULTIN, Senior Adviser, Department of Education, World Bank, Washington, D.C. USA

G. HUNNINGS, Vice-Chancellor, University of Malawi, Zomba, Malawi

GÖREL HUSÉN-STRÖMQVIST, Institute for the Study of International Problems in Education, University of Stockholm, Stockholm, Sweden

WARNER IMIG, Dean, College of Music, University of Colorado, Boulder, Colorado USA

INDUSTRIAL DESIGNERS SOCIETY OF AMERICA, McLean, Virginia USA

INTERNATIONAL ASSOCIATION OF AGRICULTURAL ECONOMISTS, Chicago, Illinois USA

INTERNATIONAL ASSOCIATION OF ART, UNESCO, Paris, France

INTERNATIONAL COUNCIL OF NURSES, Geneva, Switzerland

INTERNATIONAL FEDERATION OF INTERIOR DESIGNERS, Amsterdam, the Netherlands

INTERNATIONAL FEDERATION OF PHOTOGRAPHIC ART, Abtwil-St. Gallen, Switzerland

INTERNATIONAL HO-RE-CA, International Federation of Hotel and Restaurant Associations, Zurich, Switzerland

INTERNATIONAL INSTITUTE OF WELDING, London, England

INTERNATIONAL SOCIETY OF SOIL SCIENCE, % Food and Agriculture Organization of the United Nations, Rome, Italy

INTERNATIONAL STATISTICAL INSTITUTE, Permanent Office, The Hague-Voorburg, the Netherlands

INTERNATIONAL UNION OF PURE AND APPLIED CHEMISTRY, Secretariat, Oxford, England

R. O. H. IRVINE, Vice-Chancellor, University of Otago, Dunedin, New Zealand

BARBARA JACKIER, Librarian, Forsyth Dental Center, Boston, Massachusetts USA

ARLYNE A. JACKSON, Reference Librarian, Baker Library, Harvard Business School, Boston, Massachusetts USA

MOHAMMED FADHEL JAMALI, University of Tunis, Tunis, Tunisia

A. WILLIAM JASPER, President, World's Poultry Science Association, % American Farm Bureau Federation, Park Ridge, Illinois USA

GERT JANSSEN, Association of Mining Engineers, Dusseldorf, Federal Republic of Germany

A. W. JOHNS, Director of Education, Gibraltar

JO ANNE JOHNSON, Publications Manager, American Society for Industrial Security, Washington, D.C. USA

ABDELKADER EL KADIRI, Cultural Attaché, Embassy of Morocco, Washington, D.C. USA

LEON KAREL, Executive Secretary, National Association for Humanities Education, Kirksville, Missouri USA

W. KARTOMO, Embassy of Indonesia, Washington, D.C. USA

JANET KATZ, Charlestown, Massachusetts USA

WARD M. KELLER, Executive Director, American Society of Radiologic Technologists, Chicago, Illinois USA

KARL R. KESSLER, Public Information Officer, American Veterinary Medical Association, Schaumburg, Illinois USA

O. ALBERT KEVER, Optician I.O.R.T., Brussels, Belgium

MOHAMMED SARWAR KHAN, Data Center, Ministry of Education, Riyadh, Saudi Arabia

HUSSAM AL-KHATEEB, Vice-Minister, Higher Education, Damascus, Syrian Arab Republic

JOHN B. KLIS, Director, Publications, Institute of Food Technologists, Chicago, Illinois USA

K. KÖCHLE, General Secretary, International Association for the Exchange of Students for Technical Experience, Zurich, Switzerland

FANTA KOUROUMA, Cultural Attaché, Embassy of the Republic of Guinea, Washington, D.C. USA

IBRAHIMA KOUROUMA, Director, Press and Documentation Bureau, Conakry, Republic of Guinea

WALTER KRANZ, Press Officer, Press and Information Office of the Liechtenstein Government, Vaduz, Liechtenstein

EGON KRAUS, President, International Society for Music Education, Oldenburg, Federal Republic of Germany

A. M. KRISTJANSON, Director, National Programs, Association of Universities and Colleges of Canada, Ottawa, Ontario, Canada

HERMANN F. KROEGER, Consul, Information and Press Affairs, German Consulate General, Boston, Massachusetts USA

LOIS KRYGER, Division of Dentistry, Bureau of Health Manpower and Health Resources Administration, Rockville, Maryland USA

JEAN-FRANÇOIS LACRONIQUE, Science Attaché, Embassy of the French Republic, Scientific Mission at Boston, Cambridge, Massachusetts USA

R. LAMY, Registrar, University of Mauritius, Reduit, Mauritius

CHARLES C. LARSON, Commission on Forestry Education, International Union of Societies of Foresters, State University of New York College of Environmental Science and Forestry, Syracuse, New York USA

JEAN-PIERRE LASSALE, Rector, Academy of Antilles and Guiana, Fort-de-France, Martinique

G. H. LEATHERMAN, Executive Director Emeritus, International Dental Federation, London, England

MARC LEBRUN, Assistant Executive Secretary, International Union for the Scientific Study of Population, Liege, Belgium

FEDOR LEDERER, Administrative Director, CIOS–World Council of Management, Geneva, Switzerland

ROBERT LEESTMA, Associate Commissioner, Institutional Development and International Education, Office of Education, Washington, D.C. USA

EDWARD J. LEHMAN, Executive Director, American Anthropological Association, Washington, D.C. USA

FRED C. LEONE, Executive Director, American Statistics Association, Washington, D.C. USA

GARY W. LESKE, Professor of Agricultural Education, Department of Vocational and Technical Education, University of Minnesota, St. Paul, Minnesota USA

M. LEUENBERGER, Secretary-Treasurer, World Veterinary Association, Geneva, Switzerland

MARION HELENA LEVINE, Reference Librarian, Countway Medical Library, Harvard University, Boston, Massachusetts USA

CHARLES L. LEWIS, Executive Vice-President, American Personnel and Guidance Association, Washington, D.C. USA

CHING-JIANG LIN, Administrative Vice-Minister, Ministry of Education, Taipei, Republic of China

DAVID S. LINDBERG, Chairman, Education Committee, American Society for Medical Technology, Bellaire, Texas USA

J. LYNCH, Professor, Institute of Latin American Studies, University of London, London, England

AHMAD MADI, University of Jordan, Amman, Jordan

MAKENGO SAYA, Director, Division of Higher Education, Commission on Equivalencies, Department of Education, Kinshasa and Gombe, Zaire

WILLIAM M. MCCLELLAN, Music Librarian, University of Illinois at Urbana-Champaign, Urbana, Illinois USA

E. M. MCKAY, Secretary General, World Confederation for Physical Therapy, London, England

RICHARD MCLANATHAN, Director, American Association of Museums, Washington, D.C. USA

ROBERT MCLARREN, Secretary General, International Banker Association, Washington, D.C. USA

D. MCNALLY, Assistant Director, University of London Observatory, Department of Physics and Astronomy, University College, University of London, London, England

C. A. MEILICKE, Director, Division of Health Services Administration, University of Alberta, Edmonton, Alberta, Canada

S. W. B. MENAUL, Air Vice-Marshal, Director General, Royal United Services Institute for Defence Studies, London, England

M. A. MENDEZ, President, World Federation of Occupational Therapists, Pretoria, South Africa

BEN W. MILLER, Professor, Department of Kinesiology, University of California, Los Angeles, California USA

EARLYNN J. MILLER, Director, Publications Unit, National Dance Association, Washington, D.C. USA

SAMUEL C. MILLER, Director, Education and Research, American Society of Landscape Architects, McLean, Virginia USA

JAMES MILLETTE, Head, Department of History, University of the West Indies, St. Augustine, Trinidad

ROBERT R. MINARIK, Director, International Services Division, William Hood Dunwoody Industrial Institute, Minneapolis, Minnesota USA

WILLIAM M. MITCHELL, Educational Consultant, National Secretaries Association (International), Kansas City, Missouri USA

C. R. MITRA, Director, Birla Institute of Technology and Science, Rajasthan, India

MODERN LANGUAGE ASSOCIATION OF AMERICA, New York, New York USA

JOHN MOGEY, Professor and President, Committee on Family Research, International Sociological Association, Boston University, Boston, Massachusetts USA

CHRISTINE MOHRMANN, Secretary General, Permanent International Committee of Linguistics, Niméque, the Netherlands

LOIS MORAN, Director, Research and Education, American Crafts Council, New York, New York USA

RUSSELL E. MORGAN, JR., Executive Secretary, World Federation of Public Health Associations, % American Public Health Association, Washington, D.C. USA

RHOADS MURPHEY, Secretary-Treasurer, Association for Asian Studies, University of Michigan, Ann Arbor, Michigan USA

R. W. A. NAALDIJK, Acting Director, Department of Education, Netherlands Antilles

ZL. NAIDENOV, Press Secretary, Cabinet of the President, Committee for Science, Technical Progress and Higher Education, Sofia, Bulgaria

KAMAL NAJI, Director General, Ministry of Education, Doha, Qatar

JANET NASH, Graduate Assistant, Northeastern University, Boston, Massachusetts USA

NATIONAL ASSOCIATION OF BUILDING MANUFACTURERS, Washington, D.C. USA

NATIONAL ASSOCIATION OF SCHOOLS OF ART, Reston, Virginia USA

NATIONAL LEAGUE OF NURSING, New York, New York USA

IBRAHIM ABBAS NATTO, Assistant Professor, University of Petroleum and Minerals, Dhahran, Saudi Arabia

RICHARD S. NAYLOR, Professor and Chairman, Department of Earth Sciences, Northeastern University, Boston, Massachusetts USA

J. RUSSELL NAZZARO, Administrative Officer, Educational Affairs Office, American Psychological Association, Washington, D.C. USA

JEAN NEPOTE, Secretary General, International Criminal Police Organization, Saint Cloud, France

L. R. NEWBY, Secretary, Health and Education, Naura Island, Republic of Nauru

GERHARD NICKEL, Executive Secretary General, International Association of Applied Linguistics, University of Stuttgart, Stuttgart, Federal Republic of Germany

F. Nicol, Education and Training Officer, Institute of Travel Agents, Staines, England

Raymond B. Nixon, Professor Emeritus, School of Journalism and Mass Communication, University of Minnesota, Minneapolis, Minnesota USA

Daniel A. Nona, Executive Director, American Council on Pharmaceutical Education, Chicago, Illinois USA

Everett H. Northrop, Librarian, U.S. Merchant Marine Academy Library, King's Point, New York, USA

Sylestre Nsanzimana, Rector, National University of Rwanda, Butare, Rwanda

Vicente Muñiz Núñez, Rio Piedras, Puerto Rico

J. C. T. Oates, Reader in Historical Bibliography, Deputy Librarian, Cambridge University Library, Cambridge, England

Joseph O'Keefe, Professor, Department of Fire Protection and Safety, Bunker Hill Community College, Charlestown, Massachusetts USA

Ingram Olkin, Professor, Department of Statistics, Stanford University, Stanford, California USA

Hubert B. Owens, Dean Emeritus, School of Environmental Design, Professor Emeritus Landscape Architecture, University of Georgia, Immediate Past President International Federation of Landscape Architects, Athens, Georgia USA

Mark N. Ozer, President, American Society for Cybernetics, Washington, D.C. USA

Ara Oztemel, Chairman of the Board, Satra Corporation, New York, New York USA

R. O. Palmer, Chief Education Officer, Ministry of Education, St. George's, Grenada, West Indies

T. V. Palu, Ministry of Education, Nuku'Alofa, Tonga

Pan-American Health Organization, Washington, D.C. USA

Krishna Raj Pandey, Chief, Research Division, Tribhuvan University, Kathmandu, Nepal

Hee Kyoo Park, Education Attaché, Embassy of the Republic of Korea, Washington, D.C. USA

Robert W. Parry, Professor, Department of Chemistry, University of Utah, Salt Lake City, Utah USA

V. L. Parsegian, Executive Officer, Educational Bridges Project, Rensselaer Polytechnic Institute, Troy, New York USA

Dave Partington, Middle Eastern Librarian, Harvard College Library, Cambridge, Massachusetts USA

Fernando Piera, Assistant to the Director General, Intergovernmental Bureau for Information, Rome, Italy

Robert Porter, Visual Arts Department, Associated Council of the Arts, New York, New York USA

Poultry Science Association, Texas Agricultural and Mechanical

University, College Station, Texas USA

PETER R. PRIFTI, Research Associate, Massachusetts Institute of Technology, Cambridge, Massachusetts USA

J. L. PSIMHIS, Minister, Ministry of National Education and Educational Reform, Banqui, Central African Empire

RUTH M. PYNE, Senior Librarian, National Agricultural Library, Beltsville, Maryland USA

HAROLD R. RAEMER, Professor and Chairman, Department of Electrical Engineering, Northeastern University, Boston, Massachusetts USA

M. A. RAIF, Under-Secretary, Ministry of Education, Turkish Federated State of Cyprus

ANGELA RAMMSTEDT, Center for Interdisciplinary Research, University of Bielefeld, Bielefeld, Federal Republic of Germany

SAAD ABDUL-BAQI AL-RAWI, President, University of Baghdad, Baghdad, Iraq

AHMED ABDEL RAZIG, National Council for Higher Education, Khartoum, Sudan

PAUL REGAN, Director, International Research Activities, Institute of International Studies, United States Office of Education, Washington, D.C. USA

PAUL REILES, Assistant Government Counsel, Ministry of National Education, Luxembourg

MARGIT REKASI, Chief, Department of Foreign Relations, Ministry of Culture and Education, Budapest, Hungary

GEORGE J. RESNIKOFF, Executive Director, Institute of Mathematical Statistics, California State College, Hayward, California USA

JOYCE M. REY, Librarian, Smithsonian Astrophysical Observatory, Cambridge, Massachusetts USA

JAMES J. REYNOLDS, President, American Institute of Merchant Shipping, Washington, D.C. USA

EDWARD RHODE, Associate Dean, School of Veterinary Medicine, University of California, Davis, California USA

VIRGINIA J. ROCK, President Emeritus, Master of Stong College, Professor of English, York University, Downsview, Ontario, Canada

ANTONIO RODRIGUEZ-BUCKINGHAM, Librarian, Tozzer Library, Peabody Museum, Harvard University, Cambridge, Massachusetts USA

J. M. ROOP, Assistant to the General Manager, Society of Automotive Engineers, Warrendale, Pennsylvania USA

MORTON RUBIN, Professor, Department of Sociology and Anthropology, Northeastern University, Boston, Massachusetts USA

MARGARET M. RYAN, Assistant Secretary, Council on Dental Education, American Dental Association, Chicago, Illinois USA

NIBONDH SASIDHORN, former Minister of Education, Ministry of Education, Bangkok, Thailand

A. SAVELIEV, Secretary, Maritime Safety Committee, Intergovernmental

Maritime Consultative Organization, London, England

NATALIE SCHATZ, Reference Librarian, Littauer Library, Harvard University, Cambridge, Massachusetts USA

RICHARD B. SCHEETZ, Coordinator, Educational Services, Edison Electric Institute, New York, New York USA

J. SCHLITZ, Secretary, International Association for Educational and Vocational Guidance, Strassen, Luxembourg

FELIX SCHMID, International Society for Business Education, Lausanne, Switzerland

H.P. SCHMIDHAUSER, Secretary General, International Association of Scientific Experts in Tourism, Berne, Switzerland

SCHOOL OF THE ART INSTITUTE OF CHICAGO, Chicago, Illinois USA

CALVIN SCHWABE, Professor, Epidemiology and Preventive Medicine, School of Veterinary Medicine, University of California, Davis, California USA

THOMAS A. SEBEOK, Chairman, Research Center for Language and Semiotic Studies, Indiana University, Bloomington, Indiana USA

ERIC J. SHARPE, Secretary General Emeritus, International Association for the History of Religions, Department of Religious Studies, Furness College, Lancaster, England

A. AHMAD SIDDIQI, Secretary, Afghan National Commission for UNESCO, Government of the Republic of Afghanistan, Kabul, Afghanistan

MERKHALLE OULD SIDI, First Secretary, Embassy of the Islamic Republic of Mauritania, Washington, D.C. USA

ADELAIDE SIEGEL, Reference Librarian, American Personnel and Guidance Association, Washington, D.C. USA

KAREN HEGGE SIMMONS, Chief Librarian, American Institute of Certified Public Accountants Library, New York, New York USA

JEAN H. SISCO, Consultant, Government and Public Affairs, American Retail Federation, Washington, D.C. USA

WILLIAM L. SLAYTON, Executive Vice-President, American Institute of Architecture, Washington, D.C. USA

DEAN R. SMITH, Director, Administrative Services Division, International Association of Chiefs of Police, Gaithersburg, Maryland USA

JOHN J. SOROKA, Chief, Search Department, Engineering Societies Library, New York, New York USA

WALTER STERN, Head, Department of Chemistry, New South Wales Institute of Technology, New South Wales, Australia

P. STAAL, Secretary General, International Dairy Federation, Brussels, Belgium

HUGH M. STIMSON, former Secretary-Treasurer, American Oriental Society, New Haven, Connecticut USA

MUHAMMADI SISWO SUDARMO, Deputy Director, Regional Institute of Higher Education and Development, Singapore, Republic of Singapore

DONALD E. SUPER, President, International Association for Educational and Vocational Guidance, Professor Emeritus, Teachers College, Columbia University, New York, New York USA

SEYDOU MADANI SY, Rector, University of Dakar, Dakar, Senegal

DENIS SZABO, Director, International Centre for Comparative Criminology, Montreal, Quebec, Canada

CHARLES SZLADITS, Adjunct Professor of Comparative Law, Parker School of Foreign and Comparative Law, Columbia University, New York, New York USA

LÉON TABAH, Director, Population Division, Department of Economic and Social Affairs, New York, New York USA

GLEN L. TAGGART, President, Utah State University, Logan, Utah USA

AMNUAY TAPINGKAE, former Director, Regional Institute of Higher Education and Development, Singapore, Republic of Singapore

SOL TAX, Professor, Department of Anthropology, University of Chicago, Chicago, Illinois USA

TEXTILE INSTITUTE, General Secretary, Manchester, England

THEOLOGICAL EDUCATION FUND, Service of the Commission on World Mission and Evangelism of the World Council of Churches, Bromley, England

A. E. THOMPSON, Director of Studies, Institute of Travel Agents, Staines, England

LORING THOMPSON, Vice-President and Dean for Planning, Northeastern University, Boston, Massachusetts USA

ABDOULAYE TOGUYENI, Rector, University of Ouagadougou, Ouagadougou, Upper Volta

K. W. J. TOPLEY, Director of Education, Hong Kong

JACK L. TREYNOR, Financial Analysts Federation, New York, New York USA

MANUEL B. TRONOSCO, Dean, Faculty of Engineering, National University of Pedro Henriquez Ureña, Santo Domingo, Dominican Republic

JANUSZ TYMOWSKI, Professor of Production Engineering, Technical University of Warsaw, Warsaw, Poland

ANTONIO URRELLO, Secretary-Treasurer, Canadian Association of Latin American Studies, Ottawa, Ontario, Canada

J. H. V. VAN BAREN, Soil Scientist, International Soil Museum, Centre for Research and Information, Wageningen, the Netherlands

S. VAN DER HEIDE, Secretary General, International Union of Geological Sciences, Haarlem, the Netherlands

H. A. VAN LEEUWEN, Head, Sub-Department Documentation Information, Ministry of Education and Science, 's-Gravenhage, the Netherlands

JOSEPH VOCI, President, Arthur D. Little Management Education Institute, Cambridge, Massachusetts USA

F. ELEANOR WARNER, Librarian, New England College of Optometry, Boston, Massachusetts USA

DONALD A. WASHBURN, Director, Bureau of Library Services, American Dental Association, Chicago, Illinois USA

WCOTP COMMITTEE ON CONTINUING EDUCATION, Morges, Switzerland

MICHEL WEILL, Secretary General, International Union of Architects, Paris, France

S. J. WELLENSIEK, Professor Emeritus, Department of Horticulture, Agricultural University, Wageningen, the Netherlands

D. A. WELLS, Honorary Secretary, Modern Humanities Research Association, Queen's University of Belfast, Belfast, Northern Ireland

DONAT G. WENTZEL, Professor, Department of Physics and Astronomy, University of Maryland, College Park, Maryland USA

P. WERMUTH, Professor, Department of English, Northeastern University, Boston, Massachusetts USA

ELMAR WERTZ, Delegate for Education, International Union of Architects, Paris, France

BARBARA WHITE, Editor, *Physical Therapy*, American Physical Therapy Association, Washington, D.C. USA

JEAN I. WIDGER, Editor, *Radiologic Technology*, Detroit, Michigan USA

FLORENCE B. WILKINSON, Supervisory Librarian, Teachers College Library, Columbia University, New York, New York USA

ALFRED B. WILLCOX, Executive Director, Mathematical Association of America, Washington, D.C. USA

CHARLES WILLET, former Head, Orders and Receipts, Widener Library, Harvard College Library, Cambridge, Massachusetts USA

MARY B. WINE, Executive Associate, Association of Independent Colleges and Schools, Washington, D.C. USA

WILMA E. WINTERS, Librarian, Center for Population Studies, Harvard University, Boston, Massachusetts USA

JOHN WOLFE, President, Northwestern College of Chiropractic, St. Paul, Minnesota USA

WORLD CRAFTS COUNCIL, New York, New York USA

WORLD METEOROLOGICAL ORGANIZATION, Office of the Secretary General, Geneva, Switzerland

WORLD PEACE THROUGH LAW CENTER, Washington, D.C. USA

JOHN H. WOTIZ, Professor, Department of Chemistry and Biochemistry, Southern Illinois University, Carbondale, Illinois USA

C. GILBERT WRENN, Professor Emeritus, Counseling Psychology, Arizona State University, Tempe, Arizona USA

A. C. WRIGHT, President, Canadian Association of Slavists, Department of Russian, Queen's University, Kingston, Ontario, Canada

CHI-YUEN WU, Professor of Public Administration, New York University, New York, New York USA

JEAN-JACQUES WYLER, Counselor, International Communications and Public Relations, Honorary Secretary, International Public Relations Association, Geneva, Switzerland

Brian J. Wynne, Executive Director, American Society of Consulting Planners, McLean, Virginia USA

Nancy M. Yedlin, Director, College and Community Relations, Fashion Institute of Technology, New York, New York USA

Enrico Zanelli, Professor, Law School, University of Genoa, Genoa, Italy

Constantine K. Zurayk, American University, Beirut, Lebanon

A Final Thank You

I especially wish to thank key members of the editorial staff—including the senior editor, special editors, associate editors, and the project secretary and coordinator—for their unselfish devotion to this project. They gave generously of their time outside regular working hours and very often allowed *Encyclopedia* work to take precedence over personal recreation and family relationships. To the members of their families who were so patient and understanding, my heartfelt appreciation.

My gratitude is also due the editorial staff of Jossey-Bass Publishers. Special thanks go to Gracia A. Alkema, who supervised and coordinated the editorial-production work of the *Encyclopedia;* to Dorothy Conway, who edited the essays on national systems, fields of study, centers and institutes, and who developed a style guide and checked the entire *Encyclopedia* for consistency in both style and facts; to Paige Wickland, who did the final editing of the topical essays; and to Earline Hefferlin, for her painstaking compilation of the comprehensive name and subject indexes.

Although encyclopedias and reference works are not usually dedicated to individuals, I am making an exception in this instance and dedicate these volumes to my wife, Edna; my daughter, Margaret K. Browning; my granddaughter, Margaret E. Browning; my son, Asa W. Knowles, and his wife, Margaret; and my grandchildren, Douglas, Dianne, and William Knowles.

Asa S. Knowles

Acronyms

AAALAC   American Association for Accreditation of Laboratory Animal Care

AAAS   American Association for the Advancement of Science

AAASA   Association for the Advancement of Agricultural Sciences in Africa

AAC   Association of American Colleges

AACJC   American Association of Community and Junior Colleges

AACRAO   American Association of Collegiate Registrars and Admissions Officers

AACSB   American Assembly of Collegiate Schools of Business

AACTE   American Association of Colleges for Teacher Education

AAEA   African Adult Education Association

AAFRC   American Association of Fund-Raising Council

AAGS   Association of African Geological Surveys (*see* ASGA)

Note: American denotes a United States association.

AAHE	American Association for Higher Education
AAHPER	American Alliance for Health, Physical Education, and Recreation
AAI	African-American Institute, United States
AAI	*Association actuarielle internationale* (*see* IAA)
AAM	American Association of Museums
AAPS	African Association of Political Science, Tanzania
AAS	American Astronomical Society
AAS	Association for Asian Studies (including four regional councils: SEARC, ARC, CIARC, NEARC)
AASA	American Association of School Administrators
AASCU	American Association of State Colleges and Universities
AASSREC	Association of Asian Social Science Research Councils, India
AAU	Association of African Universities
AAU	Association of American Universities
AAU or AArU	Association of Arab Universities
AAU	Association of Atlantic Universities, Canada
AAUA	American Association of University Administrators
AAUCS	Australian Asian Universities' Co-operation Scheme
AAUP	American Association of University Presses

AAUP	American Association of University Professors
ABED	*Associação brasileira de economistas domesticas*, Brazil
ABEO	*Associação brasileira de escolas de arquitectura*, Brazil
ABI	*Association des bibliothèques internationales* (*see* AIL)
ABT	*Arbeitsstelle für Bibliothekstechnik* (Center for Technical Services), Federal Republic of Germany
ABU	Asian Broadcasting Union, Japan
AC	*Akademikernes centralorganisation* (Association of Graduates from Institutions for Higher Education), Denmark
ACA	American Chiropractic Association
ACAAE	Australian Council on Awards in Advanced Education
ACAD	American Conference of Academic Deans
ACBCU	*Association canadienne des bibliothèques de collège et d'université* (*see* CACUL)
ACCU	Asian Confederation of Credit Unions
ACE	American Council on Education
ACEA	*Association canadienne des études africaines* (*see* CAAS)
ACHA	American College Health Association
ACHE	Association for Continuing Higher Education, United States

ACHS	Association of College Honor Societies, United States
ACIPA	American Consortium for International Public Administration
ACLA	American Comparative Literature Association
ACLS	American Council of Learned Societies
ACME	Association of Consulting Management Engineers, United States
ACOF	*Association des conseillers d'orientation de France,* France
ACOSCA	African Cooperative Savings and Credit Association
ACPA	American College Personnel Association
ACPE	*Agrupación nacional sindical de constructores promatores de edificios urbanos,* Spain
ACRL	Association of College and Research Libraries, United States
ACS	American Chemical Society
ACSC	Association of Christian Schools and Colleges, the Philippines
ACT	American College Testing Program
ACTFL	American Council on the Teaching of Foreign Languages
ACU	Association of Commonwealth Universities
ACU-I	Association of College Unions—International, United States
ACUIIS	Association of Colleges and Universities for International—Intercultural Studies, United States

ACURIL	Association of Caribbean University and Research Libraries (*Asociación de bibliotecas universitarias y de investigación del Caribe*)
ADA	American Dental Association
ADESPE	*Association pour le développement de la science politique européenne* (Association for the Development of European Political Science)
ADETEM	*Association pour le développement des techniques de marketing,* France
AEA	Adult Education Association of the U.S.A.
AEAI	Association of Engineers and Architects in Israel
AEC	Atomic Energy Commission, United States
AECT	Association for Educational Communications and Technology, United States
AEDP	*Association européenne pour la direction de personnel* (*see* EAPM)
AFB	*Arbeitsstelle für das Bibliothekswesen,* Federal Republic of Germany
AFCUL	Australian Federation of Credit Union Leagues
AFGRAD	African Graduate Fellowship Program (African-American Institute), United States
AFIRS	American Federation of Information Processing
AFL-CIO	American Federation of Labor-Congress of Industrial Organizations
AFROTC	Air Force Reserve Officer Training Corps, United States
AFSCME	American Federation of State, County, and Municipal Employees

AFT	American Federation of Teachers
AGB	Association of Governing Boards of Universities and Colleges, United States
AGS	Association of Graduate Schools, United States
AHEA	American Home Economics Association
AIAA	American Institute of Aeronautics and Astronautics
AIB	Academy of International Business, United States
AIBM	*Association internationale des bibliothèques musicales* (*see* IAML)
AICA	*Association internationale pour le calcul analogique* (International Association for Analog Computation)
AICCU	Association of Independent California Colleges and Universities, United States
AICS	Association of Independent Colleges and Schools, United States
AICT	*Association internationale des critiques de théâtre* (International Association of Theatre Critics)
AICU	Association of International Colleges and Universities
AID	Agency for International Development, United States
AIDBA	*Association internationale pour le développement de la documentation des bibliothèques et des archives en Afrique* (International Association for the Development of Documentation, Libraries and Archives in Africa)

AIDELA
Association internationale d'éditeurs de linguistique appliquée (International Association of Publishers of Applied Linguistics) (defunct)

AIDP
Association internationale de droit pénal (International Association of Penal Law)

AIED
Association internationale des étudiants dentaires (*see* IADS)

AIESEC
Association internationale des étudiants en sciences économiques et commerciales (International Association of Students in Business and Economics)

AIESEP
Association internationale des écoles supérieures d'éducation physique (International Association of Higher Schools of Physical Education)

AIGI
Association internationale de géologie de l'ingénieur (*see* IAEG)

AIIC
Association internationale des interprètes de conférence (International Association of Conference Interpreters)

AIISUP
Association internationale d'information scolaire, universitaire et professionnelle

AIL
Association of International Libraries (*see* ABI)

AILA
Association internationale de linguistique appliquée

AILC
Association internationale de littérature comparée (*see* ICLA)

AIM
Asian Institute of Management
AIM
Australian Institute of Management

AIMA
All India Management Association

AIMAV
Association internatiónale pour la recherche et

la diffusion des méthodes audio-visuelles et struc-
turo-global

AIMEA   *Association internationale des métiers et en-
                      seignement d'art* (International Association for
                      Crafts and the Teaching of Art)

AIOSP   *Association internationale d'orientation scolaire
                      et professionnelle* (*see* IAEVG)

AIPA   *Association internationale de psychologie analy-
                      tique* (*see* IAAP)

AIPCN   *Association internationale permanente des congrès
                      de navigation* (*see* PIANC)

AIPCR   *Association internationale permanente des congrès
                      de la route* (*see* PIARC)

AIPEA   *Association internationale pour l'étude des ar-
                      giles* (International Association for the Study
                      of Clays)

AISF   All India Students' Federation

AISM   *Association internationale de signalisation mar-
                      itime* (*see* IALA)

AIT   *Alliance internationale de tourisme* (Interna-
                      tional Touring Alliance)

AITC   *Association internationale des traducteurs de
                      conférence* (International Association of
                      Conference Translators)

AITI   *Associazione italiana traduttori et interpreti*
                      (Italian Association of Translators and
                      Interpreters)

AIU   *Association internationale des universités* (*see*
                      IAU)

AIU   Association of Indian Universities

AIVPA   *Association internationale vétérinaire de produc-
                      tion animale* (*see* IVAAP)

ALA	American Library Association
ALAFO	*Asociación latinoamericana de facultades de odontología,* Guatemala
ALAM	*Asociación latinoamericana de museos,* Ecuador
ALAMAR	*Asociación latinoamericana de armadores (see* LASA)
ALEBCI	*Asociación latinoamericana de escuelas de bibliotecología y ciencias de la información* (Latin American Association of Schools of Library and Information Sciences)
ALECSO	Arab League Educational, Cultural and Scientific Organization
ALFAL	*Asociación de lingüística filología de América Latina* (Linguistic and Philological Association of Latin America)
AMA	American Management Association
AMA	American Medical Association
AMAT	*Association des musées d'Afrique tropicale (see* MATA)
AMMA	*Associazione industriali metallurgici meccanici affini,* Italy
AMSA	Association of Medical Schools in Africa
AMTEC	Association for Media and Technology in Education in Canada
AMV	*Association mondiale vétérinaire (see* WVA)
AMVMI	*Association mondiale des vétérinaires microbiologistes, immunologistes et spécialistes des maladies infectieuses (see* WAVMI)
ANIES	*Asociación nicaragüense de instituciones de educación superior,* Nicaragua

ANOP
Association nationale d'orientation profession-nelle, Belgium

ANPUR
Associazione nazionale professori universitari di ruolo (National Association of University Professors), Italy

ANUIES
Asociación nacional de universidades e institutos de enseñanza superior (National Association of Universities and Institutes of Higher Education), Mexico

ANVAR
Agence nationale pour la valorisation de la recherche (National Agency for the Promotion of Research), France

AOE
Association of Overseas Educators, United States

AOTA
American Occupational Therapy Association

AP
Advanced Placement Examination, United States

APEDE
Asociación panameña de ejecutivos de empresas, Panama

APETI
Asociación profesional española de traductores e interpretes (Spanish Professional Association of Translators and Interpreters), Spain

APEUCH
Asociación de profesores y empleados de la Universidad de Chile (Association of Professionals and Technicians of the University of Chile)

APGA
American Personnel and Guidance Association

APP
Advanced Placement Program, United States

APPA
Association of Physical Plant Administrators of Universities and Colleges, United States

APSA	American Political Science Association
APT	Association of Polytechnic Teachers, United Kingdom
ARAVEG	Asian Regional Association on Vocational and Educational Guidance, Japan
ARC	South Asian Regional Council (of AAS)
ARGC	Australian Research Grants Committee
ARL	Association of Research Libraries, United States
ARS	Agricultural Research Service (of the Department of Agriculture), United States
ASA	African Studies Association, United States
ASAIHL	Association of Southeast Asian Institutions of Higher Learning
ASA-UK	African Studies Association of the United Kingdom
ASB	*Afrikaanse Studentebond* (Union of Afri-caans-speaking South African Students), South Africa
ASCE	American Society of Civil Engineers
ASCUN	*Asociación colombiana de universidades* (Colombian Association of Universities)
ASEAN	Association of Southeast Asian Nations
ASGA	*Association des services géologiques africains* (*see* AAGS)
ASITEJ	*Association internationale du théâtre pour l'enfance et la jeunesse* (International Association for Children's and Youth Theatres)
ASLA	American Society of Landscape Architects

ASOS	*Association suisse d'organisation scientifique*, Switzerland
ASPA	American Society for Public Administration
ASRT	Academy of Scientific Research and Technology, Egypt
ASTA	American Society of Travel Agents
ASTEC	Australian Science and Technology Council
ASTI	*Association suisse des traducteurs et interprètes* (Swiss Association of Translators and Interpreters)
ASTMS	Association of Scientific, Technical and Managerial Staffs, Great Britain
A-T	Audio-tutorial (method of instruction)
ATA	American Translators' Association
ATCDE	Association of Teachers in Colleges and Departments of Education, Great Britain
ATE	Association of Teacher Educators, United States
ATEA	Association for Teacher Education in Africa
ATRUM	Association of Teachers of the Royal University of Malta (in 1977 renamed University Teachers' Association)
ATTI	Association of Teachers in Technical Institutions, Great Britain
AUA	Argonne Universities Association, United States
AUB	American University of Beirut
AUC	American University in Cairo
AUCC	Association of Universities and Colleges of

Canada (*Association des universités et collèges du Canada*)

AUDECAM   *Association universitaire pour le développement de l'enseignement et de la culture en Afrique et à Madagascar* (University Association for the Development of Education and Culture in Africa and Madagascar)

AUEFW   Amalgamated Union of Engineering and Foundry Workers, United Kingdom

AUFS   American Universities Field Staff

AUIE   Associated Universities for International Education, United States

AULLA   Australian Universities Language and Literature Association

AUPELF   *Association des universités partiellement ou entièrement de langue française* (Association of Partially or Wholly French-Language Universities)

AUPHA   Association of University Programs in Health Administration, United States

AUS   Australian Union of Students

AUT   Association of University Teachers, New Zealand

AUT   Association of University Teachers, United Kingdom

AVA   American Vocational Association

AVCC   Australian Vice-Chancellors' Committee

AVE   *Asociación venezolana de ejecutivos*, Venezuela

AVI   *Association universelle d'aviculture scientifique* (*see* WPSA)

B

BAC	Buenos Aires Convention
BACIE	British Association for Commercial and Industrial Education, United Kingdom
BAPPENAS	*Badan perancang pembangunan nasional* (National Development Planning Agency), Indonesia
BASIC	Computer language
BBC	British Broadcasting Corporation
BDIA	*Bund deutscher Innenarchitekten* (Association of German Interior Architects), Federal Republic of Germany
BEC	Business Education Council, United Kingdom
BEOG	Basic Education Opportunity Grant, United States
BEPC	*Brevet d'études du premier cycle* (Certificate of lower secondary study—French-language systems)
BESCT	*Brevet d'enseignement du second cycle technique* (Certificate of completion of second technical cycle—French-language systems)
BFI	British Film Institute
BID	*Banco interamericano de desarrollo* (*see* IDB)
BIM	British Institute of Management
BIMCO	Baltic and International Maritime Conference
BITEJ	*Bureau international pour le tourisme et les échanges de la jeunesse* (International Bureau for Tourism and Youth Exchanges)

BLADE   Basic Literacy for Adult Development, Canada

BLK   *Bund-Länder-Kommission für Bildungsplanung* (Federal-State Commission for Education Planning), Federal Republic of Germany

BLLD   British Library Lending Division

BMBW   *Bundesministerium für Bildung und Wissenschaft* (Federal Ministry for Education and Science), Federal Republic of Germany

BNI   *Beroepsvereniging van Nederlandse interieurarchitekten,* the Netherlands

BÖIA   *Bund österreichischer Innenarchitekten,* Austria

BRISMES   British Society for Middle Eastern Studies, United Kingdom

BSL   Bavarian State Library, Federal Republic of Germany

BTS   *Brevet de technicien supérieur* (Certificate of higher technician), France

BUP   *Bachillerato unificado y polivalente* (Certificate of secondary education), Spain

BVB   *Beroepsvereniging voor binnenhuisarchitekten,* Belgium

C

CAAS   Canadian Association of African Studies (*see* ACEA)

CAB   Central Advisory Board (of the Association of Indian Universities)

CACUL   Canadian Association of College and University Libraries (*see* ACBCU)

CAE	Commission on Advanced Education, Australia
CAEL	Cooperative Assessment of Experiential Learning (of the Educational Testing Service), United States
CAFRAD	*Centre africain de formation et de recherches administratives pour le développement* (African Training and Research Center in Administration for Development)
CAI	Computer-assisted instruction
CAIM	*Syndicat national des créateurs d'architectures intérieures et de modèles*, France
CAL	Computer-assisted learning
CAMES	*Conseil africain et Malgache pour l'enseignement supérieur* (African and Malagasy Council for Higher Education)
CAMPUS	Comprehensive Analytical Methods of Planning
CAP	*Certificat d'aptitude professionnelle* (Certificate of professional aptitude—French-language systems)
CAP	Commonwealth Association of Planners
CAPA	Confederation of Asian and Pacific Accountants
CAPES	*Certificat d'aptitude au professorat de l'enseignement secondaire* (French-language systems)
CARICOM	Caribbean Community
CARL	Canadian Academic Research Libraries
CASC	Council for the Advancement of Small Colleges, United States
CASE	Commission on Accreditation of Service Experiences, United States

CASE	Council for the Advancement and Support of Education, United States
CASTARAB	Conference of Arab Science and Technology at Rabat (1976)
CAT	College Achievement Test, United States
CAT	College of Advanced Technology, United Kingdom
CAUT	Canadian Association of University Teachers
CBAT	Central Bureau for Astronomical Telegrams, United States
CBI	Confederation of British Industry
CCA	Cacchetti Council of America, United States
CCC	Council for Cultural Cooperation (of the Council of Europe)
CCCU	Caribbean Confederation of Credit Unions
CCEA	Commonwealth Council for Educational Administration, Australia
CCIC	Canadian Council for International Co-operation/*Conseil canadien pour la coopération internationale*
CCICH	*Confédération internationale catholique des institutions hospitalières* (International Catholic Confederation of Hospitals)
CCIPA	*Comité inter-americano de protección agricola*, Argentina
CCIVS	Co-ordinating Committee for International Voluntary Service (*see* CCSVI)
CCR	Cooperative College Registry, United States
CCSM	Czechoslovak Committee for Scientific Management

CCRST   *Comité consultatif de la recherche scientifique et technique* (Central Advisory Committee on Scientific and Technological Research), France

CCS   College Scholarship Service (of the College Entrance Examination Board and the American College Testing Service)

CCSVI   *Comité de coordination du service volontaire internationale* (*see* CCIVS)

CDG   Carl Duisberg-Gesellschaft (Carl Duisberg Society), Federal Republic of Germany

CDP   Committee of Directors of Polytechnics, United Kingdom

CEA   *Commissariat à l'énergie atomique* (Atomic Energy Commission), France

CEA   *Commission économique des Nations Unies pour l'Afrique* (*see* ECA)

CEA   Cooperative Education Association, United States

CEAP   Catholic Educational Association of the Philippines

CEC   Commission of the European Communities

CEC   *Conseil européen de l'enseignement par correspondance* (European Council for Education by Correspondence)

CED   Cooperative Education Division (of American Society for Engineering Education)

CEDCA   *Centre d'études de droit comparé africain* (Center for the Study of Comparative African Law), Zaire

CEDEP   *Centre européen d'éducation permanente* (European Center for Continuing Education)

CEDO	Center for Educational Development Overseas, United Kingdom
CEEB	College Entrance Examination Board, United States
CEG	*Collège d'enseignement général* (General secondary school—French-language systems)
CEI	*Centre d'études industrielles* (International Management Development Institute), Switzerland
CEI	*Commission électrotechnique internationale* (International Electrotechnical Commission)
CELTA	*Centre d'études de linguistique théoretique et appliquée* (Center of Theoretical and Applied Linguistics), Zaire
CEMA	Council for Economic Mutual Assistance, Eastern Europe
CEMT	*Conférence européenne des ministres des transports* (*see* ECMT)
CEN	*Comisión estatuaria nacional* (National Statute Commission), Peru
CENIDE	*Centro nacional de investigaciones para el desarrollo de la educación* (National Center for Educational Research and Devleopment), Spain
CENTO	Central Treaty Organization, Turkey
CENTRO	*Centro latino-americano de pesquisas em ciências sociais*, Brazil
CEPCI	*Conseil international des practiciens du plan comptable international* (International Council of Practitioners of the International Plan of Accounts), Belgium
CEPE	*Certificat d'études primaires élémentaires* (Certificate of primary study—French language systems)

CEPES   *Centre européen pour l'enseignement supérieur* (European Center for Higher Education)

CEPICT   *Centros de promoción de la investigación científica y tecnológica* (Centers for the Promotion of Scientific and Technological Research), Bolivia

CEPTA TV   Centre for Production and Training for Adult Education Television, Singapore

CER   *Centre d'éducation revolutionnaire* (Center of Revolutionary Education), Guinea

CERDIA   *Centre d'études et de recherches des industries agricoles et alimentaires*, France

CERI   Centre for Educational Research and Innovation (of OECD)

CERN   *Centre européen pour la recherche nucléaire* (European Center for Nuclear Research)

CESO   *Centrum voor de studie van het onderwijs in veranderende maatschappijen* (Center for the Study of Education in Changing Societies), the Netherlands

CET   *Collège d'enseignement technique* (Technical secondary school—French-language systems)

CEU   Continuing Education Unit (of credit measurement), United States

CEUUCA   *Centro estudiantil universitario de la Universidad centroamericana* (Center of University Students of the Central American University), Nicaragua

CFAE   Council for Financial Aid to Education, United States

CFHE   Consortium on Financing Higher Education (New England), United States

CFR	Code of Federal Regulations, United States
CGIAR	Consultative Group on International Agricultural Research (of World Bank)
CGEP	*Collèges d'enseignement général et professionnel* (Secondary schools of general and vocational education), Canada
CGLI	City and Guilds of London Institute, United Kingdom
CGMW	Commission for the Geological Map of the World
CGP	Comparative Guidance and Placement Program (of CEEB), United States
CGS	Council of Graduate Schools in the United States
CHEAR	Council on Higher Education in the American Republics, United States
CIA	Central Intelligence Agency, United States
CIADEC	*Confédération internationale des associations de diplômés en sciences économiques et commerciales* (International Confederation of Associations of Graduates in Economic and Commercial Sciences)
CIAM	*Congrès internationaux d'architecture moderne* (International Congresses for Modern Architecture)
CIARC	China and Inner Asia Regional Council (of AAS)
CIAT	*Centro internacional de agricultura tropical* (International Center of Tropical Agriculture) (of CGIAR), Colombia
CIB	*Counseil international du bâtiment pour la re-*

	cherche, l'étude et la documentation (International Council for Building Research, Studies and Documentation)
CIC	Committee on Institutional Cooperation, United States
CIC	*Consejo interamericano cultural* (Inter-American Cultural Council) (of Organization of American States)
CICRED	Committee for International Coordination of National Research in Demography, France
CICRI	Cooperative Industrial and Commercial Reference Service, United Kingdom
CIDA	Canadian International Development Agency
CIDEM	*Consejo inter-americano de música* (Inter-American Music Council)
CIDESA	*Centre international de documentation économique et sociale africaine* (International Centre for African Economic and Social Documentation)
CIDIUTI	*Conférence internationale permanente des directeurs des instituts universitaires de traducteurs et interprètes* (Permanent International Conference of Directors of University Institutes of Translators and Interpreters)
CIDSS	*Comité international pour la documentation des sciences sociales* (International Committee for Social Science Information and Documentation)
CIEE	Council on International Educational Exchange, United States
CIEPS	*Conseil international pour l'éducation physique*

	et le sport (International Council of Sport and Physical Education)
CIES	Comparative and International Education Society
CIES	Council for International Exchange of Scholars, United States
CIFE	*Conseil international du film d'enseignement* (*see* ICEF)
CIGR	*Commission internationale de génie rural* (International Commission of Agricultural Engineering)
CIGRE	*Conférence international des grands réseaux électriques à haute tension* (International Conference on Large High Tension Electric Systems)
CIHED	Center for International Higher Education Documentation, United States
CII	*Conseil international des infirmières* (*see* ICN)
CIIR	Cameroon Institute of International Relations (of Federal University of Cameroon)
CIJE	Current Index to Journals in Education, United States
CIMMYT	*Centro internacional de mejoramiento de maize y trigo* (International Maize and Wheat Improvement Center) (of CGIAR), Mexico
CIO	*Comité interministériel d'orientation* (Interministerial Orientation Committee), Ivory Coast
CIOS	*Conseil international pour l'organisation scientifique* (International Council for Scientific Management)
CIP	*Centro internacional de la papa* (International Potato Center) (of CGIAR), Peru

CIPL	*Comité international permanent des linguistes* (Permanent International Committee of Linguists)
CIPM	Council for International Progress in Management, United States
CIRB	International Centre for Biological Research, Switzerland
CIRF	*Centre international d'information et de recherche sur la formation professionnelle* (International Center for Information and Research for Professional Education)
CIRM	*Comité international radio-maritime* (International Maritime Radio Association)
CISS	*Conseil international des sciences sociales* (*see* ISSC)
CIT	Chartered Institute of Transport, United Kingdom
CIT	*Comité international de la télévision* (International Television Committee)
CIT	*Comité international des transports par chemins de fer* (International Rail Transport Committee)
CIUS	*Conseil international des unions scientifiques* (*see* ICSU)
CLACSO	*Consejo latinoamericano de ciencias sociales* (Latin American Social Science Council)
CLAD	*Centre de linguistique appliquée de Dakar* (Center of Applied Linguistics of Dakar), Senegal
CLADEA	*Comité latinoamericano de decanos de escuelas de administración* (Latin American Committee of Deans of Schools of Administration), Colombia

CLAF	*Centro latinoamericano de física* (Latin American Centre for Physics), Brazil
CLAR	*Confederación latinoamericana de religiosos* (Latin American Confederation of Religious)
CLEP	College-Level Examination Program, United States
CMEA	Council for Mutual Economic Assistance
CMI	*Comité maritime international* (*see* IMC)
CMOPE	*Confédération mondiale des organisations de la profession enseignante* (*see* WCOTP)
CMRSS	*Conseil mediterranéen de recherches en sciences sociales* (*see* MSSRC)
CNAA	Council for National Academic Awards, United Kingdom
CNES	*Centre national d'études spatiales* (National Center for Space Research), France
CNOF	*Comité national de l'organisation française,* France
CNOS	*Comitato nazionale per l'organizzazione scientifica,* Italy
CNPq	*Conselho nacional de pesquisas* (National Research Council), Brazil
CNRS	*Centre national de la recherche scientifique* (National Center for Scientific Research), France
COE	*Conseil oecuménique des églises* (*see* WCC)
COLAC	*Confederación latinoamericana de cooperativas de ahorro y crédito* (Latin American Confederation of Savings and Credit Cooperatives)

COLCIENCIAS	*Fondo colombiana para investigaciones científicas* (Colombian Fund for Scientific Research)
COM	Computer Output Microfilm, United States
COMLA	Commonwealth Library Association, Jamaica
CONACYT	*Consejo nacional de ciencia y tecnología* (National Council for Science and Technology), Mexico
CONICET	*Consejo nacional de investigaciones científicas y técnicas* (National Council of Scientific and Technical Research), Argentina
CONICIT	*Consejo nacional de investigación científica y tecnológica* (National Council for Scientific and Technological Research), Costa Rica
CONICIT	*Consejo nacional de investigaciones científicas y tecnológicas* (National Council for Scientific and Technological Research), Venezuela
CONICYT	*Comisión nacional de investigación científica y tecnológica* (National Commission for Scientific and Technological Research), Chile
CONSAL	Conference of Southeast Asian Librarians
CONUP	*Consejo nacional de la Universidad peruana* (National Council of Peruvian Universities)
COPA	Council on Postsecondary Accreditation, United States
COPARMEX	*Confederación patronal de la República Mexicana*
CORD	Committee on Research in Dance, United States
COSERV	National Council for Community Services to International Visitors, United States
COSPAR	Committee on Space Research (of ICSU)

COST	Committee on Science and Technology, India
COTA	Certified Occupational Therapy Assistant
COU	*Curso de orientación universitaria* (University orientation program), Spain
CPC	China Productivity Center, Republic of China
CPEP	College Proficiency Examination Program, United States
CPEPIP	*Centre populaire d'éducation, de perfectionnement, et d'initiation à la production* (People's Center for Education, Further Training, and Introduction to Practical Work), Benin
CPIUA	Committee for the Promotion of an International University in America (now Committee for the World University), United States
CRE	*Conférence permanente des recteurs et vice-chanceliers des universités européennes* (Standing Conference of Rectors and Vice-Chancellors of European Universities)
CREAA	*Conseil régional pour l'éducation et l'alphabétisation des adultes en Afrique* (Regional Council for Adult Education and Literacy in Africa)
CREN	*Centre régional d'études nucléaires* (Regional Center for the Study of Nuclear Science), Zaire
CRESU	*Consejo representativo del sistema universitario* (Representative Council of the University System), Peru
CRIDE	*Center de recherches interdisciplinaires pour le développement de l'éducation* (Center for Interdisciplinary Research for the Development of Education), Zaire

CRL	Center for Research Libraries, United States
CRS	Congressional Research Service, United States
CRUTAC	*Centro rural universitario de treinamento e de acção comunitaria* (Rural University Center for Training in University Action), Brazil
CS	Cambridge School Certificate, Kenya
CSBO	*Centraale voor studie-en beroepsorientering,* Belgium
CSE	Certificate of Secondary Education, United Kingdom
CSIR	Council of Scientific and Industrial Research, India
CSIRO	Commonwealth Scientific and Industrial Research Organization, Australia
CSS	College Scholarship Service (of College Entrance Examination Board), United States
CSSF	*Société des africanistes*, France
CSUCA	*Consejo superior universitario centroamericano* (Central American Higher University Council)
CTCL	Community and Technical College Libraries, Canada
CTFT	*Centre technique forestier tropical* (Center of Tropical Forestry), Upper Volta
CUAG	*Centre universitaire des Antilles-Guyane* (University Center of Antilles-Guiana)
CUB	*Confederación universitaria boliviana* (Bolivian University Confederation)
CUES	College and University Environment Scales, United States

CUMBIN   City University Mutual Benefit Instructional Network, United States

CUMIS   Credit Union Insurance Society, United States

CUNA   Credit Union National Association, United States

CUNADATA   Credit Union National Association Data Corporation, United States

CUNY   City University of New York, United States

CUP   Committee of University Principals, South Africa

CUPA   College and University Personnel Association, United States

CUPU   Committee of Urban Public Universities, United States

CUUN   *Centro universitario de la Universidad nacional* (University Center of the National University), Nicaragua

CVC   Committee of Vice-Chancellors and Principals of the Universities of the United Kingdom

CVRS   *Centre voltaïque de la recherche scientifique* (Volta Center for Scientific Research), Upper Volta

CWOIH   Council of World Organizations Interested in the Handicapped

D

DAAD   *Deutscher akademischer Austauschdienst* (German Academic Exchange Service), Federal Republic of Germany

DAC   Development Assistance Committee (of OECD)

DAE	Department of Atomic Energy, India
DAIR	Dual Access Information Retrieval System, United States
DANTES	Defense Activity for Non-Traditional Education Support, United States
DBV	*Deutscher Bibliotheksverband* (German Library Association), Federal Republic of Germany
DCSM	Danish Council for Scientific Management
DEA	*Diplôme d'études approfondies* (Diploma of advanced study), France
DESS	*Diplôme d'études supérieures spécialisées* (Diploma of specialized higher study), France
DEUG	*Diplôme d'études universitaires générales* (Diploma of general university study)
DGRST	*Délégation générale à la recherche scientifique et technique* (General Delegation for Scientific and Technical Research), France
DEST	*Diplôme d'études supérieures techniques* (Advanced technical diploma), New Caledonia
DISUP	*Direction de l'enseignement supérieur et de la recherche* (Office of Higher Studies and Research), France
DKNVS,M	*Det kongelige norske videnskabers selskab, Museet* (Royal Norwegian Society of Sciences and Letters)
DNA	Deoxyribonucleic acid
DOS/VS	Disc-Operated System with Virtual Storage (IBM system)
DPCE	*Diplôme du premier cycle économique* (Diploma of economics, first cycle), New Caledonia

DPCT	*Diplôme du premier cycle technique* (Diploma of technical study, first cycle, New Caledonia
DPRK	Democratic People's Republic of Korea
DRDO	Defence Research and Development Organisation, India
DSF	*Danske studerendes faellesraad* (National Union of Danish Students), Denmark
DSI	Dairy Society International
DTE	Diploma in Teacher Education, Zambia
DUEL	*Diplôme universitaire d'études littéraires* (University diploma of literary study)—French-language systems)
DUES	*Diplôme universitaire d'études scientifiques* (University diploma of scientific study—French-language systems)
DURENAS	*Departmen urusan research nasional* (Ministry of National Research), Indonesia
DUSO	Dar es Salaam University Students' Organization, Tanzania
DUT	*Diplôme universitaire de technologie* (University diploma of technology), France
DVB	*Deutscher Verband für Berufsberatung,* Federal Republic of Germany
DVPW	*Deutsche Vereinigung für politische Wissenschaft* (German Association of Political Science), Federal Republic of Germany
DVTA	*Deutscher Verband technischer Assistentinnen und Assistenten* (German Association of Technical Assistants), Federal Republic of Germany
DVV	*Deutscher Volkshochschul-Verband* (German

Adult Education Association), Federal Republic of Germany

E

EAACE	East African Advanced Certificate of Education
EAAFRO	East African Agricultural and Forestry Research Association, Kenya
EACE	East African Certificate of Education
EAEC	East African Examinations Council
EAPM	European Association for Personnel Management (*see* AEDP)
EARDHE	European Association for Research and Development in Higher Education
EAROPH	Eastern Regional Organization for Planning and Housing, India
EBU	European Broadcasting Union, Switzerland
ECA	Economic Commission for Africa (of the United Nations) (*see* CEA)
ECAFE	United Nations Economic Commission for Asia and the Far East
ECBO	European Cell Biology Organization
ECE	Economic Commission for Europe (of the United Nations)
ECFMG	Educational Commission for Foreign Medical Graduates, United States
ECIS	European Council of International Schools
ECLA	Economic Commission for Latin America (of the United Nations)

ECMT	European Conference of Ministers of Transport (*see* CEMT)
ECPD	Engineers Council for Professional Development, United States
ECS	Education Commission of the States, United States
EDI	Economic Development Institute (of World Bank)
EDUCOM	Interuniversity Communications Council, United States
EEC	European Economic Community
EEOC	Equal Employment Opportunity Commission, United States
EFMD	European Foundation for Management Development, Belgium
EFTS	Electronic Funds Transfer System
EGB	*Educación general básica* (Basic education), Spain
EIER	*Ecole inter-états des ingénieurs de l'équipement rural* (Interstate School of Engineering and Rural Engineering), Upper Volta
ELS	English Language Service centers
EMBO	European Molecular Biology Organization
EMC	Educational Media Council, United States
ENAG	*Escuela nacional de agricultura y ganadería* (National School of Agriculture and Animal Husbandry), Nicaragua
ENE	*Escuela nacional de enfermería* (National School of Nursing), Nicaragua

EPA	Environmental Protection Agency, United States
EPF	*Ecole polytechnique fédérale de Lausanne* (Federal Institute of Technology), Switzerland
ERIC	Educational Resources Information Center, United States
ERIC-HE	Educational Resources Information Center-Clearinghouse on Higher Education
ERISA	Employment Retirement Income Security Act, United States
EROPA	Eastern Regional Organization for Public Administration, the Philippines
ERP	European Recovery Program (Marshall Plan)
ESAN	*Escuela superior de administración de negocios* (Higher School of Business Administration), Peru
ESAPAC	*Escuela superior de administración pública de América Central* (Central American Higher School of Public Administration), Costa Rica
ESCAP	Economic and Social Commission for Asia and the Pacific (of the United Nations)
ESF	European Science Foundation
ESLAT	English as a Second Language Achievement Test
ESOMAR	European Society for Opinion and Marketing Research
ESSEC	*Ecole supérieure des sciences économiques et commerciales* (Higher School of Economic Sciences and Business Administration), France
E-SU	English-Speaking Union of the United States

ETH	*Eidgenössische technische Hochschule* (Federal Institute of Technology), Switzerland
ETS	Educational Testing Service, United States
EURARPIA	European Association for Research on Plant Breeding
EURATOM	European Atomic Energy Community
EURIM	European Conference on Research into the Management of Information Services and Libraries
EUTA	Ethiopian University Teachers Association

F

FAC	*Fonds d'aide et de coopération technique et économique* (Fund for Aid and Technical Cooperation), France
FAGS	Federation of Astronomical and Geophysical Services
FAIB	*Fédération internationale des associations de bibliothécaires* (*see* IFLA)
FAO	Food and Agriculture Organization (of the United Nations)
FAPA	Federation of Asian Pharmaceutical Associations
FAPUASA	Federation of All-Pakistan Universities Academic Staff Associations
FDI	*Fédération dentaire internationale* (International Dental Federation)
FDJ	*Freie deutsche Jugend* (Student Division of Free German Youth), German Democratic Republic
FEANI	*Fédération européenne d'associations nationales*

d'ingénieurs (European Federation of National Associations of Engineers), France

FEI   Financial Executives Institute, United States

FEPC   Fair Employment Practices Committee, United States

FERES   *Fédération internationale des instituts de recherches socio-religieuses* (International Federation of Institutes for Socio-Religious Research)

FESAC   *Fondation de l'enseignement supérieur de l'Afrique Centrale* (Central African Foundation for Higher Education)

FEU   *Federación estudiantil universitaria* (Federation of University Students), Cuba

FECH   *Federación estudiantil de la Universidad de Chile* (Student Federation of the University of Chile)

FEUH   *Federación de estudiantes universitarios de Honduras* (Honduran Federation of University Students)

FFRDC   Federally Funded Research and Development Centers, United States

FHA   *Félag húsgagnaarkitekta,* Iceland

FIA   *Fédération internationale de l'automobile* (International Automobile Federation)

FIACC   Five International Associations Coordinating Committee (IFIP, IFAC, IFORS, IMEKO, AICA)

FIAI   *Fédération internationale des associations d'instituteurs* (International Federation of Teachers' Associations)

FIARO   *Federazione italiana associazioni regionali os-*

pedaliere (Italian Federation of Regional Hospital Associations)

FICEPS   *Fédération internationale catholique d'éducation physique et sportive* (Catholic International Federation for Physical and Sports Education)

FIEA   *Fédération internationale des experts en automobile* (International Federation of Automobile Experts)

FIEP   *Fédération internationale d'éducation physique* (International Federation for Physical Education)

FID   *Fédération internationale de documentation* (International Federation for Documentation)

FIH   *Fédération internationale des hôpitaux (see* IHF)

FIL   *Fédération internationale de laiterie (see* IDF)

FILA   Federation of Indian Library Associations

FILLM   *Fédération internationale des langues et litteratures modernes* (International Federation of Modern Languages and Literatures)

FIMS   *Fédération internationale de médecine sportive* (International Federation of Sportive Medicine)

FINEP   *Financiadora de estudos e projetos* (Financing of Studies and Projects), Brazil

FIP   *Fédération internationale pharmaceutique* (International Pharmaceutical Federation)

FIPACE   *Fédération internationale des producteurs autoconsommateurs industriels d'électricité* (International Federation of Industrial Producers of Electricity for Own Consumption)

FIPESO   *Fédération internationale des professeurs de*

l'enseignement secondaire officiel (International Federation of Secondary Teachers)

FIPLV   *Fédération internationale des professeurs de langues vivantes* (International Federation of Modern Language Teachers)

FIPP   *Fondation internationale pénale et pénitentiaire* (*see* IPPF)

FISP   *Fédération internationale des sociétés de philosophie* (*see* IFPS)

FISTA   *Fédération internationale des sociétés d'ingénieurs des techniques de l'automobile* (International Federation of Automobile Engineers' and Technicians' Associations)

FISU   *Fédération internationale du sport universitaire* (International University Sports Federation)

FIT   *Fédération internationale des traducteurs* (International Federation of Translators)

FIYTO   Federation of International Youth Travel Organizations

FLACSO   *Facultad latinamericana de ciencias sociales* (Latin American Faculty of Social Sciences), Chile

FMOI   *Fédération mondiale des organisations d'ingénieurs* (*see* WFEO)

FONAPE   *Fondo nacional de préstamos para educación* (National Fund for Loans to Education), Costa Rica

FORTRAN   Computer language

FPAA   *Federación panamericana de asociaciones de arquitectos,* Uruguay

FSA   Faculty, Student, Administration stores (of New York State University), United States

FSZMP	*Federacja socjalistycznych związków młodzieży polskiej* (Federation of Socialist Unions of Polish Youth)
FTC	Federal Trade Commission, United States
FUACE	*Fédération universelle des associations chrétiennes d'étudiants* (*see* WSCF)
FUN	*Fondo universitario nacional,* Colombia
FUPAC	*Federación de universidades privadas de América Central y Panamá* (Federation of Private Universities of Central America and Panama)

G

GAIT	Guatemalan Association of Interpreters and Translators
GAL	*Gesellschaft für angewandte Linguistik* (Society for Applied Linguistics), Federal Republic of Germany
GATT	General Agreement on Tariffs and Trade
GBE	General Baccalaureate Examination, Iraq
GCE	General Certificate of Education, United Kingdom
GCE, A-level	General Certificate of Education, advanced level, United Kingdom
GCE, O-level	General Certificate of Education, ordinary level, United Kingdom
GED	General Educational Development Testing Program, United States
GED	General Equivalency Diploma, United States
GFCM	General Fisheries Council for the Mediterranean (of FAO)

GMA	Greek Management Association
GMC	General Military Course (of the United States Air Force)
GNOE	*Groupement du nursing de l'Ouest Européen* (West European Group of Nurses)
GNP	Gross National Product
GRE	Graduate Record Examination, United States
GREM	*Groupement romand pour l'étude du marché et du marketing,* Switzerland
GUAU	*Grupo unificado de admisiones universitarias* (United Group of University Admissions), Colombia
GULERPE	*Grupo universitario latinoamericano de estudios para la reforma y perfeccionamiento de la educación* (Latin American University Group of Studies for the Reform and Perfection of Education)

H

HEA	Higher Education Act, United States
HEA	Higher Education Authority, Ireland
HEGIS	Higher Education General Information Survey (of HEW), United States
HEW	(Department of) Health, Education and Welfare, United States
HIS	Hochschule Information System, Federal Republic of Germany
HKFS	Hong Kong Federation of Students
HKMA	Hong Kong Management Association

HLR	*Hushållslärarnas riksförening,* Sweden
HNC	Higher National Certificate, United Kingdom
HNCE	Higher National Certificate of Education, Sri Lanka
HND	Higher National Diploma, United Kingdom
HRCC	*Conseil canadian de recherches sur les humanités/* Humanities Research Council of Canada
HSC	Higher School Certificate, Kenya
HSC	Higher Secondary Certificate, Bangladesh
HTL	*Höhere technische Lehranstalten* (Higher technical colleges), Switzerland
HTU	Hungarian Teachers' Union, Hungary

I

IAA	International Actuarial Association (*see* AAI)
IAA	International Association of Art-Painting, Sculpture, Graphic Art
IAAB	Inter-American Association of Broadcasters, Brazil
IAAE	International Association of Agricultural Economists
IAAER	Now WAAER, World Association for the Advancement of Educational Research
IAAF	International Amateur Athletic Federation
IAALD	International Association of Agricultural Librarians and Documentalists
IAAP	International Association of Analytical Psychology (*see* AIPA)

IAAP	International Association of Applied Psychology
IAAS	International Association of Agricultural Students
IACA	Inter-American College Association
IACA	International Association of Consulting Actuaries
IACD	International Association of Clothing Designers
IACME	International Association of Crafts and Small and Medium-Sized Enterprises
IACP	International Association of Child Psychiatry and Allied Professions
IACS	International Association of Classification Societies
IACUSD	International Association of College and University Security Directors
IADC	International Association of Dentistry for Children
IADC	International Association of Dredging Companies
IADR	International Association for Dental Research
IADS	International Association of Dental Students (*see* AIED)
IADIWU	International Association for the Development of International and World Universities
IAEA	International Atomic Energy Agency
IAEG	International Association of Engineering Geology (*see* AIGI)

IAESTE	International Association for the Exchange of Students for Technical Experience
IAEVG	International Association of Educational and Vocational Guidance (*see* AIOSP)
IAEWP	International Association of Educators for World Peace
IAGC	International Association of Geochemistry and Cosmochemistry
IAH	International Association of Hydrogeologists
IAIAS	Inter-American Institute of Agricultural Sciences, Costa Rica
IAKS	*Internationaler Arbeitskreis Sportstädtenbau* (International Working Group for the Construction of Sports Facilities)
IALA	International Association of Lighthouse Authorities (*see* AISM)
IALL	International Association of Law Libraries
IAMG	International Association for Mathematical Geology
IAML	International Association of Music Libraries (*see* AIBM)
IAMLT	International Association of Medical Laboratory Technologists
IAMS	International Association of Microbiological Societies
IAOS	International Association of Oral Surgeons
IAP	International Association of Planetology
IAPA	Inter-American Press Association, United States

IAPESGW	International Association of Physical Education and Sports for Girls and Women
IARF	International Association for Religious Freedom
IASI	Inter-American Statistical Institute
IAS	International Association of Sedimentologists
IASL	International Association of School Libraries
IASP	International Association of Scholarly Publishers
IASP	International Association of Social Progress
IASSW	International Association of Social Science Workers
IATA	International Air Transport Association
IATTC	Inter-American Tropical Tuna Commission, United States
IATUL	International Association of Technological University Libraries
IAU	International Association of Universities (*see* AIU)
IAU	International Astronomical Union
IAUP	International Association of University Presidents
IAUPL	International Association of University Professors and Lecturers
IBA	Institute of Business Administration (of Federal University of Cameroon)
IBE	International Bureau of Education (of UNESCO)

IBEDOC	International Bureau of Education Documentation Center
IBM	International Business Machines
IBI	Intergovernmental Bureau of Informatics
IBRD	International Bank for Reconstruction and Development (World Bank)
ICA	International Chiropractors Association
ICAE	International Council for Adult Education
ICAP	*Instituto centroamericano de administración pública* (Central American Institute of Public Administration), Costa Rica
ICAR	Indian Council of Agricultural Research
ICARDA	International Center for Agricultural Research in Dry Areas
ICARE	*Instituto chileño de administración racional de empresas*, Chile
ICCC	Intercouncil Coordinating Committee, Canada
ICCE	International Council for Correspondence Education
ICDO	International Civil Defence Organization (*see* OIPC)
ICE	*Institutos de ciencias de la educación* (Institutes of educational research), Spain
ICECU	*Instituto centroamericano de extensión de la cultura* (Central American Institute for the Extension of Culture), Costa Rica
ICED	International Council for Educational Development

ICEF	International Council for Educational Films (*see* CIFE)
ICEM	Intergovernmental Committee for European Migration, Switzerland
ICETEX	*Instituto colombiano de crédito educativo y estudios técnicos en el exterior* (Colombian Institute for Educational Credit and Technological Studies Abroad), Colombia
ICFES	*Instituto colombiano para el fomento de la educación superior* (Colombian Institute for the Promotion of Higher Education)
ICFU	International Council on the Future of the University
ICHCA	International Cargo Handling Co-ordination Association
ICLA	International Comparative Literature Association (*see* AILC)
ICM	International Confederation of Midwives
ICMR	Indian Council of Medical Research
ICN	International Council of Nurses (*see* CII)
ICNAF	International Commission for North West Atlantic Fisheries, Canada
ICOM	International Council of Museums
ICOMOS	International Council of Monuments and Sites
ICP	International Council of Psychologists
ICPHS	International Council for Philosophy and Humanistic Studies
ICPO	International Criminal Police Organization

ICRISAT	International Crops Research Institute for the Semi-Arid Tropics (of CGIAR), India
ICSHB	International Committee for Standardization in Human Biology
ICSPE	International Council of Sport and Physical Education
ICSU	International Council of Scientific Unions (*see* CIUS)
ICU	International Christian University, Japan
ICU	International Credit Union
ICUAE	International Congress of University Adult Education
ICVA	International Council of Voluntary Agencies
IDA	Institute of Defense Analysis (Research Consortium), United States
IDA	International Development Association (of World Bank)
IDB	Inter-American Development Bank (*see* BID)
IDC	International Dairy Committee
IDC	Interior Designers of Canada
IDEA	*Instituto para el desarrollo de ejecutivos en la Argentina*
IDEF	*Institut international de droit d'expression française* (International Institute of Law of the French-Speaking Countries), France
IDEP	International and Development Education Program Clearinghouse
IDF	International Dairy Federation (*see* FIL)

IDORT	*Instituto de organização racional de trabalho*, Brazil
IDSA	Industrial Designers Society of America, United States
IEDP	African Institute for Economic Development and Planning (of ECA)
IEE	Institution of Electrical Engineers, United Kingdom
IEEE	Institute of Electrical and Electronic Engineers, United States
IEHE	International Encyclopedia of Higher Education
IESE	*Instituto de estudios de la empresa* (Institute of Graduate Business Studies), Spain
IFAC	International Federation of Automatic Control
IFAN	*Institut fondamental d'Afrique noire* (Institute of Black African Studies), Senegal
IFC	Interfraternity Council, United States
IFC	International Finance Corporation (of the World Bank) (*see* SFI)
IFCB	International Federation of Cell Biology
IFCU	International Federation of Catholic Universities
IFHE	International Federation for Home Economics
IFHP	International Federation for Housing and Planning
IFIP	International Federation of Information Processing

IFLA	International Federation of Landscape Architects
IFLA	International Federation of Library Associations (*see* FAIB)
IFMBE	International Federation for Medical and Biological Engineering
IFORS	International Foundation of Operational Research Societies
IFPRA	Inter-American Federation of Public Relations Associations, Venezuela
IFPS	International Federation of Philosophical Societies (*see* FISP)
IFSEG	International Federation of Societies of Economic Geologists
IFSPO	International Federation of Senior Police Officers
IFUW	International Federation of University Women
IFWEA	International Federation of Workers' Educational Associations
IFWL	International Federation of Women Lawyers
IGOs	International Governmental Organizations
IGU	International Geographical Union
IHA	International House Association
IHCA	International Hebrew Christian Alliance
IHF	International Hospital Federation (*see* FIH)
IIALM	International Institute for Adult Literacy Methods

IIAS	International Institute of Administrative Sciences (*see* IISA)
IIC	International Institute for Conservation of Historic and Artistic Works
IIE	Institute of International Education, United States
IIEP	International Institute of Educational Planning (*see* IIPE)
IIHL	International Institute of Humanitarian Law, Italy
IIID	Indian Institute of Interior Designers
IIIL	International Institute of Iberoamerican Literature, United States
IIIT	International Institute of Instructional Technology
IIP	International Institute of Philosophy
IIP	Israel Institute of Productivity
IIPE	*Institut international de planification de l'éducation* (*see* IIEP)
IIS	*Institut international de sociologie* (International Institute of Sociology)
IISA	*Institut international des sciences administratives* (*see* IIAS)
IIT	*Institut international du théâtre* (*see* ITI)
IITA	International Institute of Tropical Agriculture, Nigeria
ILAFA	*Instituto latinoamericano del fierro y el acero* (Latin American Iron and Steel Institute), Chile

ILAT	*Instituto latino-americano del teatro* (Latin American Theatre Institute)
ILCA	International Livestock Center for Africa, Ethiopia
ILCE	*Instituto latinoamericano de la communicación educativa* (Latin American Institute for Educational Communication)
ILO	International Labour Organisation
ILPES	*Instituto latinoamericano de planificación económica y social* (Latin American Institute for Social and Economic Planning)
ILRAD	International Laboratory for Research on Animal Diseases, Kenya
IMA	International Management Association
IMA	International Mineralogical Association
IMAJ	International Management Association of Japan
IMC	International Maritime Committee (*see* CMI)
IMC	International Music Council
IMCO	Inter-Governmental Maritime Consultative Organization (*see* OMCI)
IMDI	International Management and Development Institute, United States
IME	International Management Education
IMEDE	*Institut pour l'étude des méthodes de direction de l'entreprise* (Management Development Institute), Switzerland
IMEKO	International Measurement Conference
IMF	International Monetary Fund

IMI	Industrial Management Institute, Iran
IMI	Irish Management Institute, Ireland
IMMYT	*Centro internacional de mejoramiento de maize y trigo* (International Maize and Wheat Improvement Center) (of CGIAR), Mexico
INABEC	*Instituto nacional de becas y crédito educativo* (National Institute of Scholarships and Educational Credit), Peru
INBTP	*Institut national des bâtiments et des travaux publics* (National Institute of Construction and Public Works), Zaire
INCAE	*Instituto centroamericano de administración de empresas* (Central American Institute for Business Administration), Nicaragua
INCAP	*Instituto de nutrición de centroamérica y Panamá* (Institute of Nutrition of Central America and Panama)
INCIE	*Instituto nacional de ciencias de la educación* (National Institute of Educational Sciences), Spain
INCOLDA	*Instituto colombiano de administración,* Colombia
INEA	International Electronics Association
INGOS	International Non-Governmental Organizations
INNOTECH	Regional Center for Educational Innovation and Technology, Southeast Asia
INQUA	International Union for Quarternary Research
INRA	*Institut national de la recherche agronomique* (National Institute for Agronomic Research), France

INS	Immigration and Naturalization Service, United States
INSA	International Shipowners' Association
INSEA	International Society for Education Through Art
INSEAD	*Institut européen d'administration des affaires* (European Institute of Business Administration)
INSERM	*Institut national de la santé et de la recherche médicale* (National Institute for Health and Medical Research), France
INTA	*Instituto nacional de technología agropecuaria* (National Institute of Agricultural Technology), Argentina
INTECAP	*Instituto técnico de capacitación y productividad*, Guatemala
INTER-CENTRE	International Centre for the Terminology of the Social Sciences
INTERTANKO	International Association of Independent Tanker Owners
INTI	*Instituto nacional de technología industrial* (National Institute of Industrial Technology), Argentina
INTSOY	International Soybean Program, United States
IOMP	International Organizations for Medical Physics
IPA	International Paleontological Association
IPA	International Phonetic Association
IPA	International Publishers Association

IPFE   *Instituto peruano de fomento educativo* (Peruvian Institute for Educational Development), Peru

IPPF   International Penal and Penitentiary Foundation (*see* FIPP)

IPPF   International Planned Parenthood Federation

IPSA   International Passenger Ship Association

IPSA   International Political Science Association

IPVS   International Pig Veterinary Society

IRA   International Recreation Association

IRAL   International Review of Applied Linguistics in Language Teaching, Federal Republic of Germany

IRANOR   *Instituto nacional de racionalización y normalización*, Spain

IRC   International Revenue Code, United States

IRCT   *Institut de recherches du coton et des textiles exotiques* (Institute of Cotton and Exotic Textile Research), Upper Volta

IRES   *Institut de recherches économiques et sociales* (Institute for Economic and Social Research), Zaire

IREX   International Research and Exchanges Board, United States

IRHO   *Institut de recherches pour les huiles de palme et oléagineux* (Research Institute for Oils and Oilseeds), Upper Volta

IRIA   *Institut de recherche d'informatique et automatique*, France

IRRD	International Road Research Documentation (of OECD)
IRRI	International Rice Research Institute (of CGIAR), the Philippines
IRSAC	*Institut des recherches scientifiques en Afrique Centrale* (Institute of Scientific Research), Zaire
IRTAC	International Round Table for the Advancement of Counseling
ISA	International Sociological Association
ISCED	International Standard Classification of Education (UNESCO sponsored)
ISDS	International Serials Data System (UNESCO sponsored)
ISER	Institute of Social and Economic Research, Barbados
ISI	International Statistical Institute
ISIC	International Student Identity Card
ISME	International Society for Music Education
ISMUN	International Student Movement for the United Nations
ISO	International Student Office
ISRRT	International Society of Radiographers and Radiological Technicians
ISSC	International Social Science Council (*see* CISS)
ISSMP	International Society for the Study of Medieval Philosophy (*see* SIEPM)
ISSN	International Standard Serial Number

ISSS	International Society of Soil Science
ISTA	*Institut supérieur des techniques appliquées* (Institute of Applied Sciences and Technology), Zaire
ISTC	International Student Travel Conference
ISTI	*Institut des sciences et techniques de l'information* (Institute for the Science and Techniques of Information), Zaire
ISVS	International Secretariat for Volunteer Service
ITC	International Training Center, the Netherlands
ITI	International Theatre Institute (*see* IIT)
ITO	International Trade Organization (*see* GATT)
ITT	International Telephone and Telegraph Corporation, United States
ITU	International Telecommunications Union
ITV	Instructional Television, El Salvador
IUA	International Union of Architects (*see* UIA)
IUBS	International Union of Biological Sciences (*see* UISB)
IUC	Inter-University Council for Higher Education Overseas, United Kingdom
IUCN	International Association for Conservation of Nature and Natural Resources (*see* UICN)
IUCW	International Union for Child Welfare (*see* UIPE)

IUFOST	International Union of Food Science and Technology
IUFRO	International Union of Forestry Research Organizations
IUGG	International Union of Geodesy and Geophysics
IUGS	International Union of Geological Sciences
IUHPS	International Union of the History and Philosophy of Science
IULA	International Union of Local Authorities (*see* UIV)
IUPAP	International Union of Pure and Applied Physics (*see* UIPPA)
IUPS	International Union of Psychological Sciences
IUR	International Union of Railways (*see* UIC)
IUS	International Union of Students
IUSSP	International Union for the Scientific Study of Population
IUT	*Instituts universitaire de technologie* (University institutes of technology), France
IVAAP	International Veterinary Association for Animal Production (*see* AIVPA)
IVIC	*Instituto venezolano de investigaciones científicas* (Venezuelan Institute for Scientific Research)
IVS	International Voluntary Services
IWC	International Whaling Commission

J

JAIMS	Japan-American Institute of Management Science, United States
JCEE	Joint Council for Economic Education, United States
JCET	Joint Council for Educational Telecommunications, United States
JICE	Japan International Cultural Exchange
JLA	Jordan Library Association
JMB	Joint Matriculation Board, South Africa

K

KAIS	Korea Advanced Institute of Science, Republic of Korea
KFEA	Korean Federation of Educational Associations, Republic of Korea
KIST	Korea Institute of Science and Technology, Republic of Korea
KJSE	Kenya Junior Secondary Education Examination
KKN	*Kuliah Keya Nyata* (a rural volunteer program in Indonesia)
KORSTIC	Korea Scientific and Technological Information Center, Republic of Korea
KPC	Korea Productivity Center, Republic of Korea

L

LAEA	Language Association of Eastern Africa

LASA	Latin American Shipowners Association (*see* ALAMAR)
LASPAU	Latin American Scholarship Program of American Universities, United States
LAWASIA	Law Association for Asia and the Western Pacific, Australia
LEA	Local Education Authority, United Kingdom
LEAA	Law Enforcement Assistance Administration, United States
LEEP	Law Enforcement Education Program, United States
LIBER	*Ligue des bibliothèques européennes de recherche* (League of European Research Libraries)
LIFIM	Finnish Institute of Management, Finland
LIPI	*Limbaga ilmu pengetahuan* (Indonesian Institute of Science)
LLBA	Language and Language Behavior Abstracts, United States
LNSU	Liberian National Students Union
LO	*Landsorganisationen i Sverige* (Confederation of Swedish Trade Unions), Sweden

M

MAFF	Ministry of Agriculture, Fisheries, and Food, United Kingdom
MARC	Machine Readable Cataloging (for libraries)
MASUA	Mid-American State Universities Association, United States

MATA   Museums Association of Tropical Africa (*see* AMAT)

MAWEV   *Verband der Maschinen-und Werkzeughändler,* Austria

MBO   Management by Objectives

MCEI   Marketing Communications Executives International

MDTA   Manpower Development and Training Act, United States

MEDLARS   Medical Literature Analysis and Retrieval System, United States

MHS   Military Historical Society, United Kingdom

MIPI   *Madjelas ilmu pengetahuan indonesia* (the Council Sciences of Indonesia)

mips   Million instructions per second

MIT   Massachusetts Institute of Technology, United States

MLA   Modern Language Association, United States

MNC   Multinational Corporation

MOBRAL   *Movimento brasileiro de alfabetização* (Brazilian litcracy movement)

MOS   Military Occupational Specialty, United States

MOSST   Ministry of State for Science and Technology, Canada

MPG   *Max-Planck-Gesellschaft zur Förderung der Wissenschaften* (Max Planck Society for the Advancement of Science), Federal Republic of Germany

MSAR	Model of Simulation and Allocation of Resources (cost and resource model)
MSSRC	Mediterranean Social Sciences Research Council (*see* CMRSS)
MTAC	Management Training and Advisory Center, Kenya
MUASA	Makarere University Academic Staff Association, Uganda
MUCIA	Midwest Universities Consortium for International Activities, United States

N

NAACP	National Association for the Advancement of Colored People, United States
NABA	North American Ballet Association, United States
NABM	National Association of Building Manufacturers, United States
NACAC	National Association of College Admissions Counselors, United States
NACCU	National Association of Canadian Credit Unions
NACILA	National Council of Indian Library Associations
NACS	National Association of College Stores, United States
NACUA	National Association of College and University Attorneys, United States
NACUBO	National Association of College and University Business Officers, United States
NAEB	National Association of Educational Broadcasters, United States

NAFCU	National Association of Federal Credit Unions, United States
NAFSA	National Association for Foreign Student Affairs, United States
NAG	Nursery Action Groups (for promotion of nursery facilities in Europe, the United States, Australia)
NAHAL	*No'ah halutzi lochem* (Pioneering Fighting Youth), Israel
NAL	National Agricultural Library, United States
NAME	National Association of Media Educators, United States
NAMRU	(United States) Naval Medical Research Unit in Egypt
NAPCAE	National Association for Public Continuing and Adult Education, United States
NARS	National Archives and Records Service, United States
NAS	National Association of Schoolmasters, United Kingdom
NASA	National Aeronautics and Space Administration, United States
NASULGC	National Association of State Universities and Land-Grant Colleges, United States
NATFHE	National Association of Teachers in Further and Higher Education, United Kingdom
NATIST	National Translation Institute of Science and Technology, Japan
NATO	North Atlantic Treaty Organisation

NAVA	National Audio-Visual Association, United States
NAWDAC	National Association for Women Deans, Administrators, and Counselors, United States
NCAA	National Collegiate Athletic Association, United States
NCAVAE	National Committee for Audio-Visual Aids in Education, United Kingdom
NCCE	National Commission for Cooperative Education, United States
NCEA	National Catholic Educational Association, United States
NCEE	National College Entrance Examination, the Philippines
NCGE	National Certificate of General Education, Sri Lanka
NCHE	National Council of Higher Education, Sri Lanka
NCHEMS	National Center for Higher Education Management Systems, United States
NCICU	National Council of Independent Colleges and Universities, United States
NCPEA	National Conference of Professors of Educational Administration, United States
NCR	National Council for Research, the Sudan
NCST	National Committee on Science and Technology, India
NCTA	National Council for Technological Awards (replaced by CNAA), United Kingdom

NCURA	National Council of University Research Administrators, United States
NCUSI	National Council of University Students of India
NDEA	National Defense Education Act, United States
NDMF	National Development and Management Foundation of South Africa
NDS	National Direct Student Loans, United States
NEA	National Education Association, United States
NEA	Nuclear Energy Agency (of OECD)
NEARC	Northeast Asia Regional Council (of AAS)
NEC	National Education Committee, Nepal
NEC	National Education Commission, Thailand
NELINET	New England Library Network, United States
NEPA	National Environmental Policy Act (of 1969), United States
NES	National Education Society of Sri Lanka, Sri Lanka
NFER	National Foundation for Educational Research in England and Wales
NFS	National Federation of Students, Ecuador
NGOs	National Non-governmental Organizations
NHK	*Nippon hoso kyokai* (Japan Broadcasting Corporation)

NHSC	National Home Study Council, United States
NIC	National Interfraternity Conference, United States
NIDA	National Institute for Development Administration, Thailand
NIE	National Institute of Education, Japan
NIH	National Institutes of Health, United States
NIKKYOSO	*Nippon kyoshokuin kumiai* (Japan Teachers Union)
NIL	*Norske interiørrarkitekters landsforening*, Norway
NIOSH	National Institute of Occupational Safety and Health, United States
NISS	National Institute of Social Sciences, United States
NIST	National Institute of Science and Technology, the Philippines
NITCC	National Industrial Training Council and Committee, Kenya
NIVE	*Nederlandse instituut voor efficiency*, the Netherlands
NIVTC	National Industrial and Vocational Training Centers, Kenya
NKI	*Norske Korrespondensinstitutt-Skolen* (Norwegian Correspondence Institute), Norway
NLRA	National Labor Relations Act, United States
NLRB	National Labor Relations Board, United States
NNCAE	Nigerian National Council for Adult Education

NNE	Northern Nurses Federation, Sweden
NNEB	Nursery Nurses Examination Board, United Kingdom
NNFS	Nepal National Federation of Students
NNRO	*Norske rasjonalkomite for rasjonell organisasjon*, Norway
NORAD	Norwegian Agency for International Development
NOW	National Organization for Women, United States
NPA	National Personnel Authority, Japan
NPA	National Planning Association, United States
NPC	National Panhellenic Conference, United States
NRC	National Research Council of Canada
NRC	Nuclear Regulatory Commission (formerly Atomic Energy Commission), United States
NROTC	Naval Reserve Officer Training Corps, United States
NRTA	National Retired Teachers Association, United States
NSB	National Science Board, the Philippines
NSB	National Science Board, United States
NSDB	National Science Development Board, the Philippines
NSF	National Science Foundation, United States
NSSFNS	National Scholarship Service and Fund for Negro Students, United States

NSU	*Norsk Studentunion* (Norwegian Student Union), Norway
NUEA	National University Extension Association, United States
NUES	National Union of Ethiopian University Students
NUFFIC	Netherlands Universities Foundation for International Co-operation
NUIS	National Union of Iraqi Students
NUMAB	*Nederlandsche unie van metaalgieterijen en aanverwante bedrijven*, the Netherlands
NUNS	National Union of Nigerian Students
NUS	National Union of Students, Papua-New Guinea
NUS	National Union of Students, United Kingdom
NUSAS	National Union of South African Students
NUT	Nigeria Union of Teachers
NUZS	National Union of Zambian Students
NVBF	*Nordiska vetenskapliga bibliotekarieförbundet* (Scandinavian Association of Research Librarians)
NVGA	National Vocational Guidance Association, United States
NYU	New York University, United States
NZIM	New Zealand Institute of Management
NZLA	New Zealand Library Association
NZTCA	New Zealand Teachers Colleges Association

| **NZUSA** | New Zealand University Students' Association |

O

OAS	Organization of American States
OAU	Organisation of African Unity
OCAM	*Organisation commune africaine, Malgache et mauricienne* (Common Afro-Malagasy and Mauritian Organisation)
OCLC	Ohio College Library Center
OCR	Office of Civil Rights (of United States Department of Health, Education and Welfare)
ODC	Overseas Development Council, United States
ODECA	*Organización de estados centroamericanos* (Organization of Central American States)
ODUCAL	*Organización de universidades católicas de América Latina* (Organization of Catholic Universities in Latin America)
OECD	Organisation for Economic Co-operation and Development
OEI	*Oficina de educación iberoamericana* (Ibero-American Bureau of Education), Spain
OFI	*Orientation à la fonction internationale* (International Civil Service Training Organization)
OFICEMA	*Oficina central marítima* (Central Maritime Office), Spain
OFRATEME	*Office français des techniques modernes d'éducation*, France
OH	*Österreichische Hochschülerschaft* (Austrian National Union of Students)

OHE	Office of Higher Education, Papua-New Guinea
OIE	*Office internationale des épizooties* (International Office of Epizootics)
OIPC	*Organisation internationale de protection civile* (*see* ICDO)
OIRT	*Organisation internationale de radiodiffusion et télévision* (International Radio and Television Organization)
OLC	Overseas Liaison Committee (of American Council on Education), United States
OMB	Office of Management and Budget, United States
OMCI	*Organisation inter-gouvernementale consultative de la navigation maritime* (*see* IMCO)
OMEP	*Organisation mondiale pour l'éducation présco- laire* (World Organization for Early Child- hood Education)
ONC	Ordinary National Certificate, United Kingdom
OND	Ordinary National Diploma, United Kingdom
ONISEP	*Office national d'information sur les enseigne- ments et les professions* (National Office for Information on Education and the Profes- sions), France
OPEC	Organization of the Petroleum Exporting Countries
OPS	*Organización Pan-Americana de salud* (*see* PAHO)
OPSU	*Oficina de planificación del sector universitario* (Office for University Planning), Venezuela

ORSTOM	*Office de la recherche scientifique et technique d'outre-mer* (Office of Scientific and Technical Research Overseas), France
OSHA	Occupational Safety and Health Administration, United States
OTC	Officer Training Corps, United Kingdom
OTR	Occupation Therapists Registered

P

PAA	*Preueba de aptitud academica* (Academic Aptitude Test), Chile
PAASCU	Philippine Accrediting Association of Schools, Colleges and Universities, the Philippines
PACU	Philippine Association of Colleges and Universities
PADT	*Programas andinos de desarrollo tecnológico* (Andean Programs for Technological Development)
PAEC	Philippine Atomic Energy Commission
PAHO	Pan American Health Organization (*see* OPS)
PAIGC	*Partido africano da indepencência de Guiné e Cabo Verde* (African Party for the Independence of Guinea and Cape Verde), Guinea-Bissau
PAIGH	Pan-American Institute of Geography and History, Mexico
PAR	Policy Analysis Review, United States
PBEC	Pacific Basin Economic Council
PCS	Parents' Confidential Statement (for financial aid), United States

PERB	Public Employment Relations Board, United States
PERMANIN	Indonesian Management Association
PGC	Planning and Grants Committee, Israel
PGRI	*Persatuan guru Republik Indonesia* (Teachers Union of the Republic of Indonesia)
PHILCOMAN	Philippine Council of Management
PIANC	Permanent International Association of Navigation Congresses (*see* AIPCN)
PIARC	Permanent International Association of Road Councils (*see* AIPCR)
PIRG	Public Interest Research Groups, Australian, Canadian, and United States campuses
PL	Public Law, United States
PLANDES	*Sociedad chilena de planificación y desarrollo,* Chile
POC	Professional Officer Corps (of the Air Force), United States
POLI	*Instituto politecnico de Nicaragua* (Polytechnic Institute of Nicaragua)
POSDCORB	Library Management functions (Planning, Organizing, Staffing, Directing, Coordinating, Reporting, and Budgeting)
PPB	Planned Program Budgeting, United States
PPBS	Program, Planning and Budgeting System, United States
PRC	People's Republic of China
PREDE	*Programa regional de desarrollo educativo* (Re-

gional Educational Development Program) (of OAS)

PSA   Political Studies Association of the United Kingdom

PSAC   President's Science Advisory Committee, United States

PSAT-NMSQT   Preliminary Scholastic Aptitude Test-National Merit Scholarship Qualifying Test, United States

PSI   Personal System of Instruction, United States

Q

QPA   Quality point average, United States

R

RAEC   Royal Army Educational Corps, United Kingdom

RAI-TV   *Radiotelevisione Italiana* (Italian broadcasting company)

RCRF   *Rei Cretariae Romanae Fautores* (Association of Roman Ceramic Archeologists)

RFB   Recording for the Blind, United States

RFP   Requests for Proposals (by government agencies), United States

RFQ   Requests for Quotations (by government agencies), United States

RIE   Resources in Education, United States

RIHED   Regional Institute of Higher Education and Development, Singapore

RIPA   Royal Institute of Public Administration, United Kingdom

RKW	*Rationalisierungs-Kuratorium der deutschen Wirtschaft*, Federal Republic of Germany
RLG	Research Libraries Group, United States
ROTC	Reserve Officers Training Corps, United States
RRPM	Resource Requirements Prediction Model, United States

S

SACC	Scientific Advisory Committee to the Cabinet, India
SACO/SR	*Sveriges akademikers centralorganisation/Statstjänstemännens riksförbund* (Central Organization of Swedish Professional Workers), Sweden
SAD	*Société des artistes décorateurs*, France
SAE	Society of Automotive Engineers, United States
SAF	*Svenska arbetsgivareföreningen* (Swedish Employers' Confederation), Sweden
SAHR	Society for Army Historical Research, United Kingdom
SAINT	Symbolic Automatic Integrator, United States
SALAIM	Seminar on the Acquisition of Latin American Materials, United States
SASO	South African Students Organization
SAT	Scholastic Aptitude Test, United States
SATA	Student Air Travel Association, Denmark
SCAAP	Special Commonwealth African Assistance Plan

SCANUS	Student Community Action-National Union of Students, United Kingdom
SCAULEA	Standing Conference of African University Librarians Eastern Area
SCAULWA	Standing Conference of African University Librarians Western Area
SCIBP	Special Committee for the International Biological Programme
SCITEC	Association of Scientists, Technologists, and Engineers of Canada
SCONUL	Standing Conference of National and University Libraries, United Kingdom
SDC/ERIC	Systems Development Corporation/Educational Resources Information Center, United States
SDS	Students for a Democratic Society, United States
SEARC	Southeast Asian Regional Council (of AAS)
SEATO	South-East Asia Treaty Organization
SECUSSA	Section on United States Students Abroad (of NAFSA), United States
SEAMEO	Southeast Asian Ministers of Education Organization
SFAE	Swiss Federation for Adult Education
SFI	*Société financière internationale* (*see* IFC)
SFS	*Sveriges förenade studentkårer* (Swedish National Union of Students), Sweden
SGEN	*Syndicat général de l'éducation nationale*, France
SHI	*Studentara Háskóla Íslands* (National Union of Icelandic Students)

SIAD   Society of Industrial Arts Designers, United Kingdom

SIBMAS   *Société internationale des bibliothèques et musées des arts du spectacle* (International Society of Libraries and Museums of Performing Arts)

SID   Society for International Development, United States

SIDA   Swedish International Development Authority

SIEPM   *Société internationale pour l'étude de la philosophie médiévale* (*see* ISSPM)

SIM   Singapore Institute of Management

SIO   *Sisustusarkkitehdit-Inredningsarkitekter,* Finland

SIP   *Sociedad interamericana de psicologia*, Colombia

SIR   *Svenska inredningsarkitekters riksförbund,* Sweden

SITES   *Sociedad interamericana de psicologia,* Colombia

SNAF   *Société nationale d'horticulture de France*

SNDT   Shreemati Nathibai Damodar Thackersey Women's University, India

SNESup   *Syndicat national de l'enseignement supérieur* National Union of Higher Education), France

SNP   *Servicio nacional de pruebas* (National Testing Service), Colombia

SOC   Servicemen's Opportunity Colleges, United States

SOFA   Students Overseas Flights for Americans/ European Student Travel Center

SOLINET	Southeastern Library Network, United States
SPEPADUC	*Sindicato profesional de empleados, profesores y administradores de la Universidad católica* (Professional Association of Employers, Professors and Administrators of the Catholic University), Chile
SPPB	*Statens psykologisk-pedagogiska bibliotek* (National Library for Psychology and Education), Sweden
SRC	Students Representative Council, Malta
SRCC	Scandinavian Research Council of Criminology
SREB	Southern Regional Education Board, United States
SRHE	Society for Research into Higher Education, United Kingdom
SSC	Secondary School Certificate, Bangladesh
SSM	*Socialisticky svaz mládeže CSSR* (Socialist Union of Youth of Czechoslovakia)
SSRCC	Social Science Research Council of Canada (*Conseil canadien de recherche en sciences sociales*)
SSTS	Scandinavian Student Travel Service
SSU	Swaziland Students' Union
SUL	Small University Libraries, Canada
SUNU	Student Union of Nairobi University
SVTRA	*Schweizerische Vereinigung technischer Röntgenassistentinnen und Röntgenassistenten,* Switzerland

SYL	*Suomen ylioppilaskuntien liitto/Finlands studentkårers förbund* (National Union of Finnish Students)
STEIA	*Comité français de science, technologie, et économie des industries alimentaires* (French Committee of Science, Technology, and Food Industries), France

T

TAC	Technical Advisory Committee (of CGIAR)
TAFE	Technical and Further Education, Australia
TAGER	Texas Association for Graduate Education and Research, United States
TANCA	Technical Assistance to Non-Commonwealth Countries in Africa, United Kingdom
TBV	*Tjänstemännens bildningsförening* (Salaried Employees Education Association), Sweden
TCO	*Tjänstemännens centralorganisation* (Central Organization of Salaried Employees), Sweden
TEC	Technician Education Council, United Kingdom
TEC	Tertiary Education Commission, Australia
TEDRO	Test Development and Research Office
TESOL	International Association of the Teachers of English to Speakers of Other Languages
TCCIT	A comprehensive research program in computer-assisted instruction at the MITRE Corporation, United States

TIS	Technical Information Service (of National Council for Science and Technology), Mexico
TMA	Turkish Management Association
TNO	*Organisatie voor toegepast natuurwetenschappelijk onderzoek* (Organization for Applied Scientific Research), the Netherlands
TOEFL	Test of English as a Foreign Language, United States
TTINTEC	*Instituto de investigación tecnológica, industrial y de normas técnicas* (Institute of Industrial Technological Research and Standards), Peru
TUC	Trades Union Congress, Great Britain
TURK	*Türk üniversite rektörleri konferansi* (Conference of Rectors of Turkish Universities)
TUSS	Total University Simulation Systems, the Netherlands

U

UAI	*Union académique internationale* (International Union of Academies)
UAP	Universities Authorities Panel (of the CVC), United Kingdom
UAS	University Air Squadrons, United Kingdom
UASCR	*Uniunea asociatiilor studentilor comunisti din Romania* (Union of Communist Students' Associations of Romania)
UATI	*Union des associations techniques internationales* (*see* UIEO)
UBLS	University of Botswana, Lesotho and Swa-

ziland (now University of Botswana and Swaziland)

UCA	*Universidad centroamericana* (Central American University), Nicaragua
UCC	Universal Copyright Convention
UCCA	Universities Central Council on Admissions, United Kingdom
UCEA	University Council for Educational Administration, United States
UCHS	University Center for Health Services (of Federal University of Cameroon)
UCNS	Universities' Committee for Non-Teaching Staffs, United Kingdom
UCPTE	*Union pour la coordination de la production et du transport de l'électricité* (Union for Coordinating Production and Distribution of Electricity)
UDUAL	*Unión de universidades de América Latina* (Union of Universities of Latin America)
UEC	*Union européenne des experts comptables économiques et financiers* (European Union of Public Accountants)
UER	*Unités d'enseignement et de recherche* (Units of teaching and research), France
UFRC	Universities Finance Review Committee, Papua New Guinea
UFTAA	Universal Federation of Travel Agents' Associations
UGC	University Grants Committee or Commission (Various Commonwealth Countries)

UGE	*Union des grandes écoles,* France
UGEC	*Union générale des élèves congolais* (General Association of Congolese Students), The Congo
UGET	*Union générale des étudiants de Tunisie*, Tunisia
UHA	*Universitets- och Högskoleämbetet* (National Board of Universities and Colleges), Sweden
UIA	*Union internationale des architects* (*see* IUA)
UIA	*Union internationales des avocats* (International Association of Lawyers)
UIC	*Union internationale des chemins de fer* (*see* IUR)
UICB	*Union internationale des centres du bâtiment* (International Union of Building Centres)
UICN	*Union internationale pour la conservation de la nature et des ses ressources* (*see* IUCN)
UIEO	Union of International Engineering Associations (*see* UATI)
UIFA	*Union internationale des femmes architectes* (International Union of Women Architects)
UIMA	University Insurance Managers Association, United States
UIO	*Union internationale des orientalistes* (International Union of Orientalists)
UIOP	*Unione italiana per l'orientamento professionale*, Italy
UIPE	*Union internationale de protection de l'enfance* (*see* IUCW)
UIPPA	*Union internationale de physique pure et appliquée* (*see* IUPAP)

UISB	*Union internationale des sciences biologiques* (*see* IUBS)
UITP	*Union internationale des transports publics* (International Union of Public Transport)
UIV	*Union internationale de villes et pouvoirs locaux* (*see* IULA)
UJC	*Union des jovenes communistas* (Union of Young Communists), Cuba
UJSC	*Union de la jeunesse socialiste congolaise* (Union of Congolese Socialist Youth), The Congo
UMA	University of Mid-America
UMSU	University of Malawi Students' Union
UN	United Nations
UNAM	*Universidad nacional autónoma de México* (National Autonomous University of Mexico)
UNAN	*Universidad nacional autónoma de Nicaragua* (National Autonomous University of Nicaragua)
UNCTAD	United Nations Conference on Trade and Development
UNDP	United Nations Development Programme
UNED	*Universidad de educación a distancia* (National University of Distance Education), Spain
UNEF	*Union nationale des étudiants de France*
UNEP	United Nations Environment Programme, Kenya
UNESCO	United Nations Educational, Scientific and Cultural Organization
UNFPA	United Nations Fund for Population Activities, United States

UNICA	Association of Universities and Research Institutes from the Caribbean
UNICARE	University Child Club Center, Australia
UNICEF	United Nations International Children's Emergency Fund
UNIDO	United Nations Industrial Development Organization
UNIDRAT	International Institute for the Unification of Private Law, Italy
UNIPEDE	*Union internationale des producteurs et distributeurs d'énergie électrique* (International Union of Producers and Distributors of Electrical Energy)
UNITAR	United Nations Institute for Training and Research
UNRISD	United Nations Research Institute for Social Development
UNRWA	United Nations Relief and Work Agency for Palestine Refugees
UNSDRI	United National Social Defence Research Institute
UPADI	*Union panamericana de asociaciones de ingenieros* (Pan American Federation of Engineering Societies)
UPGC	University and Polytechnic Grants Committee, Hong Kong
UROEA	UNESCO Regional Office for Education in Asia
USAFI	United States Armed Forces Institute
USAID	United States Agency for International Development (*see* AID)

USC	United States Code
U68	Swedish Education Commission established in 1968
USI	Union of Students in Ireland
USMCR	United States Marine Corps Reserve
USNSA	United States National Student Association
USOE	United States Office of Education
USPSIS	United States Political Science Information System
USUAA	University Students' Association of Addis Ababa, Ethiopia
UTASA	University Teachers' Association of South Africa
UWI	University of the West Indies
UWW	University Without Walls, United States
UYA	University Year for Action, United States

V

VA	Veterans Administration (a United States federal bureau)
VAD	*Vereinigung der Afrikanisten in Deutschland*, Federal Republic of Germany
VAK	*Vyshaya attestationaya komissia* (Supreme Attestation Commission), Union of Soviet Socialist Republics
VCOAD	Voluntary Committee on Overseas Aid and Development, United Kingdom
VDZI	*Verband deutscher Zahntechniker Innungen*, Federal Republic of Germany

VISTA	Volunteers in the Service of America, United States
VESKA	*Verband schweizerischer Krankenanstalten* (Association of Swiss Hospitals), Switzerland
VNUS	Vietnam National Union of Students, Vietnam
VSI	*Vereinigung schweizer Innenarchitekten* (Association of Swiss Interior Architects)
VSO	Voluntary Service Overseas, United Kingdom
VTUZ	Factory higher technical education institution, Union of Soviet Socialist Republics
VUZ	*Vysshee uchebhoe zavedenie* (Higher Educational Institute), Union of Soviet Socialist Republics
VVS	*Vereniging der vlaamse studenten* (Association of Flemish Students), Belgium

W

WAAS	World Academy of Art and Science
WAAVP	World Association for the Advancement of Veterinary Parasitology
WAB	World Association Buiatrics
WAC	Women's Army Corps, United States
WACTE	West African Council for Teacher Education
WAEC	West African Examinations Council
WAF	Women's Air Force, United States
WALS	West African Linguistic Society

WAPOR	World Association for Public Opinion Research
WARDA	West African Rice Development Association, Nigeria
WATBOL	Computer language used in problem solving
WATFIV	Computer language used in problem solving
WAVA	World Association of Veterinary Anatomists
WAVFH	World Association of Veterinary Food Hygienists
WAVMI	World Association of Veterinary Microbiologists, Immunologists, and Specialists in Infectious Diseases (*see* AMVMI)
WAVP	World Association of Veterinary Pathologists
WAVPPB	World Association of Veterinary Physiologists, Pharmacologists and Biochemists
WAY	World Assembly of Youth
WCC	World Council of Churches (*see* COE)
WCC	World Crafts Council
WCOTP	World Confederation of Organizations of the Teaching Profession (*see* CMOPE)
WCPT	World Confederation for Physical Therapy
WEA	Women's Equity Action League, United
WEA	Workers Educational Association (*Arbetarnas bildningsförbund*), Sweden
WEAL	Women's Equity Action League, United States

WFEO	World Federation of Engineering Organizations (*see* FMOI)
WFOT	World Federation of Occupational Therapists
WHO	World Health Organization
WICHE	Western Interstate Commission for Higher Education
WIGUT	West Indies Group of University Teachers
WMO	World Meteorological Association
WPSA	World Poultry Science Association (*see* AVI)
WR	*Wissenschaftsrat* (Science Council), Federal Republic of Germany
WRK	*Westdeutsche Rektorenkonferenz* (West German Rectors Conference), Federal Republic of Germany
WSAVA	World Small Animal Veterinary Association
WSCF	World Student Christian Federation (*see* FUACE)
WSDB	World Studies Data Bank, United States
WUJS	World Union of Jewish Students
WUS	World University Service
WVA	World Veterinary Association (*see* AMV)
WVPA	World Veterinary Poultry Association

Y

YMCA	Young Men's Christian Association
YWCA	Young Women's Christian Association

Z

ZANUT   Zambia National Union of Teachers

ZAV   *Zentralstelle für Arbeitsvermittlung* (Central Placement Office of Ministry of Labor and Social Affairs), Federal Republic of Germany

ZVS   *Zentralstelle für die Vergabe von Studienplätzen* (Central Admissions Office), Federal Republic of Germany

Glossary

This glossary of postsecondary education terminology presents a selected alphabetical listing of educational terms that relate to or are specifically ancillary to postsecondary education. Included are terms that appear in the topical essays and national systems articles. Also included are terms in ordinary usage in higher education throughout the world and those that are essential to understanding various systems of postsecondary education and educational concepts.

The glossary includes both English and non-English terms. For non-English terms, the language of origin (1) is indicated at the beginning of the definition (used primarily when the definition consists of a brief translation), (2) is apparent from the context of the definition itself, or (3) can be determined by the country name or language system in parentheses at the end of the definition (for example, Federal Republic of Germany, French-language systems).

Specification of the country name or language system at the end of the definition also indicates the term is used primarily—but not necessarily exclusively—in that country or language system.

Italicization has been used for all foreign expressions within definitions and as a cross-referencing system to key words defined elsewhere in the glossary.

Of necessity, the definitions are brief. Readers who wish more information should consult one or more of the following sources:

American Association of Collegiate Registrars and Admissions Officers. *A Glossary of Terms Used by Registrars and Admissions Officers.* Washington, D.C., 1956.

American Association of Collegiate Registrars and Admissions Officers. *Handbook of Data and Definitions in Higher Education.* Washington, D.C., 1962.

Bartholomew, C. A. *Epithetology*. Red Bank, New Jersey: Commercial Press, 1948.

Blishen, E. (Ed.) *Encyclopedia of Education*. New York: Philosophical Library, 1970.

Council for Cultural Co-operation of the Council of Europe. *Structure of University Staff*. Strasbourg, 1966.

Garciá Laguardia, J. M., *Legislacíon Universitaria de América Latina*. Mexico City: Universidad Nacional Autónoma de Mexico, 1973.

Good, C. V. (Ed.) *Dictionary of Education*. New York: McGraw-Hill, 1973.

Grandpré, M. *Glossaire International*. Paris: UNESCO, 1969.

International Federation of University Women. *International Glossary of Academic Terms*. Paris, 1939.

Knowles, A. S. (Ed.) *Handbook of College and University Administration*. New York: McGraw-Hill, 1970.

Means, H. W., and Semas, P. W. (Eds.) *Faculty Collective Bargaining*. 2nd ed. Washington, D.C.: Chronicle of Higher Education, 1976.

Onushkin, V. G. (Ed.) *Planning the Development of Universities II*. Paris: UNESCO; International Institute for Educational Planning, 1973.

Renetzky, A. (Ed.) *Yearbook of Higher Education*. Los Angeles: Academic Media, 1969.

United States Department of Health, Education and Welfare. Education Division. National Center for Educational Statistics. *Combined Glossary*. Washington, D.C., 1974.

United States Department of Health, Education and Welfare. Office of Education. *Definitions of Student Personnel Terms in Higher Education*. Washington, D.C., 1968.

UNESCO. *The UNESCO/IBE Education Thesaurus*. Paris. 1975.

UNESCO. *International Standard Classification of Education (ISCED)*. Paris, 1976.

UNESCO. *World Guide to Higher Education*. Paris, 1976.

A

A-level.

Advanced level of the *General Certificate of Education* examination, taken by students in form VI at age eighteen (United Kingdom). See also *General Certificate of Education, O-level*.

Ability.

(1) The quality or state of being able; (2) natural talent or acquired proficiency in a particular work or activity. See also *aptitude, academic aptitude, artistic aptitude, mechanical aptitude*.

Ability grouping. Grouping of students within programs of study based on ability measured by special *examinations* and *tests*. See also *aptitude test*.

Ability testing. See *aptitude test*.

Abitur. Examination at the end of secondary schooling (German-language systems). See also *Matura, Reifeprüfung, Reifezeugnis*.

Absence. The failure of a student to be present for the entire period of a scheduled class. See also *absence regulations, excessive absences, excused absence, unexcused absence*.

Absence regulations. Rules governing nonattendance at class; usually promulgated by the faculty.

Academia. (1) Latin: name of the olive grove north of Athens where Plato (in the fourth century B.C.) gathered around him a group of scholars to discuss philosophy; the place came to denote this particular type of school; (2) also used generically to refer to the system or total aspect or atmosphere of higher education in humorous or flowery speech.

Academic. (1) Individual who is a member of, or is associated with, an organized community of intellectuals such as a higher education institution; may be an independent scholar, student, fellow, or temporary or permanent member of the teaching staff of an institution; (2) term used to describe programs of study and courses, usually referring to the theoretical, literary, classical, or liberal.

Academic ability. A combination of abilities with emphasis on verbal or linguistic accomplishment and numerical or mathematical facility. See also *academic aptitude*.

Academic acceleration. A procedure permitting qualified students to progress faster than average students in a specified program. In contrast to *academic* *enrichment,* this procedure permits the student to finish a course of study and begin the next higher one in advance of his or her chronological peers. Also called *scholastic acceleration.*

Academic achievement.   Knowledge attained or skills developed in school subjects, usually designated by test scores or by marks assigned by the teacher, or both. See also *grade.*

Academic administration.   Supervision and control of instructional activities and academic personnel in a higher education institution.

Academic aptitude.   The *ability* of a person to deal in abstractions and to engage successfully in advanced learning.

Academic calendar.   See *academic year, calendar.*

Academic community.   (1) The totality of personnel and students at all higher education institutions in a country, as well as at other institutions where academics are active in traditional academic pursuits (teaching and/or research); (2) all members of one specific university including students, teachers and researchers, administrators, academic staff, and nonacademic personnel.

Academic degree.   See *degree.*

Academic discipline.   (1) Faculty action taken to indicate that a student's academic achievement is unsatisfactory; see also *disciplinary action;* (2) a broad field of study.

Academic dismissal.   Involuntary separation of a student from his or her institution by administrative or faculty action because the student has not met academic requirements.

Academic dress.   Garments and articles that are used to indicate an office in a university, a degree, or some other qualification awarded by a university or similar institution or body.

Academic education. Study oriented toward the acquisition of theoretical, literary, classical, or liberal knowledge and pure research, as opposed to professional knowledge and applied research. Also called academic study, academic program.

Academic enrichment. Modification of a curriculum by introducing additional material of special interest, for the purpose of adding depth of knowledge to a particular segment of that curriculum, either for an entire student body or for those students who are capable of progressing more quickly than the general student population.

Academic failure. Inability to maintain a predetermined minimum level of accomplishment as designated by a *grade* or by *examination;* thus, failure to progress to the next stage of learning.

Academic freedom. The right of the teacher and student to be free from external or institutional coercion, censorship, or other forms of restrictive interference in teaching and research. See also *Lehrfreiheit, Lernfreiheit, libertad de cátedra.*

Academic goal. Objective sought by a student based on a planned program of study.

Academic governance. The control of policies and regulations pertaining to all aspects of academic affairs of an institution.

Academic insignia. Any article, such as a coat of arms, badge, mace, staff, or seal used to indicate an office in a university or a degree or other qualification awarded by a university or similar institution or body. See also *academic dress.*

Academic performance. The demonstrated achievement of learning as opposed to the potential for learning;

documented by *grade* or *examination*. See also *performance test, test.*

Academic personnel. Members of a university or college concerned with the teaching and research functions of the university, including administrators whose responsibilities center on the academic functions of the university. (Administrators and staff concerned with the business operations of the university usually are not accorded academic rank and title.) See also *nonacademic personnel.*

Academic probation. (1) The opportunity for students to "prove" themselves by being allowed to perform under supervision at a level higher than that indicated by *grade* or *examination;* (2) the act of suspending disciplinary action, such as expulsion, pending a student's improvement of his or her grades. Also called scholastic probation.

Academic program. See *academic education.*

Academic progress check. Tabulation and analysis of *credit hours* earned toward degree requirements.

Academic rank. The title of an individual member of a teaching or research staff; each title defines its major responsibilities. The academic ranks most commonly used in colleges and universities are *professor, associate professor, assistant professor, senior lecturer, lecturer, instructor, assistant, and tutor.* Also called faculty rank.

Academic record. A record of courses completed and grades achieved by a student. See also *transcript.*

Academic research. All university-based research, whether applied or basic, undertaken by members of a higher education institution.

Academic standards. Specific levels of *academic achievement* selected as (a) *goals* or (b) *norms* for *academic performance.*

Academic standing. The status of a student based on his or her scholastic performance. See also *good standing.*

Academic standing committee. A committee that establishes policies and makes decisions on questions relating to the academic status of students (United States).

Academic study. See *academic education.*

Academic tenure. An arrangement under which faculty appointments in a higher education institution are continued until *retirement* for age or physical disability, subject to *dismissal* only for adequate cause or unavoidable termination on account of financial exigency or change of institutional program.

Academic travel abroad. Travel outside one's home country by students, faculty, or staff of institutions of higher education, undertaken primarily in pursuit of activities of an educational or research nature rather than a commercial or recreational nature.

Academic warning. A notice given to a student to advise him or her that demonstrated performance is not satisfactory and, unless improved, may result in *academic dismissal* or *probation.*

Academic year. In most countries, a period usually of eight to ten months when university or college is in session; in the United States, for example, the academic year generally extends from September through May, divided into two semesters or three quarters, although year-round calendars also exist, usually in the form of four quarters. See also *calendar, four-one-four, intersession, quarter, semester, term, trimester.*

Académie.   *Academy;* an administrative unit consisting of elementary, secondary, and higher education departments organized into one administrative unit, headed by a rector (France).

Academy.   (1) Institution of higher education, such as the United States Military Academy; (2) in Europe, generally a higher institution of fine or dramatic arts or music; (3) body of scholars, such as the National Academy of Sciences; (4) secondary-level school, such as the Concord Academy.

Accelerated college entrance.   The admission of capable students prior to completion of secondary school; programs vary with colleges, but some enroll *freshmen* after only three of the usual four years of secondary school (United States).

Acceptance.   Notification to the applicant of approval for admission. See also *admission.*

Acceptance fee.   A fee required when notice of admission is received; usually not refundable but generally applicable to tuition or other fees (United States). See also *application fee.*

Accepted student.   A student who has met *admission requirements* and has been invited to enroll in a higher education institution. Also called admitted student.

Access to education.   (1) A distribution process: the determination of who or how many are to attend higher education institutions; depends on whether system is elite or offers mass access; (2) the ease or difficulty of gaining access to higher education institutions often determined by selection processes at the lower levels of education.

Accountability.   (1) Traditionally, fiscal responsibility; (2) currently, higher education's answerability to public authority and society for its objectives and performance (in relation to monies spent). Thus, in education, teachers and school systems may be required to prove actual improvement in performance by means of teacher effectiveness tested by an outside agency. See also *performance contract.*

Accredit.

(1) To admit an institution to membership in an association requiring specific standards for admission, with membership constituting *accreditation*; (2) to grant approval of the quality of a program by a national, regional, or professional agency responsible for setting academic standards as well as for measuring how well individual institutions meet these standards.

Accreditation.

Assessment and regulation of *academic standards* of educational institutions or programs, either by a government agency with the advice of representatives from these institutions (as in most European systems), by professional bodies, or directly by boards or associations composed of representatives from these institutions (United States).

Accreditation criteria.

The established qualitative and quantitative standards by which an agency or association evaluates an educational institution to determine whether it merits *accreditation* (United States).

Accredited institution.

An institution that meets the standards established by an accrediting agency and is thereby authorized to announce its accreditation or approval.

Accrediting association.

An organization that exists solely to establish criteria for judging the quality of programs and services offered by educational institutions; to determine the extent to which institutions meet these criteria; and to issue a list of the institutions, courses, or programs found to be of acceptable quality. Member institutions voluntarily meet the criteria of membership as defined by the organization. An institution's *accreditation* status determines in large measure the acceptability of its *credits* (or courses completed) by other institutions as partial fulfillment of degree requirements (United States).

Acharyas.
The ablest teachers; title used in ancient Hindu education.

Achievement.
(1) Accomplishment or proficiency in a skill or body of knowledge; (2) progress in a program of study.

Achievement motivation.
Desire or ambition of individuals to accomplish or achieve, such as to improve the quality of, or to excel in, the performance of academic or practical work.

Achievement test.
Test designed to measure a person's knowledge, skill, and understanding of a body of knowledge or program of study. Contrast *aptitude test.*

Active student.
A student who is currently enrolled in a higher education institution.

Activism.
Any theory or procedure that emphasizes physical activity rather than intellectual debate; exemplified by the student activism movement of the 1960s to bring about student participation in educational, academic, and administrative affairs and in social change.

Ad hoc teachers.
Part-time teachers employed, as needed, in *independent study programs.*

Additive credit.
Academic credit, awarded by an institution to students for work experience under *cooperative education*, which is added to those credits normally required for graduation

but which does not take the place of such credits. Contrast *nonadditive credit*. See also *credit granted for off-campus experience* (United States).

Adjunct professor. A professor appointed for a specific purpose on a part-time basis. A doctorate and active professional or research activity are usually required.

Aðjunkt. Faculty rank: part-time lecturer (Iceland).

Adjunktus. Faculty rank: lecturer (Hungary).

Administration. All techniques and procedures used in operating an institution, including organization of duties and responsibilities of officers for efficient management; and establishment of policies, principles, rules, and regulations to be followed in carrying out these duties and responsibilities. See also *academic administration, fiscal administration*.

Administrative officer. A person who directs and supervises activities of a higher education institution. May either be elected or appointed by institutional boards or councils, or appointed by the chief officer of a national government agency. Administrative officers may include: *visitor, chancellor, vice-chancellor, president, rector, vice-president, vice-rector, director, principal, dean, chairman, registrar, bursar*.

Administrative personnel. Those persons responsible for making and executing policy. Administrative personnel may be classed as general, in terms of serving the institution as a whole, or as departmental or divisional, in terms of engaging in the administration of a department, division, or component part of the institution.

Administrative policy. The principles adopted by the governing board or administration of a higher education institution outlining the principles to be followed with respect to the administration of the institution.

Administrator.   See *administrative officer.*

Admission.   Acceptance of an applicant for enrollment in a higher education institution upon proof of satisfaction of specified criteria, such as a secondary school-leaving certificate indicating successful completion of secondary school. According to policy of the individual institution or other responsible authority, admission may be *open* or *restricted/selective*. See also *admission condition, admission examination, admission requirements, numerus clausus, selective admission.*

Admission application fee.   See *application fee.*

Admission by certificate.   The method by which graduates of accredited secondary schools are admitted to many colleges, particularly the public colleges, on the basis of school credentials (United States). In some nations a secondary school-leaving certificate is in reality a certificate of admission for those wishing to enter the university.

Admission by certificate and examination.   College admission granted on the basis of examinations that supplement the secondary school certificate; for those students whose secondary school backgrounds lack some ordinarily required subjects or for those students who are from any unaccredited secondary schools (United States).

Admission certificate.   The secondary school record that signifies that the candidate meets the school's certification and recommendation standard (United States). Also called entrance certificate.

Admission condition.   A temporary withholding of full clearance for admission because of lack of certain required credentials (United States). Also called entrance condition.

Admission deficiency.   Lack of a specific subject requirement that the student must satisfy to gain unconditional admission to an institution or to a particular program. The deficiency may be removed by completing work in a secondary school; by taking courses without credit on campus; by doing extra work in the field of the deficiency; by completing courses through correspondence, extension, or summer school; by examination; or by attaining a specified level of scholarship in some other manner (United States). Also called entrance deficiency.

Admission deposit.   A fee paid in advance by a candidate for admission; shows intention to enroll in an institution. The fee may be refundable, until a certain date, on cancellation of proposed registration.

Admission examination.   An appraisal of ability or education achievement (oral or written) that an applicant to a higher education institution must satisfy at a certain level to be admitted. See also *concours d'entrée, examen de admisión.*

Admission policy.   The criteria established to determine the qualifications to be required of applicants for admittance to an institution.

Admission procedure.   The sequence of review and approval of a candidate's eligibility for entrance to the institution.

Admission quota.   A set number of students to be admitted to a college, university, or program. See also *numerus clausus.*

Admission requirements.   Specifications regarding the educational preparation or such other prerequisites as age, legal residence, or special examinations to be fulfilled by an applicant to a higher education institution. See also *admission examination.*

Admission to advanced standing.

Status granted to incoming student that recognizes college-level work completed in secondary school or at another higher education institution (United States). See also *advanced placement.*

Admission to graduate standing.

Acceptance for graduate study based on undergraduate or other graduate work with satisfactory grade average or achievement. Admission may be by examination. Acceptance permits the undertaking of course work and, although regulations differ among institutions, usually implies acceptance as a degree candidate (United States).

Admission to special standing.

Status granted to those students who do not meet the general minimum *admission requirements* but who have other special qualifications (United States).

Admission with deficiency.

Admission to a college or university of a candidate who has not completed all *admission requirements* (United States).

Admissions attrition.

A reduction in admissions resulting from the failure of those who are granted admission to actually enroll (United States).

Admissions center.

A central agency that provides information about various colleges and their admissions requirements for prospective applicants (United States). Used in a number of countries, such as Sweden and the Federal Republic of Germany, where *numerus clausus* exists in many fields.

Admissions counselor.

One who advises prospective applicants, parents, school counselors, and other interested persons on matters pertaining to admission to a college(s) (United States).

Adult.

A person who has completed his or her formal or informal education and who has assumed responsibility and a productive role in society; certain educational programs are organized around the special needs and interests of adults. See also *adult education.*

Adult education.

Any activity or program deliberately designed by a providing agent to satisfy the learning needs or interests of persons who are over statutory school-leaving age and whose principal activity is no longer in education. Adult education spans nonvocational, vocational, general, formal, and nonformal studies, as well as education with a collective social purpose. Also known as *continuing education, extension education, lifelong learning, permanent education, recurrent education.*

Adult educators.

Educators having special training and experience in teaching adults.

Adult students.

See *adult education.*

Adult vocational education.

Theoretical and practical training in semi-skilled, skilled, or trade occupations to serve the special needs of *adults,* usually given on a part-time basis so that employed adults may attend.

Advanced course.

A course introducing materials and concepts that require previous mastery of the elementary and/or intermediate courses.

Advanced degree.

A degree, such as a *master's* or a *doctorate,* awarded following successful completion of a *program of study* beyond the first degree.

Advanced placement.

The status accorded a student who has undertaken college-level work in a secondary school for which credit is given by a college or university. For example, a student may enter college with sophomore standing (United States). See also *admission to advanced standing, advanced standing credit.*

Advanced Placement (AP).
A national testing program of the College Entrance Examination Board and Education Testing Service whereby high school students about to enter a college or university can be tested on prescribed university-level material and receive college or university-level credit if they receive acceptable scores (United States).

Advanced professional degree.
A second-level degree, such as a *master's* or *doctoral*; may require completion of a first professional degree.

Advanced professional school.
A semiautonomous school, usually at the graduate level, requiring previous undergraduate work and providing programs leading to one or more professional degrees in a field of study; examples are *law school, medical school.*

Advanced standing credit.
Credit granted for work done at another higher education institution; for military service; for college-level courses taken in secondary school; or for competence demonstrated by examination (United States).

Advanced standing examination.
Examination taken to obtain *credit* for self-study, employment experience, or courses taken in other colleges or postsecondary schools. See also *advanced placement, examination for credit.*

Advisory board.
See *advisory committee.*

Advisory committee.
A group of persons, sometimes from outside the educational community, who are called upon by that community to offer advice about an educational program. Such a

group does not have final decision-making powers. Also called advisory board.

Afdelningsleder. Faculty rank: head of department; teaches and conducts research (Denmark).

Affiliated college. A college that offers programs of study but has no power to award degrees. Degrees are conferred by an *affiliating university*.

Affiliating university. A university that awards degrees for programs conducted by *affiliated colleges*.

Affirmative action. Actions required by federal law that are undertaken by an institution to overcome existing discriminatory practices, primarily by making additional efforts to recruit, employ, and promote qualified members of groups (principally *women* and *minority groups*) previously excluded from employment or attendance (United States).

Age group. Used broadly to refer to enrollment in the three stages of education: primary school age group, roughly ages 6/7 to 12/13; secondary school age group, roughly ages 12/13 to 17/18; and tertiary age group 17/18 to 21/22 or 19/20 to 23/24.

Aggregation. See *enrollment*.

Agrégation. Competitive examination to qualify for (a) teaching in secondary schools (*agrégation de l'enseignement secondaire*) or (b) for a post in certain fields in higher education: law, economic sciences, medicine and pharmacy (*agrégation de l'enseignement supérieur*). Success in the examination gives right to the title *agrégé* (French-language systems).

Agrégé. See *agrégation*.

Agricultural education. (1) Instruction, including degree-level courses and programs, leading to vocational proficiency in agriculture; (2) preparation for teaching in agriculture.

Ahlicipta.
Senior fellowship scheme at the University of Science, Malaysia, in which retired men and women write about their work experience. The writings are then studied by students.

Aims.
See *educational aims.*

Aiúto.
Faculty rank: instructor's aide (Italy).

Akademi.
Academy (Sweden, Turkey).

Aldines.
A book or edition published by Aldus Manutius of Venice in the sixteenth century; usually a fine edition of a Greek, Italian, or Latin classic.

Allmennfag.
Interdisciplinary study (Norway).

Alma mater.
Latin: fostering mother. (1) A college or university which one has attended or from which one has graduated; (2) the song or hymn of a university or college.

Almuce.
A hood with furred edges and small tails worn by high church dignitaries in Oxford during the fifteenth century.

Alphameric number.
Assignment of numbers in sequence to correspond with alphabetic listing.

Altalános iskola.
General primary school of eight years' duration (Hungary).

Alternative freshman year.
A self-paced, flexible pattern of instruction, allowing first-year students to take as few or as many courses as they can handle successfully (United States).

Alternative higher education.
See *alternative programs.*

Alternative programs.   Nontraditional studies at higher education institutions such as *experiential education, continuing education, lifelong learning, distance education*, and different types of outreach programs.

Alumni.   Masculine plural of alumnus. Feminine: alumna, alumnae. Graduates of an institution of higher education (United States).

Alumni college.   Formal and informal education programs provided for graduates of the institution, often during summer vacations (United States).

Alumni financial support.   See *annual giving*.

Alumni fund.   Funds provided annually by graduates of an institution of higher learning to help meet the institution's operating and capital costs.

Alumni placement bureau.   A college or university office that assists *alumni* of the institution to obtain full-time employment and to transfer to new professional positions.

Alumni publication.   Publication published for the benefit of, and containing information for, graduates of an institution. See also *class notes*.

Amanuensis.   Faculty rank: assistant to *afdelningsleder* (department head) (Denmark, Norway).

Ancillary services.   See *auxiliary enterprise*.

Anglophone.   English speaking. Generally used in reference to African nations, formerly under British rule: anglophone Africa. See also *francophone*.

Annual giving.   Annual donation to a college or university by *alumni* and others in response to a drive by the institution for financial support (United States). See also *key alumni.*

Annual giving funds.
Funds collected yearly from *alumni* and others. See also *annual giving.*

Antinepotism rules.
Rules established to strike down *nepotism* rules that forbid the employment of a husband and wife in the same institution. Nepotism rules have been seen by women academics as a barrier to *equal opportunity* in employment (United States).

Apartheid.
A South-African policy of *segregation* and political, economic, and educational *discrimination* against non-European population groups. Euphemistically called separate development.

Apolytarion.
Greek term for a secondary school-leaving certificate required for higher study at home or abroad (Cyprus).

Application.
(1) The act of filing the appropriate records and forms required for an applicant to be considered for admission to a higher education institution; (2) the appropriate credentials and forms filed.

Application blank for admission.
A form for collecting and reporting data on candidates for admission; usually the first formal communication between the candidate and the school or college.

Application fee.
A fee charged by most colleges to defray the costs of handling the candidate's papers and to discourage excessive multiple applications. The fee is usually nonrefundable but is sometimes applied to tuition or fees at registration. Also called evaluation fee (United States). See also *acceptance fee.*

Applied arts courses.
Skill-oriented courses in such fields as crafts, painting, design, and home economics for practical or utilitarian ends.

Applied research.   Research for discovery of new scientific knowledge that has specific applications with respect to products or processes.

Appropriation.   Funding of authorized or recommended expenditures.

Aptitude.   The projected *ability,* often indicated by the results of appropriate tests, to succeed in specific fields of endeavor. Special tests are given to ascertain *academic, artistic, mechanical,* and other *aptitudes.*

Aptitude test.   Test designed to ascertain a person's potential to succeed in a field of endeavor. Contrast *achievement test.*

Arbeiter-und Bauern Fakultäten.   Special educational institutions for young farmers and workers who have been recommended for attendance by their employers, organizations, or local authorities (German Democratic Republic).

Arbitration.   Settlement of grievances or disputes by a third party, designated as arbitrator. See also *collective bargaining.*

Archives.   (1) Documents, whatever their form or date, produced and/or received by any public or private person and/or institution and preserved for future use; (2) the repository, whether public or private, for such documents.

Area studies.   (1) Academic programs of study offered by some universities, dealing with a geographical area, such as Latin America, Southeast Asia, or Subsaharan Africa; (2) research articles or books dealing with such selected geographical areas.

Articulation.   (1) The coordination of the policies and practices of one educational level or system with those of another educational level or system or with work opportunities to produce a smooth flow of students from one educational sector to another or from education to employment; (2) the organizing of the educational system so that the whole educational process becomes an unbroken flow with the rate of flow different for each individual.

Artistic aptitude.

An *ability* to succeed in artistic expression such as painting, designing, drawing, music.

Arts and sciences education.

See *liberal arts.*

Asamblea.

Assembly; a common name for a governing board in higher education institutions in Spanish-language systems. The exact nomenclature varies: *asamblea universitaria* (university assembly), *asamblea general universitaria* (general university assembly), *asamblea general de claustro* (general assembly of teaching staff), *asamblea de claustro de facultad* (faculty assembly), *asamblea universitaria nacional* (national university assembly).

Asistans.

Faculty rank: assistant to professor (Turkey).

Asistent.

Faculty rank: assistant to professor (Yugoslavia).

Aspiranty.

Postgraduate students working toward the degree of *Kandidat nauk* (Union of Soviet Socialist Republics, Czechoslovakia, Bulgaria).

Aspirantura.

Postgraduate program leading to the degree of *Kandidat nauk* (Union of Soviet Socialist Republics, Czechoslovakia, Bulgaria).

Assignment sheet.

Written directions covering assignments given to students; includes procedures, definitions of requirements, supplementary readings.

Assimilado.   Before 1961 an African person enjoying the constitutional rights of Portuguese citizens in the African colonies of Portugal.

Assistant.   In French-language systems, (1) the entry or lowest rank in hierarchy of teaching staff; (2) in English-language systems, a person below the rank of instructor who assists a regular faculty member. Also called *graduate assistant* in the United States.

Assistant lecturer.   Faculty rank: a junior member of the teaching staff.

Assistant professor.   Third level of faculty rank in descending order from professor (United States). See also *profesor adjunto.*

Assistantship.   A position made available to a graduate student in part-time teaching, administration, or research while the student continues his or her studies for an advanced degree.

Assistent.   Faculty rank: *assistant* (Sweden, Denmark).

Assistente.   Faculty rank: *assistant* (Brazil, Portugal, Angola, Mozambique).

Associate degree.   A credential or qualification generally awarded after a two-year program in a junior college or technical institute but also awarded by some four-year institutions; thus, it may be a terminal degree as well as an intermediate qualification. Refers to Associate in Arts (A.A.), Associate in Science (A.S.), and others (United States and United States-derived systems).

Associate professor.   Generally, the second highest *faculty rank* (United States and United States-derived systems). See also *profesor asociado.*

Associateship.   Professional qualification awarded by a professional body bestowing the right to practice a profession. Other professional qualifications are *graduateship, licentiateship, fellowship* (United Kingdom, Australia).

Association.

An organization of persons or institutions having a common interest, such as a national or regional teachers association, a university association of teachers, or a local association of colleges and universities.

Atheneum.

Modern secondary school with programs qualifying graduates for university study (the Netherlands).

Athletic conference.

An association of colleges and/or universities for purposes of conducting intercollegiate sports according to agreed-upon rules and schedules for contests. Conference organization is made up of official representatives of each college or university (usually the president). All members of the conference are governed by regulations concerning conduct of games and contests, financial aid for athletes, and total number of players who may be squad members (United States).

Athletic scholarship.

A financial grant for further higher education for those proficient in *athletics*.

Athletics.

Games and sports engaged in on a competitive or noncompetitive basis by teams or individuals in colleges and universities, or in organizations and groups.

Attendance.

The act of being present as a student in an educational institution. See also *compulsory education*.

Attestation d'études approfondies (AEA).

A diploma awarded for one year of successful study in the third cycle of higher education in sciences (French-language systems).

Attrition.

The decline from year to year, because of *dropout,* expulsion, or other reason, of the number of students in *attendance,* in an institution of education; the opposite of *holding power*. See also *wastage*.

Attrition rate. The rate by which the number of students attending an institution declines from one period to another because of disciplinary dismissal, dropout, death, transfer, and other reasons.

Auditor. Student in regular attendance at class who does not participate fully or expect to receive credit or grades. See also *noncredit student*.

Aufbaustudium. Advanced university programs (Federal Republic of Germany, Austria).

Automatic salary increase. Established salary increase awarded annually to all teachers or staff according to rank and title. Also called step increase.

Autonomy. Independence of universities to act without external controls by state, federal, municipal, or local authorities. In continental Europe autonomy has been a characteristic of the senior professor; in Britain and the United States autonomy has generally accrued to the institution; (2) the exercise of freedoms in the learning process (freedom to select programs, channels of learning). See also *academic freedom, fiscal autonomy*.

Auxiliary enterprise. Activities of a business nature (such as bookstore, cafeteria, and student residences) operated for the service of students, staff, and faculty but not directly related to the instructional cost structure of the university. Such activities are generally budgeted separately in universities in the United States.

Average active enrollment. The number of enrollments calculated by averaging actual enrollments on specific dates, such as beginning, midpoint, or end of term.

Average full-time equivalent enrollment.	The average part-time enrollment converted to a *full-time equivalent;* equivalency is established by dividing the total of average part-time student *credit hours* or courses in which students are enrolled per academic year or term by the normal full-time load per student in *credit hours* or courses per academic year or term (United States). See also *student credit-hour.*
Award.	(1) Certificate or prize given for achievement; (2) recognition of the completion of an educational program; (3) a grant of financial aid.
Ayudante de cátedra.	Faculty rank: teaching aide; supervises laboratory work and practical assignments (Spanish-language systems).

B

Baccalauréat.	Secondary school-leaving certificate generally awarded after successful completion of thirteen years of study and a national examination. The *baccalauréat* is awarded in different specialties or sections distinguished by letters—A, B, C, D, E, T. The *baccalauréat de technicien* is awarded for technical study. The *baccalauréat* generally gives access to all fields of university study; the exception is that students who have a specialty in arts or economic and social sciences may not enroll directly in science faculties but must first pass an examination (French-language systems).
Baccalaureate.	(1) A term relating to the bachelor's degree; (2) the religious service preceding the *commencement.* See also *bachelor's degree.*
Baccalaureate sermon.	A traditional service for graduates of colleges and universities; usually held the Sunday before *commencement* exercises in a church or chapel (United States).

Baccalaureatus. First degree offered in Iceland; for instance, *baccalaureatus artium* (bachelor of arts). See also *formal academic degree*.

Baccalaureus. Degree awarded after three and a half years of study at a technical university (the Netherlands).

Bacharel. Title awarded in fields such as law (five years), administration, economics (four years). The degree is called *bacharelado* (Brazil). Also first university qualification after three years of study (Portugal, Angola, Mozambique).

Bacharelado. See *bacharel*.

Bachelor's degree. The first degree in arts and sciences and in certain professional and technical fields awarded after three or four years (United Kingdom and British-derived systems) or four years (United States) of study; for example, Bachelor of Arts (B.A.), Bachelor of Science (B.S.).

Bachiller. Title of secondary school graduate who holds the secondary school certificate *bachillerato* (Spanish-language systems).

Bachillerato. Secondary school certificate awarded in Spanish-language systems, generally after twelve years of study. It can also carry a designation of specialty: *bachillerato en educación* (education), *bachillerato en humanidades* (humanities), *bachillerato especializado* (specialized), *bachillerato general superior* (general higher certificate), *bachillerato industrial* (industrial), *bachillerato en ciencias y letras* (science and humanities), *bachillerato técnico* (technical), *bachillerato comercial* (commercial). Can also be the first university degree (Peru, Argentina).

Bachillerato profesional. First university degree awarded after six to eight semesters (Peru).

Bachillerato unificado y polivalente (BUP). Certificate of secondary education after a three-year upper-secondary program (Spain).

Bachillerato universitario. Degree awarded in some private universities after four years of study (Argentina).

Bagrut. Secondary school-leaving certificate awarded after twelve years of study (Israel).

Bargaining. See *collective bargaining.*

Basic education. (1) A level of education that includes those basic and specific skills needed for a person to function adequately as a member of society; (2) in collegiate circles, usually general programs or survey courses offered during the first two years of a four-year baccalaureate program (United States).

Basic research. Study or investigation to develop new knowledge that may have no apparent immediate practical application. Contrast *applied research.*

Basket three. One of the sections of the Helsinki Agreement, signed by thirty-five countries at conclusion of the intergovernmental Conference on Security and Cooperation in Europe in August 1975, which deals with increased cultural contact among Eastern Europe and the Western nations.

Behavioral objectives. The aims and objectives of a program or course of study stated as actual *performance criteria* or as descriptions of observable and measurable behavior.

Bibliographer. (1) A person who compiles bibliographies; (2) one who writes about or is informed about books, their publication, contents, authors, and other details, relative to a particular topic.

Bibliographic service. (1) The provision, publication, and dissemination of sources of information by means of abstracts, directories, indexes, catalogs, and bibliographic periodicals; (2) a chief function of a library, documentation center, or archival institution.

Bibliography. (1) The identification and systematic description or classification of publications; (2) a list or catalog of books or writings related to a particular topic.

Bid. (1) An invitation to a student to join a fraternity (United States); (2) a guaranteed total price for construction of a facility or for furnishing supplies, submitted by a contractor or a supplier in response to an invitation (advertising for bids). Usually a required procedure in tax-supported institutions.

Bienestar estudiantil. Spanish: student *welfare services.*

"Big bang" theory. The concept of the origin of the universe by chemical explosion; term used to indicate the massive governmental intervention to get university reform under way in the 1960s in Japan.

Big Ten. The Mid-Western Conference Athletics League, which consists of Illinois, Indiana, Iowa, Michigan, Michigan State, Minnesota, Northwestern, Ohio State, Purdue, and Wisconsin universities (United States).

Big Three. Traditionally used for Harvard, Princeton, and Yale universities, specifically in reference to athletic activities (United States).

Bilateral aid. Provision of financial or human assistance by one country to another, most often between an industrialized nation and a developing nation.

Bilateral programs.
Exchange or assistance programs between two countries, institutions, or organizations.

Bilingual.
Facility in the use of two languages.

Binary system of education.
The organization of education in two sectors; in particular, the division of financing and function between the university sector and the sector comprising the programs and institutions controlled by local education authorities (United Kingdom).

Block-release courses.
Programs that involve college attendance of employees for periods averaging eighteen weeks in a year, either (a) in two or more short periods of full-time study, between which students return to their firms, or (b) one or more short periods of full-time study supplemented by study one or two days a week during another part of the session (United Kingdom). See also *day-release courses.*

Board.
A group of persons, appointed or elected, functioning in an advisory or decision-making capacity at many levels within an institution of higher education. Such a board may be an academic board, *advisory board, governing board,* board of directors, *board of trustees,* faculty board.

Board of studies.
Academics (professors, readers, and other recognized teachers) in a subject, responsible for the general organization and content of the teaching and examining in that subject (United Kingdom and Commonwealth countries).

Board of trustees.
A group of individuals, officially designated by charter or statute, who have general, fiscal, and academic responsibility for the operation of a college or university.

Bonded student.
A student who is legally bound to repay a government- or industry-sponsored educa-

tion by means of a specified number of years of service; especially customary in teacher training.

Bonding. The legal requirement that a student repay a government- or industry-sponsored education by a stipulated number of years of service.

Brahmacharin. Religious student mentioned in the *rig-veda*, the primary sacred scripture of Hinduism.

Brahmin. The highest of the four Hindu castes; comprising intellectuals, scholars, and priests.

Brain drain. The emigration of highly skilled professionals, generally from a developing country to a developed country; results in economic, developmental, and social loss to the developing nation, which has expended scarce resources on the training of the professional.

Branch campus. A unit of a university located separately from the main campus but under the direction of the central university administration. Generally does not offer a full university curriculum but includes specific programs or faculties, such as arts or law. Also called *university branch*.

Brevet. Certificate awarded at the conclusion of basic, technical, or vocational programs at different levels (French-language systems). See also *brevet élémentaire, brevet d'études du premier cycle, brevet d'enseignement industriel, brevet d'études professionnelles, brevet de technicien, brevet de technicien supérieur.*

Brevet d'enseignement industriel. Certificate of industrial study awarded after completion of the long secondary program. Does not give access to university study (French-language systems).

Brevet d'études du premier cycle (BEPC). Certificate awarded after successful completion of the first (generally four-year) cycle of secondary education in francophone African countries.

Brevet d'études professionnelles (BEP).   Certificate of professional study awarded after two years of secondary study; either national or departmental certificates (French-language systems).

Brevet de technicien.   Technical certificate awarded after the full secondary program. Does not generally give access to university study (France).

Brevet de technicien supérieur.   Certificate of higher technician. Awarded after two years of postsecondary study (France).

Brevet élémentaire.   Elementary school certificate awarded after completion of six years of elementary education in some francophone African countries.

Brevis.   Certificate awarded after completion of tenth grade of a vocationally oriented secondary program as signified by the *réalexamen* (Denmark).

Budget.   An estimate of an institution's proposed sources of income and expenditures for a given period or for a specific purpose.

Budgeting.   Estimating in detail the income and expenditures for a specific period and for specific purposes. Estimate approved by proper financial and administrative authorities becomes the institutional budget. When related to a specific educational program, this procedure is known as program budgeting.

Bureau of institutional reasearch.   An office or staff responsible for gathering and analyzing data for use of administrators, governing boards, and faculty in reaching decisions relative to the operation of an institution (including inauguration of new programs, development of special facilities, and other policies) and for forecasting future trends in such areas as enrollments and manpower needs, which may affect the operation and growth of the institution.

Bursar. (1) Generally the financial officer, or treasurer, of an institution or college; (2) a student holding a scholarship (United Kingdom and Commonwealth countries).

Bursaries examination. Examination taken by students at the end of the fifth year of secondary education. Successful candidates obtain bursaries (grants) for full-time university study. The grants vary according to the level of attainment in the examination (New Zealand).

Bursary. (1) Government financial assistance awarded to a student in need of such aid (United Kingdom and Commonwealth countries); (2) the treasury of an institution of higher education (United Kingdom). See also *scholarship*.

Business college. A public, private, or proprietary institution offering programs leading to careers in business office occupations, such as stenography and accounting. Programs vary in length from a few weeks to four years. In the United States proprietary schools are empowered by many states to grant degrees. Also called business schools.

Business education. Programs of instruction, offered by business colleges and proprietary institutions, leading to careers in office occupations and middle management.

C

Calendar. The structure of the school year. For colleges and universities the calendar is usually designated as an *academic year*, which may consist of two semesters or terms, three terms, or possibly two terms with an intersession lasting three or four weeks. The *quarter system* calendar divides the calendar year into four quarters, with three quarters being the academic year and the fourth usually a summer term. The *trimester* calendar is usually three terms of equal length. See also *academic year*.

Calotte.

In *academic dress*, a cap worn by canons and other church dignitaries in twelfth- and thirteenth-century Europe.

Campus.

The grounds of an educational institution on which its buildings are situated. The *main campus* is where the principal business and programs of the institution are conducted; the *branch campus* is a unit of the institution located separately from the main campus but under the central institutional administration. The *branch campus* often offers specialized programs, such as a medical or an engineering program. See also *facilities*.

Campus Panhellenic.

An organization made up of representatives from Greek-letter *sororities* on a campus to promote cooperation and establish standards for its members. More than two hundred Campus Panhellenics are joined in the National Panhellenic Conference that meets biennially (United States).

Campus security.

A security force, composed of campus and/or municipal police, for the protection of students, employees, and campus property (United States).

Campus yard.

The open area of the grounds fully or partially surrounded by the college or university buildings.

Cancelled registration.

The removal of a student's name from the official roster of registered students.

Candidate.

One who seeks admission, sits for an examination, or competes for a scholarship.

Candidature.
First university qualification awarded after two or three years at the end of a broadly based program; essential for further studies and specialization (Belgium, Burundi).

Candidatus.
(1) In Denmark, first university degree, requiring four and one half to eight years of study. *Candidatus magisterii* is the degree required for teaching. (2) In Norway, first degree *candidatus magisterii* awarded after three to five years of study in liberal arts, sciences, or social sciences. Higher degrees are *candidatus* plus mention of the appropriate field, such as *candidatus medicinae, candidatus theologiae, candidatus sociologiae.* (3) In Iceland, *candidatus* with appropriate field of specialization also is the first degree, awarded after four and one half to seven years of study. Examples are *candidatus medicinae et chirurgiae* (medicine and surgery) and *candidatus theologiae* (theology). See also *kandidaatti, kandidat.*

Candlemas.
Sometimes used to denote the second term of a three-term academic year (*Martinmas, Candlemas,* and *Whitsunday*) (United Kingdom).

Canon law.
The body of ecclesiastical rules or laws used as a guide in church organization and administration. One of the earliest fields of study.

Cap and gown.
Academic dress or regalia worn on special academic occasions by students, graduates, faculty, governing board members and public officials in higher education institutions.

Capability.
The limit of a student's academic, artistic, or practical development at a given time.

Capacité en droit.
Below-degree-level certificate awarded after two years of the study of law. *Baccalauréat* is not necessary for entry to program (French-language systems).

Capacity.
(1) The number of students that can be accommodated in an educational institution or in a classroom; (2) the limit to which a student can develop a function, given optimum educational and environmental support.

Capital expenditures.
Funds spent on physical facilities, land, and equipment that will be in use for a period of not less than one year.

Capital giving.
Donations of money or property for capital purposes such as construction of buildings, acquisition of land, and additions to endowment funds.

Capitation funding.
See *capitation grant.*

Capitation grant.
A grant provided to an institution of higher education in proportion (per head) to the number of students enrolled from a given area (United States).

Cappa.
A cape used in *academic dress.*

Cappa clausa.
Earliest official dress of masters, academic rather than ecclesiastical in origin. As of 1533, bachelors and doctors of divinity, doctors of canon or civil law, and doctors in sciences could wear the "sleeveless cote" in scarlet, violet, or mulberry. (Doctors at Oxford still retain their scarlet habits as a convocation dress, worn over gown, with hood worn over the habit.)

Capuchons rouges.
Scarlet robes granted to doctors in theology and canon law at the University of Paris by Pope Benedict XII in the fourteenth century. Doctors at Oxford began to wear scarlet robes in the middle of the fourteenth century.

Caput.
The administrative officer who is concerned with the conduct and discipline of students (Canada).

Career.
The totality of work in a given vocation or profession by a person in his or her lifetime.

Career choice.
See *guidance.*

Career education.
(1) The totality of experiences through which one learns about, and prepares to engage in, work as part of one's way of living; (2) a philosophy of education that permeates all instruction, emphasizing the relationship between the subject matter and the career development of each student; (3) postsecondary education that encompasses all the planned educational experiences of the public or private higher education system, in concert with the community, to ensure that each person is prepared to work according to his or her chosen life style.

Carnegie unit.
A measure of secondary school work used as guideline in admitting students to college. The name is derived from the 1908 report of a conference sponsored by the Carnegie Foundation for the Advancement of Teaching, which defined the unit. One unit normally represents a year's study of one subject in a class meeting comprising not less than 120 sixty-minute recitation hours or the equivalent. Originally, the system assumed sixteen units of work in a four-year period as a minimum for high school certification (United States).

Carrera.
Spanish: career or profession.

Carta.
(1) Spanish: charter, ordinance, or decree. (2) Portuguese: certificate, such as *carta de ensino primario elementar* (certificate of primary education) (Mozambique).

Case-history method.
See *case system of instruction.*

Case system of instruction.
Instruction based on the use of cases; used in teaching law, business, and journalism.

Legal education uses court cases that are selected because they illustrate application of the law and interpretation of the law in specific situations. Cases used in business and journalism are written descriptions of actual experiences and events in a given organization or situation, from which the student may deduce general theoretical principles.

Cassock. Ankle-length, close-fitting garment worn under habit in the early *academic dress* of undergraduates and holders of bachelor's degrees. Also called *sub-tunica* (fifteenth century); adopted from religious dress.

Catalog. A pamphlet or book generally issued annually by a university, college, or subunit within a university giving the curricula, academic calendar, and such other information as administrative officers, statutes, tuition, and programs of study. See also *calendar.*

Cataloging. The process of classifying all the books or other materials in a library; bibliographic data for each work is included.

Cátedra. Spanish: chair or professorship.

Catedrático. Faculty rank: full professor in charge of a *chair* (Spanish-language systems).

Cathedral schools. Medieval schools in Europe that prepared students for priesthood and/or civil service; continued as university preparatory schools into the nineteenth century.

Catholic college. College owned and operated by the Roman Catholic Church or a Roman Catholic religious order. See also *Jesuit institutions.*

Censors. Examiners who held oral examinations at the end of secondary school (*gymnasium*), thereby determining whether a student could graduate (Sweden, 1868–1968).

Census date.   The date when a count is made of enrollments for report purposes.

Center.   (1) A college or department, at an institution of higher education, which specializes in study and/or teaching of a specific subject (center for pedagogical studies, center for linguistics, adult education center); (2) a space within an institution designed for a particular educational purpose (learning center, reading center, student service center, center for continuing education, guidance center); (3) a location off campus where educational programs are conducted.

Central education agencies.   Central offices of governments or school systems that exercise control over and provide services to subordinate school units.

Centralization.   The practice of concentrating in one place or center under few authorities the administration and supervision of an institution or system of higher education.

Centralized administration.   A single, as opposed to diffused, authority for control and management; for example, where policy control of an education system is vested in one agency, such as a ministry of education.

Centre.   *Center.* (1) An educational institution such as *centre d'éducation revolutionnaire* (center of revolutionary education), a term applied to all educational institutions in Guinea, or *centre universitaire* (university center), an institution generally offering a limited number of fields of study; (2) a part of an institution such as *centre de recherche* (research center) (French-language systems).

Centro.   *Center;* for instance, *centro de bienestar* (student welfare center) (Spanish-language systems).

Ceremonies.

The conducting of special events (commencements, dedications, inaugurations) incorporating traditional academic rituals, dress, and procedures (such as carrying the mace of authority). Academic ceremonies have common features in all nations.

Certificado.

Certificate. Generally a secondary-level qualification awarded in Spanish-language systems such as *certificado de profesor normal* (normal school teacher certificate) (Paraguay); *certificado de estudios superiores* (certificate of higher education) awarded after short-cycle programs in technological programs (Venezuela); *certificado de técnico* (technician certificate), secondary school-leaving certificate (Argentina and other Spanish-language systems).

Certificat.

Certificate. Educational qualification at all levels of education in French-language systems. For example, *certificat d'aptitude professionnelle* (CAP), professional certificate; *certificat d'aptitude au professorat de l'enseignement secondaire* (CAPES), secondary school teachers certificate.

Certificate.

(1) A document signifying satisfactory completion of a program of undergraduate, graduate, or post-graduate study; for example, a certificate may be issued for at least one year of study beyond the master's degree; (2) a credential awarded for completion of a short-cycle program, generally in technical institutions (United States); (3) a secondary school-leaving qualification, such as the General Certificate of Education (GCE) (United Kingdom). Contrast *degree*. See also *certificate of completion*.

Certificate course.

A course leading to a certificate as opposed to a degree.

Certificate of completion. A formal statement to the effect that a course or program has been satisfactorily completed (United States). Also called certificate of training.

Certificate program. A sequential program of study leading to a certificate or other similar formal nondegree award, such as a diploma or professional designation.

Certificate student. A student enrolled in a certificate course.

Certification. A procedure by which a governmental agency or professional association grants licenses or certificates that permit individuals to practice a profession or use an authorized title such as psychologist. See also *associateship, esame di stato, fellowship, graduateship, licentiateship, Staatsexamen*.

Chair. A teaching position in an institution of higher education; the professor holding the *chair* is eminent in the field; often used for *endowed chairs* (United States); older European and Latin American universities are divided into faculties and subdivided into chairs for each discipline. Each chair is held by a full professor; thus the term often signifies the professorship itself. See also *cátedra*.

Chairman. Head of an academic department or discipline.

Chancelier. *Chancellor;* represents the ministry of education and functions as rector of the *académie* in which the university is located (French-language systems).

Chancellor. (1) Chief executive for a group of institutions of higher education; (2) honorary title given to a president of an institution of higher education upon retirement from presidency; may involve some duties; (3) chief administrative officer of each campus of a multicampus institution (United States);

(4) head and chief officer of a university and president of a council and guild of graduates, often a ceremonial position (United Kingdom and Commonwealth countries).

Chancellor's assessor. The chancellor's representative or substitute on governing bodies (United Kingdom).

Change of course. Change in registration from original subjects or courses by substituting new subjects or courses (United States).

Chargé de cours. Faculty rank: member of the teaching staff who, whether or not the holder of a doctorate, carries out the duties of a lectureship (*maître de conférences*) or of a vacant chair (French-language systems). Also called *chargé d'enseignement*.

Chargé d'enseignement. See *chargé de cours*.

Charitable gift annuity. See *annual giving*.

Charter. Legal document defining the organization of a higher education institution; grants certain powers and specifies duties, responsibilities, and liabilities of the individual or group to whom the charter is issued; granted by a specially empowered authority of a nation, state, or municipality.

Chatauqua movement. A summer series of lectures, concerts, and other programs of adult education that began in Chatauqua, New York, in 1874 and became the basis of a national movement. Established patterns for the development of adult education programs by colleges and universities (United States).

Chef de travaux. Faculty rank: covers different types of posts. Usually the person at this rank organizes practical exercises and/or research under the supervision of a professor (French-language systems).

Chimère. See *habit.*

Ching-hsueh. Study of classics. Style of learning associated with Confucianism, which dominated the Chinese academic world from the Han age (202 B.C.–A.D. 22) to the twentieth century.

Chŏnmun-hakkyo. Specialized postsecondary schools (Democratic People's Republic of Korea).

Church-affiliated college. A college that has ties to a specific religious denomination, generally through a church-controlled governing board. An affiliated church organization usually has financial responsibility for the institution.

Church-owned college. A college that is founded and owned by a religious denomination; often emphasizes strongly the doctrine of the denomination. The church finances the college (United States). See also *Catholic college, denominational college.*

Church-related college. A college that is identified with a denomination but not controlled by it. The denomination may provide some funding. Sometimes designated as a church-sponsored college.

Ciclo. *Cycle;* used to indicate level of a program of study, generally at the secondary level, such as *ciclo básico común* (common basic cycle) or *ciclo diversificado* (specialized cycle) (Spanish-language systems).

Cité universitaire. French: university city. A residential and dining complex for students.

City and Guilds of London Institute. Founded in 1878, the largest examining body in vocational education, mainly in crafts. Also undertakes external examinations for students from Commonwealth countries (United Kingdom).

Civic university.   A university established through local civic-mindedness but not under civil or municipal control (United Kingdom). See also *redbrick universities*.

Class.   (1) A group of students who report regularly and at a scheduled time to the same teacher, such as a biology class; (2) all students who enter a college or university at the same time and expect to graduate at the same time. The four classes of undergraduates are termed *freshman class, sophomore class, junior class,* and *senior class.* Each class also uses as reference its year of graduation; for instance, class of '78 indicates those students who graduate with their *first degree* in 1978 (United States).

Class attendance.   A student's presence at a meeting of a class or course for which the student is registered.

Class card.   A form used in assigning students to sections of courses. May also be used as a ticket of admission to class or as a device to collect grades at the end of the term (United States).

Class notes.   (1) Section of university *alumni publication* that brings graduates up to date on the whereabouts and activities of classmates around the world; (2) summaries written by students of information presented in a lecture or demonstration (United States).

Class schedule.   A listing of time and place of meeting of classes. May also include name of instructor, days, hours, and credits.

Class size.   The number of students enrolled in a class; often limited by number of seats in a classroom or by stations at laboratory benches. Standard class size is the number of students that a faculty establishes as the optimum number for effective teaching. Lecture classes can be as large as several hundred students, whereas discussion classes usually are limited to a small number. Most colleges have established their own norms for class size.

Class standing.

Rank or position of a student in class based on *grade point average*. Also called class rank.

Classe terminale.

Final year of study for the *baccalauréat* (French-language systems).

Classes préparatoires aux grandes écoles.

Preparatory classes for the *grandes écoles* requiring the *baccalauréat* for entry (France).

Classical education.

(1) Education based on the intellectual heritage of the ancient world (Greek, Latin, Arabic, Hebrew) and emphasizing the cultured person; flourished in the Western world from 1450 to 1850; (2) educational programs at all levels concerned with the ancient world.

Classical languages.

Ancient Latin and Greek.

Classification system.

Systematic grouping of library and other materials according to predetermined categories and characteristics.

Classified student.

A student who is regularly enrolled and is pursuing an associate, bachelor, or higher degree program. Sometimes called regular student, member of one of the regular classes, or degree credit student.

Claustro.

Assembly. Name for governing bodies, commonly used in Spanish-language universities, such as *claustro universitario* (university assembly), *claustro facultativo* (faculty assembly), *claustro docente* (teachers assembly).

Clearance.

Removal of obstacles or restrictions that prevent students from registering or attending classes (United States).

Clock hour.   Class period of fifty-to-sixty-minutes duration.

Club of Rome.   An informal group of some eighty-five scientists, humanists, economists, and industrialists from throughout the world who explore long-term global, economic, and political trends to inform political and other decision makers. In order to be free of influence, the group has no officers or budget.

Cluster college.   (1) Group of colleges in close physical proximity that cooperate in providing educational programs and that make facilities available to students of all the colleges in the cluster; in clusters cooperation is closer than in a *consortium* (United States); (2) in France, prior to the establishment of regional universities, doctoral candidates, provincial university professors, and residential staff members joined a "cluster" around a holder of a chair at the Sorbonne, who was a patron of the cluster.

Coach.   (1) In athletics, an instructor in one or more sports; (2) in academic subjects, generally a junior member of the teaching staff or a graduate student who instructs and aids students in the techniques of studying or in the basic facts of the subject.

Coaching.   (1) The instruction of students to compete in sports events and games; (2) the act of instructing one or more students who are preparing for a special examination or who are failing in a subject.

Cocurricular activities. Organized student projects, events, and groups, such as student newspapers, plays, and orchestras sponsored by an educational institution to supplement the academic program or curriculum. See also *extracurricular activities*.

Coeducation.
A system of education in which both sexes attend the same school, begun in Protestant elementary schools during the Reformation and at the tertiary level in the United States in the early part of the nineteenth century. In many countries, especially Muslim countries, single-sex schools are still prevalent, especially at the secondary level.

Coeducational housing.
Sharing of dormitories by students of both sexes, whereby men and women are (a) located in separate buildings in the same dormitory complex but share common lounge and dining areas; (b) housed on separate floors in the same building but share common lounge and dining areas; (c) housed in adjacent rooms and fully share the living facilities (except bathrooms) of a dormitory.

Cogobierno.
Spanish: co-governance. The principle of eligibility of students for participation on all university committees and governing boards as advocated by the Córdoba Manifesto (1918).

Colegio.
University college. Institutions offering the first cycle of university education (Spain).

Colegio profesional.
Spanish: professional association. Composed of practitioners of a profession, such as architects, engineers.

Colegio universitario.
Spanish: university college. Institutions offering the first cycle of university education.

Collaborative programs.
Programs offered collaboratively by several universities that have joined together to more effectively provide experiential programs to students.

Collective bargaining.
Negotiations by college or university teachers and staff with administrative officers or other institutional officials to reach an agreement on salaries, working conditions, and fringe benefits. Faculty and staff

are generally represented by a *faculty union* (United States). Also called collective negotiations.

College.   Derived from Latin *collēgium:* an association, guild, or corporation. (1) In the United Kingdom, from the Middle Ages on, the term applied to secondary or higher education, such as Seton College at the secondary level and Oxford and Cambridge at the higher level; also used as a name for such bodies as Royal College of Surgeons, which offer limited teaching facilities; (2) in the United States (a) a four-year institution of higher education, usually offering programs in the liberal arts leading to a bachelor's degree or a two-year institution offering lower qualifications; (b) a major division of a university, such as the College of Education; (c) sometimes, an association or group, such as an electoral college; (d) used generically, higher education, as "go to college," although the institution attended might be a university; (3) in other countries, use of the word is similar to the above, generally (a) an independent institution such as a college of education; (b) a unit within a university; (c) a teaching institution not authorized to grant degrees, such as an *affiliated college* (Bangladesh, India, Pakistan). See also *community college, denominational college, junior college, land-grant college, nondenominational college, nonsectarian college, sectarian college, private college, public college.*

College.   (1) Secondary school, generally offering the first or four-year cycle, in French-language systems; in France and many other French-language systems, this schooling is offered in a *collège d'enseignement général, collège d'enseignement secondaire,* or *collège d'enseignement technique;* in Quebec, Canada, the school is called *collège d'enseignement général et professionelle;* (2) *collège* is also used to refer to the prestigious *Collège de France,* one of the French *grandes établissements.*

College Board Examinations. Tests offered by the College Entrance Examination Board, a private testing service, to high school students to determine the students' ability to succeed in higher education study. Taking of these examinations and submission of scores is a requirement for admission to some institutions. Consists of a general test and optional tests per students' choice (United States).

College clearinghouse. A center that obtains the records and credentials of selected students who are seeking college admission and makes the information available to admissions officers of accredited institutions (United States). Also called college clearing center.

College corporation. The legal entity of a college as defined in the *charter;* usually consists of the president and trustees.

College credit. Academic credit awarded on the completion of a course of study; each course of study carries a certain number of *credit hours;* one credit hour is one hour of class and two hours of preparation each week for a semester or term of fifteen or more weeks, three credit hours is three hours of class plus six hours of preparation each week for a semester or term of fifteen or more weeks. Laboratory courses usually carry one half or two thirds the amount of credit awarded for lecture-recitation courses.

College day. An event held at a high school to acquaint students with the programs and services offered by a specific institution of higher education (United States). Also called college night.

College Entrance Examination Board. The private organization that contracts with the Educational Testing Service to prepare, administer, and transmit the results of standardized achievement and aptitude tests required for admission by many institutions of higher education (United States).

College examiner.

(1) The administrative officer who evaluates credentials and administers tests to determine the eligibility of candidates for admission; see also *director of admissions;* (2) person who evaluates the performance of a college's students to determine the award of credits or degrees.

College graduate.

Person who holds a college degree. In the generic sense, refers to anyone holding a first or advanced degree, whether from a college or university.

College-level course.

Courses above the secondary school level. Normally taken to earn a certificate or degree offered by a postsecondary or tertiary institution. See also *university-level education.*

College-Level Examination Program (CLEP).

A college-credit-by-examination testing program developed by the College Entrance Examination Board and the Educational Testing Service to validate learning and competency attained outside the classroom for use by institutions in awarding *college credit*. The program currently includes five general examinations and forty-seven specialized examinations (United States).

College-level student.

A student pursuing postsecondary studies with credits applicable to a certificate or degree.

College of Education.

College specializing in the training of teachers for nursery school and primary and secondary education.

College of the Air.

A series of college courses broadcast as lessons on a regular schedule with provision for directed study and supplementary course outlines and materials (United States). See also *distance education*.

College placement.   A service that aids college students in planning employment or future education.

College Proficiency Examination Program (CPEP).   A college-credit-by-examination testing program administered by the American College Testing Program and designed to allow colleges to award *college credit* to students for learning obtained outside the classroom, in order to shorten the time required to achieve an academic degree (United States).

College publications.   All publications (catalogs, brochures, leaflets, and reports) of a college. Those designed to attract new students are called promotional publications.

College survey.   Study of a college or university to appraise how well the institution meets its aims and objectives and to determine adequacy of instruction, facilities, course offerings, and resources. See also *accreditation*.

College union.   A social center, often known as a student center or *commons*, providing social and recreational programs for the student community. Also called student center.

College/university adult education student.   One who is enrolled in a college or university full-time or part-time adult education program. See also *continuing education*.

College within a college.   An undergraduate instructional unit in which students and faculty live and study in the same physical area; attempted in some institutions as a means of overcoming problems attributed to large enrollments and depersonalization (United States).

Colleges of advanced education.   Institutions distinguished from universities by their emphasis on vocational programs, their orientation to teaching rather than research, and their primarily technical programs that lead to a diploma rather than to a degree. They are categorized into large multidisciplinary metropolitan colleges, small single-discipline metropolitan colleges, multidisciplinary nonmetropolitan colleges, and small single-discipline country colleges (Australia).

Collegiality.

In college or university governance, the joint sharing of responsibility for policy decision making by governing board members, administrators, faculty, and students.

Collegiate hostel.

A boarding house for students that is under the direct and exclusive control of one college, that is regarded as an integral part of that college, and that admits only those students who are studying in that particular college.

Colloquium.

(1) Reading course on important books, usually with group discussion led by a panel of experts from different subject areas; (2) also an advanced-level lecture presented by invited scholars for the benefit of graduate students and research-oriented faculty.

Combination courses.

Courses that combine study at the secondary and higher education levels, called *Kombinationsutbildning* (Sweden).

Combined course.

A program of study that includes courses from two or more curricula, schools, or colleges. For example, a combined business-law program consists of courses offered by the College of Business Administration and the College of Law. The program may combine general education and professional education. A student may receive the bachelor's degree on completing three years in the liberal arts college and the first year in the professional school. The professional degree is awarded after all remaining professional requirements have been met (United States). See also *interdisciplinarity.*

Combined degree.   See *combined course.*

Commencement.   The ceremony at which certificates, diplomas, or degrees are awarded and conferred on students who have successfully completed their program of study. Also called *graduation exercises.*

Committee system.   Use of committee to determine policies, procedures, or regulations.

Common room.   (1) A room reserved for the informal and exclusive use of the teaching staff of a college or university; (2) used colloquially, indicates the members of the staff collectively (United Kingdom).

Commons.   A student center or *college union.* Sometimes refers to a dining hall.

Community college.   A publicly financed two-year institution of postsecondary education offering both terminal training and preparation for entering a four-year institution on a transfer basis. Programs of community colleges usually offer liberal arts and professional programs to meet the needs of a particular community or local area (United States). See also *junior college.*

Community development programs.   University extension programs, such as agricultural or urban extension programs, aimed at improving economic and/or social conditions in the community or work place.

Community junior college.   See *community college.*

Commuter.   A student who lives at home and travels to the institution he or she attends for classes, study, and other activities. See also *resident student.*

Commuter college. A higher education institution primarily serving nonresident students.

Comparative education. The analysis in two or more national environments of educational systems and problems in terms of sociopolitical, economic, cultural, ideological, and other variables, in order to understand the factors that underlie similarities and differences in these countries.

Compensation. (1) Payments to faculty and staff members for services rendered, including *salary* and *fringe benefits;* (2) pay to individuals who are injured or disabled and who cannot carry on regular duties.

Compensatory education. A program of study that seeks to overcome deficiencies in a student's educational background and develop latent potential by stressing activities, experiences, and materials especially designed to motivate the student. See also *remedial programs.*

Compensatory recompense. Terminal payment, in addition to regular salary, provided to an employee because of an official act that reduces personnel or closes an educational institution (United Kingdom).

Competency-based education. A program whereby students demonstrate, by examination, a level of competency required for a particular occupation or a particular degree (United States).

Competitive admission. A type of *selective admission* in which only a few of the applicants are admitted, based on level of success in an examination or on grade averages, because of limitations on the number which can be accommodated. See also *numerus clausus.*

Complexe polytechnique. Comprehensive polytechnic school at the secondary level (Benin).

Comprehensive examination.

(1) An examination that measures knowledge in several fields; (2) an examination required for admission to candidacy for an advanced degree. See also *qualifying examination.*

Comprehensive higher education institution.

An institution offering both academic and occupational fields of study; the model of many United States institutions. Program offerings include two-year terminal and transfer programs leading to certificates and degrees, bachelor's and first professional degrees, graduate level programs leading to certificates and graduate degrees; basic and applied research is conducted in a variety of fields. Adult education and public service programs are offered. See also *comprehensive university.*

Comprehensive secondary school.

A secondary school that, in addition to accredited programs, has a number of departments, such as business, vocational, and industrial arts, designed to meet the needs of students of varying interests and abilities.

Comprehensive university.

(1) A university stressing natural and social sciences (People's Republic of China); (2) an institution incorporating both shorter, vocationally oriented programs and longer, research-oriented programs (Federal Republic of Germany).

Comptroller.

An administrative officer who is responsible for the general supervision of operations of accounting records and financial transactions, including the preparation of financial reports; and who is also responsible for handling all matters pertaining to remuneration, relationships with banks, and all the financial transactions that relate to students (United States). See also *bursar, treasurer.*

Compulsory education.

School attendance, generally in primary school, required by law in many countries for a specified period varying from four to twelve years.

Computer-assisted instruction.

An instructional technique utilizing computer equipment to (a) present information to student; (b) receive and evaluate student's responses; (c) based on steps a and b, present additional information. The instruction can be programmed to permit the student to proceed at his own pace (computer-assisted individually paced instruction).

Computer-managed instruction.

A computer-based system of testing that is used to manage the instruction of students by monitoring students' individual achievement, pinpointing instructional problems, and prescribing additional assignments.

Computer Output Microfilm (COM).

Microphotographic image produced directly from information recorded on magnetic tape.

Computer simulation.

An instructional model that uses computers; it is intended to make the learning situation or learning materials conform as closely as possible to an actual or hypothetical situation in which the learning can be applied.

Concours d'entrée.

Entrance examination that might be required for entry to educational institutions at different levels; for example, for entry to secondary or to postsecondary institutions (French-language systems).

Concurrent cooperative education.

See *parallel cooperative education.*

Concurrent registration.

Registration in more than one college in the same institution or in two separate institutions, or registration in day and evening programs at the same time.

Concurso vestibular. Examination for entry to higher education institutions (Brazil).

Condition. A grade indicating deficiency in work that must be removed prior to receiving either a passing or failing grade (United States).

Condition grade. A temporary grade allowing the student to complete assignments and additional work after the close of the term. The final grade assigned is usually D or F (failure).

Conditional admission. See *admission condition*.

Conference. An organized gathering for purposes of hearing lectures, conducting discussions, and sharing information and views. Also called *institute, workshop*.

Conference center. A facility owned and controlled by a university, where university adult education or extension courses are held. Largely used in the United States; in the United Kingdom a number of institutions, either owned by or associated with universities, perform similar functions. Centers may have residential facilities, food service, and specially equipped classrooms and lecture rooms.

Confidentiality of records. A basic principle binding the university not to expose or release official documents or other student and faculty records except by consent of the individual or through legal processes.

Congregation. Name of the general assembly of senior members of certain United Kingdom universities. At the University of Oxford the congregation receives proposals from the Hebdomadal Council concerning university regulations, which the congregation may adopt, reject, or amend. Confers honorary and ordinary degrees.

Conseil. *Council.* Common in French-language universities are such councils as *conseil d'administration* (administrative council) and *conseil academique* (academic council).

Consejo. *Council.* Common in Spanish-language universities are such councils as *consejo academico* (academic council), *consejo superior* (higher council), *consejo universitario* (university council), *consejo facultativo* (faculty council).

Conselho. *Council.* Common in Portuguese-language universities are such councils as *conselho administrativo* (administrative council), and *conselho directivo* (directive council).

Consortium. A voluntary, formally organized association of higher education institutions that cooperates in offering academic programs and services, employs at least one professional administrator, and requires either annual contributions from members or other evidence of long-term commitment. See also *cluster college.*

Constituent college. One of several colleges forming a university.

Continuation study center. A facility for conducting short courses for adults (United States).

Continuing education. Educational programs, usually *noncredit* and of short duration, offered for adults who are seeking education for professional advancement or for personal reasons other than professional advancement. See also *adult education, recurrent education.*

Continuing professional education. Offering of courses of a professional nature to keep members of a profession abreast of new information and developments. Sometimes known as state-of-the-art courses.

Contract learning. A program based on a written agreement between a student and a faculty member outlining the objectives of the program, the activities of the student that will meet these objectives, the criteria for evaluating these activities, and the credit to be granted on successful completion (United States).

Contract of enrollment. The agreement to pay financial charges when enrolling in a higher education institution (United States).

Contract programs. (1) Programs offered or conducted under contracts with the national government, a foreign government, an industry, or other funding agency that define the instructional services to be provided by the institution; the nature of courses, and other conditions of instruction; (2) programs based on an agreement between instructor and student pertaining to the amount of work to be accomplished in a specified period on a self-study basis.

Contract relationship. An understanding between student and institution regarding regulations. degree requirements, residence, and other matters, which are usually set forth in the catalog and which are in effect when the student enrolls.

Contracted research. Research conducted by academic personnel for a specific outside contractor (industry or government) under terms of a legal contract.

Contractual relationship degree requirements. The agreement an institution is considered to have made with the student to award a degree when the student has completed the requirements stated in the catalog in effect at the time of his or her *matriculation*.

Convenience loan. A loan by a business office or other agency to students or parents without demonstrated financial need. Commercial interest rates are usually charged.

Convocation. (1) A legislative assembly in certain United Kingdom universities consisting of all holders of master of arts and senior degrees; at the University of Oxford, the convocation elects the *chancellor* and professor of poetry; (2) an organized gathering, often for ceremonial purposes.

Cooperative bookstore. A university bookstore operated on the principle of a refund to its members; the refund is achieved by dividing profits on the basis of patronage.

Cooperative education. A process that formally integrates a student's academic study with work experience (in cooperating employer organizations) related to the student's field of study. The program is based on alternating periods of work and study, with alternating quarters or semesters being most common (United States). See also *sandwich plan, education alterné, work-study program.*

Cooperative education calendar. An academic calendar that integrates off-campus experience (usually paid jobs) with academic study in one of several ways. The *alternating plan* operates on a full calendar year as opposed to the traditional academic year and permits students to spend a specific number of weeks on campus and a specific number of weeks in off-campus experience, alternating periods of study and work. The *parallel plan* provides for students to work half a day and attend classes half a day. The *extended day plan* incorporates a more traditional calendar because students work a full day and attend classes in the late afternoon or evening. The *field experience plan* stops academic work entirely for a period of four to six weeks when all students leave the campus to gain off-campus experience.

Cooperative Extension Service. An educational system to transfer information from the university to the public through extension agents, established by the Smith-Lever Act in 1914 as a joint enterprise of federal, state, and local governments. Funded one half from federal funds and one half from state, local, and other sources to link the university closely with the community, it was orginally conceived as an agricultural extension program but now includes urban extension programs, community development in cities and villages, health care, and assistance to business (United States).

Cooperative student contract.

A written agreement sometimes made between a cooperative education institution and business, professional, or industrial employers, providing for the employment of certain cooperative students according to the provisions of the federal vocational acts (United States).

Coordinadores de especialidad.

Coordinators of specialty; an administrative rank at the professorial level (Bolivia).

Coordinate college.

An institutional arrangement, which consists of a college enrolling women located in close proximity to a men's college, that permits both men and women to take classes jointly in both institutions as undergraduates.

Coordinated course.

(1) A course that involves the presentation of material by two or more academic departments or disciplines (also termed *interdisciplinary course*), agencies, institutes, or committees, of a given higher education institution; (2) a course involving presentations by college and industry as a joint program.

Coordinator of cooperative education.

A member of the college staff responsible for administering the *cooperative education* program and placement of students. The coordinator acts as liaison between the college and employers in programs of cooperative education and handles all problems connected with on-the-job activities.

Copyright.

A legal convention that gives authors of literary, dramatic, musical, artistic, and other creative works exclusive right to reproduce and publish such works while denying this right to others. Copyright is based on both statutory and common law. Common law copyright protects unpublished work; statutory copyright protection should be properly noted on or in the published work. Copyright has to be applied for country by country.

Córdoba reform.

A reform movement, started in Córdoba, Argentina, in 1918, which spread through all of Latin America. Among its goals were university autonomy and democratization, that is, participation of all the members of the university in its governing bodies.

Corporate grant.

Voluntary monetary contribution of a corporation to a higher education institution.

Corporation.

The legal entity of a college or university as defined in the *charter;* usually consists of the president and trustees.

Correction of grade.

Change of an already-recorded grade because of error in reporting or recording.

Correspondence course.

A course conducted primarily by written communication between instructor and student. See also *correspondence study.*

Correspondence institution.

Institution offering courses and programs by correspondence; the mails are used to provide course outlines, instructional materials, and lessons. Students are assigned to faculty who read completed reports and examinations, grade the student's work, and answer questions raised by students. Programs may lead to degrees, certificates, and titles.

Correspondence student. A student who is enrolled in a program of study or a course that is conducted by mail. Students enrolled in credit courses are included in total enrollment figures of the institution. See also *distance education*.

Correspondence study. A method of instruction conducted by correspondence using the mails. Students enrolled in courses and programs receive lessons and assignments by mail and return written lessons and examinations for grading. A period of attendance on campus for examinations may be required. Programs lead to standard degrees. See also *independent study, distance education*.

Corsi a fini speciali. Specialized, below-university level courses taken at the university; generally vocationally oriented (Italy).

Cost accounting. Compilation and analysis of expenditures related to a task, activity, or unit of work to determine cost incurred.

Cost-of-education grant. A grant of funds to a college or university by which a public or private agency matches in whole or in part a sponsored scholarship or fellowship award; of financial benefit to the college itself. Known also as supplemental grant.

Cost-of-education supplement. A grant to a college or university by an organization or agency that sponsors employee scholarship, fellowship, or tuition-grant programs. The purpose is to pay part or all of the difference between the cost of instruction and tuition charge.

Costs per student. The total expenditure for a program or college divided by the total number of students enrolled or by the number of full-time equivalent students enrolled.

Council. A group of individuals, elected and/or appointed, that (a) advises an executive officer, such as the rector, president, or dean; or (b) sets policy for the institution or a subunit within it, such as a faculty, department, or school. Typical councils are the *university council, administrative council, faculty council, department council.*

Council of Trent. A council summoned by Pope Paul III in 1545. Sometimes referred to as the beginning of the Catholic Counter-Reformation since it concentrated on the challenges of the Protestant Reformation. It reaffirmed an emphasis on education and, to this end, recommended the establishment of a *seminary* for each diocese.

Counseling. (1) A procedure often involving conversation and questioning by which a specially trained individual, the *counselor,* assists students, individually or as a group, to make decisions such as those involving their programs of study or career choices; (2) individualized and personalized assistance in which educational and community resources are used by a counselor to help a student achieve the best success of which he is capable. See also *guidance, faculty counseling, group counseling.*

Counseling group. A situation in which counseling is accomplished by grouping students together rather than working with students individually.

Counselor. An individual specially trained to assist students to make adjustments and choices regarding educational and vocational matters; sometimes members of a faculty are assigned a number of students as counselees.

Cours complémentaires. Postprimary studies (Togo). See also *adult education.*

Course. (1) Information and organized materials pertaining to a specific subject or area of knowledge designed for presentation in a term or semester (United States); (2) a *program of study* that leads to the award of a diploma or degree (United Kingdom). Degree requirements specify completion of certain courses, either required or elective.

Course description.
A written explanation of the offerings in a specific *program of study.* Descriptions of all courses offered by a university, generally with a statement of the number of *credits* awarded for the particular course, are contained in the college or university *catalog* (United States).

Course examination.
The test generally given at the end of a course and used for assigning grades or credits.

Course number.
A number assigned to identify a course. It may designate the department offering the course, the level of the course, prerequisites for enrollment, and the level of students eligible to enroll.

Course of study.
An area of subject matter organized to permit a teacher to transmit fundamental facts and principles to a student. Courses may be either *academic* or *vocational;* they may also be *required* or *elective;* and they may be offered as *credit courses* or *noncredit courses.*

Course repetition.
Taking a course more than once to make up a failing grade, to raise a grade, or to gain a more thorough knowledge of the subject.

Course title.
The name of a course, which gives prospective students an idea of the contents of the course.

Courses in absentia.
Courses taken by *matriculated students* unable to attend regular classes but who do the work by appointment with a resident instructor.

Coursewriter.   A computer language used for the preparation of tutorial computer programs.

Court.   A formal legislative and advisory body of a university (United Kingdom, India).

Craft advisory committee.   Persons, selected from a specific trade or occupation, who advise the institution pertaining to teaching particular occupations or trades.

Crèche.   Day nursery for children one to three years of age. First started in France in 1884. Popular in Israel and East European countries.

Credentials.   Certificates or statements in the form of (a) degrees, certificates, or diplomas giving evidence that a course or academic program has been completed; (b) licenses that give the holders the right to perform certain tasks based on education and experience.

Credit.   A quantitative measure of academic work; for instance, three credits might indicate three hours of in-class instruction plus six hours of outside preparation a week for one semester. Laboratory courses usually have one half or two thirds credit value of lecture-recitation courses. See also *advanced standing credit, credit by examination, deferred credit, extension credit, military credit, professional credit, resident credit, transfer credit.*

Credit by examination.   The award of academic credit on the basis of successful completion of approved tests, often used by capable students to shorten the time required to earn a degree (United States). See also *college credit, College-Level Examination Program.*

Credit conversion.   The translation of credit earned on the basis of one type of academic calendar to equivalent credits that would have been earned on a different type of academic calendar. For example, nine hours credit in a quarter system is equal to six semester hours credit on a semester system.

Credit course.
A postsecondary course that carries credit toward an associate, bachelor's, or higher degree, whether in the given institution or by transfer to another institution (United States).

Credit granted for off-campus experience.
Academic credit awarded by an institution to students for the satisfactory completion of off-campus work or the demonstration of prior learning. Such credit may sometimes be substituted for other academic credits (*nonadditive credits*) or may be added to other credits as extra credit but not counted toward meeting degree requirements (*additive credits*).

Credit-granted unit.
In unit-cost studies, the number of students in each class who completed the term with satisfactory grades, multiplied by the number of credits earned by each student (United States).

Credit hour.
The unit used to measure the work completed by a student at a college or university. Usually one credit hour refers to one hour of classroom work, lecture, demonstration, or recitation a week, plus two hours of outside preparation, for the length of the academic term. Credit hours for laboratory work are usually calculated at one half or two thirds the amount of time worked in the laboratory. Quarter credit hours and semester credit hours are the two most common systems of measuring course work in the United States and in other countries using credit hour systems. Institutions on the *trimester plan* generally use the semester credit hour system. Courses offered in a calendar other than semester or quarter, including summer sessions, may be measured in term credit hours or stated in semester or quarter credit hours (United States). See

also *credit, semester, term, trimester, quarter credit hour, semester credit hour.*

Credit point. See *credit hour.*

Credit union. A financial association formed and controlled by the faculty and staff of an institution for the purpose of saving money and making small loans at low interest rates to members (United States).

Credit unit. See *credit hour.*

Credit validation. Conditional acceptance of a student's degree credits from an unaccredited college or university pending a student's satisfactory performance at an accredited institution.

Crédito educativo. Educational financial credit for students, which may consist of a monthly allowance, waivers for registration fees, low-cost meals, and others (Spanish-language systems). See also *educational credits, educrédito.*

Critical mass. (1) The core of high-level personnel needed to assume key positions in all aspects of society—governmental leaders and professionals such as doctors, lawyers, teachers, engineers, clergy, scientists—in order for the society to progress; (2) the number of *faculty members* needed at an institution in order to stimulate each other intellectually and scholarly. Term derived from nuclear physics.

Critique. An evaluation process whereby the professor reviews a student's work for strengths and weaknesses and offers suggestions for improvement.

Crombie code. A formula for working out the exact amounts of *compensatory recompense* for faculty and staff whose services are being terminated; takes into consideration rates of pay and length of service (United Kingdom).

Cross-cultural research. A type of research that involves studying a phenomenon in more than one cultural setting. See also *cross-cultural study*.

Cross-cultural study. Studies contrasting two or more cultures for the purpose of comparing how the cultures operate and how each attempts to solve specific problems; the comparison may be of existing cultures, ancient cultures, or ancient and existing cultures.

Cultural exchange. The reciprocal exchange of people, either individuals or groups, and the trading of exhibits and artistic performances from two or more countries in an effort to enhance appreciation of the cultures involved in the exchange.

Culturally disadvantaged. See *disadvantaged student*.

Curator. A guardian or overseer of art objects, rare books, documents, library collections, or other valuables.

Curriculum. (1) A systematic sequence of courses and materials of instruction that qualify a student for *graduation* or *certification* in a particular field, such as a liberal arts curriculum or business curriculum; (2) the total course offerings of an institution. See also *program of study, occupational curriculum, open-ended curriculum, transfer curriculum*.

Curso de orientación universitaria. A preuniversity orientation course that students must complete to be *matriculated* at a university (Spain).

Cutoff score. The point in a range of test scores that identifies minimum acceptable performance.

Cycle.

A plan of organizing the curriculum of a school system into units, generally leading to a certificate, diploma, or degree for each completed cycle or unit. For instance, secondary education in most francophone African countries is divided into a long cycle leading to the *baccalauréat* and a short cycle leading to the *brevet d'études du premier cycle* (BEPC); secondary education in Spanish systems may be divided into a basic cycle and a diversified cycle. The French university and its derived systems offer three cycles: leading to the *diplôme d'études universitaires générales* (DEUG) and equivalent qualification, the *maîtrise,* and advanced diplomas and the doctorate.

D

Daigaku.

College, university, or institute (Japan).

Dar al-hadith.

Arabic: house of religious traditions. Early type of Islamic higher education with set sectarian course contents. Attached to or independent of mosques. This type of education had almost died out by the eighteenth century.

Dar al-Hikmah.

Arabic: place of wisdom. The Cairo research center that transformed Arabic from a language of poetry and song in the pre-Islamic period into a richly renovated language, capable of translating philosophic, scientific, and technological works.

Data.

All concepts, facts, and principles used as a basis for drawing conclusions, making inferences, or carrying out investigations. Grouped data are those that have been tabulated into class intervals; ungrouped or raw data are those in the form in which one gathers them.

Data processing.

(1) The use of data processing machines for

the systematic handling of information; (2) the production of records, reports and data; (3) the classifying, sorting, calculating, summarizing, and recording of data using machines.

Dates of attendance. Calendar days designating the dates when terms or semesters begin and end, as well as the holidays, vacations, and other days when classes are not held and instruction does not take place. See also *academic year, calendar*.

Day classes. Courses conducted during the day for persons regularly enrolled in a full-time institution. See also *evening classes, part-time classes*.

Day-release courses. Courses taken by young school leavers who are released for study by their employers for one or two days a week; some of these courses include periods of evening instruction. Courses generally qualify students for technical examinations (United Kingdom and Commonwealth countries).

Dean. (1) Officer of an independent college or of a division, college, or school of a university, who is responsible, under direction of the president or other executive officer, for the administration and supervision of instructional activities (United States). The title is also used to note an administrative officer in charge of specific functions, such as academic dean—the officer in charge of instructional programs in a school or college, who may be called chief academic officer, dean of faculties, dean of instruction. Other examples include dean of students—the person in charge of student services (such as counseling and discipline) in regard to male and female students; dean of student services—the official in charge of all student services including student housing, extracurricular activities, social calendar, counseling; dean of women—the person in charge of all student services as they pertain to female students (title now in use in the United States is Associate Dean of Students). (2) Head of a faculty, often appointed or elected for a set period with eligibility for reappointment. Usually a member of the senate of the university; often a member of the university council as well (most countries).

Dean's list.

A list of students whose *grade point averages* deserve special recognition. Students so listed often receive special privileges regarding class attendance, absences, and other matters (United States).

Debating or literary society.

Generally considered the forerunner of the *fraternity* in the United States. Existing debating societies were united into a union in 1815 at the University of Cambridge, which thereby became the birthplace of the student union.

Decano.

Spanish: *dean*.

Decentralization.

A process whereby a central source of administrative responsibility allows certain functions and duties to be handled by subordinate agencies or personnel. See also *centralization*.

Decision making.

The process of choosing among alternative courses of action or policies. For example, academic decisions are traditionally made by faculties, faculty senates, and councils; administrative decisions are made by administrators with the advice of faculty bodies if the decisions involve academic policy; and general institutional policy decisions are made by ministries of education, governing boards, or other legal entities.

Dedicación exclusiva.

Exclusive dedication. Used in relation to professors who devote themselves to teaching and research full time with no outside employment (Spanish-language systems).

Dedication.

(1) Exercise held by a college or university naming a campus, area, building, or room in honor of, or in memory of, a person or persons who have given long service to the institution or made financial donations to the facility being dedicated; (2) devotion to or zeal in fulfilling one's responsibility.

Defense Activity for Non-Traditional Education Support (DANTES).

A Department of Defense agency that gives some of the standardized tests and correspondence course examinations previously administered by the United States Armed Forces Institute (United States).

Deferred credit.

Credit accepted provisionally (for instance, from an unaccredited college) until after advanced work has demonstrated the competence of the student (United States).

Deferred giving.

A program whereby individuals agree to make gifts to an institution at a future time. Involves the irrevocable transfer of funds or property by an individual by will at death (bequest) or at a specific time during the lifetime of the donor in exchange for life income either to the donor or another individual. Also called planned giving.

Deferred remuneration.

Part of the annual salary or special salary of an administrator, faculty member, or staff person that is set aside and held as a special fund until retirement. The accumulated amount paid in installments after retirement according to the agreement made when deferred salary payments began. Payments are taxable at the time they are made.

Deficiency report.

A notice informing a student that his academic performance is unsatisfactory. Deficiency reports are prepared at midterm and may be sent to parents, advisers, and other authorized persons (United States).

Degree. A title conferred by a college or university on an individual as official recognition that a program of studies has been completed or the competence equal to that gained by these studies has been attained. The degree may be a first degree, first professional degree, master's degree, doctoral or equivalent degree. See also *external degree, formal degree, honorary degree, informal degree, professional degree*.

Degree check. Reviewing courses or credits completed by students to determine students' progress toward meeting *graduation* requirements (United States).

Degree-credit student. A student whose program of study consists wholly or principally of work that is creditable toward an associate, bachelor's, or higher degree (United States).

Degree-granting authority. The power derived from governments to grant degrees. May be exercised by the president or chancellor of a university, by the university council, or by an external agency, such as a ministry of education. In the United States this power is vested in an institution's governing board which authorizes an official (usually the president or chancellor) to confer degrees.

Degree mill. See *diploma mill, fraudulent school*.

Degree of autonomy. Extent to which a governing board, ministry of education, or other authority grant academic and fiscal independence to administrative officers and faculty of an educational institution. See also *autonomy*.

Degree requirements. The educational and other standards (established by faculties or appropriate authorities) that a student must complete satisfactorily to be eligible to receive a degree.

Degree with distinction. A degree awarded to those students who have given evidence of unusual achievement in their studies and examinations, such as the bachelor's degree *summa cum laude*. See also *graduation honors, honors,* and *honours degree*.

Dekan.	*Dean* (Germany, Denmark, Norway, Switzerland, Czechoslovakia, Yugoslavia); also *dékán* (Hungary).

Democratization of education.	(1) The extension of educational opportunity to all applicants regardless of sex, or of socioeconomic, ethnic, or racial background; (2) the inclusion of representatives of all factions of the institution (faculty, administrators, students) in the governance of the institution through membership on governing boards. See also *Cogobierno, Drittelparität*.

Demonstration plot.	A special area of land used to give students practical experience in agricultural techniques or to illustrate different agricultural techniques and crops.

Demonstration program.	A program, often in the form of experiments, that has been carefully designed and prepared to illustrate specific principles, procedures, or concepts.

Demonstrator.	(1) Faculty rank: a temporary auxiliary member of the teaching staff, often chosen from among senior students; see also *graduate assistant*; (2) a person who teaches by illustration or by reproducing experiments.

Denominational college.	A college financed and administered by a religious denomination or sect.

Denominational institution.	College or university closely affiliated with or controlled by a specific religious denomination or sect.

Denominational university.	A university financed and administered by a religious denomination or sect.

Department.	(1) A major subdivision within a university

(Department of Arts and Sciences); (2) an administrative subdivision within a faculty or school (Department of Physics); (3) a noninstructional unit within an institution (personnel department).

Department chairman. A faculty member who, in addition to teaching duties, is designated to preside over departmental meetings of faculty and staff members and to perform certain administrative duties.

Department head. Synonymous with *department chairman*.

Deposit. Payment made by a student to cover certain contingencies. All or part may be refunded, depending on the charges incurred by the student. Examples include a laboratory breakage deposit or a deposit on a locker key assigned to a student (United States).

Dépôt legal. Deposition law of 1537; stipulated that a copy of every French publication be deposited with the *Bibliothèque nationale (France)*.

Deputy-chancellor. An honorary officer acting for the chancellor in his absence.

Desegregation. Elimination or modification of practices that separate (segregate) or classify students in educational institutions or programs on the basis of race (United States).

Developed country. A country that is technologically advanced and has a relatively high living standard.

Developing country. A country in a relatively early stage of industrial and educational development but working toward greater industrialization and expanding and upgrading educational opportunities.

Development. (1) Growth, expansion, maturation, as in student development or intellectual development; (2) in the United States, efforts to increase institutional resources through fund raising and increased public support. See also *institutional development, educational development, manpower development.*

Development officer. The title of an officer of a higher education institution whose responsibility is raising funds and conducting activities designed to increase resources of the institution (United States).

Dhamma. The canonical teachings of Buddha.

Dharma. Sanskrit: the destiny of the human soul, the study of which is a principal aim of Hindu and Buddhist education.

Dharmashastra. Sanskrit: the sacred laws of the Hindu religion, the study of which is an important part of Hindu education.

Diagnostic test. A *test* that yields detailed information about a student's achievement in one or more fields and is used to point out weaknesses so that remedial instruction can be given.

Didactic method. (1) A method of instruction that emphasizes authoritative guidelines; (2) any method of teaching or instruction.

Dimorphics. Science of two forms, usually applied to sex-role research, although some researchers in contemporary women's studies now are enlarging their focus.

Diplom. *Diploma.* Qualification of higher education awarded to students who have passed successfully the terminal examination, *Diplomprüfung,* in certain faculties (Austria, Federal Republic of Germany, German Democratic Republic).

Diploma. (1) A credential or qualification awarded upon successful completion of (a) secondary-level education, for instance, *diploma de* *maturità* (Italy) or high school diploma (United States); (b) postsecondary-level education, where diplomas may be awarded at below degree level, for instance, *higher national diploma*, the qualification awarded after three years of professional study in technological subjects (United Kingdom), or at degree level, such as *Diplom* (Austria and Eastern European nations); or (c) postgraduate education, for instance *diplôme d'études supérieures*. (France). (2) The document signifying the award of a degree or other academic credential.

Diploma mill.

An institution that offers diplomas and degrees without demanding usual academic achievement on the part of students. See also *fraudulent school*.

Diplomado.

Title for holder of diploma (Spanish-language systems).

Diplomarbeit.

Thesis or other work required for the award of a *Diplom* (Austria; Federal Republic of Germany, German Democratic Republic).

Diplôme.

Diploma. (1) Higher education qualification, such as *diplôme d'état de pharmacien*, a professional qualification; (2) qualification awarded after the first two years of study at a university or institute of. technology; (3) also postgraduate-level award, such as *diplôme d'études supérieures*, *diplôme d'études approfondies* (French-language systems).

Diplomeksamen.

An examination in those fields that leads to a professional qualification, such as the fields of engineering or business (Denmark).

Diplomprüfung.

Terminal examination offered by certain faculties and leading to a *Diplom* (Austria, Federal Republic of Germany, German Democratic Republic).

Diplomstudien.	Studies for the *Diplom* (Austria, Federal Republic of Germany, German Democratic Republic).
Direct cost of higher education.	Total resources allocated to higher education, including government subsidy derived from taxation (amounting to 20 percent of total educational expenditures in many countries) and the costs borne by individual students.
Direct financial aid.	A program of financial assistance designed to help students pay for the costs of acquiring an education. Direct financial aid is given to individual students in the form of *fellowships*, *scholarships*, *grants-in-aid*, *loans*, *work-study* opportunities, and others. See also *indirect financial aid*.
Directed study.	(1) The study of a specific discipline related to national manpower needs for which students may receive government scholarships; (2) a form of learning whereby a student works closely with a faculty member who assigns specific programs, courses, or research work and indicates specific steps to be followed to complete the academic work.
Director.	An administrator of a unit within an institution (for example, director of a center or institute or of a specific administrative function (for example, director of research, director of personnel).
Director of admissions.	An administrative officer charged with the responsibility of admitting students. Other titles used for the same function are: admissions officer, examiner, dean of admissions, or *registrar*.
Directory.	A university publication that contains an alphabetical listing of the names of stu-

dents, faculty, and administrative staff with their home addresses, campus addresses, and telephone numbers. Separate directories for students, faculty, and staff are also published (United States).

Disability.

A defect in physique, intellect, or behavior that makes achievement difficult or impossible. Academic or learning disabilities refer to a condition that hinders or prevents a student from making normal progress in completing standard curricula. Also called *handicap*.

Disability population.

Those members of a nation who have a *disability* that makes educational achievement difficult or impossible. See also *handicapped student*.

Disadvantaged student.

A student whose financial (economic) or cultural background is such that he or she cannot compete on an equal basis with other students in organized educational activity. A financially or economically disadvantaged student comes from a low-income family that is generally not able to provide an educational opportunity equivalent to that provided by more affluent families; the economic disadvantage is often exacerbated by cultural disadvantage, that is, the student is a member of a class or group whose values and experiences differ from those of the majority culture; thus, not knowing the values and expectations of the dominant culture, the disadvantaged student experiences rejection and frustration. See also *attrition, discrimination, dropout, wastage*.

Disciplinarity.

Specialized investigation through teaching and research of homogeneous subject matter. See also *interdisciplinarity, transdisciplinarity*.

Disciplinary action.

A measure, accompanied by penalties, imposed by officers of the institution responsible for handling student *disciplinary problems* on a student who has not followed prescribed conduct regulations. See also *discipline, disciplinary problem*.

Disciplinary dismissal. Involuntary separation of the student from the institution as a result of the student's conduct. See also *disciplinary problem*.

Disciplinary probation. A status resulting from a student's unsatisfactory conduct (excepting academic performance). The student continues to be enrolled in the institution but is required to subject himself to specific rules and regulations to avoid dismissal. See also *disciplinary problem*.

Disciplinary problem. Unacceptable conduct or behavior of a student (apart from unsatisfactory academic achievement) that is serious enough to be referred to the administrative officer, staff, or student agency responsible for *disciplinary action*. See also *discipline*.

Disciplinary standing. Status of a student based on his conduct as a member of the student body. The student may be in *good standing*, be on *disciplinary probation*, or have been subject to *disciplinary dismissal*. See also *disciplinary action*.

Disciplinary warning. An action, less stringent than *disciplinary probation*, taken by an institutional authority to warn a student that his behavior (apart from academic performance) is unacceptable. If not improved, student faces *disciplinary probation* or *dismissal*. See also *discipline*.

Discipline. (1) A broad, logically organized body of subject matter distinguished by its scholarly prestige; see also *field of study*; (2) authoritative control of student behavior through punishments or rewards; (3) self-directed efforts to pursue a course of action in the face of difficulty.

Discrimination.   (1) Ability to perceive or distinguish a given stimulus, such as a specific type of sound, smell, or visual pattern, from among similar stimuli; (2) policy of using nonrelevant factors, such as race, religion, sex, and economic background in admission, hiring, promotion, grading, and other activities that results in unfavorable treatment of an individual or a group and therby hinders or retards the individual's achievement and success. See also *disadvantaged student, equalization of access to education, integration, minority groups, racial discrimination, segregation, social discrimination.*

Discussion.   A method of instruction for a small number of students in which the emphasis is on the intellectual interaction of group members.

Discussion section.   A subdivision of a larger class that, by virtue of its restricted size, allows individual contribution in the form of discussion, question-and-answer, and other participation techniques.

Dismissal.   (1) The refusal of the institution to allow a student to continue in the institution unless he is formally readmitted; usually *academic dismissal* or *disciplinary dismissal*; (2) termination of a faculty member's employment; in relation to tenured faculty, may only be for adequate cause. See also *academic tenure.*

Dissertation.   A written report or document based on original research required to achieve the doctoral degree; generally, must be defended orally before a jury of experts in the field. Some countries (United States, Sweden) require a two- to three-year formal program of study prior to preparation of the dissertation. *Thesis* is sometimes used as a synonym.

Distance education.   Education using different media (correspondence, radio, television, or others) but requiring little or no physical attendance at the institution offering the education and the degree. Increasingly common in Europe. Referred to as *Fernunterricht* in the Federal Republic of Germany and *télé-enseignement* in France. See also *extramural education, independent study.*

Distance study.

See *distance education*.

Distance university.

See *extramural education, independent study, Open University.*

Distributive education.

A program of instruction in marketing, merchandising, and management.

Division.

A grouping for administrative purposes of two or more departments in a college or university (United States).

Docent.

Faculty rank: a member of teaching staff, often part time, below professorial rank in a university.

Doctor Honoris Causa.

An honorary degree awarded by a university for outstanding service to scholarship or society, solemnly conferred during a public ceremony.

Doctoral degree.

Usually the highest degree awarded by a university or college for completion of a specific program or for other attainment. Duration of study varies from country to country and from discipline to discipline. Requirements also vary: an examination plus a thesis (Federal Republic of Germany); two to three years of study, an examination, and a thesis (United States); a thesis based on research (the Netherlands). Distinction is also made between a research doctorate, such as the *Doktorgrad* (Denmark) or the Doctor of Philosophy (Ph.D), and a professional doctorate, such as the Doctor of Medicine (United States). The degree may also be divided into lower and higher levels: the lower is Doctorate of Philosophy (D.Phil. or Ph.D.); the higher is Doctor of Letters (Litt.D.), generally conferred for outstanding scholarship (United Kingdom). In the Soviet Union the equivalent levels are *Kandidat nauk*, awarded for three years of postgraduate study and research; and *Doktor nauk*, which is the highest degree and requires outstanding contributions. The doctoral degree or doctorate is conferred in almost every country having university-level programs of postsecondary education. Some of the foreign degree terms are *doctorat* (French-language systems); *doctorado* (Spanish-language systems); *doctorandus* (the Netherlands). See also *honorary degree*.

Doctoral thesis.   See *dissertation*.

Doctorate.   See *doctoral degree*.

Doctor's degree.   See *doctoral degree*.

Documentation center.   A center, generally specializing in a discipline such as education or medicine, either independent or attached to a university for (a) the collection of information, (b) the diffusion or dissemination of information, and (c) research and investigation in the center's area of expertise. A national education documentation center generally serves as the repository for educational publications and studies generated nationally and as the major center for national research on education.

Domicile.   The place where one has his true, fixed, and permanent home and principal establishment. A person resides there not for a special or temporary purpose but with the intention of making it a permanent home for an unlimited or indefinite period. Domicile is an important factor in relation to tuition and student fees, for tuition and fees for out-of-state students are frequently higher than for state residents in many of the states in the United States. Establishing domicile in a state often enables a student to pay the lower tuition and fee rates set by a state college or university for its own domiciliaries.

Don. Colloquial term for a university teacher (United Kingdom).

Dormitory. A residential building controlled by an institution of higher education that provides rooms and often board for its resident students. See also *cité universitaire, hostel.*

Double registration. The enrollment by a student having a superior scholastic record in undergraduate and graduate courses at the same time. Permission for such is usually granted to a student in his last term or year of undergraduate work.

Drittelparität. The sharing of decision making in university governance by a tripartite division between administrators, faculty, and students (Federal Republic of Germany).

Droit d'auteur. French: right of the author. See also *copyright, Urheberrecht.*

Dropout. A student who leaves an institution of education voluntarily before graduation or before completion of a program of study without transferring to another institution and with no expectation of returning to complete a program of study.

Dropout prevention. Activities and programs undertaken to motivate and stimulate a student's interest in his education and thereby prevent him from becoming a *dropout.*

Dropout rate. An expression of a comparison between the number of students entering a program of study on the first-year level and the number of students successfully completing the program. See also *attrition, wastage.*

Dual enrollment. Enrollment in two colleges at the same time, either in a single institution or in two separate institutions.

Due process. Procedural guarantees on constitutional and nonconstitutional grounds to citizens, as members of public or private institutions, which said institutions cannot act "arbitrarily," "capriciously," or with "manifest unfairness." In academic circles refers to grievance procedures established jointly by governing bodies, administrators, and faculty by which students, faculty, or staff who claim their rights have been violated or abrogated may obtain redress (United States).

Dueling societies. Secret societies of students that engage in the *Mensur* (duel). Dueling societies existed for centuries at universities such as Heidelberg, Hamburg, and Munich; some still exist, but the custom of dueling is dying out. Membership is for life and is reputed to assure social status.

Duplicated record. A transcribed or mechanically reproduced copy of a student's record. See also *transcript.*

E

Early admission. *Matriculation* of superior high school students prior to completion of high school. Such students may be admitted to a college or university after finishing the *junior year* of secondary school (United States).

Early decision admission. Consideration by a college or university of an application submitted earlier than usual, giving the applicant a decision in advance, usually in the applicant's *junior year* or early part of the *senior year* of secondary school (United States).

Earned degree.

A degree awarded in recognition of the fulfillment of certain academic requirements. Contrast *honorary degree.*

Easter.

One of four designations of religious origin for quarters of the academic calendar—*Hilary*, Easter, *Trinity*, and *Michaelmas*—starting in August with the Trinity quarter. Such designations were used by Oxford and Cambridge universities and later, in the United States, by Harvard College. In other United States institutions such as the College of William and Mary, a three-term calendar was adopted and the Easter term dropped; universities in the United Kingdom also later dropped the Easter term.

Ecole ménagère.

School of home economics at the secondary level (French-language systems).

Ecole normale.

Teacher training school, generally at the secondary level (French-language systems).

Ecole normale supérieure.

Advanced teacher training institution (French-language systems). Also, one of the most famous of the French *grandes écoles*, which trains highly qualified researchers and university lecturers.

Econometrics.

The application of mathematical form and statistical techniques to the testing of economic problems.

Economic effect of higher education.

Impact of education, or lack of same, on individuals and society, as reflected in individual income distribution and the national growth rate. See also *educational benefits, individual return of higher education.*

Educable mentally retarded.

A person, who because of slow mental development, needs special educational instruction to become socially adequate and literate.

Educación básica.	Basic or primary education (Spanish-language systems).
Educación media.	Secondary school, generally academically oriented (Spanish-language systems).
Educación superior.	Higher or postsecondary education in Spanish-language systems.
Educación universitaria.	University education (Spanish-language systems).
Education.	(1) Organized and sustained communication designed to bring about *learning;* (2) making available to each generation the organized knowledge of the past; (3) the socialization of the individual into his culture and environment. See also *comparative education, continuing education, cooperative education, elementary education, extension education, formal education, general education, higher education, international education, liberal education, mass education, nonformal education, postgraduate education, preprimary education, primary education, private education, professional education, public education, secondary education, technical education, terminal education, undergraduate education, vocational education.*
Education at the first level.	See *elementary* and *primary education.*
Education at the second level.	See *secondary education.*
Education at the third level.	See *higher education, postsecondary education, tertiary education.*
Education for an elite.	See *elite higher education.*
Education for the masses.	See *mass education.*
Education permanente.	*Lifelong learning;* an opportunity for *adults* to pursue education conducive to individual

advancement throughout their lives (French-language systems). See also *adult education, lifelong learning, recurrent education.*

Education recurrente. See *recurrent education.*

Educational aims. The directions set for a system of education, or an individual institution, by the educators or individuals directly concerned with that system or institution. More limited than *educational goals.*

Educational background. The previous educational experience of a candidate for admission or for employment as evidenced by school *records, certificates, diplomas,* or *degrees.*

Educational benefits. Individual or public benefits obtained from the acquisition of an advanced education. Generally used in cost-benefit analyses of the private and public costs of education.

Educational certificates. Qualifications awarded on successful completion of a specified program of education, for instance, primary, secondary, and vocational school certificates. See also *certificate.*

Educational corporation. Any chartered enterprise engaged in educational activities.

Educational credits. A 1976 national plan to provide loans to students in private institutions and to supply partial living expenses for students in public institutions (Brazil). See also *crédito educativo, educrédito.*

Educational development. (1) The implementation and further improvement of education at any level; (2) the extent of educational opportunities available to citizens of a country, often measured by the country's literacy rate.

Educational equality. A balanced access to educational facilities for all citizens without regard to economic background, race, religion, sex, or other nonacademic criteria. See also *equal oppor-tunity, equalization of access to education.*

Educational exchange. Systematic interchange of students, teachers, researchers, administrators, equipment, and materials among educational institutions and organizations in different countries. See also *exchange programs.*

Educational expenditure. Total charges incurred in running an educational institution. Includes both capital and recurrent (operating) costs.

Educational facilities. See *facilities.*

Educational finance. (1) The raising and expending of revenue for education; (2) management of the financial affairs of colleges and universities.

Educational goals. (1) Societal goals that express the values of a particular country or institution and set the direction for the education system or enterprise as a whole; (2) level of aspiration of the individual student.

Educational guidance. The process of assisting the student and his family in relating the student's interests, aptitudes, and abilities to available course options and program and career choices through counseling and informational materials.

Educational history. See *history of higher education.*

Educational innovation. Any change in educational structures and programs that differ from previously established forms. Innovations in one country or institution thus can be tradition in another. Among some twentieth-century innovations are satellite or branch campuses, academic consortia, short-cycle programs, the *Open University*, and *interdisciplinary programs.*

Educational institution. An organization such as a school, institute, college, or university created for the express purpose of formally imparting instruction.

Educational legislation.   Laws, decrees, and statutes established by the appropriate governmental legislative bodies or institutional authorities concerned with a system of education. Such laws refer to school attendance, compulsory education, and authorized levels and types of education.

Educational loan.   See *student loan.*

Educational maladjustment.   (1) Student's achievement falling below that anticipated as a result of aptitude tests; (2) poor fit between the individual's level of training and his or her career needs; (3) overproduction of manpower in certain fields and underproduction in other fields.

Educational media.   The means of communication designed to accomplish *learning.* Generally refers to audiovisual materials and technological equipment such as television, radio, computers, films, slides, and teaching machines.

Educational methods.   See *teaching methods.*

Educational mission.   A group of specialists who, under the auspices of international agencies, provide a country with technical assistance as planners, administrators, or faculty.

Educational mobility.   (1) The free movement of students, teachers, and other personnel among educational institutions within a country and across national boundaries; (2) the ability to move freely among various programs within a system of education, principally between the two main divisions of academic and vocational study.

Educational opportunity.   The ability to attend an educational institution; generally used in terms of *equal op-*

portunity. See also *access to education, equal opportunity*.

Educational placement. (1) Assignment of a student to an appropriate course, level, or institution; (2) assistance to a student in terms of improving his or her scholarship and career choices. See also *guidance*.

Educational planning. (1) On a national basis, studying and determining suitable educational institutions and programs to fulfill a nation's educational goals in terms of educational opportunities and manpower requirements; (2) on an institutional basis, allocating resources to fulfill the institution's developmental goals.

Educational policy. The general plan that guides educational decisions about how to attain a nation's or institution's *educational goals*.

Educational reform. Altering a nation's or institution's educational policy so as to cause significant improvement in financial allocation among levels of education, enrollment patterns, the nature of the curricula, or other factors.

Educational research. Study and investigation concerned with the field of education or bearing on educational problems. See also *applied research, basic research, research*.

Educational resources. Available finances, educated and trained manpower, and facilities needed to fulfill the *educational goals* of an institution, a community, or a nation.

Educational statistics. Quantitative data that describes or characterizes enrollment figures in a given institution or nation. May be based on enrollments by level of education, by sex, or by other categories.

Educational technology. (1) Application of scientific principles in designing and implementing educational programs; (2) audiovisual equipment, computers, multimedia presentations, and other equipment-oriented instructional techniques. See also *computer-assisted instruction, computer-managed instruction.*

Educational television. Preparation of instructional programs for closed-circuit or broadcast television for (a) use as an integral part of a school, college, or university course, or (b) as ancillary material designed to enrich the viewer's understanding of a subject.

Educational tests. See *achievement tests, aptitude tests, tests.*

Educational trends. Educational changes, national or international, that persist for a relatively long period and that affect the character of existing national educational institutions or education systems. Examples include the international move toward greater decentralization of decision making in the 1960s and the greater mobility of faculty and staff in the 1970s.

Educator. A teacher or educational administrator who contributes to the educational development of other persons.

Educrédito. A special fund offering loans to students at low interest rates and with adequate grace periods (Nicaragua). See also *crédito educativo, educational credit.*

Egresado. A student who has completed course requirements but not his or her thesis and thus does not receive the *licenciatura* (Spanish-language systems).

Election card. A card on which the student lists the courses for which he or she plans to register (United States).

Elective courses. Courses not required for completion of a specific program of study but selected by a student for his general interest and recognized as meeting degree requirements (United States). See also *required courses.*

Elective program.
The part of a study program selected by the student, as opposed to the part specifically required for graduation or for a degree in a particular field of study (United States).

Elementary education.
Education at the first level, generally beginning at age five to seven and lasting five to six years; in some countries a learning certificate is awarded. Also called *primary education.*

Eleven-plus.
The age of transition from primary to secondary education in British practice, originally recommended in the 1926 Hadon Report, *The Education of the Adolescent*, and a source of much controversy later when demands were made for comprehensive secondary schooling (United Kingdom).

Elite higher education.
An education system in which only a select few have access to higher education; characterized by rigid selection mechanisms at the lower educational levels, which allow only a diminishing number of students to continue from one level to another. Contrast *mass higher education.*

Elitism in higher education.
The view that a small proportion of the population possessing the highest intellectual capacity should benefit most from educational resources and from the educational efforts of society. See also *elite higher education, mass education.*

Elzevirs.
Editions of the Greek New Testament and the classics published from about 1583 to 1680 by the Elzevier Publishing House (the Netherlands).

Emergency loan.
A small loan made to a student to assist him with temporary financial difficulty; gener-

ally, does not require a formal note, carries no interest, and is repayable within the same academic term or year (United States).

Emeritus professor. A title conferred on a professor as a mark of special distinction at retirement. Emeritus status is also granted to other academic ranks. Also called *professor emeritus; professeur émérite* (French-language systems); *professor emérito* (Spanish-language systems).

Emigration. See *brain drain.*

Empirical research. Research emphasizing experience and observation, in contrast to conceptual or theoretical research.

Employee matching fund programs. Financial aid awarded by a company to employees and consisting of some percentage sharing of educational costs when the employee takes higher education courses.

Employment counseling. See *placement service.*

Encyclopedia. One or more volumes containing extensive information on all branches of knowledge or on one discipline only (*Encyclopedia of Philosophy*); articles are generally arranged alphabetically.

Endowed chair. A professorship that has a special endowment for its support. See also *chair, endowed professorship.*

Endowed college. See *endowed institution.*

Endowed institution. An institution receiving considerable income from *invested endowment funds.* Also called endowed college, endowed university.

Endowed professorship. A permanent financial provision by a benefactor to a university; the income from the provided funds supports a specific professorship. See also *endowed chair.*

Endowed scholarship.
A scholarship perpetuated by income from a fund established by a donor, who may impose specific conditions or restrictions on the recipient.

Endowed university.
See *endowed institution.*

Endowment fund.
A fund from which the income may be expended but whose principal must remain intact.

Enfermera graduada.
Graduated nurse. Title conferred on graduates of a three-year program in the School of Nursing (Nicaragua).

Engineer.
An occupational title awarded to a person who has completed the required study for a degree in engineering. In Spanish, *ingeniero*; in French, *ingenieur*.

Enrollment.
(1) The total number of students attending a given school unit, or the total attending all colleges and universities in a country (enrollment may be full-time or part-time); (2) the act of registering in an institution. See also *dual enrollment.*

Enrollment influences.
Factors that affect or influence the number of students who enroll on a particular educational level; may be economic, cultural, racial, or ethnic. See also *equal opportunity, discrimination.*

Enrollment percentage.
See *enrollment rate.*

Enrollment projections.
Forecasts of future numbers of students in an institution, group of institutions, or a nation, based on past enrollment data and demographic information.

Enrollment rate.
(1) The ratio of total school enrollment to total school-age population; (2) the ratio of students actually enrolled at a specific level

of education to the total number of persons in the appropriate age-group.

Enrollment trends. Long-term changes in the number of students who enter (a) various types of institutions, such as university education rather than technical education; (b) specific fields of study, such as arts rather than sciences. Changes in enrollment patterns may require changes in educational planning.

Enseignement alterné. Alternate education—a period of practical work alternated with a period of theoretical study (French-language systems). See also *cooperative education, sandwich plan*.

Enseignement de base. Basic education (Benin).

Enseignement en alternance. See *enseignement alterné*.

Enseignement moyen. Intermediate or middle school (Benin).

Enseignement secondaire général. General secondary education divided into a lower cycle of four years and a higher cycle of three years that leads to the *baccalauréat* (French-language systems).

Enseñanza media. Academically oriented secondary education (Latin American countries).

Ensino basico. Six-year program of basic education (Guinea-Bissau).

Ensino de adaptação. Portuguese primary schools for African students during the colonial period (Angola, Mozambique).

Ensino geral polivalente. Secondary education program with a technical emphasis (Guinea-Bissau).

Ensino medio polivalente. Intermediate level of vocational training (Guinea-Bissau).

Entrance evaluation.   The procedure that determines whether a candidate is eligible for admission under the institution's entrance requirements and what status the candidate will get under the curriculum requirements applicable to him (United States). See also *freshman standing, advanced standing*.

Entrance examination.   See *admission examination, examen de admisión*.

Entrance requirements.   See *admission requirements*.

Environmental education.   (1) The study of values, attitudes, and influences affecting a person's relationship to his or her culture and physical environment; (2) instruction in ecology.

Environmental health program.   Efforts to maintain a wholesome physical environment for students, faculty, and staff in a higher education institution. These efforts include inspection and safety measures related to food, water, air, swimming pools, and waste disposal.

Epithetology.   The study of degrees, professional titles, and designations by professional societies.

Epomidas.   A scarf, adapted to the graduate's degree and faculty, required as part of the *academic dress* for all graduates of Oxford after 1636, according to *Laudian statutes*.

Equal opportunity.   A principle that all qualified applicants be considered for postsecondary admission or employment without regard to nonscholastic criteria such as race, sex, or socioeconomic class.

Equalization of access to education.   The opening up of access to higher education to students previously excluded, such as minorities, women, and students from the lower socioeconomic classes.

Equivalence of qualifications.   A principle that stresses the acceptability, recognition, and validation by the state, by institutions of higher education, or by professional bodies of qualifications acquired in other institutions or nations. Equivalence does not imply that courses and programs of study or degrees are identical but rather that they compare favorably in level and content.

Éréttségi. School-leaving certificate awarded after twelve years of general, technical, or artistic education (Hungary).

Esame di laurea. Higher education degree awarded after four to six years of study. To qualify for the degree and the title *dottore,* students must pass prescribed courses and submit a thesis. Before being allowed to practice their profession, holders of the *laurea* must pass a state examination, *esame di stato* (Italy).

Esame di stato. State examination required for holders of the *laurea* before they can practice a profession (Italy).

Escuela normal. Secondary-level school for the training of primary school teachers (Spanish-language systems).

Escuela técnica superior. Advanced technical school offering the full three cycles of higher education and leading to titles such as architect and engineer (Spanish-language systems).

Escuela universitaria. University school offering in one cycle only, education for teachers in elementary education, business studies, and various technical areas (Spanish-language systems).

Ethnic group. A group with a common cultural tradition and a sense of identity; exists as a subgroup of a larger society.

Ethnic studies programs. Sequences of multidisciplinary courses that emphasize the language and culture of ethnic groups and that attempt to understand these cultures in their entirety. Such programs are usually characteristic of ethnically plural societies. In contrast to *foreign area studies* attention is focused more on indigenous groups and on having students from these groups understand their own origins than on understanding people of another society.

Evaluation.

(1) The process of appraising the performance of students or staff at an institution. Involves a standard, goal, or set criteria and consideration of evidence in light of these criteria. In relation to student achievement, evaluation may involve judgment of merit based on test scores but more frequently a cumulative judgment arrived at through measurements, impressions, and careful appraisals. (2) For transfer students, the study by institutional staff of academic records from another institution to estimate whether courses completed by the students are comparable to those required at their new institution.

Evaluation criteria.

The standards (a) against which a student or teacher is measured when undertaking an *evaluation* of progress or achievement; (b) the rules applied when considering a transfer student's records.

Evening class.

A course generally held during evening hours and offered in a separate division; intended both for matriculated and non-matriculated students on a part-time basis; usually leads to a degree. See also *continuing education, evening college, extension education.*

Evening college.

An independent institution, or a division of a college or university, offering classes for part-time students but maintaining academic parity with full-time programs; enables working people to take programs otherwise limited to day-time clientele. Also called evening institute. See also *extramural education.*

Evening lectures. A program continuing for nine university terms, leading to a Pass Bachelor of Arts degree, offered mainly to teachers and certain other carefully selected students who are at least twenty-one years old (Ireland).

Examen artium. Secondary school-leaving examination for formal entry to higher education (Norway).

Examen d'access à l'enseignement moyen. *Admission examination* to enter intermediate education (Algeria).

Examen de admisión. *Admission examination* to enter higher education (Latin American countries).

Examen philosophicum. Preliminary examination in philosophy given after the first or second semester of university study; permits successful students to continue their studies (Norway).

Examination. An appraisal of ability or achievement that must be met at a certain specified level by a candidate for a certificate, diploma, or degree. See also *admission examination, test.*

Examination for credit. See *credit by examination.*

Examination schedule. A schedule showing the days, hours, and places assigned for specific examinations, based usually on the class schedule or on a prearranged grouping plan.

Ex cathedra lectures. A specific way of teaching by lecture without practical demonstration and without student participation in discussions of subject matter.

Excess student credit load. *Credit hours* beyond the normal student load of twelve to fifteen credits per semester. To enroll for excess credits, a student may have to seek special approval and show high scholastic success (United States).

Excessive absences. Nonattendance to the extent that achievement in a course or program of study may be impaired; withdrawal from the course or program may be required.

Exchange of students.
Programs that deal with the interchange of students among countries for a limited time, usually one year, generally under the sponsorship of private or international agencies. See also *educational exchange.*

Exchange professor.
A professor temporarily employed in another institution or country, often trading duties with a professor from that institution or country. See also *exchange programs.*

Exchange programs.
Programs that deal with the interchange of students, teachers, and research staff among institutions of higher education in the same country or in different countries. The exchange may be directly between two institutions or under the sponsorship of private, public, or international agencies or organizations. See also *educational exchange, Fulbright Exchange Program.*

Exchange student.
A student who temporarily exchanges places with a student in another country, under the sponsorship of private or international agencies.

Exchange-visitor program.
A program authorized by the United States Department of State for students, scholars, and specialists to enter the United States for specific purposes under the sponsorship of United States institutions and agencies.

Exclusivity doctrine.
The granting of sole representation for *collective bargaining* to a teacher's union.

Excused absence.
Nonattendance that is legitimate according to the regulations of the institution.

Executive officer.
The person in charge of day-to-day administration of an institution or a subunit within an institution. The chief executive officer of an institution is called president, chan-

cellor, principal, or rector. See *administrative officer.*

Exhibition. A financial award, usually for merit, but of less value and standing than a scholarship, made to a secondary-level or university student; generally based on a competitive examination (United Kingdom and Commonwealth countries).

Exhibitioner. Winner of an *exhibition* award or a lesser scholarship (United Kingdom and Commonwealth countries).

Ex officio. Latin: by virtue of the office. A position attained by election or appointment to another council or committee, or the holding of a particular office. A president or rector may be an *ex officio* member of a governing board or council.

Expatriate teacher. A teacher employed on contract by an institution when the teacher is not a native or national of the country where the institution is located. A common arrangement in a number of former colonial countries.

Experiential education. Off-campus learning undertaken by college or university students as partial fulfillment of requirements for certificates or degrees (United States). See also *cooperative education.*

Exploratory course. Course designed to give students firsthand knowledge of a variety of disciplines and occupations and to help students in their occupational and educational choices.

Expulsion. See *disciplinary dismissal.*

Extended day cooperative education. See *cooperative education calendar.*

Extension center. An on- or off-campus facility where undergraduate, graduate, or postgraduate courses are offered but where complete curricula are not usually available. See also *extension education*.

Extension class.   A class offered under the auspices of a college, university, or adult education agency to adults who are enrolled in *extension courses* for *extension credit*. See also *extension education, extramural education*.

Extension course.   A course offered on a part-time basis in an extension center. Extension courses may or may not have counterpart courses offered on campus, but generally they are of the same level and credit value as the institution's regular courses.

Extension credit.   Credit granted for the completion of a course offered in *extension education* (United States).

Extension division.   A division of a higher education institution established to provide off-campus education.

Extension education.   Instructional activities other than those offered in regular classes on campus. Extension education includes *correspondence study*, classes for part-time students, and *evening classes*. In the United States this type of education started as courses offered for *credit* to external students in the *land-grant colleges*.

Extension services.   See *extramural education*.

Extension work.   Courses offered by the university as a community service; generally held off campus. Such courses are designed to bring people up to date in their respective fields but do not lead to a degree. See also *extramural education*.

External degree.   A degree validated by an agency or institution independent of the university offering the instructional program. See *external examination*.

External examination. Examination administered independently of the institution offering the instructional program, so that the competence of the student is certified by an independent judging agency. The University of London has served as such an agency for a number of former British colonial countries. See also *external examiner, external degree.*

External examiner. A person or agency not connected with an institution selected to administer the examinations of an institution independently. An external examiner is generally selected to ensure that examinations maintain international standards or standards equivalent to those of institutions authorized to grant degrees.

External governing authority. Agencies external to the institution, such as a government ministry or a church organization, that control the policy and decision-making powers of the institution.

External student. (1) A student who is allowed to take the examinations of a university without attending lectures; (2) a secondary school graduate unable to gain matriculation at a university but attending as a special or non-degree student.

Extracurricular activities. Out-of-class pursuits that do not fall within the scope of the academic curriculum such as student government and athletics; generally supervised or financed by the institution but not offered for academic credit.

Extramural education. Courses conducted for part-time adult students by colleges or universities, on or off campus. Seen as a method of extending the resources of the university to the community for developmental purposes (United Kingdom and Commonwealth countries). See also *extension education, independent study.*

Extraordinary professor. A professor who is employed temporarily under special contract.

F

Face-to-face tuition.   Individual instruction provided by part-time tutorial staff; one of the channels that provides feedback on a student's progress in the *Open University*. Each student is assigned to a local study center, where he meets with the tutor of the course (United Kingdom).

Fachbereich.   Study field, the equivalent of a university department (Federal Republic of Germany).

Fachbereichsrat.   Council in charge of a *Fachbereich* (Federal Republic of Germany).

Fachhochschule.   College of technology not requiring *Abitur* for entry, offering vocationally oriented programs lasting three to four years (Federal Republic of Germany).

Fachoberschule.   Two-year higher technical schools at the secondary level (Federal Republic of Germany).

Fachschule.   Colleges that train medium-level skilled personnel and confer nonacademic degrees (German Democratic Republic).

Facilities.   The buildings and outdoor areas used by a higher education institution for instruction, administration, and supportive services. See also *campus*.

Facoltà.   Italian: *faculty*.

Factory colleges.   Narrowly specialized postsecondary institutions that are totally integrated with a factory; the factory director serves as president of the college and specialists within the factory serve as faculty (Democratic People's Republic of Korea). See also *mother factory*.

Factory schools.   Schools established at factories under specific Factory Acts in nineteenth-century Britain. The 1833 Factory Act, for instance, made attendance at school a prerequisite for employment with school fees deducted from the student's wages.

Faculdad. (1) Portuguese: *faculty*; (2) an institution offering instruction in one field of study (Brazil). See also *instituições isoladas*.

Facultad. (1) Spanish: *faculty*; (2) an institution offering instruction generally in one field of study (Spain).

Faculty. (1) A major division of a university, termed a college, school, or department in some countries; sometimes it may be a separate institution similar to a college, for example, *faculdad* (Brazil), *facultad* (Spain), *fakultet* (Yugoslavia); (2) teachers and academic staff who teach, conduct research, and engage in other activities within the framework of a broad field of study; (3) the teaching staff of a postsecondary institution; (4) an ability, capacity, or skill.

Faculty adviser. A member of a teaching staff assigned to counsel students in academic and sometimes nonacademic matters.

Faculty association. A group of faculty members banded together for professional reasons. See also *faculty unionization, teacher association*.

Faculty counseling. Advising by staff members of students who are not members of their classes. Many institutions assign a given number of students to a faculty member for counseling in addition to his or her teaching duties.

Faculty member. An academic staff member who is engaged in instruction, research, or related educational activities in an educational institution. Contrast *nonacademic personnel*.

Faculty mobility. See *educational mobility*.

Faculty rank. The status of an academic staff member in relation to other staff members of the same university, for instance, *professor*, *associate professor*, *instructor* (United States); *professor*, *reader*, *lecturer* (United Kingdom).

Faculty recruitment.

Seeking out qualified persons to fill positions available on the teaching and/or research staffs of an educational institution. *Affirmative action* procedures are required in faculty recruitment in the United States.

Faculty research.

Investigation and study carried on by staff members in search of new knowledge; this may be supported by an outside agency. Usually no compensation is received by the staff member beyond his or her academic salary.

Faculty/student ratio.

The ratio of the number of teachers to the number of students in a given class, institution, or country. Also called teacher/student ratio.

Faculty teaching load.

(1) In terms of an individual staff member, the number of hours spent per week on instruction and instruction-related activities excluding nonteaching functions such as research, administration, and counseling; (2) in terms of a department, faculty, or institution, the aggregate of teaching hours spent by staff members taking into account levels of courses, full-time and part-time faculty, and other variables. See also *full-time teacher*, *part-time faculty*, *dedicación exclusiva*.

Faculty union.

An organization authorized, usually by a vote among faculty members at an institution, to represent the faculty in negotiations with the ministry, governing boards, and administration concerning terms and conditions of employment, *remuneration*, and *fringe benefits*. The faculty supports the union by paying dues. Each union has a number of officers, elected for a set period by the union members.

Faculty unionization. The organizing of faculty members into a *faculty union* as dues-paying members, allowing the union to handle negotiations with governing boards and administration regarding remuneration, fringe benefits, terms and conditions of employment. See also *collective bargaining*.

Fagrad. Subject or departmental council consisting of faculty members from a specific subject area or department (Denmark).

Failing grade. A mark in a subject that indicates performance below the level required by the department in order to be counted as credits toward *graduation*.

Fair dealing. See *fair use*.

Fair use. Rule of reason applied to the use of copyrighted material; essentially it implies that an author may quote from another author's work to illustrate or buttress his points. The new copyright law, effective January 1, 1978, specifies certain conditions that exempt a user from liability in reproducing copyrighted material (United States). In other English-speaking countries it is often called fair dealing.

Fakultet. (1) Postsecondary faculty offering instruction for four to five years in a field of study; grouped together, faculties form a university, the function of which is to coordinate the affairs of the faculties and to deal with matters of common interest (Yugoslavia); (2) faculty (Sweden and Finland).

Federãcao. Portuguese: federation; a type of university-level institution (Brazil).

Fee. A charge in lieu of tuition (in United States public institutions) or a charge for special services, such as processing admission applications, use of library, special laboratory courses, matriculation, registration, late registration, special examinations, activities programs, use of student centers, and other special services. See also *acceptance fee, admission application fee, application fee, incidental fee, matriculation fee, nonresident fee, out-of-state fee, penalty fee, privilege fee, registration fee, regular fee, special fee, tuition fee.*

Fee concession.   Waiver of fees for special reasons, such as for children of faculty members. See also *tuition remission.*

Fee refund.   A return of all or part of the fees to students who have withdrawn according to regulations (United States).

Fee waiver.   A cancellation of fees for certain students, such as student assistants, faculty, and faculty dependents (United States). See also *tuition remission, fee concession.*

Fellow.   (1) The holder of a fellowship; (2) a member of a learned society; (3) in some universities a trustee or member of the *corporation*; (4) a distinguished scholar selected to hold a teaching or research position in a college (United Kingdom).

Fellowship.   (1) A gift of money to a student generally for graduate study to support his or her enrollment as a full-time student; (2) a position in a university held by a graduate student having teaching duties as part of his or her educational program; (3) the status and emolument of a distinguished scholar (United Kingdom). See also *research fellowship, sponsored fellowship, teaching fellowship.*

Felsöfokú szakiskolák.   Higher technical institution providing advanced technical training (Hungary).

Felsöfokú technikumok.   Higher *technikum*, or technical school, providing advanced technical training (Hungary).

Feminism. Activities that promote the interests of women; in education, this is principally manifested by efforts to equalize faculty promotions and salaries of women with those of men and to make all educational programs for men (including athletics) equally available to women. See also *equal opportunity, equalization of access to education*.

Fernuniversität. An institution, similar to the British Open University, offering higher education programs leading to degrees by means of correspondence study, radio, and television (Federal Republic of Germany). See also *distance education, Open University*.

Fernunterricht. Distance teaching. Education offered via correspondence, radio, and television (Federal Republic of Germany). See also *Fernuniversität*.

Field agent. A staff member employed to represent the institution off campus and secure enrollments (United States).

Field experience. Off-campus practice, observation, or other learning activities related to a program of study. See also *cooperative education*.

Field of concentration. The area of knowledge or academic discipline that is the primary subject of a student's program. See also *major field of study*.

Field of study. An academic discipline, including both introductory and advanced courses. See also *field of concentration*.

Field study. A plan whereby students leave the campus for a specified period to undertake practical work in their area of concentration. Also called field work. See also *cooperative education*.

Field work. See *field study*.

Fifth-year student.	A student enrolled in the last year of a five-year program leading to a bachelor's degree, or a student in the last year of a *cooperative education* program (United States).
Fihrist al-ulum.	Index of Sciences. An annotated bibliography of thousands of original and translated works in Arabic by Mahmud ibn al-Nadim in the tenth century.
Final examination.	The last test given in a class or a degree program.
Final oral examination.	The last test given to a candidate for a doctoral degree, which is conducted by a faculty committee and administered orally. The candidate must defend his *thesis* or *dissertation* and otherwise satisfy the examining committee that he is qualified to receive the degree.
Finance officer.	Officer in a college or university responsible for the administration of funds and the supervision of the preparation of financial records and reports.
Financial aid.	Assistance to students to meet the costs of an education. It may be direct, that is, awarded directly to the student, or it may be indirect, that is, awarded to the institution for the benefit of all students. See also *bursary, grant-in-aid, scholarship, student loan, work-study*.
Financial aid office.	The office in a university or college responsible for providing monetary assistance and advice to students (United States).
Financial aid officer.	The person responsible for administering the financial aid program of an institution of higher education. Also called director of financial aid (United States). See also *financial aid office*.
Financial aid package.	The total assistance granted a student by an institution, including *scholarship* or *grant-in-*

aid, student loan, and *work-study* (United States).

Financial aid tender.   The offer made by a college or university to a student applying for assistance, specifying the total amount of the *financial aid package* for which he or she is eligible (United States).

Financial need.   The funds required by a student to balance his or her budget in addition to the student's own money and that available from parents and other outside sources.

Financial planning.   Planning capital outlay and operational costs of an institution.

Financial support.   Actual and in-kind funds provided for the operation, maintenance, development, and other activities of a higher education institution.

Finishing schools.   Private secondary schools or *junior colleges* that emphasize liberal arts; formerly considered the culmination of general education for women (United States).

First degree.   The initial degree conferred by a postsecondary institution, generally after three to six years of study. May be a *general* or *academic degree*, such as the *bachelor's*, or a first *professional degree* or title, such as engineer. Also called first-level degree.

First professional degree.   In the United States, a specialized degree in such fields as law, engineering, or medicine that often requires completion of a four-year general bachelor's degree before professional study. In other nations such degrees are awarded to students who directly enter four to six years of professional study and graduate with a title such as architect, agronomist, or engineer. See also *advanced degree, postgraduate degree.*

First-time student.   A student enrolling in an institution of higher education who has not previously attended any other college or university (United States).

Fiscal autonomy.

The authority vested in governing bodies or faculties to handle the financial affairs of an institution without interference by government or outside agencies.

Fiscal policy.

(1) A statement, adopted by the appropriate internal or external governing body of an institution, that outlines the principles to be followed in financial matters; (2) fixed procedures and practices regarding financial matters of an institution with changes made only by specific authorization.

Fiscal year.

A twelve-month period at the end of which financial accounts are closed and reports made. Usually either July 1 to June 30 or January 1 to December 31.

Folkhögskola.

Swedish: folk high school. A typically Scandinavian form of adult education that also achieved limited success in heavily Scandinavian-populated areas of the United States. Started in the mid nineteenth century to provide education for rural youths during the winter months, these boarding schools have remained popular; today, in addition to traditional civic education, they often also provide transitional education between basic education and higher education.

Foregone income.

Earnings forfeited by a student by not holding a job during period of study; taken into account in cost/benefit studies of postsecondary education as part of the cost to the student of continued schooling.

Foreign area studies.

The study of societies and cultures of regions of the world other than the native area of the student, emphasizing a multidisciplinary approach, indigenous languages and culture, and an understanding of the foreign society and its culture.

Foreign language requirement.

An essential requisite for a degree, such as a reading knowledge of or fluency in a modern or classical language. Such requirements have been dropped from many *undergraduate programs* but have been more commonly retained in *graduate study* (United States).

Foreign student.

(1) A student enrolled in an institution of higher education in a country of which he is not a native; also called *international student*; (2) a status governed by the type of visa held by a student. Those having immigrant status are generally not considered foreign students (United States).

Foreign student adviser.

A faculty or staff member who counsels foreign students in academic and personal matters as well as in matters concerning their alien status, such as visas, registrations, entrance permits, and employment.

Foreign student office.

The office responsible for providing counsel, guidance, and other services to foreign students in all necessary matters including entry regulations, visas, and registrations. See also *foreign student adviser*.

Forgiveness loan.

Cancellation of a loan, in whole or in part, when the student has fulfilled certain conditions, thus converting this portion of the loan retroactively into an outright *grant-in-aid* or *scholarship*. Also called loan conversion.

Form.

One of the units of the secondary school program. In Britain, form I generally enrolls students of ages eleven to twelve; in other Commonwealth countries the ages can vary widely. The *General Certificate of Education*, ordinary level, is generally taken at about age sixteen to seventeen in forms IV or V; the advanced level, after form VI (United Kingdom and Commonwealth countries). See also *grade, sixth form*.

Formal academic degree.

A Latin degree that originated prior to the twentieth century; examples are Magister Artium and Litterarum Doctor. See also *informal academic degree, formal professional degree, informal professional degree, formal honorary degree, informal honorary degree*.

Formal education.

An institutionalized program of education, prescribed by appropriate authorities, that is offered by schools, institutes, colleges, and universities established for the sole purpose of offering instruction in an orderly, planned, and systematic fashion. See also *adult education, compulsory education, informal education, nonformal education*.

Formal honorary degree.

A Latin degree conferred *honoris causa* in recognition of outstanding personal achievement; examples are Juris Civilis Doctor and Musicae Doctor. These degrees are also conferred as *earned degrees*. See also *honorary degree, informal honorary degree*.

Formal professional degree.

A Latin degree of pre-twentieth-century origin conferred in recognition of successful completion of a specific professional curriculum; examples are Chirurgiae Doctor and *Pedagogiae Magister*.

Formation professionnelle continue.

Continued professional training. A part of the recurrent educational programs designed for working adults in France. It was established by law on July 16, 1971, to provide additional training for professionals, financed by the employers to the amount of one percent of the payroll of a company.

Forum.

A program format in which two or more specialists discuss an assigned subject in a lecture-hall setting; discussants are placed on a platform before an audience, which may ask questions and give comments.

Foundation.
See *philanthropic foundation*.

Four-one-four (4-1-4).
An academic calendar consisting of two terms of four months each that are separated by a term of one month (United States). See also *calendar, semester term*.

Four-year institution.
A college or university offering four years of postsecondary-level work leading to a *bachelor's degree*. The curriculum may be in liberal arts, occupational fields, or a combination of both. See also *liberal arts college*.

Four-year junior college.
An institution combining the last two years of high school or preparatory school with the first two years of college-level study, organized and operated as a single unit (United States).

Francophone.
French speaking. Generally used in reference to African nations formerly under French rule, that is, francophone Africa. See also *anglophone*.

Franklin Book Program.
Booklift of over forty tons of books, provided by major publishing firms in the United States, to Bangladesh under the auspices of the United States Agency for International Development in 1974.

Fraternity.
Student society with a social or professional emphasis; membership usually by invitation only. Usually affiliated with other chapters on a national basis. Fraternity refers to a male society, while a women's group, popularly called a *sorority*, is more correctly known as a women's fraternity (United States).

Fraudulent record.
A record that has been intentionally altered so that it is not a true copy of the original permanent record. Usually refers to an altered *transcript*.

Fraudulent school.   A nonaccredited educational institution making unsupported, exaggerated claims about its educational program and offering certificates and degrees to individuals without requiring the academic standard of work that the certificate or degree is intended to certify. See also *diploma mill*.

Free education.   Education provided at public expense without charge to the student.

Free universities.   (1) Programs set up by dissident students and faculty, especially during the student unrest of the 1960s (United States); (2) a term used synonymously with *private* or *independent* institutions to denote institutions not primarily supported by a government and therefore free to pursue their own interests, for example, Belgian and Dutch free universities.

Freedom of speech.   See *academic freedom*.

Freedom of student press.   The right of students to publish journals and newspapers without prior censorship or fear of reprisals by institutional or governmental authorities. See also *academic freedom, Lehrfreiheit, Lernfreiheit*.

Freshman.   A student regularly enrolled in the first year of a four-year bachelor's degree program or a four-year high school program. See also *sophomore, junior, senior* (United States).

Freshman class.   All students enrolled in the first year of a four-year bachelor's or undergraduate program of study or a four-year high school program (United States).

Freshman standing.   Acceptance into a college or university as a regularly enrolled first-year student (United States).

Freshman week.   An orientation program, held before the start of the academic year, for students entering college; purpose is to familiarize them with the institution, the principles governing the wise use of time and effort, methods of study, and other pertinent facts of college life. It is also a period for tests and examinations that provide the faculty with a basis for advising and assisting freshmen in planning their programs (United States).

Fringe benefits. Compensation for faculty and staff members other than salary, such as life insurance, pension plan, medical care, *tuition remission*, and accident insurance. See also *nonfinancial fringe benefits*.

Fulbright Exchange Program. A United States program initiated by the Fulbright Act of 1946 and later expanded by the Mutual Educational and Cultural Exchange Act of 1961 (popularly known as the Fulbright-Hays Act). The purpose of the program is the exchange of students, teachers, lecturers, and researchers between the United States and more than 120 participating countries in order to improve international understanding.

Fulbright scholar. A student, teacher, researcher, or other specialist from the United States or another designated country who has been awarded a Fulbright financial grant for study, teaching, or research and travel in other countries. See also *Fulbright Exchange Program.*

Full-time day classes. Classes conducted during the day for students enrolled full-time.

Full-time equivalent enrollment. Conversion of part-time enrollments to equivalent full-time enrollments. It is determined by dividing the total number of credit hours earned by part-time students by the number of credit hours of the average full-time course load. Thus thirty hours of credit earned by ten part-time students at an institution where fifteen credits is the average full-time course load results in a full-time equivalent enrollment of two students.

Full-time student. (1) A student who is carrying a full course load as determined by the institution. Study is considered full-time when a student carries at least 75 percent of a normal course load (three to five courses) (United States); (2) a student whose primary activity is study. See also *part-time student*.

Full-time teacher. An instructor whose primary activity is teaching and research. In many Latin American countries full-time teaching is clearly defined, for example, a miminum of five hours a day in Peru; thirty hours a week in Ecuador; and forty hours a week in Brazil. See also *part-time teacher, dedicación exclusiva*.

Functional education. Education for which there is an anticipated job applicability without need for further training or study.

Functional literacy. The condition of having essential word-recognition skills for reading, and a mastery of letter forms for writing, and thus possessing the tools necessary to obtain information and express thoughts. See also *illiteracy, literacy*.

Functionally illiterate. (1) The condition of being unable to read, write, and compute sufficiently well to meet the requirements of adult life; (2) a person of such condition.

Fundamental research. See *basic research*.

Funds. See *educational finance*.

Further education. Primarily used in the United Kingdom to legally denote all full-time and part-time education for persons beyond compulsory school age, but in practice often excludes higher education provided in universities and colleges of education and is generally confined to the more technically and vocationally oriented programs of the polytechnics, regional colleges, and special colleges of further education.

G

Gakka.   Department of a faculty (Japan).

Gakubu.   Faculty, college, or school within a university (Japan).

Gakushi.   *Bachelor's degree* (Japan).

Geaggregeerde.   The most highly qualified scientific personnel who assist professors in supervising practical work, teaching, and conducting research. Appointment to this position is achieved by passing a special faculty examination. This type of appointment is slowly disappearing (Belgium). See also *agrégé*.

General Certificate of Education.   A credential earned by passing an examination set by seven university boards and the Associated Examining Board at one of two levels—the ordinary, or O-level, taken by students in form IV or V at ages 16–17, and the advanced, or A-level, taken by students in form VI at ages 18–19. This examination is nationally validated and constitutes the basis of entry requirements for universities and *further education* colleges (United Kingdom). Commonwealth countries that have not yet established their own examining boards give the Overseas General Certificate of Education Examination of Cambridge or London, also at ordinary and advanced levels.

General college.   See *general education*.

General continuation class.   A part-time class for persons under eighteen years of age who have left full-time instruction to enter the labor force; it provides general instruction rather than specific occupational training (United States).

General degree.

A university degree awarded for completion of a curriculum with a wide variety of courses and subjects. The opposite of a special degree (United Kingdom).

General education.

Instruction involving knowledge basic to all learning, as opposed to specialized education needed only by those in a particular occupation or with particular responsibilities.

General Educational Development Test.

An examination, administered to adults over nineteen who have not completed their formal high school education. It enables such adults to earn a *General Equivalency Diploma*, which qualifies them for further education opportunities or a license for different types of occupations. The test is offered through the department of education of each state or through the United States Armed Forces Institute (United States).

General Equivalency Diploma.

A credential comparable to a *high school diploma* obtained in the United States by taking the *General Educational Devleopment Test* offered through each state's department of education to students who are at least nineteen years of age and have not completed their secondary education (United States).

General examination.

A test necessary to receive a degree, covering either a variety of subjects or subjects pertinent to a specialized field of knowledge. It may be given at any level of educational achievement—bachelor's, master's, or doctoral.

Gerente.

University manager who handles financial and administrative duties and supervises nonteaching staff (Spain).

Gesamthochschule.

New comprehensive university that brings

together previously independent institutions (for example, a university, a teacher-training college, and an engineering school) and thus integrates long- and short-cycle programs and academic and professional courses (Federal Republic of Germany).

Gesamtschule. Comprehensive secondary school (Federal Republic of Germany).

Gesellenprüfung. An apprenticeship examination ending formal apprenticeship (*Lehre*) undertaken by some students in secondary stage II (Federal Republic of Germany). Also called *Gehilfenprüfung*.

G.I. Bill. Popular name for the Serviceman's Readjustment Act of 1944, which provided financial assistance for higher education to veterans of World War II. The act was amended in 1952 and 1966 to apply to veterans of the Korean and Vietnam conflicts (United States).

Gift. Money, an art object, equipment, books, or other property received from a philanthropic foundation, private individual, or private organization for use by an institution for its own purposes.

Gifted student. A student of unusual intellectual ability. See also *academic aptitude*.

Gimnazia. Academic secondary schools prior to 1959 (Bulgaria).

Gimnazija. Four-year secondary school of general education with two or more tracks (Yugoslavia). See also *gymnasium*.

Glossary. A listing and definition of terms in a specific field or language.

Goals. See *educational goals*.

Good standing.　A classification indicating that a student's achievement is satisfactory and that his or her records are clear of restrictions, thus enabling the student to continue academic studies (United States). See also *academic probation*, *disciplinary probation*.

Governance.　The exercise of authority to operate colleges and universities, delegated by constitution, charter, or statute to a person, body, or government agency. See also *academic governance*.

Governing board.　A group of persons with the responsibility of controlling and managing an educational institution; usually delegates executive functions to appointed or elected administrators and academic affairs to faculties while reserving final approval authority. Deals primarily with matters of policy. See also *board of trustees*, *corporation*.

Governmental agencies.　Any subdivisions of any local, state, or national government.

Gown.　(1) The robe of the *academic dress*; (2) a collective term meaning students, faculty, and administrators, as in "town and gown."

Grade.　(1) A rating or evaluation of a student's progress as expressed by assigning a *letter grade* or *numerical grade* or by some other method; (2) a major division of educational programs at the primary and secondary levels of education (United States). See also *form*, *mark*, *standard*.

Grade appeal process.　Procedure for appealing unfavorable grades.

Grade index.　Average of a student's reported grades, weighted according to credit and letter value (United States). See also *grade point*.

Grade point.　Numerical value assigned to a letter grade.

In the United States the grade points most commonly used are A = 4, B = 3, C = 2, D = 1, F = 0. The total grade points earned in a course are found by multiplying the numerical equivalent of the letter grade by the hours of credit in the course. See also *grade, grade point average*.

Grade point average. A measure of scholastic achievement in several courses obtained by dividing the sum of the total grade points earned by the total number of hours of course work (United States).

Grade report. (1) A teacher's evaluation of a student's achievement during a specified period of time in a specific course. (2) The official notification to a student of his or her grades at the end of a semester or term. Copies are sometimes sent to the student's parents, adviser, or other individuals or agencies authorized to receive such information. A grade report becomes part of a student's permanent academic record. See also *supplementary grade report*.

Graduado escolar. School graduate. Title conferred on graduates of the eight-year basic school (Spain).

Graduand. A student who has completed the necessary examinations and is awaiting graduation (United Kingdom and Commonwealth countries).

Graduate. (1) A student who has successfully completed an educational program and has been awarded a certificate, diploma, or degree. See also *alumni*. (2) The act of receiving an award for completion of a program of study.

Graduate admission examination. See *Graduate Record Examination*.

Graduate assistant. Faculty rank: a person below the rank of instructor who assists an instructor by performing such duties as grading students' papers, keeping records, and preparing and arranging laboratory materials. See also *teaching assistant*.

Graduate degree. See *advanced degree*.

Graduate problems course. A course allowing a *graduate student* to work on a problem independently of other graduate students. It may result in a thesis, although usually it is not so extensive a report (United States).

Graduate Record Examination. A test widely used by graduate schools to determine the qualifications of candidates for graduate study. It is administered by an outside agency, the Educational Testing Service, and designed to examine both *aptitude* and *achievement* (United States).

Graduate school. A separate school or major division of a university that administers programs for degrees beyond the first degree or the first professional degree and that may also have administrative responsibility for research programs carried out by faculty members. See also *advanced degree, advanced professional degree*.

Graduate student. A student holding a first degree who is enrolled in a program leading to a graduate degree, such as a master's or doctoral degree.

Graduate study. Pursuit of a program that leads to an *advanced degree*. It is the most specialized form of study and is oriented primarily toward thorough scholarship and proficiency in research. See also *postgraduate study*.

Graduateship. A professionally awarded qualification that gives the right to practice a profession. The terminology varies among different professional bodies. See also *associateship, licentiateship, fellowship*.

Graduation. (1) Formal recognition by an institution of a student's completion of a program of study, usually in the form of a certificate, diploma, or degree; (2) the ceremony at which such an award is conferred. See also *commencement, graduation exercises*.

Graduation check. Review of a student's records to determine whether the student has met the specified minimum educational requirements to be eligible for graduation; these requirements usually consist of total *credit hours*, hours in certain subject matter fields, semesters or quarters of residence, minimum grades, and comprehensive examinations covering major areas of study.

Graduation exercises. The formal ceremony, also called *commencement*, at which certificates, diplomas, or degrees are conferred by an educational institution upon those students who have successfully completed its requirements; after this conferral such students are called *graduates* of the institution.

Graduation honors. Recognition of outstanding achievement in an academic program or in a student's field of specialization. This is usually indicated on the diploma by the phrases "summa cum laude" (highest honor), "magna cum laude" (high honor), and "cum laude" (honor) (United States). See *degree with distinction, honors*.

Graduation requirements. See *degree requirements*.

Gradué. *Graduate* of a university (France).

Grammar school. (1) A publicly provided university preparatory school for pupils from ages eleven to nineteen (United Kingdom); (2) an elementary school (United States).

Grandes écoles. Highly competitive, elite institutions at the university level that prepare graduates for careers in commerce, industry, and specific areas of the civil service. The majority are public institutions under the secretary of state of higher education or an appropriate ministry; about 25 percent are private. Entrance examinations are highly competitive and candidates for admission have generally attended one of the *classes préparatoires aux grandes écoles* before taking the entrance examination (France).

Grandes établissements. State-funded institutions such as the *Collège de France, Observatoire de Paris*, and *Muséum national d'histoire naturelle* that are responsible for basic research of the highest order (France).

Grant. (1) An appropriation of funds by a foundation or government agency to an individual or institution; the amount and purpose of the grant and the period during which the grant is expendable are usually specified at the time the grant is made; (2) a term used synonymously with *scholarship*, a stipend given to a student for specific academic, artistic, or athletic achievement. See also *bursary, scholarship, grant-in-aid*.

Grant-in-aid. (1) Funds awarded in periodic payments to students in need of financial aid; does not imply academic distinction; (2) assistance from government or industry to an individual or institution for a specific purpose, such as a research project.

Great congregation. During the first centuries of the university, a meeting of all the masters at Oxford. Later called *convocation* (United Kingdom).

Greek letter society. See *fraternity, sorority*.

Grievance. (1) A complaint by an employee, union, or employer that a contract has been violated;

	(2) more generally, any complaint of an injustice.
Grievance procedure.	The stages by which a labor grievance is settled or appealed.
Gross National Product (GNP).	The total value of goods and services produced in a nation during a specific period (usually one year), including the total expenditures by consumers, government, and gross private investment.
Gross wastage.	The difference in numbers of all those students who enrolled in an individual institution or in all institutions of higher education in a country minus all those who actually *graduated*; this difference is used regardless of the reasons for not completing the programs (such as dropping out, failing, or enrolling in another program or institution). See also *attrition*, *dropout*, *net wastage*.
Ground breaking.	Informal ceremony to commemorate the beginning of construction of a new building. Participants generally include the donor of the building, officers of the college or university, members of the board of trustees, representatives of the architects or contractors, and public officials.
Group counseling.	The guidance and advising of groups of students on academic and career matters (United States).
Group study.	Independent study done by a group of students. There are four basic variations: (a) informal group study, in which the group organizes and conducts its own sessions; (b) informal group study with visits by the instructor; (c) directed or supervised study, in which the group is under the direction of a teacher who meets with it periodically; and (d) individual counseling in a group

study format, which differs from the other three types in that students may pursue different purposes and courses. See also *independent study*, *correspondence study*, *distance education*, *home study*, *open education*.

Grundschule. Four-year basic school for ages six to ten (Austria, Federal Republic of Germany).

Grundskolan. Nine-year comprehensive basic school (Sweden).

Guidance. Activities that aim to help students assess and understand their abilities, interests, and educational needs; formulate realistic goals for education and careers; and increase their knowledge of career opportunities. Guidance includes *counseling* and evaluating students, assisting with their personal and social adjustment, and planning and conducting guidance programs (United States). See also *educational guidance*, *placement service*, *precollege guidance*, *vocational guidance*.

Guidance personnel. People employed to carry out the guidance program of an institution; includes counselors, personnel deans, placement counselors, and guidance specialists (United States).

Guild. In medieval times, a group of masters that jointly controlled a trade or territory of work, elected one of their own as head, took oaths of obedience and fealty, and individually exercised personal control over journeymen and apprentices.

Guild organization. In higher education, a combination of personal and collegial governance that was the first organizational base for the university and has endured over the centuries. It is still apparent in those institutions that adhere to a chair-based organization.

Guru.	A teacher in a *gurukula* in ancient Hindu education (India).
Guru vidalaya.	Specialized teacher-training college (Sri Lanka).
Gurukul universities.	Independent universities, specializing in Hindu religion and philosophy and the comparative study of religions (India).
Gurukula.	A method of teaching in ancient Hindu education. Under the leadership of a teacher, *guru*, a group of not more than fifteen students studied the sacred scripts (India).
Gymnasieskolan.	Upper secondary school of two to four years based on nine years of basic education (Sweden). See also *gymnasium*, *gymnasieskole*.
Gymnasieskole.	Upper secondary school (Denmark). See also *gymnasium*, *gymnasieskolan*.
Gymnasion.	Greek term for a lower general secondary school (Cyprus).
Gymnasium.	(1) Academic secondary school; (2) nine-year academic secondary school (Federal Republic of Germany); (3) a building or room devoted to physical education (United States).

H

Habilitation.	Qualification to teach in universities, which requires a minimum of three years of work after the doctorate, a special examination, and a thesis written under the guidance of a professor (Federal Republic of Germany).
Habilitationsschrift.	Thesis presented by a candidate for the *Habilitation* (Federal Republic of Germany).
Habit.	Earliest *academic dress* for undergraduates and bachelors at the universities. A black gown fashioned on the dress of reli-

gious orders; its use was discontinued in England after the Reformation, although doctors at Oxford still retain the scarlet gown adopted about the middle of the fourteenth century.

Haksa. *Bachelor's degree* (Democratic People's Republic of Korea).

Hakushi. *Doctor's degree* (Japan).

Hall of residence. (1) A place of residence at a university (except Oxford, Cambridge, and Durham), college, or other higher education institution (United Kingdom). See also *dormitory, hostel.* (2) A part of the name of many college buildings, such as Richards Hall. (3) A university building devoted to a specific purpose, such as an alumni hall.

Handbook. A publication designed to give ready reference in a specific subject; examples are a handbook of administration and a student handbook.

Handicap. An atypical physical, health, sensory, mental, or psychological condition that adversely affects the performance of an individual.

Handicapped student. A student who is mentally retarded, hard of hearing, deaf, speech impaired, visually handicapped, seriously emotionally disturbed, crippled, or health impaired in some other way and thus requires special education and related services.

Harambee schools. Locally supported primary schools that do not receive governmental subsidies (Kenya).

"Hard" social science. Those social science disciplines that emphasize statistical accumulation and summation of empirical data.

Hauptschule. Five-year vocationally oriented school for students aged eleven to sixteen (Federal Republic of Germany).

Head of college. A position for which there are a variety of terms: *dean, master*, mistress, *principal, president, rector, warden*.

Headmaster. Chief administrator, or principal, of a secondary school (United Kingdom and Commonwealth countries, United States).

Health occupation education. Courses and practical experience designed to develop understanding and skills required by supportive personnel in health care and health services. Skills include providing diagnostic, therapeutic, preventative, restorative, and rehabilitative services.

Health personnel. Persons in the field of physical and mental health, such as physicians, psychiatrists, nurses, midwives, dentists, dental hygienists, psychiatric social workers, and therapists, whose services are directed primarily at individuals.

Health services for students. Physical and mental health services that provide college or university students with appropriate medical, dental, and nursing services.

Hebdomadal council. The central policy-forming and executive body of the University of Oxford, comprised of the chancellor, vice-chancellor, a member of the *congregation* who is de facto chairman of the council, immediate ex-vice-chancellor and the next vice-chancellor (if chosen), two proctors, the assessor, the vice-chairman of the general body of the faculties, and eighteen members elected by the congregation (United Kingdom).

Hierarchical order. See *faculty rank*.

Hierarchy. (1) The organization of faculty ranks in which each rank, except the highest (full professor), is subordinate to the rank or ranks above; (2) the administrative organization of a college or university.

High school.

Secondary school, generally comprising grades nine or ten to twelve. May be either academically or vocationally oriented, or may be comprehensive in offering both academic and vocational programs (United States). See also *secondary education*.

High school diploma.

The certificate received after successfully completing the program of a secondary school (United States). See also other school-leaving diplomas, such as *baccalauréat, bachiller, higher school certificate, high school equivalency certificate*.

High school equivalency certificate.

A document issued by a state department of education certifying that a person has completed the equivalent of a high school program; it fulfills entry requirements of some colleges (United States).

Higher adult education.

Programs offered by a college or university for adults and out-of-school youth with one or more of the following objectives: providing students with opportunities for professional or career advancement; assisting governmental or voluntary agencies in the study and/or solution of community, urban, state, and national problems; providing education for citizen responsibility; and expanding cultural knowledge and interests. These programs may be for credit or noncredit; at the undergraduate, graduate, or postgraduate levels; and for professional or nonprofessional training. They may be in the form of classes, conferences, short courses, or *correspondence courses* and may be held on campus or elsewhere. They are usually offered by a distinct administrative unit, such as an *extension division* or an *evening college*. See also *adult education, lifelong learning, recurrent education*.

Higher degree.

See *advanced degree*, *postgraduate degree*.

Higher education.

Education above the level of secondary school, provided by universities, colleges, academies, professional schools, graduate schools, teachers colleges, and technical institutions. See also *further education*, *postsecondary education*, *tertiary education*.

Higher National Certificate (HNC).

A higher education credential or qualification awarded after three or more years of part-time study in a technological field; entry requirement is generally the *General Certificate of Education*, ordinary level (United Kingdom).

Higher National Diploma (HND).

A higher education qualification requiring three or more years of full-time study; entry requirement is at least the *General Certificate of Education*, ordinary level (United Kingdom).

Higher school certificate.

A secondary school qualification obtained automatically and without examination on completion of form VII, after a total of thirteen years of education, comprising eight years of primary school and five years of secondary school (United Kingdom).

Highest education.

Education at the degree level or higher, as opposed to *higher education*, which in Greece is *postsecondary education* below the degree level.

Hilary.

(1) One of four designations of religious origin—Hilary, *Easter*, *Trinity*, and *Michaelmas*—for the quarters of the academic calendar. Originating at Oxford and Cambridge universities, it was later adopted by Harvard College. The Hilary term started in August. The present quarter system used by some 25 percent of the United States institutions evolved from this pattern. (2) Name of one of three school terms—Trinity, Hilary, and Easter—used by the College

of William and Mary in an academic calendar in 1736, which began with Trinity in late September. (3) In British universities, the three-term academic year consists of Michaelmas, Hilary, and Trinity, starting with Michaelmas in October. See also *Trinity*, *Easter*, *Michaelmas*, *Martinmas*, *Candlemas*, *Whitsunday*.

Hinayana.

Sanskrit: the pristine and elite form of Buddhism (called Lesser Vehicle), as opposed to *Mahayana* (Greater Vehicle), which had a wider appeal.

History.

(1) A written account of events concerning a nation, group, or institution that attempts to explain the relationships between events and the significance of events; (2) a field of study.

History of higher education.

A record of the events in the development of higher education institutions, either nationally, regionally, or internationally.

Hochschule.

Institution of higher education at the university level; examples are *technische Hochschule* (technical university) and *pädagogische Hochschule* (teacher-training college) (Austria, Federal Republic of Germany). See also *Fachhochschule, Gesamthochschule, Hogeschool, Högskola, Høgskole, Højskole*.

Hochschule Information System (HIS).

Cost and resource model using disaggregated cost functions (Federal Republic of Germany).

Hogeschool.

Professional university-level institution (the Netherlands).

Högskola.

(1) An individual higher education institution, generally offering professionally oriented education (Sweden); (2) the totality of the higher education system, encompassing

all institutions of *postsecondary education* at all levels (Sweden).

Høgskole. Professional university-level institution (Norway).

Højere forberedelseeksamen. Preparatory examination following special courses that enable students who have not completed the *realskole* or *gymnasieskole* to enter higher education (Denmark).

Højskole. Professional university-level institution (Denmark).

Hold. Withholding permission to register or have a transcript issued until a student has fulfilled some delinquent financial or other obligation to the institution (United States).

Holding power. The ability of an institution to retain its enrolled students; the opposite of *attrition* or *wastage*.

Home state. The state of permanent residence, that is, the state in which the student resided immediately prior to first registering in college. See also *domicile*.

Home study. Formal study with instruction conducted by mail, radio, or television. See also *correspondence study*, *independent study*.

Honor roll. See *dean's list*.

Honor society. (1) National organizations with chapters only in four-year degree-granting institutions; open to students who have achieved a high level of scholarship and fulfill the society's requirements in respect to a specific field of study. Phi Beta Kappa is the oldest and probably best known. (2) At the secondary level, an organization of high achievers (United States). See also *National Honor Society*.

Honor student.
A student whose academic performance is outstanding.

Honor system.
An agreement by students with representatives of an educational institution to regulate their own conduct according to a defined set of principles. The agreement requires that a student shall act honorably in all the relations and phases of student life. Lying, cheating, stealing, or breaking one's word are infringements of the honor code.

Honorable withdrawal.
Notation on a student's transcript indicating that he or she has withdrawn in *good standing* (United States).

Honorary degree.
A higher degree conferred by a college or university on persons who have made outstanding contributions to the welfare of humanity or who have made outstanding contributions to the welfare of the institution itself. See also *formal honorary degree, informal honorary degree*.

Honorary fraternity.
A society for which students qualify by meeting certain scholastic, social, or service standards. See also *fraternity*.

Honorary scholarship.
A scholarship, with or without a token stipend, that is granted in recognition of academic distinction, generally to honor those students who have no demonstrated need for financial assistance. See also *scholarship*.

Honors.
Describes a degree that recognizes outstanding achievement in an undergraduate or a graduate program of study. General honors are given to students who attain high grades in all their courses; special honors are given to students for outstanding achievement in the work of one branch

of study or field of specialization (United States).

Honors-at-entrance. A term indicating public recognition of high scholastic achievement by outstanding students who are entering college, used particularly on the West Coast; no monetary grant is involved (United States).

Honors before graduation. Recognition granted for excellence of scholarship to superior students; it is generally awarded at an *honors convocation* or on an honors day.

Honors convocation. A special university academic event designed to recognize outstanding scholars among graduate and undergraduate students, who are awarded certificates and prizes. *Alumni* who are outstanding in scholarship or the professions may be elected to honor societies or awarded honorary degrees on the occasion (United States).

Honors course. (1) A highly specialized undergraduate course with higher standards than those required for a pass degree; it often requires four years rather than three for graduation (United Kingdom); (2) a course for superior students emphasizing independent work and greater student responsibility, which usually frees the student from classroom attendance and regular requirements; direction and instruction are by individual professors (United States).

Honors program. See *honors course*.

Honosítás. Special evaluation of foreign applicants to higher education institutions (Hungary).

Honours degree. A university degree, generally in one main and one subsidiary area of concentration.

Graduates are rated according to three categories: first-class honors, second-class honors (which may be divided into an upper and a lower level), and third-class honors. A majority of students in the United Kingdom take honours degrees (United Kingdom and Commonwealth countries). See also *degree with distinction*.

Hood.

An item of *academic dress*, based on the Oxford-Cambridge tradition, that is worn over the *gown*, hangs down the back, and is kept in place by a neckband passing under the chin. Each university may have its own scheme of hoods, with varying colors, trimmings, and shapes to indicate the field of study, degree (bachelor's, master's, or doctor's), and the awarding institution.

Hospicum.

Communal housing provided by the University of Paris. See also *dormitory, hostel, residence hall*.

Hostel.

(1) A student residence associated with a university and governed by the university authorities or by an outside body under the university's supervision; (2) a term commonly used for student housing in East European countries. See also *dormitory, residence hall*.

House plan.

(1) A system of self-government for a living group, usually consisting of residents on one floor in a residence hall (United Kingdom); (2) a system of organizing some academic and extracurricular activities of an institution on the basis of separate dormitories, residence halls, or "houses," as at Harvard; (3) at the secondary level, a system of educational organization through which both an educational plan and curriculum development are implemented (United States).

Human resource development.	See *manpower planning*.
Human resources.	See *manpower*.
Humanism.	(1) The phase of the Western Renaissance that sought to restore the values of ancient Greece and Rome by recovering their literary works; (2) a philosophical theory that emphasizes human values.
Humanities.	The branches of learning considered to be mainly cultural, such as arts, languages, literature, philosophy, religion, and history. See also *liberal arts*.

I

Igazgató.	Principal or director of a college or institute (Hungary).
Ijazah.	Arabic: a license to teach granted in the early Islamic world to students who successfully completed their studies with an Islamic scholar.
Illiteracy.	(1) Complete inability to read or write; (2) inability to read and write sufficiently well to function within a certain culture or social or economic level. See also *functional literacy*, *functionally illiterate*, *literacy*.
Illiterate.	An adult who can neither read nor write. See also *illiteracy*.
Impact doctrine.	A legal ruling requiring that an employing institution negotiate with its faculty union over the impact of a decision that changes the terms and conditions of employment, even though the decision itself requires no negotiation (United States).
In loco parentis.	The legal concept that an institution of

higher education serves in lieu of the parents for students who are residents on its campus (United States).

Inactive student.
A student who, although matriculated, is not currently enrolled (United States).

Inauguration.
A ceremony to install a new chief executive. The ceremony may involve the governing boards, administrators, faculty, staff, and students of the institution, as well as the immediate family of the person being installed. In the United States, it is customary to invite representatives from sister institutions and other nearby institutions and sometimes from institutions in the rest of the nation or abroad; as well as representatives from appropriate academic, professional, and honor societies; and public officials of the city or town and the state where the institution is located.

Incidental fee.
A charge not specifically related to instruction, for example, a student union or center fee.

Income value.
The projected return to an individual on the investment in his or her education.

Incomplete grade.
A temporary grade given by an instructor when all required work has not been completed by a student for some justifiable reason. A permanent grade for the term is recorded when the work has been completed; if it is not completed, a failing grade may be given (United States).

Incorporated college.
A college established as a corporate body under the laws of the appropriate governmental authority.

Increment.
See *salary*.

Incunabula.
(1) Books printed before 1501; (2) works of

art or records of an early period of art or human activity.

Independent institution.   See *private institution*.

Independent study.   (1) A teaching-learning arrangement in which the teacher and the learner carry out their respective tasks and responsibilities apart from each other and communicate through media such as correspondence, radio and television, and different types of audiovisual equipment (United States). In other countries such education is often called *distance education*. See also *correspondence study, external student, home study, open learning*. (2) An arrangement whereby superior students in a college or university are allowed to choose a topic or problem to study in depth under supervision of instructors in lieu of class attendance (United States). See also *internal independent student, independent study programs*.

Independent study abroad.   Academic study outside the home country, unrelated to a *group study* program, usually for credit (United States).

Independent study programs.   *Alternative programs* for superior on-campus students, originally called *honors programs*, which were renamed on a recommendation by the National Research Council in 1925 (United States); for off-campus students the first such programs were *correspondence study* programs, developed in Germany in 1856. Other programs are *open learning, distance education, home study*.

Index.   An alphabetically arranged list of the topics or subjects in a book or study in which the location of each subject is indicated, as by page number.

Indigena.   An African not enjoying citizenship rights in Portugal's African colonies before 1961.

Indirect cost of higher education.

The output lost to a country in terms of manpower hours missed when students attend higher education institutions rather than work, as well as the cost to the individual students of *foregone income*. See also *direct cost of higher education*.

Indirect financial aid.

Funds awarded by the government, such as institutional support and subsidies, which generally benefit all students collectively. See also *direct financial aid*.

Individual instruction.

Tutorial lessons given to a single student in subjects such as music, art, and speech.

Individual return of higher education.

The income derived as a direct result of a student's investment in higher education, which usually results in a higher lifetime income than that of those people who have less education. After deducting costs of *foregone income* and direct individual expenses, graduates of higher education internationally have been estimated to reap a 17.5 percent average return on their investment in higher education. See also *income value, social benefit of higher education*.

Individualized instruction.

(1) Instruction designed to suit the convenience of the learner both as to place and time; (2) usually structured learning programs with set objectives, small learning units, and a test of knowledge or skills that provides immediate feedback or reinforcement for the learner.

Infant school.

The lower division of primary school for pupils five to seven years of age and sometimes younger (United Kingdom and Commonwealth countries).

Informal academic degree.

A degree that either represents a translation of a Latin *formal academic degree* or is an academic degree of twentieth-century origin or current issue, such as Bachelor of Arts or Master of Philosophy.

Informal course.　　A *noncredit course* that provides continuing educational opportunities for adults and out-of-school youth (United States). See also *informal education, noncredit course*.

Informal education.　　Education given outside the formal, structured educational system, often in the family and other primary groups.

Informal honorary degree.　　A degree either translated from a Latin *formal honorary degree* or an *honorary degree* originated in a language other than Latin. Examples are Doctor of Agriculture, Doctor of Political Science, Doctor of Criminology, and Doctor of Finance. See also *honorary degree*.

Informal professional degree.　　A professional degree that is a translation of a pre-twentieth-century Latin degree or is a current degree of twentieth-century origin, such as Bachelor of Agriculture, Master of Pharmacy, or Doctor of Pedagogy.

Information system.　　A collection of data organized in a systematic way that is designed to facilitate decision making within an institution, as by a *management information system*.

Ingeniero.　　Engineer. Professional qualification awarded generally after five to six years of university study, often with mention of a specialty, such as *ingeniero agrónomo* or *ingeniero civil* (Spanish-language systems).

Ingenieur.　　Engineer. (1) Abbreviated *ir*, title awarded after study of at least six years at a technical university; (2) abbreviated *ing*, title awarded by technical colleges after four years of study (the Netherlands).

Ingénieur.　　Engineer. Title of person who has completed university-level study in engineering and received the *diplôme d'ingénieur*. An additional two years of study and submission of a thesis are required for the doctorate, *docteur-ingénieur* (French-language systems).

Ingénieur industriel. Industrial engineer. False Belgian diploma, often confused with authentic title *ingénieur technicien* (Belgium).

Ingénieur technicien. Technical engineer. Technical qualification awarded after four years of study (Belgium).

Inkan-kisa. Human engineers; that is, teachers trained in teacher-training institutions (Democratic People's Republic of Korea).

Innovation. See *educational innovation*.

Inservice education. Efforts to promote the professional growth and development of workers while on the job through short-term courses that emphasize changes and innovations in the subject matter and equipment of their work or that attempt to effect attitude changes through activities such as role playing, intervisitation, demonstrations, and laboratory sessions.

Inservice education for teachers. An educational process that serves both the educational development of the employed teacher and the advancement of education. Such training for the teacher focuses on curriculum, improvement of instruction, technological changes, and new techniques and materials. It is designed to be a self-reviewing mechanism and to enable teachers to obtain higher level certificates.

Instituicões isoladas. Institutions generally specializing in one field of study (Brazil).

Institute. (1) An educational institution, such as a technical institute, a mechanics institute, or an institute of technology, offering programs of study below the degree level; (2) a separate institution, within or independent of a university, designed for teaching and/or research in a particular field of study; examples are an institute of criminology or an institute of social studies; (3) a section within a university with the role of a faculty; (4) a short course or workshop consisting of lectures and discussion topics on a specific theme. See also *conference, research institute*.

Institutional survey.

Study and evaluation of an institution by a committee, often for the purpose of accreditation. It consists of a review of the purposes of the college or university and an appraisal of its programs based on established criteria. An institutional self-survey (or self-study) is conducted by a committee or committees consisting of the institution's own faculty and staff, frequently with the assistance of outside consultants. An external institutional survey relies only on outside examiners. Both types are generally used as the basis for the accreditation or reaccreditation of institutions by the regional accrediting agencies (United States).

Institutional accreditation.

See *accreditation.*.

Institutional development.

The enhancement of the academic and physical resources and services of an institution to serve particular purposes, such as the needs of a developing nation or a need for reform and modernization of existing institutions. It often includes providing new instructional programs and equipment, and, when needed, a corresponding increase in academic competency of the faculty to implement the new programs.

Institutional research.

The collection, analysis, and presentation of information about an institution of higher education to improve understanding of the institution and its operations and to facilitate administrative and policy decisions.

Institutional research bureau.

A unit within a university that conducts research on college or university operations as well as external influences and events that may affect the institution; it thereby facilitates decision making and policy determination at all levels.

Institutional seal.

The official stamp or other symbol of an institution used to authenticate transcripts and other official records and documents.

Institutional self-management.

Arrangements giving educational institutions at any level a degree of autonomy in controlling administrative and academic matters.

Institutional support.

Financial contributions in the form of capital and recurrent grants extended to an institution of higher education by a designated governmental agency or authority or through gifts from individuals, corporations, and foundations.

Institution.

See *educational institution*.

Institution of higher education.

An organization specializing in offering *postsecondary education* programs either below degree level or at *degree* and *postgraduate degree* levels. The nomenclature of such institutions varies, including *university*, *college*, *institute*, *academy*, *center*, *conservatory*, *school of dramatic arts*. See also *higher education*, *tertiary education*.

Instituts universitaire de technologie (IUT).

University institutes of technology. Two-year institutions introduced in 1966 to offer training to higher technicians. The qualification awarded is the technical *diplôme universitaire de technologie* (DUT), which in certain cases admits the holder to the second cycle of university education. Although largely independent in their structure, IUTs are embodied within the universities (France). See also *short-cycle education*.

Instruction. A teaching process that can take many forms in addition to face-to-face communication between teacher and student: Audiovisual instruction uses illustrative materials such as slides, films, records, tapes, and models; classroom instruction takes place inside an institution of higher education in the form of lectures, discussions, experiments, or demonstrations; computer-assisted instruction uses computers to present information and evaluate student responses; correspondence instruction is conducted by mail or through other media; group instruction attempts to teach a number of persons the same subject at the same time, but not necessarily within the confines of a formal institution; individual instruction allows the learner to proceed at his or her own pace; programmed instruction uses workbooks and textbooks and/or electronic devices to provide instruction in small steps with instant feedback; remedial instruction attempts to make up for previous learning deficiencies; and religious instruction imparts the tenets and views of a religious group.

Instructional feedback. Achievement, understanding, and behavior changes evidenced by student responses to an instructor's *tests*, *questionnaires*, or problem-solving situations; used by the instructor to modify instruction.

Instructional materials. A generic term used to describe conventional items such as course outlines, textbooks, and library resource materials, as well as items that generally are referred to as *instructional media*.

Instructional materials center. See *learning resources center*.

Instructional media. The means, methods, and materials (hardware and software) involved in communicating with students; *educational technology* is used to facilitate the educational process. See also *educational technology, learning resources center*.

Instructional methods.   See *teaching methods*.

Instructional staff.   All members of an educational institution who are occupied directly with teaching or with supervision of teaching within the institution. See also *faculty, nonteaching staff*.

Instructional technology.   See *educational technology*.

Instructional television.   See *educational technology*.

Instructor.   Faculty rank: in colleges and universities, a teacher holding a rank below that of an assistant professor (United States).

Integration.   (1) The process of combining subject matter content from different disciplines into one unified course project or unit, such as interrelating psychological and sociological subject matter in the study of business; (2) in *affirmative action*, activities aimed to enroll in an institution or classroom black and other minority students with white students in order to achieve *equal opportunity* in education. See also *apartheid, segregation*.

Integrierte Gesamthochschule.   Integrated *comprehensive university* (Federal Republic of Germany). See also *Gesamthochschule*.

Intellectual migration.   See *brain drain*.

Intelligence.   The ability to learn from experience, apply the learning to new situations, and deal effectively with abstractions. A certain level of ability, as measured by tests, is considered a necessity for success in academic study.

Intercollegiate program.   Any program that utilizes the resources of more than one college or university. See also *cluster college, consortium*.

Interdisciplinarity.   The interaction between two or more disciplines, related or unrelated, through teaching and/or research programs for the purpose of integrating or coordinating concepts, methods, and conclusions; the interaction is reciprocal so that one discipline is never subjugated to another. See also *disciplinarity*, *transdisciplinarity*.

Interdisciplinary approach.   A method of study by which faculty or research workers from different fields of learning collaborate to solve a particular problem. For example, a child development problem may be studied by a team composed of a psychologist, a medical doctor, a social psychologist, an educator, and a sociologist.

Interdisciplinary course.   A course that attempts to use the findings and principles of more than one academic discipline, usually focusing on some new area of concern; it is employed in both institutions of higher education and secondary schools to solve problems involving subject matter from various fields.

Interdisciplinary professorship.   Position that allows freedom to teach and to conduct research in two or more fields of study or special areas of these fields; it is sometimes designated by a special title and often pays remuneration comparable to that of an *endowed chair*.

Interdisciplinary program.   An approach by which faculty members from several disciplines or fields of study are brought together to develop and implement a program of study that correlates the subject matter from the members' several disciplines.

Interinstitutional cooperation.   (1) The sharing of resources, faculty, experiences, services, or labor by two or more higher education institutions in order to solve educational problems or accomplish some other common purpose; (2) bilateral cooperation between the colleges and universities of developed and less developed nations. See also *cluster college, consortium, intercollegiate program*.

Interlibrary loan. Lending of library materials from one library to another to bring better service to users and financial savings to the individual institutions.

Intermediate examination. (1) A test taken between the qualifying and *final examinations* (India). (2) A test taken after two to three years of study to obtain the qualification *kandidaat*, which allows students to continue into the main stage of study for the *doctorandus* degree (the Netherlands). (3) A test taken at the end of the first year of some professional courses (especially in scientific and medical fields in New Zealand). (4) A test between the qualifying and final examinations. Exemption from the intermediate B.A. and B.Sc. examination may be sometimes obtained through the *General Certificate of Education*, advanced level (United Kingdom).

Intern. An advanced student, usually in a professional field, who is working in a hospital, health clinic, industry, business, or other agency to gain experience under the supervision of an experienced worker. The work experience is often a *degree requirement*.

Internal administration. The inner structure of an institution, composed of the administrative officers and the institutional boards and councils responsible for operating the institution. See also *administrative officer, board, external governing authority, institutional self-management*.

Internal independent student. A campus-based student in regular attendance who takes some courses as *independent study*. See also *external student, internal student*.

Internal student. A student in regular attendance at an institution of higher education. See also *external student*.

International agencies.
Nongovernmental or governmental agencies involved in planning, research, and developmental efforts, including those concerning education on a global or regional basis. Examples of international agencies are all agencies of the United Nations and agencies established by groups of governments, such as the European Economic Community or the Organization of American States.

International baccalaureate.
Secondary school-leaving qualification based on a common curriculum and a uniform set of examinations; it was developed to meet the needs of students enrolled in international or multinational schools throughout the world, especially the needs of graduates planning to enter universities outside their host country.

International cooperation in education.
See *educational exchange, educational mobility, exchange of students, exchange programs, international education*.

International education.
(1) The various methods of global educational cooperation, understanding, and exchange achieved through (a) the international content of curricula, (b) the movement of information, scholars, and students across national boundaries, and (c) technical assistance and cooperation programs between and among institutions and nations; (1) the study (whether informational or comparative) of the different aspects of education between two countries, among regional groupings of countries, or on a global basis. See also *comparative education*.

International education office.
An office within an institution of higher education that coordinates, stimulates, and develops various programs and activities

that are supportive of international education. See also *foreign student office, international education*.

International educational exchange. See *exchange of students, exchange professor, exchange programs, exchange visitor program*.

International manpower planning. The identification of the variables that generate changes in the worldwide demand for the supply of different types of manpower. The purpose of international manpower planning is to effect the most productive utilization of the educated men and women in the world community.

International organizations. Nongovernmental bodies concerned with planning, research, and development in numerous fields, including education, on a global basis. Also called transnational organizations.

International research. Cooperation of scholars from several nations in conducting pure research or research on problems of concern to mankind in several, many, or all nations of the world. The United Nations University, with headquarters in Tokyo, is created to sponsor such research on world problems, such as food production, world hunger, water supply, and energy.

International student. A student who pursues an educational program outside his or her own country. See also *exchange student, foreign student*.

International university. An educational institution that conducts research, fosters teaching, promotes training, and furthers knowledge within a distinctly global context as well as within a cross-cultural context.

Internationalization of higher education. The implementation by colleges, universities, educational organizations, governments, and individual scholars and students of the concepts inherent in *international education*.

Internship. Field experience or work in a health agency, business, industry, or other agency to help the student gain insight and direct experience related to his or her field of study, usually conducted under the supervision of a coordinator; such experience is generally required for graduation. See also *cooperative education*, *work-study programs*.

Intersession. The period between the major segments of the academic year, for example, between the end of the spring term and the beginning of the summer session; between the end of the summer session and the beginning of the fall term; or between semesters, trimesters, or quarters within the academic year (United States).

Intramural education. Courses of study given by an educational institution for regularly enrolled students on its established locations or campuses, culminating in the degrees, diplomas, or certificates that the institution is entitled to award. See also *extramural education*, *internal student*.

Introductory course. A preliminary course that prepares the student for advanced courses in the same subject or specialization.

Involuntary withdrawal. See *academic dismissal*, *disciplinary dismissal*.

Isolated institutions. See *instituições isoladas*.

Istituti superiori. Higher institutes that offer the same level programs as universities but specialize in one or a few disciplines (Italy).

Ivory tower. A figure of speech referring to an aloofness and lack of concern with practical matters and a retreat from the concerns of the world that reputedly characterize academic personnel.

Ivy League. An association of eastern universities originally organized for athletic contests, primarily football. It is composed of Brown University, Columbia University, Cornell University, Dartmouth University, Harvard University, the University of Pennsylvania, Princeton University, and Yale University. The term has since become synonymous with prestigious and elite education; competition for admission to these institutions is keen (United States).

J

Jae-ee sabeum-taehak. Second normal college, which trains teachers in a four- to six-year program for the people's, or primary, schools (Democratic People's Republic of Korea).

Jae-il sabeum-taehak. First normal college, which trains teachers in a four- to six-year program for the secondary schools (Democratic People's Republic of Korea).

Janghakkeum. Financial assistance to students for living expenses, literally "money to encourage study" (Democratic People's Republic of Korea).

Jefe de departamento. Head (or chief) of a department within a faculty of a university (Bolivia).

Jesuit institutions. Institutions owned and controlled by the *Society of Jesus*.

Jesuits. The name used for the members of the *Society of Jesus*.

Job. (1) A position of employment; (2) the employment classification to which a student is assigned in *cooperative education*, *sandwich programs*, or *work-study programs*.

Job classification.	See *job description*.
Job description.	A systematic listing of the tasks and duties of a job together with such factors as the knowledge required, personnel relationships involved, and physical and working conditions. Also called job classification.
Job developer.	An employee whose primary responsibility is to find and develop jobs for students in *cooperative education programs* (United States).
Job security.	(1) In institutions with unions, job security is provided by contract provisions that protect employees from dismissal, usually through a seniority system. Job security often includes a traditional or expanded *tenure* system (United States). (2) In a number of countries where higher education faculty and staff are civil service employees, job security is protected by civil service regulations.
Jonghap-taehak.	Comprehensive university; there is only one, the Kim Il Sung Comprehensive University (Democratice People's Republic of Korea).
Juche.	The doctrine of national or self-identity on which educational policy has been based since 1956 (Democratic People's Republic of Korea).
Junior.	A student in his or her third year of study in a four-year college or university or in a high school (United States, Canada).
Junior class.	All students enrolled in the third year of a four-year program for the bachelor's degree or in the third year of a four-year high school program (United States).
Junior college.	(1) A postsecondary institution offering a two-year program, generally leading to the *associate degree*, which is either a terminal program, leading directly to employment,

or a transfer program, allowing the student to transfer and continue education at a four-year institution. Ownership of the institution may be *public* (federal, state, or municipal) or private, that is, *independent* (Japan, United States). (2) Five-year institutions admitting students from junior high school and two- and three-year institutions admitting students who have completed secondary school. In addition to full-time programs, these colleges offer part-time programs requiring an additional year of study. A diploma is awarded on completion of the program (Republic of China). See also *community college, junior normal college.*

Junior high school.

Generally the two to three years in a school system preceding *high school*, that is, grades seven to nine or seven to eight (Republic of China, United States).

Junior normal college.

A five-year teacher-training institution that prepares teachers for elementary school and kindergarten, admitting students from *junior high school* (Republic of China).

Junior staff.

Staff members of an institution of higher education, engaged in teaching and/or research, who hold appointments below the middle ranks in the *hierarchy* of faculty ranks, such as *instructor or assistant.*

Junior year.

The third year of study in a four-year college, university, or high school (Canada, United States).

Junior year abroad.

A practice of allowing students to spend their third year of college at a foreign university; a participating student follows a program of study that is related to his or her *major field of study* and recommended and supervised by the faculty of the institution where the student is regularly enrolled (United States).

Junta.   *Council, board.* Term commonly used for a number of governing bodies at different levels in Central and South American institutions, such as *junta de directores* (board of directors); *junta directiva de facultad* (faculty board); *junta de gobeirno* (governing board); *junta de planificación* (planning board); and *junta universitaria* (university council).

K

Kandidaat.   Qualification awarded after three years of nonterminal study that gives the right to complete an additional three years for the first degree (the Netherlands).

Kandidaat-examen.   An examination given after the first three years of study to qualify for the additional three years of study for the first degree (the Netherlands).

Kandidaatti.   First degree in higher education awarded after three to six years of study (Finland).

Kandidat.   (1) First degree in higher education awarded after three years of study (Sweden); (2) title of person holding the first degree (Sweden). See also *candidatus.*

Kandidat nauk.   Candidate of science. Degree awarded after three years of postgraduate study and research (Union of Soviet Socialist Republics, Bulgaria). See also *doctoral degree.*

Key alumni.   Outstanding graduates or former students of a higher education institution, who often work closely with the institution's admissions or fund-raising offices.

Kibbutzim.   Agricultural, communal settlements cooperatively managed by members (Israel).

Kindergarten.   Usually one year of preprimary education for small children aged four to six years;

generally part of the formal school system. See also *crèche*.

Knowledge.   The totality of facts, truths, principles, and information to which man has access.

Knowledge test.   An examination designed to measure the recall of specific information about a subject, that is, to bring out whatever relevant information is stored in the memory. See also *achievement test*.

Kodeung-hakkyo.   Secondary school or high school (Democratic People's Republic of Korea).

Kollel movement.   A Lithuanian movement in the late 1870s that encouraged young married Jewish scholars to study the Talmud and related literature for several years on a full-time basis.

Kombinationsutbildning   See *combination courses*.

Kommunal högskoleutbildning. A type of higher education administered by local education authorities (Sweden).

Konsistorium.   Governing board of a university (Denmark).

Kontaktstudium.   *Postexperience* courses (Federal Republic of Germany).

Konzil.   An advisory council to the rector of a university; membership is drawn from the different units of the institution (German Democratic Republic).

Koran.   The sacred book of Islam. Also spelled Qu'ran.

Korporationen.   *Fraternities* with a predominantly conservative outlook that died out during World War II but revived afterward (Federal Republic of Germany).

Kozasei.   Academic chairs, roughly comparable to departments (Japan).

Kurator.   Official, appointed by the Crown, in charge of the financial affairs of a university (Denmark).

Kürsü.   Academic chairs, several of which comprise a faculty (Turkey).

Kuttab.   Koranic school at the primary level; it is now being replaced in many Arabic-speaking countries by the general primary school.

Kyowon-taehak.   Two-year training school for kindergarten teachers (Democratic People's Republic of Korea).

L

Laboratory.   An area appropriately equipped for conducting experimental research.

Laboratory school.   A primary or secondary school generally under the direct control of, or closely associated with, a teacher-training institution, whose facilities may be used for demonstration, experimentation, and student teaching. See also *normal school*.

Laboratory studies.   Investigations that are conducted within an area equipped for experimental research.

Land-grant college.   An institution established by the first Morrill Act of 1862 and supplementary legislation, which granted public lands to the states for the establishment of colleges to provide full-time educational opportunities in agriculture and the mechanic arts; such institutions are known as colleges of agriculture and mechanic arts or land-grant colleges and universities (United States).

Language of instruction.

The language used in conducting classes in a given institution or nation.

Lapsed grade.

An incomplete grade that has been allowed to become a failure because the required work was not completed by the date specified (United States).

Lateral aid.

Assistance extended from one country or institution to another. See also *bilateral aid*, *multilateral aid*.

Latin grammar school.

A secondary school that stresses the classics in preparation for the university. First established by the Romans, it almost died out during the Middle Ages, was revived during the Renaissance, and then spread throughout Europe and to the United States. Remained popular in many countries until demands for comprehensive schools increased after World War II. See also *gymnasium, lycée, lyceum*.

Laubach reading method.

Way of teaching reading skills, developed by Frank Laubach, that is characterized by the expression "Each one teach one," that is, every literate person teaches an illiterate one. Key words and word configurations are used to represent the various sounds of a language to facilitate learning.

Laudian Statutes.

Regulations also called the Caroline Code, adopted for the University of Oxford in 1638 by William Laud, chancellor of the university and Lord Archbishop of Canterbury. They laid down, among other things, strict specifications for the dress of heads, fellows, and scholars at the colleges and stipulated the academic dress for each degree and faculty.

Laurea.

The single academic degree awarded by Italian universities after four to six years of study, depending on the field. Programs are set at the national level and require prescribed examinations and a *thesis*. The title awarded is *dottore*. In the future the laurea is expected to become the second of three university degrees. See also *esame di laurea*.

Law school.
An independent institution or a specialized unit within a university offering training for lawyers.

Layoff rights.
Rights, granted a tenured faculty member who is terminated as a result of a shift in student enrollments or because of financial exigency, to hold prior claim to his or her position if it is reinstated within two or three years (United Kingdom).

Learner.
One who acquires skills or knowledge of a field through instruction, experience, or training; student.

Learning.
Any change in behavior, information, knowledge, understanding, attitudes, skills, or capabilities that can be retained and cannot be ascribed to physical growth or the development of inherited behavioral patterns.

Learning library.
An adult education venture, made possible through the National Endowment for the Humanities, whereby educational opportunities are offered to the public through the use of library and museum resources in metropolitan areas (United States).

Learning resources center.
A specially designed area in an institution with a wide range of supplies and equipment for use by individual students or groups. Available are books, programmed materials, and audiovisual equipment and supplies.

Leave of absence.
(1) An authorized, extended absence of a

faculty or staff member with *remuneration* from the institution; it does not affect tenure. (2) Formal status signifying that a student who is not currently enrolled is in *good standing* and eligible to return at a specified date (United States).

Lecteur.

Faculty rank: *lecturer*. Temporary faculty member of foreign nationality (may be a graduate student), who serves as a language teacher for the academic year; appointment, which is renewable, is by the rector on recommendation of the faculty (France, Switzerland). See also *lecturer*.

Lecture.

(1) The oral transmittal in one session or meeting of an organized body of knowledge given by a professor or expert; (2) a method of teaching by which the professor gives an oral presentation with little class participation, such as questioning, taking place. See also *seminar*.

Lecture series.

An educational program, consisting of a number of lectures on a common theme, which may or may not be offered for credit. Although attendance for the entire sequence is usually encouraged, attendance at individual lectures is often permitted (United States).

Lecturer.

Faculty rank: (1) full- or part-time member of the faculty employed by a college or university to teach or lecture on a particular subject. Usually does not perform all functions of a full-time faculty member (United States). (2) The most common rank in higher education below those of reader and professor, which are reserved for heads of departments or higher officials (Commonwealth countries). (3) In other systems, a full- or part-time position, often for language teaching, for instance, *lecteur* (France), *lector* (the Netherlands), and *Lektor* (Austria,

Federal Republic of Germany, Switzerland, Denmark, Norway).

Legacy.

(1) Money or property left to an individual or an institution by a will; (2) the son or daughter of an alumnus or graduate of an institution (United States).

Legis doctor.

Latin: Doctor of Law. Probably the first doctoral degree, granted by the University of Bologna immediately following the charter of Bologna by Frederick I in 1158.

Legislation.

See *educational legislation*.

Lehre.

Formal full- or part-time apprenticeship, under the auspices of corporative organizations of industry, commerce, agriculture, or professions, for students in secondary stage II (ages 16–18/19) (Federal Republic of Germany).

Lehrfreiheit.

Teaching freedom. The part of a principle known as *Lehr-und Lernfreiheit*, first promulgated at the University of Halle in 1711, stipulating that university teachers should have the privilege to enjoy freedom of teaching, enquiry, and publication without coercion from any source (Federal Republic of Germany). See also *Lernfreiheit, academic freedom*.

Lektor.

Faculty rank: *lecturer* (Austria, Federal Republic of Germany, Switzerland, Denmark, Norway).

Lernfreiheit.

Learning freedom. The part of a principle known as *Lehr-und Lernfreiheit* stipulating that students should have the privilege to study and do research without hindrance through administrative coercion (Federal Republic of Germany). See also *Lehrfreiheit, academic freedom*.

Letter grading system. A method of judging students' performances on *tests* and *examinations*. See also *numerical grading system*.

Liberal arts. Form of education established in medieval times, so named because it constituted the education appropriate to free men, as opposed to slaves. The curriculum was composed of two parts: the lower level, *trivium*, consisted of grammar, rhetoric, and logic; the upper level, *quadrivium*, consisted of literature, geometry, astronomy, and music. The term refers to fields of study distinct from *technical* and *professional education*. See also *liberal arts college, liberal education, professional education, technical education*.

Liberal arts college. (1) A higher education institution in which the principal emphasis is on a program of liberal or general undergraduate education leading to a bachelor's degree. Preprofessional and professional training may be offered, but not with primary emphasis. Some institutions may also confer the master's degree, generally in only a limited number of fields and seldom in a professional field. (2) One of the major divisions of a university comprised of various components offering liberal arts or nonprofessional subjects (United States).

Liberal education. Education emphasizing general rather than professional knowledge. See also *liberal arts, liberal arts college*.

Libertad de cátedra. Freedom of the chair. Term used in Latin American countries to denote the privileges of the *catedrático*, the full professor. See also *academic freedom*.

Librarian. In a college or university library, an administrator of the acquisition and organization of materials of all kinds, as well as of the public service, reference, and bibliographical functions that give faculty and students access to those materials. Specific kinds of librarians include acquisitions librarians; catalog librarians, circulation librarians, periodicals librarians, and reference librarians.

Library. A building equipped to house books and other materials of communication, receive materials to be systematically cataloged and classified, and make the materials available to the specific public to be served, such as a college community.

Library card. A card issued by a library entitling a person to borrow books.

Library catalog. A listing of books or other materials in a library with bibliographical data for each work.

Licence. First degree received after three or four years of study in higher education. In arts and science subjects, students complete two years of basic education (first *cycle*); the *licence* is then awarded after one year in the second cycle (French-language systems).

Licencia secundaria. Secondary school-leaving qualification awarded in one of four specialties, humanities, technical, general technical, and agricultural study, after a total of twelve years of study (Chile).

Licenciado. Title of holders of the *licenciatura*, the first degree of higher education in Latin American countries.

Licenciatura. First degree of higher education in Latin American countries, awarded after studies extending from three or four years (education and social work) to six years (law and engineering). The title used is *licenciado*. In professional fields titles denoting the specialty are used, such as *arquitecto* and *ingeniero*. See also *titulo professional, professional degrees*.

Licentia docendi. License to teach bestowed on teachers by the church in medieval Europe. See also *Habilitation, venia docendi, venia legendi*.

Licentia ubique docendi. Early degree, which conferred the right to teach in other nations, awarded by European universities after the Renaissance.

Licentiateship. A qualification awarded by a professional body that gives the right to practice a profession (United Kingdom). See also *associateship, graduateship, fellowship*.

Licentiatus. Second degree awarded after five to seven years of study in fields such as law, dentistry, technology, theology, economics, engineering, and philosophy (Denmark, Norway).

Lifelong learning. The process by which an adult continues to acquire knowledge, formally or informally, throughout his or her life, either for vocational or professional advancement or for personal development. See also *adult education, recurrent education*.

Limited fiscal autonomy. Authority for fiscal affairs of an institution that is shared by internal bodies and external agencies. See also *fiscal autonomy*.

Lisans diplomasi. First higher education qualification, generally received after four years of study (five to six years in veterinary study and medicine) (Turkey).

Lise. The upper level of a secondary school, which is divided into two levels (the lower level is called the *orta okul*). The upper level provides specialization in the humanities or sciences (Turkey).

Literacy.

(1) The ability to read and write, generally at a level established by national norms; (2) a mastery of fundamental learning skills and knowledge sufficient for an individual to function in his or her own culture. Contrast *illiteracy*. See also *functional literacy*.

Literacy campaigns.

Coordinated efforts to increase the level of literacy (as expressed by the percentage of the total population that is literate) that have been undertaken by a number of developing nations. Among nations reporting almost total literacy as a result of such efforts are Cuba and the former Democratic Republic of Vietnam. Such campaigns mobilize large numbers of students and adults as teachers for short periods of time.

Literacy classes.

Courses organized, often during a *literacy campaign*, to achieve *functional literacy* among adults. In most cases, teachers are students and other volunteers under the guidance of special government authorities or personnel from schools or higher education institutions. See also *literacy*.

Literacy program.

See *literacy campaigns*.

Literary student magazine.

A journal dedicated to the encouragement of creative and artistic efforts by students, consisting of short stories, poetry, plays, photography, and line drawings by students. See also *student press*.

Lizentiat.

First degree in arts, law, and sciences granted after a minimum of six semesters in Swiss universities in the German-speaking cantons. Examinations and a short thesis are required for the degree.

Loan.

See *student loan*.

Loan commitment.

A formal agreement by an institution to make a given amount of money available to a student for a given time (United States). See also *student loan*.

Loan conversion.   See *forgiveness loan*.

Loan program.   See *student loan program*.

Local education authority.   (1) A county council required to provide stipulated educational facilities in its area. The *further education* sector, for instance, falls under local education authorities (United Kingdom). (2) A board of education or board of trustees that is appointed either wholly or in part by a municipal authority to control higher education institutions, with financing determined by the municipal authorities.

Loi d'orientation.   The Higher Education Orientation Law passed on November 12, 1968, which defines the goal of French higher education and determines the organizational framework of French universities.

Lower division.   The first two years of a four-year baccalaureate degree program. At some institutions it is an administrative unit that provides the general education portion of a student's curriculum, as distinguished from the upper division where specialization occurs (United States).

Lower division student.   Student in the first two years of a four-year program, generally a *freshman* or *sophomore*.

Lower secondary education.   The first portion of the secondary school program. Examples are *junior high school* (United States); the first *cycle* of four years of secondary school leading to the *brevet d'études du premier cycle* (ages 11–16) (French-language systems); secondary stage I (Federal Republic of Germany); four-year *ciclo básico* (Colombia). See also *secondary education*.

Luboks.   Popular Russian prints with great artistic

value displayed in the Lenin State Library. Earliest prints of the collection, printed from wooden and copper boards, date back to the seventeenth century.

Lump sum appropriation.
Government grants awarded in a single amount to an individual institution or faculty member, leaving the division or allocation of the grant to the institution or faculty member. Also called a bulk grant.

Lycée.
Upper secondary schools that award the *baccalauréat*, the traditional route to university admission (French-language systems). See also *lyceum*.

Lyceum.
(1) The gymnasium where Aristotle taught; (2) a classical, academic, upper secondary school common in many countries; also called *lukio* in Finland, *liceu* in Portuguese-language systems; (3) an organization, the Lyceum Movement, founded in Massachusetts in 1826 by Josiah Holbrook, to improve village schools. The movement achieved limited national exposure (United States). See also *lise, lykeion, lycée.*

Lykeion.
Greek term for an upper general secondary school (Cyprus).

M

Machine-readable cataloging.
A technique for converting library card-catalog data into machine-readable form for processing by computers.

Macrosociology of higher education.
A branch within the sociology of higher education that focuses on the relationship between the system of higher education and the wider social structure. An example is curricular changes in response to changes in the nation's occupational structure. See also *microsociology of higher education.*

Madrassa.
Arabic: ungraded Islamic center of ad-

vanced learning, attached to a mosque, offering advanced and specialized instruction. Most creative period of the madrassa was the five centuries following Mohammed's flight from Mecca (A.D. 622), when it became identified with the interpretation and propagation of Islam. The so-called traditional sciences (theological doctrine, jurisprudence, and codification of Arabic language and grammar) were taught in these centers, whereas the rational sciences (algebra, botany, and optics) were mostly cultivated in the hospitals and libraries. Many of the early madrassas are still in existence. Also spelled madrassah, medersa.

Maestro de educación primaria.

Primary school teaching qualification achieved in a secondary-level teacher-training institution (*escuela normal*) in some Latin American countries. The countries use somewhat different nomenclature, including *maestro normal, maestro normalista, maestro primario*, and *profesor normal*.

Maestro normal.

Primary school teacher qualification achieved in a secondary-level teacher-training institution (Argentina, Panama).

Maestro normalista.

Primary school teacher qualification awarded to a graduate of secondary-level normal school (Nicaragua).

Maestro primario.

Primary school teacher qualification achieved in a secondary-level teacher-training institution (Cuba). See also *maestro de educación primaria, maestro normal, maestro normalista*.

Magistar.

Academic qualification, generally making the holder eligible for academic research, awarded after two years of specialized training, which follows four to five years of study for the first professional qualification, or the university diploma (Yugoslavia). See also *magister, master's degree*.

Magister. (1) Degree awarded in certain fields, such as pharmacy and social and economic sciences, or after the examination for teacher certification (Austria); (2) qualification granted after a minimum of five years of study (*magister artium*) that generally prepares graduates for research (Denmark, Iceland, Norway); (3) first qualification of higher education after five years of study (Poland); (4) degree in humanities, social sciences, or education awarded to students who have fulfilled all the requirements for the doctorate but have not submitted a thesis (Federal Republic of Germany); (5) honorary title awarded to persons who have completed the first degree (Finland). See also *maisteri, magistar, master's degree*.

Magisterkonferens. The final examination for the *magister* qualification (Denmark).

Mahavihara. Sanskrit: Buddhist university composed of several *viharas* (colleges); most influential in the seventh and eighth centuries A.D. See also *vihara*.

Mahayana. Sanskrit: Great Vehicle; a branch of Buddhism primarily practiced in Tibet, Nepal, China, and Japan. Mahayanists hold it to be the earliest form of Buddhism. The ancient learning center at Nalanda was primarily oriented toward this form of Buddhism. See also *Hinayana*.

Mahayana sutras. Sanskrit: Scriptural narratives of the canonical literature of the *Mahayana* branch of Buddhism, which is made up of various syncretistic sects that usually emphasize compassion and universal salvation. See also *Mahayana*.

Main campus.   The principal land areas and facilities used by an institution of higher education for instruction, research, administration, and service. See also *branch campus*.

Maintenance of membership.   A union-security provision in a contract, whereby workers join a union voluntarily but, once they have done so, must remain members for the duration of the contract. See also *unionization*.

Maintenance of the institution.   The continuous monitoring of institutional facilities to ensure that grounds, buildings, and equipment are kept in usable condition. See also *maintenance staff*.

Maintenance staff.   Those people, including carpenters, painters, masons, tinsmiths, locksmiths, electricians, and plumbers, who ensure that buildings, grounds, and equipment stay in good repair and in usable condition. See also *maintenance of the institution*.

Maisteri.   Honorary title received by those who have achieved the first degree (Finland).

Maître-assistant.   Faculty rank: position below *maître de conférences* that involves tutoring and directing practical work as well as lecturing under the direction of professors and *maîtres de conférences* (French-language systems).

Maître de conférences.   Faculty rank: position below that of professor (French-language systems).

Maîtrise.   Higher education qualification awarded after four years of study. Gives access to the third cycle of higher education and is necessary to obtain the *agrégation de l'enseignement secondaire* (France). See also *master's degree*.

Major field of study.   The area of specialization in which a student concentrates his or her study. The number of credits or courses constituting a major are usually specified by the college or university and by state *certification* regulations (United States). See also *major-minor system, minor field of study*.

Major-minor system. A system that sets degree requirements in terms of minimum *credit hours* in the major field of study and in any minor (secondary) fields (United States). See also *major field of study*.

Makeup examination. A test given to a student who missed a final examination with an acceptable excuse or who wishes to remove a mark of incomplete from his or her records (United States).

Maktab. Arabic: a type of primary school, attached to a mosque, that was one of two major types of educational institutions exclusively for Muslims during the era of Muslim rule in India—approximately from the thirteenth to the sixteenth century. See also *madrassa*.

Management. The process of controlling, planning, and organizing the work of others in order to determine and accomplish set objectives. See also *management by objectives*.

Management by objectives (MBO). A comprehensive system for personnel and other management that minimizes the use of power and maximizes control of administrative processes through a clear specification of goals.

Management information system (MIS). Record keeping and data retrieval by an institution that provide reliable information quickly for use in administrative or management decisions.

Management of information system. Computer programming to manage a student's learning, test the student, and on the basis of test results make decisions regarding the student's program; thus it plans a complete learning sequence and selects the instructional tasks to achieve it.

Management-rights clause.

The section of a union contract that outlines management's rights to run a business. Since professors at some colleges and universities traditionally have held certain rights that in industry are considered management rights, this has presented some problems in faculty *collective bargaining* (United States). See also *collective bargaining, unionization*.

Mandatory admission.

A ruling, laid down by statute in some states, which provides that admission to state colleges and universities may not be denied to applicants who have a high school diploma from an accredited high school (United States).

Mandatory salary increases.

Automatic wage increases for university employees within a set salary scale. See also *salary*.

Manpower development.

The identification, establishment, and maintenance of educational programs in accordance with employment opportunities and societal needs, as indicated by *manpower planning* dictates. See also *manpower requirements*.

Manpower forecasting.

See *manpower planning*.

Manpower needs.

See *manpower requirements*.

Manpower planning.

(1) Identification of the variables affecting the demand for and supply of different types of manpower at a given future date, used to determine what types and levels of education are needed; (2) the process of matching the supply of manpower with the requirements of the economy and national development. See also *manpower development, manpower requirements*.

Manpower requirements.

The occupational composition of the population needed to achieve certain *manpower planning* targets for the development of a nation, industry, or community. See also *manpower development*, *manpower planning*.

Manpower resources.

Human resources; the educated personnel available to fulfill the *manpower requirements* of a nation, industry, or community. See also *manpower development*, *manpower planning*, *manpower requirements*.

Manual.

(1) A booklet or leaflet describing tests, books, or other materials and providing information about the use of the materials described; (2) a handbook containing instructional, informational, and/or reference materials relative to a specific field or area of activity, such as university administration. See also *handbook*, *teacher's manual*.

Manu-shastra.

Sanskrit: the Hindu code book of social law depicting or intending to effect the ideal human society.

MARC system.

Machine-readable cataloging in libraries (United Kingdom).

Mark.

A rating of achievement or academic progress assigned on the basis of some predetermined scale, such as letters (A, B, C, D, F), numbers (4, 3, 2, 1), words or phrases ("outstanding," "satisfactory," "needs improvement"), or percentages. See also *grade*, *letter grading system*, *numerical grading system*.

Martinmas.

In some universities the first and fall term of the academic year, named after the Feast of St. Martin, which is observed annually on November 11. The other terms are *Candlemas* and *Whitsunday*. The more common names are *Michaelmas*, *Hilary*, and *Trinity* (United Kingdom).

Mass access system.

In higher education, an educational system

that enrolls about 50 percent of the country's secondary school graduates.

Mass education.

(1) Universal schooling of all children at the elementary level; (2) various large-scale activities (by press, radio, television, and government) to disseminate information to or influence the opinion of the general public; (3) popular education offered to large, unorganized groups.

Mass higher education.

The opposite of *elite higher education*. The articulation of about 50 percent of a country's secondary school graduates to some form of postsecondary education.

Mass media.

The types of communication that reach large groups of persons with a common message, for example, radio, television, motion pictures, books, and magazines, in contrast to the types of communication used for limited communication with a single person or a small group of persons.

Master.

(1) An expert in a subject or skill; (2) the title of the chief administrative officer of certain academic institutions; (3) probably the first title awarded in early universities. From the twelfth to fifteenth centuries the titles *master* and *doctor* were often used synonymously, although master more frequently signified a practitioner in the crafts and guilds and doctor signified a teacher. During the fifteenth century the master became secondary to the doctorate. See also *master's degree*.

Master's degree.

In English-language institutions a second or higher degree following the bachelor's degree, generally requiring one to two years of specialized study, an examination, and/or a thesis. Examples are Master of Arts (M.A.) and Master of Science (M.S. or M.Sc.). See also *advanced degree, graduate degree, magistar, magister*.

Master's thesis.

A written report giving the results of study and original research undertaken to partially fulfill the requirements for a *master's degree*.

Matching funds.

A requirement that a state or community or both must match each dollar expended by the federal government for a specific educational purpose (United States).

Matching gift.

A method of voluntary gift support to universities and colleges by corporations, by which the corporation matches a gift by an employee to an institution of which he is an alumnus. Other voluntary gift support may include: matching tuition fees paid by an employee to an institution, based on the employee's length of tenure; service contract grants in which the gift by the corporation is based on services received from the institution, such as consultant and placement services, provided for in the service contract; and gifts in kind, that is, new or used equipment, or real estate (United States).

Maternity leave.

A leave of absence of varying length routinely granted by law in many countries to female staff members prior to and immediately following the birth of their child.

Mathas.

Sanskrit: temple schools mainly in southern India that were organized by outstanding teachers (*acharyas*) in the tenth century A.D. A few evolved into colleges with a structured curriculum and other resemblances to modern institutions of higher learning. The most famous flourished at Ennayiram, Southern India, in the eleventh century.

Matriculated student.   A student who, having fulfilled all requirements for admission, has been formally admitted and registered in a postsecondary institution. See also *admission requirements, maturity examination*.

Matriculation.   The formal admission and registration, which sometimes includes a formal ceremony, of a student in a higher education institution. See also *admission*.

Matriculation examination.   See *maturity examination*.

Matriculation fee.   A nonrefundable fee required by many colleges of every student at the time of first enrollment (United States).

Matura.   See *Reifezeugnis*.

Maturità.   Secondary school-leaving diploma, generally awarded after five years of secondary education and completion of the *maturity examination (esame de maturità)*. The diploma specifies the nature of the secondary studies: classical, scientific, technical, commercial, nautical, geometrical, technical study for girls, tourism, translation, vocational, applied arts, primary education, or arts (Italy).

Maturity examination.   A preparatory examination, the successful completion of which insures a student of entry into a university and the rights and privileges of the students enrolled at that particular institution. See also *Abitur, baccalauréat, bagrut, general certificate of education, maturità, Reifeprüfung*.

May 7th schools.   Residential educational establishments offering a combined work-and-study experience and upgraded training for cadres, senior civil servants, and professionals. Thousands of these schools were established in response to a letter by Mao Tse-tung on May 7, 1966 (People's Republic of China).

Measurement. Used for evaluative purposes; generally refers to *examinations* and *tests* of students' progress.

Mechanic arts. Practical knowledge and skill in the trades and related science; a term prevalent during the latter part of the nineteenth century (United States). See also *Morrill Acts*.

Mechanical aptitude. Projected ability, indicated by appropriate tests, to succeed with the study and work concerned with machines and mechanical processes. See also *aptitude*.

Mediation. A procedure in *collective bargaining*, used when negotiations have reached an impasse, that allows a third party, agreeable to both the union and the employer, to assist the parties to come to an agreement. See also *arbitration*.

Medical school. (1) A specialized unit within a university offering training for those studying to become medical doctors and occasionally nurses and allied health personnel; (2) an institution specializing in the discipline of medicine only. In some countries such schools are largely proprietary institutions.

Medical service. An on-campus service staffed by physicians, nurses, and other health personnel for the purpose of providing health care to students.

Medium of instruction. (1) The principal means by which a plan of instruction is communicated to a learner; examples are *face-to-face tuition*, books, tapes, records, mail, radio, television, or some other audiovisual means or combinations of means; (2) the principal language used to communicate in the instruction process. See also *language of instruction*.

Meester in de rechten. Master of Laws. Qualification at the level of *doctorandus* awarded by a faculty of law after six years of study; gives the right to practice law (the Netherlands).

Megaversity. See *multiversity*.

Memorial gift. A donation or establishment of a fund in memory of an individual or a family. Such gifts are made to establish salary funds, loan/fellowship/scholarship funds, and special purpose funds, as well as *endowed chairs* and professorships.

Memory. Knowledge or awareness of something previously learned or experienced; vital to the learning process.

Mensur. Duel. A common practice for centuries among students in the dueling societies at many German universities. Although the popularity of the practice is decreasing, a number of such fraternities still engage in it (Federal Republic of Germany).

Mental ability. See *ability, aptitude*.

Mental deficiency. See *mental retardation*.

Mental health service. A medical program available to students and faculty on many campuses for the prevention and treatment of mental and emotional disorders (United States).

Mental maturity. The state of full development of an individual's mental capacity or ability.

Mental retardation. A human condition characterized by one or several of the following: slow rate of maturation, low learning capacity, poor socialization, and below normal intellectual functioning. Depending on the degree of retardation, such persons are classifiable as uneducable mentally retarded or *educable mentally retarded*, the latter being those who can profit from education if given special help.

Mentally gifted.   A term describing a person who has intellectual ability well above average. See also *academic aptitude*.

Mentally handicapped.   A person whose general intellectual functioning is deficient to the extent of hindering achievement.

Merger of institutions.   (1) The absorption of one or more smaller institutions by a larger institution of higher education. For instance, in the United States specialized institutions have been merged with larger universities to form a college, school, or faculty within the larger university. In the United Kingdom some forty institutions have been formed by mergers. (2) The combination of two or more previously independent institutions into one larger institution, such as the National University of Zaire, which was formed by combining three previously independent institutions; in the United States a number of mergers of private universities with private or state universities and women's colleges with male colleges have taken place. Mergers of institutions take place for many various reasons, such as to realize economies of scale, to extend and broaden the curriculum, and to permit national control of higher education.

Merit increase.   Salary raise based on the performance of the individual employee and the employer's perceived value of the individual's services and skills. See also *salary*, *mandatory salary increase*, *step increase*.

Merit pay.   *Remuneration* paid to an employee in accordance with the perceived quality of work performed.

Merit rating program. A method of evaluating and appraising the effectiveness of teaching and nonteaching personnel against a predetermined scale of standards of performance, used in determining salary and wage increases or promotions. See also *merit increase*.

Merit scholar. A junior or senior in high school who has successfully passed the *National Merit Scholarship Qualifying Test* and is thus entitled to a scholarship from the National Merit Scholarship Corporation (United States).

Merit scholarship. A stipend or special recognition awarded to a student for certain types of proficiency (academic, artistic, or athletic) or as an encouragement toward high achievement. See also *merit scholar*, *National Merit Scholarship Program*.

Mesivta. See *yeshivah*.

Mess. A temporary boarding house run by a combination of students who desire to share expenses (India).

Mestiços. Portuguese: persons of mixed ancestry.

Michaelmas. The first of the three terms of the academic calendar in British and Commonwealth universities. See also *Easter*, *Hilary*, *Trinity*.

Microfiche. A four-by-six-inch transparent sheet of film that contains seventy to ninety pages of text optically reduced. A special machine is needed to enlarge the text so that it can be read.

Microfilm reader. A machine that can enlarge the text of *microfilm* so that it can be read.

Microforms. Microreproductions, such as microfilm and

microfiche, produced photographically on either transparent or opaque materials of a size too small to be read by the unaided eye.

Microsociology of higher education.

A branch of the sociology of higher education that is concerned with social relations within the higher education process, for example, the detailed study of the social psychology of the classroom.

Middle-level occupation.

An occupation at an intermediate level between a trade and a profession, preparation for which usually requires a two- to three-year program of postsecondary study.

Middle school.

A separately organized and administered school, usually beginning with grade five or six, with a program designed specifically for the early adolescent learner (United States).

Midmanagement.

Junior administrators usually in charge of coordinating responsibilities; the level of management below *top management*.

Migrant education.

A program of instruction and services for those children who move periodically with their families from one school district to another in order that a parent or other member of the immediate family may secure seasonal employment.

Migrant students.

Children who are forced to move from one school to another as a result of a parent's frequent changes of residence in pursuit of employment in seasonal agricultural activities. Very often such migration hinders educational progress. The same problem applies to children of nomads.

Mikhlalah.

A postsecondary institution providing courses of study accredited by recognized universities and awarding qualifications up to the first degree but not above (Israel).

Military credit.   Academic credit awarded to former service-
                              men upon admission to a college or univer-
                              sity; given for competency and learning at-
                              tained by serving in, and by attending
                              educational programs of, the armed forces;
                              system developed under egis of the Amer-
                              ican Council of Education (United States).

Military education.   Instruction to enhance an individual's
                              knowledge of the science and art of war;
                              generally taught in specialized institutions.

Military school.   An institution, the primary purpose of
                              which is to train its students in the science
                              and art of war. See also *military science*.

Military science.   (1) A generic term applied both to the in-
                              struction of *ROTC* students and to the de-
                              partment offering the instruction; (2) the
                              science of war, such as tactics and strategy;
                              (3) also a major or field of concentration in
                              a military school.

Minister.   (1) A high officer of government entrusted
                              with the management of a division of gov-
                              ernmental activity, such as a *minister of ed-
                              ucation*; (2) a person authorized to carry out
                              the various functions of the church, that is,
                              ordained clery.

Minister of education.   A cabinet-level officer in charge of the *min-
                              istry of education* and the provision of edu-
                              cation within a nation, who reports directly
                              to a cabinet, council of ministries, parlia-
                              ment, legislature, or head of the national
                              government. The responsibilities are often
                              subdivided according to educational level;
                              for instance, the minister of higher educa-
                              tion deals with postsecondary institutions.

Ministry of education.   Government agency of cabinet rank admin-
                              istering state-supported educational affairs;
                              often postsecondary institutions are di-
                              rected by a ministry of higher education.

Minor field of study. A secondary field of knowledge in which a student concentrates some study. The number of *credit hours* constituting a minor is usually specified by the college or university in state *certification* requirements (United States). See also *major field of study, major-minor system*.

Minority education. (1) Special educational programs provided for *minority groups*; (2) efforts to augment minority access to educational programs by providing financial assistance.

Minority group. Any recognizable racial, religious, ethnic, or social group in a community that suffers some disadvantage due to prejudice or discrimination. This term as commonly used is not a technical term and is often used to refer to categories of people rather than groups, and sometimes to majorities rather than minorities. For example, though women are neither a group (but rather a social category) nor a minority, some writers call them a minority group. In contrast, a group that is privileged or not discriminated against but still a numerical minority would rarely be called a minority group.

Misconduct of student. Violation by a student of implied or established rules governing student behavior.

Mishnah. A collection of Jewish laws from before the year 200 A.D., governing the religious, legal, economic, and social life of Jews. A basic subject in institutions offering an intensive program of Jewish education.

Missionary college. Educational institution established and operated by a religious body as a part of its missionary effort. Many such institutions were established during the colonial period in Africa, Asia, Oceania, and South America.

Mobility. See *educational mobility*.

Modern languages.   The study of contemporary foreign languages as contrasted with ancient or classical languages. See also *classical languages*.

Modular scheduling.   Organization of uniform portions, or modules, of time that are combined in various multiples, as appropriate for various courses and activities. Each module is generally a fraction of the usual time required for a class period.

Module.   (1) A segment of a highly complex subject area that involves less than a semester's work and that often cuts across departmental lines; see also *interdisciplinary study*; (2) unit of a flexible system of scheduling lasting fifteen to thirty minutes with classes extending over several units; (3) a group of students taking the same course in a modular system.

Moniteur.   A student responsible for tutoring a small group of junior students (French-language systems).

Monitor.   (1) In some Portuguese-language systems, generally a fifth-year student who assists with tutorials. (2) In English-language systems, a student assistant responsible for routine tasks, or a more mature student who assists a teacher or a professor in class instruction. Monitors were the mainstay of the monitorial or Lancasterian system of education, which was based on assembly-line techniques and introduced by Joseph Lancaster in the late eighteenth century. He was able to minimize the costs of education by using monitors for administrative as well as teaching tasks. The system was popular all over the world but competed with the madras system introduced by Andrew Bell, which also used monitors as teachers and tutors.

Monograph.   A complete but not extensive treatise on a subject.

Monolingual.   Knowing or using only one language. See also *bilingual, multilingual*.

Monotechnics.   Colloquially used for colleges exclusively devoted to teacher training (United Kingdom).

Morrill Acts.   Legislation passed by the United States Congress granting public lands for the establishment of colleges. The first Morrill Act, passed in 1862, specified instruction in agriculture, mechanic arts, and military tactics without excluding scientific or classical studies. The second act, passed in 1890, provided for an annual appropriation to each land-grant college; later amendments increased the original amounts. See *land-grant colleges*.

Mortarboard.   Common name for the square headdress with tassel worn as part of academic dress; a gold tassel designates the doctor's degree (United States).

Mother factory.   A large factory established in several major colleges with the task of providing equipment, machines, and tools for smaller *factory colleges* unable to produce their own materials. In 1959 each college and technical school was required by law to assemble a factory for training and production purposes (Democratic People's Republic of Korea).

Mother tongue.   The language of one's native land. Also called native tongue.

Motivation.   (1) An external or internal influence inciting a person to action; (2) the act of providing certain incentives to arouse a student's interest so that he or she will perform in a desired fashion.

Mouvement du 22 mars 1968.
The student revolt that started at the suburban campus at Nanterre on this date, later spread to other areas, and led to a complete restructuring of the French system of university education as codified in the *loi d'orientation*.

Mühendislik.
Qualification equivalent to a degree of Bachelor of Science in engineering, requiring from four to six years of study depending on the branch of study (Turkey).

Mühendislik doctora.
The degree of Doctor of Engineering (Turkey).

Mu'id.
Arabic: assistant; the lowest rank in the academic hierarchy in the early Islamic universities.

Multidisciplinary.
See *interdisciplinary*.

Multihandicapped student.
A student having more than one handicapping condition. See also *handicapped student*.

Multilateral aid.
Assistance extended to a nation or an institution by several foreign institutions or nations. See also *bilateral aid*.

Multilingual.
Having equal facility in several languages. See also *monolingual*, *bilingual*.

Multimedia instruction.
An educational process by which learning is promoted through overhead transparencies, slides, photographs, motion pictures, lectures, and tapes, which are used together with written materials (textbooks, and study sheets) and computerized programs.

Multinational corporations.
Business companies that buy, produce, and sell in many countries and often have worldwide operations or impact.

Multiple application. Simultaneous application for admission to two or more institutions of higher education for the same term.

Multiple campus institution. Public or private college or university with one *main campus* and several *branch campuses*, domestic or foreign.

Multiple-choice test. An examination in which the student is asked to choose the best answer from several possibilities; a recognition-type test.

Multiversity. A recent term used to refer to (1) a large, complex university with a wide variety of *undergraduate* and *graduate programs*, (2) a university consisting of a *main campus* and several *branch campuses*; (3) a university composed of many separate and partially autonomous institutions.

Municipal institution. An institution controlled by a local government authority; its board of trustees is appointed either wholly or in part by the local authority; its facilities are erected and maintained and its revenues determined by the municipal authority. See also *local education authority*.

Museology. The science or profession of museum organization, equipment, and management.

Museum. An institution that acquires, researches, and exhibits material evidence of man and his environment, such as objects of art, artifacts, and science, for the purpose of study, education, and enjoyment. Some colleges and universities have their own museums and operate them as part of the educational program and as a general service to the public.

Museum education. Formal and informal education programs carried on by museums.

N

Na'ib al-tadris.

Arabic: deputy professor; the second highest rank in the academic hierarchy of the early Islamic universities.

Named professor.

Appointment designed to attract distinguished scholars. The position includes an income from a fund established specifically to augment the regular salary of the professor holding this appointment. See also *remuneration*.

Napoleonic University.

The highly centralized university structure created by Napoleon Bonaparte in 1806. Faculties of the former universities were accorded legal status and financial autonomy as professional schools of medicine, pharmacy, and law, and faculties of science and letters, but were placed under the jurisdiction of a Grand Master and a council in Paris; primary and secondary institutions were also included. The institutions were uniform in curricula, teaching methods, and degrees. The Napoleonic University remained in force until 1896, when the institutions were again regrouped into universities. A number of the South and Central American universities were influenced by the professional emphasis of the Napoleonic University.

Nastavnik.

Teacher in a lower advanced school or *junior college* (*više škole*) (Yugoslavia).

Nation.

(1) Ancient territorial division of matriculated students derived from the *nationes* in the continental European universities, dividing the student body into groups according to permanent domicile. The practice was common in Germany, Finland, Sweden, and the United Kingdom. (2) An independent country.

National Council of YMCAs.

An organization within the British Young Men's Christian Association (YMCA) that helped to found residential adult education colleges in Great Britain after World War II.

National Defense Student Loan. See *national direct student loans*.

National direct student loans. Federally funded need-based loans available to students through the institution of attendance. The loans carry minimal interest after graduation (United States).

National educational system. The total organized educational structure of a nation, including private and public institutions, generally divided into three levels—primary, secondary, and postsecondary—and also including other organized educational services, such as adult education and youth programs, if they are delivered in structured programs under appropriate authorities.

National Honor Society. An organization established under the egis of the National Association of Secondary School Principals, designed to honor outstanding high school students. Selected by secret vote of the faculty; only 15 percent of students in the graduating class are eligible (United States).

National Interlibrary Loan Code. A code, adopted by the American Library Association in 1976, which governs lending relations among libraries on the national level (United States).

National Labor Relations Act. Commonly called the Wagner Act; passed in 1935, it is the basis for government oversight of labor relations between private employers, including private colleges and universities, and their employers (United States).

National Labor Relations Board. Created by the *National Labor Relations Act* to oversee labor relations; rules on disputes between private employees. Its decisions may be appealed to the federal courts (United States).

National language.

See *mother tongue*.

National Merit Scholarship Program.

A program awarding scholarships to a certain number of secondary school students who score highest on the *National Merit Scholarship Qualifying Test*, organized by the National Merit Scholarship Corporation. Of the approximately one million students who took the test in 1976, 3850 received a scholarship award and became known as National Merit Scholars (United States).

National Merit Scholarship Qualifying Test.

An examination giving seven scores, including English, mathematics, social studies, natural sciences, word usage, a selection score, and an average score, taken by second-semester juniors and first-semester seniors in high school to qualify as National Merit Scholars (United States).

National norm.

Statistic based on scores achieved by students in a representative nationwide sample; used to interpret test scores.

National scholarships.

A limited number of scholarships awarded to promising students throughout the nation by a higher education institution (United States).

National service.

The placement of recent university graduates in graduates in positions of national need as teachers, administrators, and extension agents at low salaries and for a set period of time as a form of restitution-in-kind for scholarships or free education. Such a service has been introduced in a number of developing countries. In addition to providing needed manpower, often in outlying areas, it affords valuable work experience for graduates. See also *bonding, study service*.

National teachers association.

An association of teachers within a country; the association often represents primary and secondary as well as higher education teachers, and it draws its membership from the entire nation. See also *teachers association*.

National Union Catalog.

Maintained by the Library of Congress since 1901, the National Union Catalog is the central record of the locations of important titles in the major research libraries of the United States and Canada. The catalog contains entries for more than twelve million titles cataloged before 1956, which was the year the Library of Congress began to publish current cataloging entries in book form for the easier access of scholars.

National university.

(1) A university that, by virtue of its services to a country and the quality and extent of its educational offerings, has been deemed of national importance and thus receives most or all of its funding from the national government; in many cases the funding agency also retains certain financial or administrative authority; (2) a university founded by a national government and designated as a national university.

Naturalism.

An educational philosophy which stresses that which is natural to man rather than emphasizing an imposed set of standards and values.

Naučni saradnik.

Learned fellows; the highest level of university fellows (Yugoslavia).

Need analysis.

A study of a student's total financial resources—including the student's and the parents' income, assets, expenses, and liabilities—to compare the amount of money available for the student's education with the cost of such education; determines how much financial aid the student needs. The financial need may be reassessed annually, and it varies according to the number of college-age youths within a family. For large families the need may be greater, even though the family income is substantial.

Negro colleges.

Postsecondary educational institutions established specifically for black citizens of the United States, mainly during the period of *segregated education*. These institutions still train larger numbers of black professionals than the nation's other institutions of higher education (United States).

Nepotism.

Special consideration that is given to a person's or persons' relatives for appointments to positions.

Nepotism rules.

A policy forbidding the employment of a husband and wife or other close relative in the same university or department within a university. See also *antinepotism rules*.

Net student wastage.

A concept that modifies the *gross wastage* figure by excluding students who have derived benefit from their courses and might later transfer to other institutions, carrying with them the qualifications achieved when dropping out.

Nichiren Shoshu Buddhism.

A form of Buddhism that arose in thirteenth-century Japan and is the basis for the lay movement *Soka Gakkai*, which is the most powerful and most higher education oriented of the New Religions that have arisen in Japan since World War II.

Night school.

See *evening class*.

No-currency exchange.

An exchange program involving arrangements between universities whereby students move from a university in one country to a university in another on a head-for-head, bed-for-bed basis. Tuition is paid by the student to the university in his or her own country.

No-grade course. A course that is graded not by numerical or letter grades but by a rating, such as "pass" or "fail." Such courses generally cannot be considered in determining a student's *grade point average* (United States).

No-growth enrollments. See *steady state*.

Nonacademic education. Technical and professional rather than literary or artistic education; it is practical rather than theoretical in nature. See also *academic education*.

Nonacademic personnel. A general term applying to employees of academic institutions whose functions are either to assist academic staff or to provide general services to the *academic community*.

Nonadditive credit. Academic credit, awarded by an institution to students for work experience under *cooperative education*, that takes the place of credits normally earned through formal courses or independent study. Contrasted with *additive credit* (United States). See also *credit granted for off-campus experience*.

Noncollegiate hostel. A boarding house for students, under private management as opposed to a *collegiate hostel*, that is managed by the institution of higher education (India).

Noncredit course. A course for which the student does not receive academic *credit* toward a degree or a diploma (United States).

Noncredit student. A student registered in a course to take part in discussions, exercises, and laboratory work but not to take the final examination; the student thus does not receive *credit*. Differs from an *auditor*, who does not participate in class activities (United States).

Nondegree-credit student.　See *noncredit student.*

Nondenominational college.　A college that is not funded by and has no affiliation with a religious denomination or sect. See also *denominational institution.*

Nondenominational university.　A university that is not funded by and has no affiliation with a religious denomination or sect. See also *denominational institution.*

Nondiscriminatory education.　A policy of equal opportunity, that is, no bias as to race, religion, sex, socioeconomic background, or ethnic origin, in the admission or examination of students and the employment of faculty and staff at an institution of higher education. See also *affirmative action*, *equal opportunity.*

Nonfarm agricultural occupation.　A vocation that does not require residence or experience on a farm but is concerned with the processing and distribution of agricultural products and supplies.

Nonfinancial fringe benefits.　Services and benefits other than money accruing to a faculty or staff member of an institution of higher education as a result of employment, such as the right to use the gymnasium and to attend athletic events without charge (United States).

Nonformal education.　Structured, systematic, nonschool education and training, generally of short duration, during which the educating or financing agency seeks a specific behavioral change in a target population. Examples are management training programs and rural development education. See also *formal education*, *informal education*, *lifelong learning.*

Nongovernmental organization (NGO).　Generally an international nonprofit organization that is not under the authority of a government. A number of such organizations cooperate with the United Nations and its agencies in the area of their expertise.

Nongraded system of education.
A system that allows students to progress at their own rate of speed and groups them according to their intellectual ability rather than their chronological age. Innovative methods such as flexible scheduling, the use of educational technology, team teaching, and independent study are used to bring about individualized education.

Nonmajor.
A student who enrolls in courses in a particular field of study but who does not expect to earn a degree or a diploma in that area (United States).

Nonprint teaching materials.
Learning resources such as film, tapes, cassettes, and television. See also *educational technology*.

Nonprofessional.
See *paraprofessional*, *nonacademic personnel*.

Nonpublic archives.
Repositories of nongovernmental records that may or may not be open to the public. Such archives may be records of churches; businesses; private institutions of higher education; professional, occupational, political, and social organizations; families and prominent individuals; and regional or subject matter collections.

Nonpublic institution.
An institution not supported by public funds; may be private or denominational.

Nonreader.
A person who is unable to read despite extended instruction. See also *illiterate*.

Nonreappointment.
Failure to renew the contract of an untenured or a probationary faculty member; usually involves a decision not to grant tenure. Differs from *dismissal* in that it takes effect at the end of the contract rather than

at any time during the academic year (United States).

Nonrecognition. A reading difficulty; inability to associate word symbols with their definitions and meanings.

Nonrecurrent funding. A nonrenewable appropriation of funds made by an individual, government agency, civic group, or foundation to a recipient (an institution of higher education, for example), usually for a specified time and purpose.

Nonrecurrent grants. See *nonrecurrent funding*.

Nonresident fee. An extra charge made by a public (state, district, or municipal) institution to a student whose residence is outside the area from which the institution draws its tax support (United States).

Nonresident instruction. Instruction given by a college or university away from its main campus or branch campuses (United States).

Nonresident student. (1) A student classification for the purpose of assessing additional tuition at publicly supported institutions of higher education; terms such as out-of-state, out-of-district, or international student are also used; (2) a student who does not live on campus.

Nonresident term. A term spent off campus to work and gain practical experience in the student's *major field of study*. See also *cooperative education*.

Nonsectarian college. See *nondenominational college*.

Nontraditional education. See *alternative programs*.

Nonuniversity sector. See *nonuniversity-type higher education*.

Nonuniversity-type higher education. Programs leading to a degree below university degree level. Admissions requirements, although sometimes identical to those for university education, tend to be less stringent (sometimes ten years plus practical work experience or, in the United Kingdom, General Certificate of Education, ordinary level). Duration of study is usually three years or less. This education is generally provided in *colleges of education, junior colleges, technical colleges, technicums*, or *institutes*. See also *postsecondary education, short-cycle education*.

Normal college. See *normal school*.

Normal school. An institution for training elementary school teachers primarily; also called teachers college (United States), *école normale* (for primary school teachers) and *école normale supérieure* (for secondary school teachers) (French-language systems), and *escuela normal* (Spanish-language systems).

Normal student load. The credit hours required for graduation divided by the number of semesters or terms normally required for graduation. For example, 120 credit hours divided by eight semesters equals 15 credit hours per semester as the normal student load (United States).

Normalista. Title of a graduate of a secondary-level teacher-training school entitling the graduate to teach at the primary level (Colombia).

Normality. Behavior considered typical in a certain situation.

Normalization. The process of establishing *norms* for standardized tests.

Norms. Standards or criteria derived from the average or median achievement of a large group on a test; usually an individual's test results are compared with the norm of a test in order to determine the individual's performance relative to that of the other examinees.

Numerical grading system.

A method of recording the progress of students by means of numerical grades for tests and examinations. See also *letter grading system*.

Numerus clausus.

Latin: closed or restricted number. (1) The practice of limiting enrollments in certain faculties, generally the sciences, because of space or *manpower development* considerations; (2) restrictions on foreign enrollments in certain high-priority fields, such as science and technology; winners of certain international awards may be exempt.

Nunnery school.

In the Middle Ages, a girls' school administered and taught by nuns.

Nursery school.

A preschool program for the three- to five-year-old child, offering training that will benefit the child in school and encourage social interaction with peers. Such schools are often *laboratory schools* of *teachers colleges* and *colleges of education*.

Nursing school.

Training school for nurses in *junior colleges* (two-year program), in hospitals connected with medical schools (three-year program), in universities (four-year program leading toward the Bachelor of Science in nursing or five-year program culminating in master's degree) (United States).

O

Occasional student.

A student who is admitted to classes but who is not proceeding to a degree.

Occupation. Any type of manual or nonmanual work that can provide a means of livelihood. See also *career*. Sometimes equated with *profession*, which usually refers to an occupation requiring extensive educational preparation and governed by its own code of ethics or conduct.

Occupational curriculum. See *vocational curriculum*.

Occupational education. See *vocational education*.

Occupational experience education. See *work experience education*.

Occupational experience program. See *work experience program*.

Occupational guidance. See *vocational guidance*.

Occupational information. Descriptions of the work, duties, responsibilities, and compensation involved in various vocations or professions; designed to guide persons in making a choice of vocation or professional occupation. Such information also includes employment outlook, promotional opportunities, and entrance requirements. Also called career information.

Occupational mobility. Possessing education and skills that allow a person to move from one occupation to another. See also *educational mobility*.

Occupational objective. A career goal of a student.

Occupational program. Studies designed primarily to prepare students for immediate employment or to upgrade a student's skills in a specific occupation.

Occupational title. See *title*.

Off-campus experience. Work or learning, generally of a practical nature, gained outside the university or college. May be performed on a voluntary or a paid basis. May be field experience related to an area of study.

Off-campus student. A student who resides in housing that is not operated by the institution, such as at home, in a boarding house, or in a private apartment.

Off-campus term. A term when students are pursuing studies away from the campus of the college or university where they are regularly enrolled, such as a study-abroad term, with credit awarded for work completed.

Office of the registrar. The office that maintains student records, grade reports, course descriptions, and academic regulations; collects and reports enrollment data; issues transcripts of students; maintains records of students' progress toward meeting degree requirements; and certifies candidates for graduation. See also *registrar.*

Official educational record. See *academic record.*

Oklevél. First qualification in higher education, which may require from two to six years of study (Hungary).

O-Level. See *General Certificate of Education.*

"Old boy" network. A group of friends or acquaintances, such as graduates of the same institution, relied on to recommend candidates for a university or college position instead of using public announcements of openings or competitive examinations to attract and screen candidates.

Ombudsman. An official who functions as an impartial facilitator in the resolution of complaints, grievances, and problems (whether of students, faculty, or staff) arising from university policies and procedures. The ombudsman has direct access to the chief executive officer and other administrators but functions independently of the university administration. Personal persuasion and mediation are the primary methods of correcting abuses, but the ombudsman may request executive intervention (United States).

Omnivalent certificate. A secondary school-leaving *certificate* that allows access to all fields of study.

Ön lisans. A qualification below degree level awarded by higher schools (junior colleges), generally in engineering, commerce, and economics (Turkey).

"On-the-curve." A type of evaluation whereby the performance of students who have experienced the same instruction for the same time period is compared by arranging scores or grades in a bell-shaped distribution curve.

Open admission. An admissions policy that admits to higher education all who complete secondary schooling if space permits, with little restriction on the type of secondary program completed, apart from courses required for a particular program in which a student wishes to enroll. Also called nonselective admission, or open enrollment. Contrast *restricted admission, selective admission.*

Open-ended program. An occupational program below degree level, often designed in cooperation with one or more four-year colleges or universities, so that its *credits* are applicable toward a *bachelor's degree*.

Open entry/exit. A policy of educational institutions that encourages students to leave the institution, without completing a program, for other learning or work experiences and to return for further education or upgrading of job skills without reapplication. Appropriate credentials or diplomas are generally awarded on completion of different learning stages to certify attendance and learning. See also *lifelong education, recurrent education.*

Open learning.
Ideally, learning open to people at all levels and at all ages, with learners entering and leaving educational programs as their needs for learning require, setting their own pace, and choosing their own goals. See also *enseignement en alternance, lifelong learning.*

Open University.
An institution designed to provide postsecondary education on a part-time basis by means of mass media, tutoring, correspondence, and short residential courses for those adults who have not enrolled in other postsecondary institutions (United Kingdom). See also *distance education, Fernunterricht, independent study, university without walls.*

Opening convocation.
A ceremony that observes the opening of an academic year and the welcoming of new students.

Operating expenditure.
Money expended for salaries, supplies, services, and maintenance of physical plant of an institution as opposed to *capital expenditures,* which is money expended for physical facilities, equipment, and land. Also called recurrent expenditure.

Optional course.
See *elective course.*

Oral education.
A program aimed at eliminating the need for special accommodations in teaching the deaf, such as sign language, by giving intensive early training in language, speech, speech reading, and use of residual hearing.

Oral examination.

An examination during which both questions and answers are spoken rather than written.

Oral history.

The handing down of ancient tradition and history by word of mouth rather than by documents, as exemplified by the *griot* in many African areas.

Ordenanza normal.

Teacher training (Spanish-language systems).

Ordinances of Manu.

Moral code of the Brahmans, formulated approximately 500 A.D. (India).

Organization.

An association of people for the pursuit of common interests.

Organized faculty research.

Research carried on by faculty and academic staff members that is separately budgeted and separately accounted for. All sponsored research falls into this category.

Orientation.

(1) The introduction of new students to the programs, facilities, and regulations of a college or university. Orientation may be conducted as a special course during one or two weeks at the beginning of a term or as a course with regular weekly meetings during the first term. Orientation may also include advising on courses and programs, registration procedures, and choices of field of specializations. Students living on campus in university housing are also given special programs to acquaint them with housing regulations. (2) Programs designed to acquaint new faculty and new university staff with academic and general policies and regulations of concern to employees. Also designed to acquaint new faculty and staff with remuneration policies, fringe benefits, and regulations governing such matters as parking, safety, and use of university facilities.

Országos középiskolai tanulmányi verseny. National Secondary School Studies Competition. A national competition for secondary school leavers, the top ten winners of which are exempt from customary university admittance examinations (Hungary).

Orta okul. Schools offering the first part of secondary education (Turkey, Cypress).

Out-of-state fees. Fees charged students who are not residents of the state where a college or university is located (United States).

Out-of-state student. A student who attends a college or university in a state other than the state of his legal residence. At publicly supported institutions, this student generally pays additional tuition and fees (United States).

Overseas student. See *international student.*

Overseer. A name for a university trustee or for a special governing board.

Oxbridge. Term used when referring to Oxford and Cambridge as distinct from all other universities.

P

Pädagogische Hochschulen. Teacher colleges (Federal Republic of Germany).

Paksa. Doctoral degree (Democratic People's Republic of Korea).

Paksa-won. Doctoral institute (Democratic People's Republic of Korea).

Pali. Indian language used in the most pristine form of Buddhism, especially in the Hinayana canonical scripture, *Tipitolsa.*

"Paper" university. A medieval university that was approved by papal bulls but never functioned; likewise, a contemporary university that announces its beginnings and never functions, or an institution that launches programs for a brief period of time and then ceases.

Parallel cooperative education.
A program whereby participating students attend classes during one segment of the day and work part time during the other segment.

Paraprofessional.
A person trained to assist professional personnel in carrying out their responsibilities, such as a technician in the health professions. Also called subprofessional.

Parents' confidential statement.
A form required of the parents of an applicant for financial aid. It provides information on the parents' financial condition and the student's own resources to help university officials determine the extent of financial need of the applicant. Typically the data include family income and assets, taxes and liabilities, and unusual expenses anticipated for the year (United States).

Parishad.
A type of early Hindu academy where the educational process was based on discussion among several students and teachers.

Participatory democracy.
The taking part in institutional decision making and policy determination by faculty, staff, and students. See also *Drittelparität*.

Part-time class.
A class conducted for part-time students, generally in the evening.

Part-time day class.
A class conducted during the day for part-time students.

Part-time faculty.
Faculty appointed to teach or conduct research on less than full-time basis. Part-time faculty are used extensively in evening programs and extension classes and on branch

campuses (United States). Part-time faculty usually conduct research or teach only a few hours each week and are not involved in committee work and policy making of colleges and universities. In many Central and South American countries, part-time staff comprise the majority of faculty appointments.

Part-time graduate. A graduate who obtains a degree by attending college or graduate school part time, usually while holding a full-time job (United States).

Part-time program (vocational). A vocational training program, which operates for one, two, or three hours in the day or evening.

Part-time student. A student who enrolls in fewer courses or credit hours than a *full-time student.*

Part-time teacher. See *part-time faculty.*

Pass course. A course of study that is more general than the specialized program required for Honors and that permits a lower score or grade in examinations (Canada, United Kingdom).

Pass-fail option. A course mark or grade of pass or fail in place of the more common grades of A, B, C, D, or F, used most often in instances where the course is not *required.* Such an option was established in many institutions during the 1960s in response to student protests. A "pass" grade does not ordinarily count in calculation of *quality point average.* (United States).

Passing grade. A mark showing that a course has been completed satisfactorily and that student is entitled to *credit.* (United States).

Passing withdrawal. Designation of satisfactory work in a course or courses at the time a student withdraws from a course or leaves college or university prior to completion of a course or program (United States).

Patronato.   Board of trustees (Spain).

Peer group evaluation.   Inspection and appraisal of quality and adequacy of academic programs by educators from comparable institutions for purpose of accreditation (United States). See also *voluntary accreditation.*

Peer review.   A review by a panel of a candidate's professional equals of a request for funding research or for advancement based on evidence of past performance and estimates of future potential.

Penalty.   An additional financial or academic requirement imposed for special circumstances (United States).

Penalty fee.   A payment added to normal fees as an assessment, such as a late registration fee (United States).

Pension.   Pay provided for retirees from funds contributed to a trust fund by individuals and the institution, or pay provided by government for all retirees.

People's university.   In the Soviet Union and other socialist countries, a further education (not higher education) institution that trains citizens for public service; runs courses for parents and teachers; offers instructions in special discipline; and guides clientele in their general educational, cultural, and professional development. Staffed mostly by volunteer workers.

Percentage (flat-rate) increase.   Salary increase for staff members based on a given percentage of their salaries rather than on individual merit or performance.

Percentile score.   The score of one student in relation to the percent of scores among a whole group or class of students. For example, a percentile score of 65 is equal to or better than that of 65 percent of the students in the group. See also *score*.

Performance contract.   An agreement between instructor and student concerning the amount of work to be completed in a reading program, special project, or research. Completion of the contract is recognized as partial fulfillment of degree requirements.

Performance criteria.   Standards by which the efficiency of programs, progress, or systems may be judged.

Performance record.   Record of actual achievement or production, such as yield per acre in agriculture.

Performance test.   An examination of demonstrated competency in a skill or vocation, in contrast to mere knowledge about it.

Perito.   Expert. Qualification awarded on completion of the second phase of secondary education in technical or commercial programs. Generally gives access to higher education in the appropriate fields (Central and South American countries).

Permanent education.   See *lifelong learning*.

Permanent nonacademic record.   The file record showing background, education, and experience of a student (United States).

Perquisite.   Special benefits such as services or housing, provided for staff members in addition to monetary remuneration. Perquisites, which are usually nontaxable, may include club memberships, a residence, free utilities, maid service, and an automobile and a driver.

Personalized system of instruction (PSI).

A plan introduced at the University of Brasilia in Brazil in 1964 whereby a course is divided into fifteen or twenty self-paced learning modules with objectives for each module stated in a study guide. The student sets his own pace of study, presents himself for testing on the module when he feels prepared, and does not proceed to the next module until passing the test. Also called Keller Plan after its originator, Fred S. Keller. See also *individualized instruction*.

Personnel data.

Information on individual staff members or students used for institutional decisions about them and for guidance and counseling.

Personnel program.

Services provided for all faculty and staff regarding recruitment, orientation, remuneration, benefits, promotion, transfer, and retirement. Usually a function of a special office that maintains all personnel records and provides counseling.

Petition.

A written request for consideration, which may involve relief from inequity or special exemption from specific policies or regulations.

Philanthropic foundation.

A trust or corporation created for charitable purposes that provides grants of funds to finance research, provision of facilities, equipment, and library resources. Usually the foundation defines areas of interest that it will support.

Philosophy of education.

(1) Reasons or rationale for teaching or engaging in instruction; (2) the study of the aims and objectives of education, considering education as part of the total culture and achievement of mankind and the contribution of education to human welfare and social progress.

Physical facilities.   Buildings, equipment, furniture, and grounds of an institution.

Pileus.   Small round skull cap worn by doctoral and later by other members of a college in the Middle Ages.

Pileus quadratus.   Square cap worn in *academic dress* by heads of houses, colleges, and halls at Oxford beginning in 1564; in 1601 this cap was ordered for all fellows (of all degrees) and scholars.

Pileus rotundus.   Round cap worn in academic dress by sons of nobles and gentlemen and fellow-commoners in early seventeenth-century Europe.

Pilot program.   A program, usually of small scale, that tests new ideas by establishing a model for a larger program; it enables the institution to resolve problems, and perfect methods and procedures before embarking on the large-scale program. Also a program conducted as a demonstration that others may copy or emulate. Also called experimental program.

Pirivena.   Educational unit of a Buddhist monastery that reached its height in the fifteenth century (Sri Lanka).

Placement.   (1) The assignment of students to courses, sections of courses, or classes based on scores in tests and educational achievement; also assignment of transfer students to courses and classes based on transfer credit; (2) assistance to graduates and students in finding suitable employment, often handled by a *placement office*.

Placement file.   Records of education and work experience of graduates and students registered with the *placement office*.

Placement office.   An office that provides information to employers on available candidates and counsels students and graduates on career opportunites and openings in various fields. May also provide information on graduate programs and military service. Such an office may be designated as placement or appointment service.

Placement service.
The functions handled by a *placement office* in assisting graduates to find suitable employment in their field of study.

Placement test.
A measure of knowledge and ability used to classify and place students in the level of work deemed proper for them.

Planning center.
An area or facility where professional staff conduct research to determine short-range or long-range plans and goals of a college or university. May also plan facilities and campus development and needs for new programs based on social trends.

Plate glass university.
Colloquial expression for a university founded since World War II (United Kingdom).

Pledge.
(1) A signed statement, not usually legally binding, agreeing to provide a certain amount of money in lump sum or installments for a particular purpose to an institution of higher education; (2) colloquially, a student who has been admitted to a *fraternity* but has not yet been initiated as a member (United States).

Political institution.
An educational institution usually founded by a political organization and having as its goal the indoctrination of students into the precepts of that organization in addition to vocational or academic study. It is often used for training organizational and executive personnel for the sponsoring organization.

Polytechnic.   A broadly based postsecondary academic
                            institution offering courses and programs
                            for full-time and part-time students. Pro-
                            grams include sandwich courses in which
                            students spend a part of the year in college
                            and the remainder of the year working in
                            industry receiving appropriate training.
                            Emphasis in programs is on applied sci-
                            ences, technology, and social sciences. Re-
                            lationships are strong with industry, com-
                            merce, and public services. In the United
                            Kingdom degrees for polytechnic students
                            are conferred under authority of the Na-
                            tional Council for Academic Awards.

**Polytechnischer   The ninth year of compulsory education;
Lehrgang.**   the polytechnic course is required for stu-
                            dents who do not plan to continue in a vo-
                            cational or other secondary school (Austria).

Pontifical institution.   Any educational institution, regardless of
                            location, under the jurisdiction of the
                            Vatican.

Pooled income fund.   A plan whereby a college or university ac-
                            cepts gifts of cash or securities from a num-
                            ber of donors, pools the gifts in a common
                            fund, and manages the investment of the
                            funds in a diversified portfolio. Income
                            earned by the pooled fund is paid to the
                            participants or to other beneficiaries in ac-
                            cordance with their respective shares of the
                            total fund.

**Postcompulsory   Education beyond the legal minimum re-
education.**   quired by law. See also *compulsory educa-
                            tion*.

Postdoctoral study.   Research and study beyond the *doctoral de-
                            gree*, usually on special projects. Certificate
                            may be given for completion of postdoc-
                            toral program.

**Postexperience   Education for persons who have already
education.**   completed a degree course (or gained its

equivalent through practical work) and have had professional experience. It consists of courses that update or refresh professional knowledge and may lead to a certificate or diploma but not a higher degree. Aims of postexperience education are clearly defined, and the content is clearly linked with practice. Such programs are most common in management, engineering, medicine, and teacher training. See also *postgraduate study*.

Postgraduate degree. See *advanced degree.*

Postgraduate education. Education extending beyond the first university degree.

Postgraduate student. One who has obtained a degree and is proceeding to further study.

Postgraduate study. Any study following the first general or professional or advanced degree. Usually study for members of a profession to keep abreast of new developments by taking short courses or attending institutes. See also *postexperience education*.

Postsecondary education. All types of education, both public and private, following secondary school, including general, liberal, technical, vocational, and professional education. Admission requirement is either a completed secondary school education or ten to eleven years of schooling with one to two years of practical training. Synonymous with *higher education, third level,* and *tertiary education*.

Postsecondary occupational education. Education, training, or retraining (including guidance, counseling, and placement services) for persons sixteen years of age or older who have graduated from or left elementary or secondary school. It is conducted by an institution legally authorized by the state to provide *postsecondary education* in order to prepare individuals for gainful employment as semiskilled or skilled workers or as technicians or subprofessionals in recognized occupations or to prepare individuals for enrollment in advanced technical education programs, but excluding any programs considered professional or that require a baccalaureate or advanced degree. Also called postsecondary vocational education.

Practical arts education. Education of a nonvocational type in subjects such as manual arts, family living, home economics, and consumer knowledge.

Practical nurse education. Programs designed to train licensed practical nurses who perform nursing duties that require less professional knowledge than of a registered nurse.

Practicum. A course or period of academic effort that combines study and practical work to relate theory and practice. Generally a degree requirement in professional fields.

Praktikant. A student trainee in an industry who is given a carefully designed program to follow (Federal Republic of Germany, Sweden).

Preceptorial. A small conference group directed by a preceptor that also receives specific instruction by regular instructors.

Precollege guidance. Advising and counseling students about career objectives, types of colleges and universities, programs offered, costs of attendance, and other matters relating to choice of a college and profession or career (United States).

Predavač. Faculty rank: *lecturer* (Yugoslavia).

Prefectural university. In Japan, a university funded and administered by prefectural authorities; the country is divided into forty-seven prefectures.

Prefreshman review course.

A course provided by a college to better prepare prospective students for college courses (United States). See also *curso de orientación universitaria*.

Preliminary application.

A statement of one's intention to apply for admission to a particular institution and of the desire to be a candidate for admission. Such notice is given prior to a candidate's readiness to file formal application for admission (United States).

Preparatory school.

(1) The second phase of general secondary education lasting two to three years to prepare for university study leading to the *bachillerato* (Mexico); (2) a private or public school offering a program of secondary education that is designed to meet admission requirements of colleges and universities.

Preprimary education.

Education preceding the first level of education. Although not yet widely provided by public institutions, preprimary education usually starts at age three, four, or five and lasts from one to three years. Emphasis is on learning readiness rather than learning per se. Also called preschool education. See also *crèche, nursery school*.

Preprofessional study.

A program of study basic to specialized training in a profession.

Prerequisite course.

A course that must be completed prior to enrolling in an advanced or succeeding course.

President.

The chief administrative officer of an institution of higher education. Serves as the executive officer of the board of trustees or of other governing authorities (United States).

Presidi.

Dean of faculty (Italy).

Preuniversity course.   A course offered by a university at a level below regular university courses, intended to introduce insufficiently prepared students to university work.

Primary education.   See *elementary education*.

Primary program.   One of the two broad functions performed by a higher education institution, according to the classification of higher education programs into primary and support programs. Primary programs include instruction, research, public service, and student aid; support programs include academic support services and separate operations such as auxiliary enterprises (United States). See also *program classification structure*.

Primer grado de   Introductory level of occupational prepa-
formación profesional.   ration following the eight years of basic education (Spain).

Principal.   (1) The chief executive officer of college, comparable to the president of a college or university in certain countries (Commonwealth countries); (2) the administrative head of a public school, such as a high school or a junior high school; also called headmaster.

Private college.   A college whose governing board is not subject to public (governmental) control except for charter or statutory provisions, usually because of primary financial support from private rather than public funds. Also called independent institution. See also *private institution of higher education*. Contrast *public college*.

Private education.   Education offered in private institutions, that is, institutions not supported by tax monies. Although most private institutions have to follow certain standard curricula in many countries, more flexibility in educational offerings is usually possible than in public institutions. Contrast *public education.*

Private educational sector.

That part of education consisting of institutions that are mostly privately (independently) funded rather than government funded. Contrast *public educational sector.*

Private financial support.

Funds provided for colleges or universities from nonpublic sources, such as gifts from individuals and grants from foundations.

Private governing board.

The governing board—usually self-perpetuating and variously termed board of regents, trustees, or directors—that is charged with the overall responsibility for the control and management of a private institution of higher education.

Private institution of higher education.

A postsecondary institution created by a charter or a statute that defines its functions and powers and supported primarily from tuition, fees, endowment income, and donations. Some tax funds may be received for special purposes, such as scholarships and research projects, but they have little or no influence on policies and operations. If the private institution is located in a nation where degree granting is the sole power of the national government through one of its ministries, the government will insist that the course offerings satisfy its requirements for degrees and certificates. Also, where the government having sole degree-granting authority has a policy of providing financing for private institutions, as well as those publicly controlled, the government will insist on conformity to its requirements relative to the awarding of degrees and certificates. See also *Catholic institution, denominational institution, independent institution, proprietary institution, private college.* Contrast *public institution of higher education.*

Privilege fee.	A fee for a special privilege, such as registering late or taking a special examination. See also *penalty fee.*
Privileged communication.	A confidential statement about a person that is to be used with discretion. See also *confidentiality of records.*
Prize.	An award for outstanding achievement.
Prize scholarship.	A scholarship awarded without regard to financial need.
Prizeman.	Winner of a university prize (United Kingdom).
Pro-chancellor.	An officer of a university, generally appointed by the chancellor, who assumes the duties of the chancellor in his absence (Commonwealth countries).
Proctor.	(1) An officer whose authority is that of exercising disciplinary powers over students (United Kingdom); (2) one who assists in the administration and supervision of examinations.
Proctorial board.	A disciplinary board composed of proctors.
Prodekan.	Deputy dean (Yugoslavia).
Profesor.	Faculty rank: *professor.* Titles of professors commonly used in Spanish-language institutions are *adjunto,* associate or assistant professor; *adscrito,* lecturer; *agregado,* associate professor; *asistent,* assistant professor; *asociado,* associate professor; *auxiliar,* assistant professor; *ayudante,* instructor; *extraordinario,* extraordinary, offering temporary courses under special contract; *honorario,* honorary; *libre,* free, giving courses outside the normal curriculum; *principal,* senior professor; *titular,* full professor; *titular adjunto,* assistant professor; *titular principal,*

full professor; *visitante,* visiting professor. See also *professor.*

Professeur de l'enseignement supérieur.
Faculty rank: professor of higher education (Morocco).

Professeur titulaire.
Faculty rank: a full professor responsible for formal teaching and for directing and coordinating the work of other staff in his subject area (French-language systems).

Profession.
An occupation generally requiring extensive educational preparation and governed by its own code of ethics or conduct. Examples are medicine, pharmacy, and law.

Professional association.
An organization composed of members of a profession and sometimes of subordinate professions or branches.of the profession who meet standards for admission established by its members. The purpose is to exchange information, promote professional development, and advance the welfare of members of the profession. It may establish standards for programs of study preparatory to entry into the profession; may also approve and accredit institutions and programs of study on the basis of their quality, and may also run professional credentialing programs to certify individual competence.

Professional certificate.
(1) A credential required for the practice of a particular profession, such as a teaching certificate; (2) an advanced credential indicating professional training beyond that required for initial certification, such as the certificate of advanced graduate study or "sixth year" certificate increasingly expected of public school administrators in the United States.

Professional credit.
(1) Credit earned toward a *professional degree*

credential; (2) credit awarded for in-service training or postgraduate professional education (United States).

Professional degree.

Degree awarded on completion of a professional program of study, such as Doctor of Medicine and Doctor of Dentistry.

Professional designation.

Title, such as engineer, signifying completion of program in a professional field of study. See also *title*.

Professional education.

Programs in professional fields of study designed to prepare students to enter a profession. Such programs may follow general arts and sciences education or may be the sole form of higher education undertaken by the student. See also *first professional degree*.

Professional examination.

Examination required of those who wish to obtain a license to practice a profession, usually given by state or national authorities or in some instances by professional societies.

Professional fraternity.

A fraternity that admits as members students preparing for a specific profession. Promotes high standards and ethics for members of the profession. Exists in colleges or professional schools offering programs preparatory to entering the profession. See also *fraternity, sorority*.

Professional military education.

Education in military science for those preparing for military careers.

Professional school.

An institution of higher education that prepares students for a profession; either after they have completed their first degree as in law, medicine, or theology, or in other fields, such as agriculture, education, engineering, and nursing, where students can enroll in undergraduate *professional study* (United States).

Professional society. See *professional association*.

Professional staff. Employees who are engaged in work that is predominantly intellectual and varied in character as opposed to routine mental, manual, mechanical, or physical work. Such employees must consistently exercise discretion, judgment, and knowledge of an advanced type.

Professional student. (1) A student enrolled in a *professional school* or program; (2) colloquially, a student who continues to take courses beyond those necessary for a degree, often instead of seeking employment (United States).

Professional study. Study required as preparation for entering a specific profession.

Professor. (1) Faculty rank: the highest rank accorded a faculty member in an institution of higher education. For instance, ranks in the United States are, in descending order, professor, associate professor, and assistant professor. The same spelling is used for this title in a number of non-English-speaking nations, such as Austria, Denmark, Federal Republic of Germany, German Democratic Republic, Netherlands, Norway, and Sweden. Comparable ranks in Portuguese are *professor titular* (full professor), *professor adjunto* (associate professor), and *professor assistente* (assistant professor). (2) More generally and colloquially, any university or college faculty member. See also *profesor, professeur titulaire*.

Professor emeritus. Title conferred on distinguished retired professors in many nations. Usually requires special action of appropriate authority. See also *emeritus professor*.

Prognostic test.   An examination, such as an aptitude test, used to predict a student's future success based on performance on the test.

Program.   (1) A series of related courses, usually taken in predetermined sequence from introductory to advanced level, leading to a degree; (2) the general goal or objective or offerings of an institution, as in *primary program*.

Program budgeting.   The construction of budget estimates on the basis of particular institutional programs or functions to help decision makers allocate funds for specific activities, goals, or objectives of the institution.

Program classification structure (PCS).   A taxonomy for cost analysis involving the systematic and exhaustive classification of all activities of higher education institutions into program elements. When this classification structure is equated to the functional classification used for accounting purposes in the institution, it becomes the basis of a system that associates each program element to an academic program for analytical and cost purposes. For example, a special session course in poultry science is an element in the larger instructional program in agriculture and natural resources within the primary programs of the institution. The PCS developed by the National Center for Higher Education Management Systems classifies all institutional activities into two major categories, primary programs (instruction, organized research, public services) and support programs (academic support, student services, institutional support, independent operations) (United States).

Program of early admission.   Accepting for admission to the *freshman class* selected students who have finished a prescribed amount of secondary school work (but less than that required for graduation).

Evidence of exceptional scholastic ability, emotional stability, and social maturity are indices usually considered as indicating that such students might profitably undertake college work sooner than most students (United States). See also *early admission*.

Program of study.   See *program*.

Program planning.   (1) The implementation of activities designed to fulfill the objectives of an institution; when translated into sequential actions, the objectives become programs; (2) the choosing of courses or a program of study by a student, often in consultation with an academic advisor.

Programmed instruction.   Presentation of a series of learning "frames" or items of information and questions that are carefully arranged to shape successively the desired answers or behavior. Choosing the correct response imbedded in the program provides immediate reinforcement of learning and leads to the next item of information. An incorrect answer leads to clarification and review.

Progress report.   An interim statement of the achievement of a student in a course or of work toward a goal.

Project method.   A method of teaching by assigning problems to students—individually and in groups—for which they gather data and find solutions, with the teacher assisting only when necessary.

Promotion.   (1) English: advancement from one rank to a higher one or from one *grade* to the next higher one; (2) German: graduation with the doctoral degree.

Proprietary school.   Privately owned, profit-making educational institution. In the United States most such schools specialize in practical job skill training for employment and organize their courses in short, intensive modules. Some have degree-granting authority but most award certificates or other non-degree credentials.

Prorektor.
Deputy rector (Hungary, Yugoslavia).

Pro-vice-chancellor.
Title of academic officer next in rank to vice-chancellor (Commonwealth countries).

Provincial university.
A university under the direct administrative and financial control of a provincial government or receiving most of its funding from a provincial government.

Provisional admission.
See *admission condition*.

Provisional registration.
Enrollment in classes on a temporary basis pending completion of some part of the admission or enrollment process.

Provost.
(1) A chief academic or educational administrator; (2) the chief administrator on an individual campus of a multicampus institution; (3) in the United States, more commonly an administrative officer, comparable to academic vice president, above the rank of dean of a particular college unit, in charge of all academic or educational activities under the president.

Prueba de aptitud academic (PAA).
National academic achievement test on completion of secondary school (Chile).

Public administration.
(1) The administration of governments and government agencies; (2) administrators employed by governments and paid by tax funds; (3) the field of study preparing such administrators.

Public archives.
Organized records of public universities, regional authorities, international and re-

gional organizations, and those of special agencies or ministries that maintain their own archives. Also governmental charter records, often closed to public.

Public college.
A college financed largely by tax support and sponsored by a government agency or authority. See *public institution of higher education*. Contrast *private college*.

Public control of institutions.
Government or government agency direction of an institution financed by tax monies. Officials of such institutions are elected or appointed by government. National governments, states and provinces, cities and counties exercise control of many institutions of higher education.

Public education.
Education offered in tax-supported and government-controlled institutions. See also *public institution of higher education*. Contrast *private education*.

Public educational sector.
That part of education consisting of institutions funded by and controlled by government or government agencies.

Public governing board.
A governing board, often labeled a board of regents, trustees, or directors, appointed or elected to operate a public, tax-supported college or university.

Public institution of higher education.
An institution administered or financed (or both) by government—national, state, provincial, or municipal. Administrators and faculty are usually appointed by a government agency or *public governing board*. Contrast with *private institution of higher education*.

Public junior college.
A short-cycle or two-year college in the United States operated by a governmental unit such as a state, municipality, county, or junior college district. Often designated *community college*. Serves educational needs of people in the local area by offering adult

education programs, terminal occupational programs, and transfer programs leading to higher degrees.

Public school.

(1) A secondary school administered by a government agency and supported by tax monies (United States); (2) an independent and predominantly residential school offering college preparatory education, run by a nonprofit, often denominational, board of governors (United Kingdom).

Public school system.

A school system administered by a government agency and funded by tax monies.

Public service.

Activities of college and university personnel, either in coordination or on an individual basis, aimed at aiding the public beyond classroom teaching and scholarly research. Faculty may contribute special knowledge and skills in helping to solve community problems and meeting community needs, as when members of a biology department serve on public boards or advise government agencies and citizen groups concerned with the environment. Usually such service is provided without compensation by the faculty or staff members working on their own time. Considered along with teaching and research as a *primary program* or goal of many colleges and universities.

Public service occupation.

Work that serves the whole society, as in public health and safety. Personnel in such occupations are appointed and employed by government agencies.

Public vocational school.

An educational institution, operated and controlled by a national, state, county, or other political subdivision, which emphasizes occupational or career education at less than degree level.

Puranas epics.

Ancient folk literature that was popular in Hindu learning from the first to the twelfth century A.D. Subject matter consisted of popular stories, legends, and myths about gods (puranas) and human heroes (epics).

Q

Quadrivium. The four higher disciplines of the medieval curriculum—arithmetic, geometry, astronomy, and music—in contrast to the *trivium*. See also *liberal arts*.

Qualification. A required condition, usually academic, for a position.

Qualifying examination. (1) An examination that qualifies a student for *admission* to a university, often called matriculation examination; (2) an examination used to determine a student's eligibility for candidacy for the *doctoral degree*. Generally consists of a written and an oral part. Also called *comprehensive* or preliminary examination.

Quality point. See *grade point*.

Quality point average. See *grade point average*.

Quarter. A term in the *quarter-system* calendar, usually consisting of ten weeks. Three quarters constitute the *academic year* and equal two semesters, but the total year's offerings usually consist of four quarters. See also *calendar, semester, term, trimester*.

Quarter credit hour. A unit that measures the value in credit hours toward degree requirements of a course during one *quarter* of the year. Normal student load per quarter generally is fifteen quarter *credit hours*.

Quarter system. The system of dividing the year into four *quarters* or terms.

Question-and-answer method. A procedure of instruction and of *examination* allowing the teacher to assess the progress of students by questioning in classroom.

Questionnaire.   A form with written questions, to elicit specific information from a number of persons, generally by a space provided for responses. The information collected is usually tabulated, analyzed, and presented in written form in a thesis, a journal article, or as a research study.

Quorum.   The number of members of a *council, board*, or other body required to be present to legally conduct the business of the body.

Quota.   A predetermined number of students allowed to enroll in an institution, a *faculty*, or a department; often used to permit or limit the enrollment of certain types of students, such as women, or particular ethnic groups, and to regulate enrollments in particular programs or specialties. Quotas are also used to shape the manpower supply of a country in accordance with established manpower needs, a practice especially common in socialist countries. See also *numerus clausus, selective admission*.

Qu'ran.   See *Koran*.

R

Racial discrimination.   Using a nonrelevant factor like race to deny an applicant admission to an institution or to refuse to hire a candidate for a staff or faculty position.

Racial integration.   Participation of all races in the same institutions, activities, and facilities; contrast *segregation*.

Racism.   The beliefs or assumptions of inherited superiority and purity of certain races that become the basis of discrimination.

Rating scale.   A graduated measure or set of categories for use in describing phenomena, for example in assessing such individual traits as the quantity or quality of a student's performance or staff member's work in comparison to that of others or to an ideal by checking one category from a series between two extremes, such as from "unsatisfactory" to "outstanding" (United States).

Ratio studiorum.   The codification in 1599 of Jesuit experience and educational practice. It represents the most systematic thinking on education in the European world to that date, organically linking secondary and university education, intellectual progress and spiritual growth, as well as the acquisition and use of knowledge.

Reader.   Faculty rank: a teacher in a university, appointed by the university as an expert in some special branch of study, but of lower rank than a *professor* (United Kingdom).

Reading period.   A scheduled period of several days or weeks near the close of a term, during which instructors are available to assist students but classes do not meet in order to allow students to review the materials covered during the term prior to final examinations.

Readmission.   Enrollment of a former student who has not been in attendance for one or more terms. See also *leave of absence, reinstatement.*

Realexamen.   Lower secondary school-leaving examination taken after the tenth grade and giving access to certain nonuniversity institutions of higher education (Denmark). See also *realskole.*

Realgymnasium.   Secondary science school (Austria).

Realschule.   A six-year school following basic school for students of eleven to sixteen years of age.

Graduates may continue into two-year higher technical schools (Federal Republic of Germany).

Realskole. Three years of lower secondary education following seven years of primary education and culminating in the *realexamen* (Denmark).

Recognised teacher. The title of a teacher who, although appointed by a college and not by the university, is considered by the university to be suitable for university teaching (United Kingdom).

Record. A cumulative document of an institution containing information on an individual, such as a student's grades, courses, and programs. The registrar typically has responsibility for the compilation, evaluation, checking, safe retention, and appropriate use of student records and for the preparation and issuance of transcripts and data from the records. See also *academic record, duplicated record, fraudulent record, permanent nonacademic record, transcript.*

Recorder. The official responsible for keeping all institutional records of students, courses, programs, and, often, receipt of fees; usually a member of the registrar's staff.

Recruitment. (1) The seeking by employers of employees; (2) the seeking and enrolling of new students in a college or university, often by means of a field agent; (3) the securing of players for school or college athletic teams, musical organizations, or other groups by offering inducements. See also *faculty recruitment.*

Recteur. *Rector:* the chief executive of universities in French-language universities.

Rector. The head of a school, college, or university

not organized on the hierarchical structure of institutions in the United Kingdom or the United States. Comparable to *principal, president*, and *vice-chancellor*.

Rector's assessor. The rector's representative or substitute on the *court* (United Kingdom).

Recurrent education. The intermittent enrollment of older students in educational institutions when they wish to acquire additional knowledge or qualifications. See also *lifelong education*.

Recurrent expenditure. The periodic outlay of money for continuing costs, such as staff salaries, departmental budgets, laboratory supplies, library operations, and plant maintenance, in contrast to one-time *capital expenditure* made for physical facilities, equipment, and land.

Redbrick university. Colloquial expression for urban universities established by royal charter in the late nineteenth and early twentieth centuries to serve the educational needs of the industrial centers of England. See also *civic universities*.

Redovni profesor. Faculty rank: full professor (Yugoslavia).

Redundant faculty member. A tenured faculty member released because of a shift in student enrollments or financial exigency, usually with the payment of compensation related to salary (United Kingdom).

Reeducation extension. Organized instruction designed for graduates, such as short courses for social workers, dentists, engineers, doctors, or nurses. See also *refresher course*.

Reevaluation of financial need. The annual review of the financial status of students (including the family's financial status) receiving financial aid to determine changes in financial need.

Reference material. A work that is of assistance to readers in securing information in a concentrated way, such as a dictionary, encyclopedia, thesaurus, or yearbook.

Refresher course.   A course designed to update knowledge and review basic principles. See also *reeducation extension*.

Regent House.   The legislative body at Cambridge University, consisting of all teachers and administrative staff at the university and the colleges with at least the M.A. degree (United Kingdom).

Regional college.   See *regional institution*.

Regional institution.   An institution maintained to educate all qualified students within a specific geographical region or to offer education and extension services to the general population of that region. Such an institution, which allows students to pursue their education at a larger, more advanced level than in local institutions associated with it, is often organized and maintained by a group of countries or by state or provincial governments and often gives priority for admission to students within the specified region.

Regional scholarship.   A scholarship awarded to qualified students residing within a specific geographical region, often used to broaden the geographic background of the student body (United States).

Regional school.   An institution that is physically and academically separate from local public schools in its area; usually specializing in occupational programs at the secondary level but offering some postsecondary adult programs. Some such schools are classified by the United States Office of Education as vocational/technical schools, others as technical institutes; the determining factors being the level of instruction and the granting of associate degrees by technical institutes (United States).

Registered graduate.

Holder of an academic degree whose name is on the university register (the official electoral roll). Registration may be automatic on graduation if fee is paid, or application for registration may be required (United Kingdom).

Registrar.

(1)The official who controls the registration and enrollments of students by enforcing official action of faculties regarding degree requirements, course requirements, residence requirements, and quality point average requirements for graduation; by authorizing certification of completion of academic work; and by issuing transcripts. In addition, the registrar may compile statistical reports on students, including number of first-time enrollments and rates of retention; may supervise the admission of students; and may also serve as university examiner. In some countries, the registrar is the principal administrator responsible to the vice-chancellor, principal, or rector in directing the day-to-day operation of the university or college. Large institutions may have a registrar and assistant registrars for each undergraduate college and graduate school as well as for evening and part-time programs. (2) In a museum, the official responsible for accessioning and cataloging objects in the collection, supervising packing and storing of collections, and providing for transportation and insurance coverage of loaned objects (United States). See also *office of the registrar*.

Registration.

The enrollment of students in various courses or programs for a specific term. Registration of full-time students involves enrollment in several courses or subjects, whereas enrollment of part-time students may involve enrollment in only one course or subject. Preregistration involves the selection by students of their courses for one term during the preceding term and is often used to assign students to convenient sections of multisection courses. See also *cancelled registration, concurrent registration, double registration, provisional registration* and *full-time equivalent enrollment.*

Registration fee.

A charge for the privilege of registering, sometimes assessed in lieu of tuition.

Regius professor.

The holder of a chair that is under the patronage of the crown by reason of royal foundation or the right of patronage having devolved upon the Crown (United Kingdom).

Regular class.

A university-level class that is designed for full-time students working toward a degree or other formal award.

Regular fee.

A fee paid by all students for educational services.

Regular program.

A standard set of classes that leads to a degree.

Regular session.

The semesters, quarters, or other terms that comprise the customary *academic year.*

Regular student.

(1) A student who has been admitted as a candidate in a regular program to work toward a degree; contrast *special student;* (2) an enrolled student who is in *good standing.*

Reifeprüfung.

Secondary school-leaving examination on completion of thirteen years of schooling to obtain the *Reifezeugnis* (German-language systems).

Reifezeugnis.

Secondary school-leaving certificate (German-language systems).

Reinstatement. Permission to reenroll following suspension or dismissal (United States).

Reitor. *Rector* (Portuguese-language systems).

Rektor. *Rector* (Denmark, Hungary, Sweden, Yugoslavia).

Rektor helyettesek. Vice-rector (Hungary).

Related subject. A course of instruction outside of but relevant to a field of study, taken either as a required or as an *elective course* in meeting degree requirements.

Relative standing. The rank or standing of a student in relation to a group or class of students.

Remedial course. An introductory-level class given by an educational institution for students not prepared to take a *regular class* given by that institution.

Remedial program. Course of instruction designed to overcome academic and cultural deficiencies and to qualify students for admission or to assist them in making normal progress in academic work.

Removal of deficiency. See *admission deficiency, incomplete grade*.

Remuneration. Salary and financial benefits accorded faculty and staff for services rendered.

Renaissance. The period of artistic and intellectual activity beginning in the fourteenth century in Italy and lasting into the seventeenth century, characterized by the revival of humanistic learning, the growth of arts and literature, and the beginning of modern science.

Report. A compilation of information or a statement prepared by one organization or person for use by others. See also *progress report*.

Required course.

A class that must be completed satisfactorily to qualify for a degree or certificate (United States). Contrast *elective course*.

Requirement.

An obligation, such as the payment of registration fees or the maintenance of satisfactory grades, that must be met to qualify for a degree, certificate, or credit (United States).

Research.

Critical, disciplined inquiry into a problem, whether contracted for and supported by industry or government or conducted independently by faculty members of universities as part of the total work-load assignment. Along with education and service, one of the three principal functions of many colleges and universities. See also *applied research*, *basic research*.

Research and development (R and D).

Disciplined inquiry and the creation of materials stemming from this inquiry, often sponsored by major national and international scientific agencies and government ministries to assure the application of research to practical problems.

Research fellowship.

Financial support given to graduate students to support their research work; contrast *teaching fellowship*. See also *fellowship*.

Research institute.

An organization, either part of a university or operated independently, that conducts research in specialized fields or for special purposes. For example, a Forensic Science Institute.

Research Libraries Group.

A consortium of the libraries of Columbia University, Harvard University, Yale University, and the New York Public Libraries in the United States. Originated to share resources and investigate possibilities (such as shared acquisition programs) for cooperative approaches toward the growing financial problems of large research libraries.

Research project.   A specific endeavor of disciplined inquiry, usually covering a planned length of time and focusing on a defined problem or area of study.

Research report.   A report presenting the results of concluded research.

Research staff.   The professional personnel employed by a college or university or other research organization exclusively to conduct research.

Residence hall.   A building serving as the living quarters of students, providing sleeping, study, social, recreational, and, frequently dining facilities. See also *dormitory, hostel.*

Residence requirement.   An institutional policy requiring a period of on-campus attendance in order to be eligible for a degree.

Resident assistant.   A student who is a member of the proctoring and advisory staff of a residence hall or dormitory (United States).

Resident credit.   *Credit* earned while in residence at a college or university.

Resident instruction.   Instruction provided on the main or branch campuses by the regular instructional staff of a college or university.

Resident student.   (1) A student who lives in university housing or residence on campus; (2) a student who is a legal resident of the division of the government (state, province) supporting an institution and therefore entitled to lower fee assessments than nonresidents.

Residential adult education center.   A special facility where adult students may take courses for their continued professional education or in traditional areas of liberal adult education, with tuition costs heavily subsidized by the central government (United Kingdom). See also *conference center*, *residential conference center*.

Residential college.   A college that provides living quarters for its students or that limits enrollment primarily or exclusively to those students who live in its residence halls.

Residential conference center.   A facility for adult education and conference programs, with audiovisual equipment, lecture halls, classrooms, conference rooms, and living accommodations. See also *conference center*.

Resource allocation.   The distribution of financial and other resources among programs, departments, and divisions of a college or university.

Resource requirements prediction model (RRPM).   A cost function or simulation model developed by the National Center for Higher Education Management Systems using disaggregated cost functions in its first operational version (United States).

Restricted admission.   Admission to an institution of higher education based on success in entrance examination or other specified requirements set by the institution or government authority (in addition to secondary school-leaving certificate or high school diploma). See also *selective admission*. Contrast *open admission*.

Restricted scholarship.   A scholarship limited to applicants who meet particular requirements, such as geographical or family origin, religious affiliation, or a specific choice of curriculum. See also *scholarship*.

Retention rate.   (1) The percentage of an entering class that enrolls for each succeeding academic year and graduates within the normal time period; (2) the proportion of learned material remembered or retained during successive periods.

Retirement.   The relinquishing by a person of his or her employment responsibilities and activities on attainment of a certain age, usually 65 or 70, either voluntarily or because of employment policy.

Retraining.   The pursuit of courses of study, practical work, or on-the-job training to acquire new skills and knowledge necessary to retain a present position or to gain a new position.

Retraining program.   Courses of instruction that give students or workers up-to-date knowledge in their field of specialization or prepare them to undertake new responsibilities.

Retread course.   (1) A course offered a second time for students who were unable to attend the first course because of schedule difficulties; (2) a course designed to update the knowledge of professionals.

Rettore.   *Rector* (Italy).

Revenue.   Income such as from tuition, fees, rents, ancillary enterprises, and tax monies.

Rigorosum.   The final examinations organized by a university as partial fulfillment of requirements for the doctoral degree (Austria).

Rig-veda.   The primary sacred scripture of Hinduism, consisting of 1028 hymns, mainly addressed to various Aryan deities.

Risk management.   The identification, analysis, prevention, reduction, or neutralization of potential changes or damages so as to protect an institution against all or part of the possible financial consequences of a given action.

Rolling admission.   The notification of applicants of their acceptance or rejection for admission throughout the year, as soon as decisions are made on their applications, as opposed to notifying all of them at one time (United States).

Rorschach ink blot test. A projective test devised by a Swiss psychiatrist, H. Rorschach (1884–1922), to identify psychological disorders or personality factors based on subjects' responses to otherwise meaningless ink blots.

Rural conscription. A one-year period of work in rural or poor urban areas required of new medical doctors and dentists (Ecuador).

Rush. To entertain a group of students to secure pledges of membership; both *fraternities* and *sororities* use this method of gaining members (United States).

S

Sabbatical leave. See *sabbatical teaching year*.

Sabbatical teaching year. A leave of absence, usually after six years of teaching service, for teaching staff with full or partial compensation to provide opportunity for professional development.

Salary. The amount of money paid to administrators, faculty, and staff. Adminstrative salaries are usually paid for a calendar year (twelve months). Faculty and staff salaries may be paid for a calendar year or for the academic year (two semesters or three quarters). Many institutions establish ranges or minimum and maximum salaries for each faculty rank, and many systems of higher education under the control of ministries of education relate salaries to the salary rates of civil servants holding comparable positions. See also *remuneration*.

Salary analysis. The study of salaries paid to administrators, faculty, and staff in order to make salaries equitable in terms of job requirements and the performance of individuals in meeting these requirements. Salary analysis may also include comparisons with salaries paid by similar or related institutions.

Salary scale. The range of salaries paid to faculty and staff on the basis of rank, length of service, or other criteria.

Sandwich course. A class taught under the *sandwich plan* whereby a student spends his time partly in a job and partly in a university or other institution that offers training in the theory of a subject; normally the student spends an alternate period of weeks or months, full-time, in one sector or the other (United Kingdom and Commonwealth countries). See also *cooperative education.*

Sandwich plan. A program that alternates periods of full-time work off campus and full-time study at an educational institution and combines this work and study as an integrated program leading to a degree. Courses are known as *thick sandwich* and *thin sandwich* according to the amount and length of work experience in the program.

Satellite college. A college that is affiliated with a larger institution. Such a college may use some facilities of the larger institution but has its own staff and programs and is usually autonomous in controlling its own programs and finances.

Satisfactory grade. A *passing grade* that meets requirements for graduation.

Schedule. See *calendar.*

Scholar. (1) A student enrolled in a university who holds an academic scholarship; (2) a faculty member who has achieved mastery of highly organized academic studies and subject matter.

Scholarship. (1) The quality of a student's achievement in his studies; (2) a financial grant that does not involve repayment, usually based on the student's performance (or potential for performance) in the educational program of the institution. Financial need is sometimes a consideration in establishing the amount of the award. See also *athletic scholarship, endowed scholarship, honorary scholarship, national scholarship, prize scholarship, regional scholarship, restricted scholarship, sponsored scholarship, state scholarship.*

Scholarship committee. Members of the administrative staff and faculty charged with reviewing faculty and academic records; scholastic requirements, with a view to maintaining desirable standards; or the performance, potential, and financial need of students to whom honors, prizes, and money may be awarded. An institution may have special committees to deal with special awards and needs.

Scholastic acceleration. Completion of an academic program in a shorter period of time than that normally expected or allowed, either by enrolling in more courses than the number usually taken by full-time students or by enrolling in summer sessions or evening courses in addition to the normal course load.

Scholastic achievement. See *academic achievement.*

Scholastic aptitude. See *academic aptitude.*

Scholastic aptitude test. See *academic aptitude test.*

Scholastic deficiency. Failure to achieve the necessary *quality point average* or other standards required for graduation.

Scholastic motivation. The degree to which students are encouraged to strive for superior academic achievement. See also *motivation*.

Scholastic probation. The status of a student whose academic work is unsatisfactory. Probation warns the student that he or she must improve the quality of academic achievement to become a student in good standing (United States).

School. (1) A division within a higher educational institution, such as an undergraduate or graduate school; (2) an educational institution at the primary or secondary levels and occasionally at the postsecondary level.

School-age population. The *age group* toward which educational efforts are primarily directed.

School attendance law. See *compulsory education*.

School-leaver. (1) A student who leaves school, either prior to or after completion of a program of study; (2) a student who leaves school after completion of compulsory education (United Kingdom).

School-leaving certificate. A credential or diploma denoting successful completion of secondary education, awarded in all countries. Examples include *Abitur* (German-language systems), *baccalauréat* (French-language systems), *bachillerato* (Spanish-language systems), high school diploma (United States).

School newspaper. A student publication, or an official publication of an institution, that provides a medium for communication within the school community.

School of art. A professional institution that offers programs specializing in painting, drawing, sculpture, design, or other arts.

Science. (1) Knowledge that has been formulated and systematized with reference to general truths and the operation of general laws; (2) organized knowledge in a specific branch of study, such as biological science, military science.

Scientific manpower.   The totality of scientists available in a particular area, such as a region or nation.

Scientific research.   Research conducted in order to advance knowledge.

Scientist.   (1) A person learned in science; (2) a person who engages in scientific research.

Score.   The rating or rank of an individual's or group's performance expressed in terms of a standardized scale of units, as opposed to a mark that describes performance in terms of qualitative measures. See also *percentile score.*

Second bachelor's degree.   A bachelor's degree earned at the same time as, or subsequent to, a first bachelor's degree, usually by completing an additional academic year and requirements for the additional degree.

Second-level degree.   See *advanced degree.*

Second-level school.   See *secondary education.*

Secondary education.   The educational level immediately preceding the tertiary or higher education level —comprised of such schools as high school, *colegio*, *lycée*, and *preparatory school*—for youths generally between twelve to thirteen and seventeen to eighteen years of age. Usually consists of a general introductory program of three to four years, followed by two to three years of more specialized study, depending on the system of education.

Secondary program.   See *secondary school.*

Secondary school.   An educational institution offering academic or vocational programs following primary or elementary schooling and prior to college- or university-level work, such as a high school, comprehensive secondary school, general secondary school, lower secondary school, technical secondary school, and vocational secondary school. See also *lyćee, lyceum, lykeion, secondary education.*

Secondary school certificate.

See *school-leaving certificate.*

Secondary school graduate.

A student who has completed secondary school and has been awarded a diploma or other school-leaving certificate.

Sectarian college.

A college controlled or sponsored by a religious group or church organization. See also *denominational college.*

Segregated education.

Programs of education in which students are separated into different programs or locations depending on educationally nonrelevant factors, such as race, religion, or sex. See also *discrimination, racial discrimination.*

Segregation.

The separation of one group of individuals from an otherwise mixed group of individuals on the basis of some predetermined factor, such as age, race, religion, or sex. See also *discrimination.*

Segundo grado de formación profesional.

The intermediate level of occupational preparation corresponding to the level of *bachiller* (Spain).

Selective admission.

Exercise of discretionary powers in admitting students to a higher education institution, usually on the basis of merit as determined by the institution and in terms of those applicants judged to have the best probability of success in their chosen program of studies. Evidence of previous achievement, recommendations regarding character and personal studies, and entrance examination scores are important elements in the selective admission procedure, and personal interviews may be required. See also *restricted admission*.

Semester.

A *term* constituting half of the *academic year*, usually fifteen to eighteen weeks. Contrast *quarter, trimester*.

Semester credit hour.

One hour of class plus two hours of preparation each week during a *semester*. See also *credit hour*.

Seminar.

(1) An organized group of students working under the supervision of an instructor and holding scheduled meetings for reports and discussion. (2) A meeting of a small group for the presentation and discussion of research or scholarship.

Seminary.

An institution of higher learning that prepares persons to become priests, clergymen, and church workers, usually sponsored and controlled by a church or religious organization but sometimes nondenominational.

Semiprofession.

A class of occupations closely related to a profession, whose practitioners are supervised by professionals in carrying out some professional responsibilities. Specialized education beyond secondary school is usually required and is often regulated by the related profession.

Semiprofessional school.

A postsecondary school that offers programs leading to semiprofessional employment requiring special skills and knowledge. Ordinarily the duration of a program is one or two years, and certificates or diplomas are given at completion of the program. In some instances degrees, such as the Associate of Science or Associate of Business, are awarded. Credits and courses are often applicable to the bachelor's degree (United States).

Senate. The highest academic policymaking body in most universities, responsible for standards of research, instruction, examinations, and awards. Membership usually includes chief administrative officers, full-time professors, deans, and heads of departments, and may include some students, nonacademic staff and occasionally laymen.

Senior. A student enrolled in the last year of a four-year undergraduate degree program or high school program (United States). See also *freshman, sophomore, junior.*

Senior Cambridge Examination. Secondary school-leaving certificate examination (United Kingdom).

Senior class. Members of the class comprised of those students enrolled for the final year of their four-year program, whether high school, college, or university (United States). See also *class.*

Senior lecturer. Faculty rank: in universities following the British university tradition, the rank immediately below *reader;* in other institutions, such as some polytechnics, the rank below principal lecturer as well as reader (United Kingdom and Commonwealth countries).

Senior student. (1) In some universities, a student who enjoys special status in view of previous studies; (2) the leading student in a university or college, generally holding office as president of the junior common room or as president of the students' union (United Kingdom).

Senior teaching and research staff. Those staff members of the university who hold academic positions above the middle rank in the academic hierarchy.

Senority system.

A personnel system that accords certain privileges and rights, such as preference in salary, tenure, promotion, choice of courses, and leaves of absence, to staff members based on their length of service.

Senmong-gakko.

Specialized postsecondary institutions (Japan).

Sequential learning.

The cumulative increase of knowledge or skills stemming from the satisfactory completion of one *module* or *course* as a prerequisite before beginning the next.

Sequential program.

In higher adult education, a series of courses to be taken in sequence as specified, leading to a nondegree formal award, such as certificate, diploma, or professional designation.

Session.

(1) A working period of about twenty weeks (winter session) and/or about ten weeks (summer session); (2) sometimes used as equivalent to the *academic year* (United Kingdom); (3) a meeting of a class or seminar (United States). See also *regular session*.

Seven College Conference.

See *Seven Sisters*.

Seven Sisters.

A group of selective women's colleges in the Northeastern United States—including Barnard, Bryn Mawr, Mount Holyoke, Radcliffe, Smith, Wellesley, and Vassar—considered similar because of common interests. Some of the seven have now merged with universities, and hence the number retains largely historical significance at this time (United States). Known formerly as the Seven College Conference.

Shared services.

Joint use of such services as library resources by two or more institutions.

Shari'a.

Arabic: Islamic law.

Sheltered workshop. A place of employment that provides paid jobs, usually at skilled and semiskilled levels, for persons who have physical, mental, or emotional handicaps.

Shopwork. Practical experiences obtained in laboratory and/or shop facilities in such areas as woodwork, metalwork, or other industrial processes and procedures.

Short course. An intensive course scheduled for a period shorter than the ordinary semester or quarter (United States).

Short-cycle education. Postsecondary study that offers career preparation for middle-level, semiprofessional, or technical employment; usually comprises the initial two years of university and culminates in a degree, such as the associate degree, a certificate, or a diploma.

Short-unit course. A course or training program, usually on a special phase of a subject that is shorter duration than the usual *term*.

Shushi. The *master's degree* (Japan).

Simulation. Role playing that imitates actual situations; used as a method of instruction.

Single-field industrial laboratory. A shop used in teaching industrial arts that is limited to a particular craft or group of industries.

Sixth form. The final year of secondary education, involving study for the advanced-level or A-level of the *General Certificate of Education* and university entry (United Kingdom). Also called top form. See also *General Certificate of Education*.

Sixth form certificate. Secondary school qualification obtained without examination on completion of form six, normally after eight years of primary and four years of secondary education (New Zealand).

Social background.

The status of an individual generally described in terms of social class, that is, his or her standing within the sociocultural system, usually based on the income and occupation of the head of the family. Most often classified as either upper class, middle class, or working class, although subdivisions can be made within each of these categories. See also *disadvantaged student.*

Social benefits of higher education.

Society's return on its investments in higher education, estimated at approximately 10 percent annually.

Social discrimination.

(1) Exclusion of an individual from a group or from an institution because of the individual's *social background*; (2) inhibition of upward social mobility, that is, the movement from a lower social class to a higher social class. See also *discrimination.*

Socialization of education.

(1) The introduction of discussion, student government, and other democratic procedures into educational institutions; (2) the shaping of a course, program, or the administration of an institution to meet the needs of society.

Society.

(1) An association or organization of people having a common purpose or mutual interests; (2) an enduring group of people that maintains and perpetuates itself.

Society of Jesus.

(Jesuits.) A Roman Catholic order, founded in 1540 by St. Ignatius of Loyola (1491–1556), particularly active in education and which founded a great number of institutions of higher education throughout the world, the first in Spain in 1546. When the order was dissolved by Clement XIV (1773–1814), a number of its institutions were closed or transferred to other ownership.

Since its reestablishment early in the nineteenth century, the Society has been persecuted and suppressed for varying periods in a number of countries but today it has seminaries, colleges, and universities in most nations with sizable Catholic populations, except in the East European socialist nations.

Socioeconomic background. See *social background*.

Soka gakkai. See *Nichiren Shoshu Buddhism*.

Sophomore. A second-year student enrolled in a four-year undergraduate or high school program (United States). See also *freshman, junior, senior*.

Sophomore class. The students enrolled in the second year of a four-year undergraduate or high school program (United States).

Sorority. A group of female students associated for social or professional reasons; usually designated by Greek letters (United States). See also *fraternity*.

Special education. Specialized programs for students with severe physical or mental handicaps, geared to their particular needs.

Special fee. A charge for a particular service or purpose.

Special honors class. A class designed for a superior group of students, with attendance required.

Special probation. The academic status of students who have been permitted to reenter after dismissal or suspension for academic reasons. The status changes when the student's cumulative grade-point average raises to that of *good standing* (United States).

Special student. A student who is not a candidate for a degree or certificate or who not yet demonstrates sufficient proficiency in academic work to be a candidate. Also called non-matriculated or unclassified student. Constrast *regular student.*

Specialist degree.   See *professional certificate.*

**Sponsored faculty
research.**   Research conducted by a faculty member under a financial grant from an outside source such as government or industry; usually separately budgeted.

Sponsored fellowship.   A fellowship provided by an organization or individual outside the institution; usually nontaxable.

Staatsexamen.   State examination required in order to teach or to practice in the fields of law, medicine, pharmacy, and secondary school teaching (Federal Republic of Germany). Called *Staatsprüfung* in Austria.

Standard.   (1) Level or *grade*, such as standard VI; (2) the goal or objective of education expressed as an ideal of education; (3) a norm by which students, teachers, or institutions are judged.

Standardized test.   An examination with uniform methods of administration and scoring, set norms, and content empirically selected and thus possible to score with high objectivity. Also called objective test.

Standing committee.   A permanent committee established for continual operation, as opposed to an ad hoc committee, created for a limited period.

State scholarship.   A scholarship provided by law or maintained by state funds and usually granted to some residents of the state for attendance at an institution in the state. Recipients in some states may be selected by members of the legislature; in others by the state board of education, the regents, presidents of institutions, or on recommendation of designated local school officials; in still others, through competitive examinations or rank among high school graduates (United States).

Statement of graduation. Written evidence that a student has been awarded a degree, including date and major field of study, if any. See also *diploma*.

Statement of standing. Certification of a student's academic achievement and status with respect to class rank and disciplinary actions, if any (United States). See also *good standing*.

Steady state. (1) A lack of growth in higher education enrollments resulting either from a deliberate policy adopted by an institution or a government agency or from student responses to such factors as downturns in the economy or higher costs; (2) the situation of an institution that as a policy plans to remain at a specific size with little or no changes in total enrollments or academic offerings.

Step increase. An increase in salary in an amount specified as a standard increment within a salary range or schedule that has a minimum and a maximum salary rate. Salaries are usually increased step by step until the maximum is reached.

Stipend. The amount of financial award for a scholarship, fellowship, or assistantship.

Streaming. The practice of placing pupils in different groups, tracks, or streams according to aptitude and/or achievement. Also called ability grouping.

Structural organization. The arrangement of administrative and decision-making bodies of a university or college.

Student. A person registered in an educational institution and pursuing a course of study. See also *accepted or admitted student, active student, classified student, college-level student, college/ university adult education student, correspondence student, degree-credit student, fifth-year student, first-time student, foreign student, full-time student, graduate student, inactive student, lower division student, migrant student, noncredit student, nondegree-credit student, nonresident student, off-campus student, out-of-state student, part-time student, postgraduate student, professional student, regular student, resident student, special or unclassified student, transfer student, transient student, undergraduate student, upper division student.*

Student activities. The extracurricular functions, events, and organizations of students—including all interest groups and student government agencies, such as the student cabinet—that occur under the auspices of an institution of higher education. See also *extracurricular activities, co-curricular activity.*

Student activities card. A card issued to a student that entitles him to admission to campus functions and events, including athletic events (United States).

Student activities center. See *student union*.

Student activities program. The total range of student functions, events, and organizations that supplements the organized academic program of an institution, usually operated and managed by students.

Student body. All of the students enrolled in an institution.

Student budget. The estimated income and expenditures of a student for an academic term or year. Used to determine financial aid.

Student classification. The status of a student based on progress in an academic program, quality of achievement, and credit hours completed (United States). See also *good standing*.

Student clock-hour. See *credit hour*.

Student costs. The amount of money required by a student for expenses such as tuition, fees, room and board, books and supplies, clothes, travel, recreation, and incidentals. As used by an institution's financial aid office, the term implies approval of the *student budget* (United States).

Student council. The general decision-making agency of student government at an institution, consisting of students elected on a representative basis; its functions vary considerably among institutions but most typically are concerned with policies regarding student activities, conduct, and discipline. Its decisions may be subject to review by the faculty or administration. Also called student senate, student cabinet. See also *student government*.

Student court. A student tribunal within institutional government, whereby selected students hear evidence and propose or impose penalties for student violations of institutional regulations.

Student credit hour. In unit-cost studies, represents one student enrolled for one hour of *credit* per term (usually one hour of class week with two hours outside preparation or two laboratory hours per week). The total student credit hours for a course is determined by multiplying the credit-hour value of the course by the number of students registered in the course—for example, a three-credit course enrolling fifteen students yields forty-five student credit hours. The total credit hours for an institution is the sum of student credit hours for all courses offered during the term (United States). See also *class size, credit hour*.

Student credit load. The total number of *credit hours* for which a student is enrolled in a term (United States).

Student credit load requirement. The number of *credit hours* an admitted student is required to carry per term. Normally a full-time program is defined as a minimum of twelve to a maximum of fifteen hours for undergraduates and nine hours for graduate students (United States).

Student exchange. See *exchange of students*.

Student evaluation of faculty. The appraisal by the students in a course of the teaching effectiveness of the faculty member, including classroom presentations, readings, and organization of course material.

Student federation. A state or national organization of college students intended to further the interests of students usually in one or more specialized problem areas; not prevalent in the United States. See also *student union*.

Student government. The student boards, committees, and organizations authorized to act on behalf of students regarding student life and student activities. See also *student council, student union*.

Student handbook. A book of information and guidance for students, published by the institution or a student organization.

Student housing. See *cité universitaire, dormitory, hostel*.

Student identification card.

An official card issued by an institution that identifies the student by name, address, birth date, signature, often with a photograph of the student.

Student learner.

A participant in a *cooperative education* program, legally employed as a part-time worker and so classified by the Wage and Hour and Public Contracts Divisions of the United States Department of Labor for wage and hour regulation purposes (United States). See also *trainee*.

Student loan.

Funds loaned to a student as financial aid and carrying low or no interest charges, with the expectation that the loan will be repaid on graduation or termination of studies.

Student loan program.

The policies and practices of an institution or agency in making *student loan* funds available.

Student migration.

The movement of students among institutions, states, and nations. See also *migration*.

Student organization.

A student group or association officially recognized by an institution of higher education. See also *student federation, student union*.

Student organization adviser.

A staff member assigned or invited to assist students in the conduct of affairs of a *student organization*.

Student personnel record.

See *permanent nonacademic record*.

Student personnel service.

The supportive, noninstructional programs conducted by an institution to assist students in utilizing academic offerings; offers a wide variety of assistance, including counseling, aptitude testing, health service, housing, food service, student activities, travel service, and placement.

Student placement.   See *placement*.

Student power.   The influence of students in campus af-
                                  fairs, institutional policymaking, and society
                                  in general. See also *cogobierno, Drittelparität,
                                  democratization of education*.

Student press.   The student journals, newspapers, maga-
                                  zines, and other publications sponsored, fi-
                                  nanced, edited, and controlled by students.
                                  Also called student publications.

Student rank.   The position of a student in class in relation
                                  to other students based on *grade-point aver-
                                  age* (United States).

Student rights.   The guarantee of protection of students by
                                  the institution against improper institu-
                                  tional actions or decisions in such areas as
                                  academic freedom, due process, disclosure
                                  of records, discrimination, or violation of
                                  civil liberties and citizenship rights (United
                                  States).

Student teacher.   A student who is preparing for a teaching
                                  career by completing a required period of
                                  supervised practice teaching in the
                                  classroom.

Student/teacher ratio.   An index of the number of students relative
                                  to the number of teaching staff in an insti-
                                  tution or a system (excluding those mem-
                                  bers of staff engaged exclusively in re-
                                  search). A ratio of 15:1 equals fifteen
                                  students for each teaching staff member.
                                  Reverse of *teacher/student ratio*.

Student teaching.   Practicum or classroom experience re-
                                  quired of candidates enrolled in teacher
                                  training programs, including observation
                                  and actual teaching in the classroom under
                                  the guidance of a master teacher. Also called
                                  practice teaching.

Student union.

(1) An organization of students concerned with student matters, often supported by a fee levied on all students and governed by a board of elected student members; (2) the building where student activities take place.

Student unit cost.

The average expenditure per student for a period of time, determined by dividing total instructional cost by total *full-time equivalent* enrollment.

Student wastage.

See *wastage*.

Student welfare service.

The program of guidance and counseling planned to meet the varying needs of students in obtaining the maximum benefits from college life. Includes such activities as orientation, educational advisement, vocational guidance, personal and social guidance, and health guidance. See also *bienestar estudiantil, student personnel service*.

Students' representative council.

See *student council*.

Studentship.

Synonym for *fellowship*.

Studium generale.

The medieval university in France, Germany, Italy, and England.

Study-service.

A program incorporating a period of civic or development service as an optional or compulsory part of the course of study in an educational institution. Students spend a specified period of time in productive work primarily intended to benefit the local or national community, such as rural or urban development, adult literacy training, agricultural extension, health education, or other non-formal educational activities including improving roads, bridges, water supplies, and the like. The tasks assigned are not necessarily related to the student's own field of study, and the period of service is unremunerated, except for a modest allowance sometimes paid to help students cover their living expenses.

Subject-matter requirement.

See *admission requirement*.

Sub-tunica.

The plain black cassock worn by undergraduates and bachelors in the early European universities.

Summer class.

A course offered during the summer *term* or *quarter*.

Summer session.

The summer *term*. See also *session*.

Supervisory teacher.

A teacher who directs the work of one or more *student teachers*. Also referred to as cooperating teacher, master teacher, or supervising teacher.

Supplementary examination.

A second examination, at which students who have failed to pass the yearly examination are afforded another opportunity to complete their year. Popularly called post mortem (Australia).

Supplementary grade report.

A grade report issued in addition to the regular term grade report in order to award *credit* through the removal of an incomplete mark or condition or through a special examination for credit during the course of a term (United States).

Supplementary instruction.

Vocational instruction generally provided on a part-time day or evening basis for adults wishing to prepare for an occupation or to refresh, update, or upgrade competencies needed for continued employment or for increased responsibility. See also *adult education*.

Survey.

An investigation to discover current practices and trends in a specific field for which data are gathered through questionnaires or interviews. Surveys can be international, national, regional, or local, but involve a number of samples or cases, in contrast to *case* studies.

Survey course. A broad overview of one or several subjects or fields of study (United States).

Suspension. Required temporary separation of a student from the institution as disciplinary action, as opposed to indefinite or permanent *dismissal.*

Symposium. A teaching method consisting of lecture presentations by two or more speakers representing different viewpoints. A moderator typically introduces the speakers and invites questions and comments from the audience after the formal presentations.

Syndicate. The executive board of a university (India).

System of education. The total educational programs and institutions of a nation or other area.

System of instruction. The particular type or plan of teaching, as by classroom lectures or computer-assisted instruction, used in a course or institution to fulfill set objectives.

T

Taehak. A college or university (Democratic People's Republic of Korea).

Talmud. A collection of rabbinic law and discussion comprising the *mishnah* developed by scholars in the academies of higher learning in Judea and Babylon, knowledge of which is required of any Jew who is to be considered a learned person.

Tanár. Faculty rank: *professor* (Hungary).

Tanárseged.   Faculty rank: *assistant* (Hungary).

Tantrism.   Form of Sanskrit: Hinduism and Buddhism that originated out of Indian folk religion. Manuals of instruction known as tantras make use of magic, incantation, and the occult and incorporate the psychology of *Hinayana* and the metaphysics of *Mahayana*.

Tawjihi.   The general secondary education examination taken at the conclusion of secondary school and a prerequisite for admission to postsecondary education (Jordan).

Taxi professor.   Colloquially, a professor who rushes via taxi from his professional office to the university only to taxi back to the offices immediately following his university lecture (Latin America).

Taxonomy.   (1) The science of classification; (2) a system for classifying similar entities, such as animals, plants, or educational fields, according to specific laws or principles.

Teach-in.   Colloquially, a conference of one or more days, during which students and faculty engage in speeches and debates about a controversial issue and for which regular classes may sometimes be canceled. (United States).

Teacher.   (1) Person employed by an educational institution to instruct students, generally after he or she completes an established program of study, participates in practice teaching, and is credentialed by appropriate authorities; (2) the generic term for instructional staff at all levels of the educational system.

Teacher aid.   A semiprofessional or paraprofessional staff member who assists a teacher in routine, noninstructional tasks.

Teacher certification. Official recognition, granted by a government agency or other appropriate body, of

an individual's qualifications to teach, usually accorded on presentation of academic
credentials or demonstration of competence. In the United States, mainly applicable in primary and secondary public
school systems.

Teacher education. An academic field of study and a branch of
educational science that includes all studies
and experiences involved in preparing a
person to teach, to organize learning experiences, to administer educational institutions, and to provide supportive services
for the learning process at all levels.

Teacher-educator. One who is responsible for the preparation
and in-service training of teachers in such
a way as to enable them to meet certification
requirements or to advance in teaching positions. See also *supervisory teacher*.

Teacher shortage. A situation that arises when the available
supply of trained and licensed teachers is
less than the number of vacancies, resulting, in many cases, in an unfavorable ratio
of teachers to students.

Teacher status. The position or rank of a teacher in relation
to his peers in terms of his legal, profes-
sional, or social status. See also *faculty rank*.

Teacher/student ratio. An index of the number of teaching staff
in relation to the number of students in an
institution or system—ratio of 1:10 is one
faculty member for every ten students. Re-
verse of *student/teacher ratio*.

Teacher-trainer. See *teacher-educator*.

Teachers association. Professional organization of teachers in a
specific field or in a system for the purpose
of promoting the professional and economic interests of the members and of
teachers in general.

Teachers college. An institution established for the purpose

of preparing teachers and support personnel for the elementary and secondary
schools. May be an autonomous institution,
a division of a state system of education, or
a professional school within or affiliated
with a university. See also *école normale, escuela normal*.

Teacher's manual.   A guide to the presentation of subject matter and related topics in a given field. Often
designed as a companion reference to a specific textbook.

Teachers organization.   See *teachers association*.

Teaching.   The process of helping learners acquire
knowledge, skills, and appreciations by
means of systematic instruction.

**Teaching and research
staff.**   All staff members of a college or university,
other than administrative or supportive
staff, who are engaged in teaching, research, or both.

Teaching assistant.   (1) An undergraduate or graduate student
who assists in instruction and in handling
clerical work incidental to teaching classes.
Remuneration may be in cash or by tuition
remission for courses in which the student
is registered. A graduate teaching assistant
is usually working for an advanced degree
(United States). (2) A staff member at the
primary or secondary level who performs
teaching duties under the supervision of a
teacher.

Teaching assistantship.   Financial support accorded an advanced
degree student as remuneration for college
or university part-time teaching. See also
teaching fellowship.

Teaching experience.   Knowledge, skill, and practice derived from
observation and participation in the trans-
mittal of information to students.

Teaching fellow. The recipient of a *teaching fellowship*.

Teaching fellowship. A fellowship requiring that a given portion of the recipient's time be spent in teaching. Since the teaching is a required aspect of the recipient's educational program, the monies received are not taxable. See also *teaching assistantship*. Contrast *research fellowship*.

Teaching load. The time spent by a teacher on all teaching-related activities, such as classroom teaching; preparation of lectures, assignments, and examinations; grading; student counseling; professional development; and creative activity. Usually expressed in terms of hours spent per week. See also *workload*.

Teaching method. A procedure, technique, or use of apparatus for the presentation of instructional materials. See also *colloquium, computer-assisted instruction, computer-managed instruction, educational technology, educational television, lecture, programmed learning, seminar, symposium, tutorial course*.

Teaching staff. The teaching personnel at a university, who may also be engaged in research. See also *faculty, teaching and research staff*.

Team teaching. A collaborative teaching method whereby two or more members of the teaching staff share the instructional duties of a class, with each teacher being responsible for a specific segment of the topic, usually in accordance with his or her special area of expertise.

Technical. (1) A high level of knowledge and skills required to perform certain techniques or duties; (2) a level of skill or occupation needed for a semiprofession (that is, between the skilled trades and the professions), generally attained in a two-year or other short-cycle education institution.

Technical assistance. Bilateral or multilateral aid programs in the form of personnel or training sponsored by a college or university in a developed nation or international agencies or organizations on behalf of a less-developed country.

Technical college. A postsecondary institution offering training in applied sciences or industrial or mechanical arts, usually for occupations at a level between the skilled trades and the professions. See also *polytechnic, technical education, technical institute*.

Technical education. Formal study oriented toward the practical application of knowledge in technical subjects, usually offered in technical institutes, junior colleges, or other special institutions of postsecondary education. Includes all occupational education for semiprofessional fields. In the United States, technical education *credits* are usually applicable toward the *associate degree* and increasingly toward the *bachelor's degree* as well.

Technical high school. A secondary school specializing in vocational as opposed to academic or liberal arts course offerings (United States). See also *technical education, technical secondary school*.

Technical institute. An independent two-year postsecondary institution or a division within a two-year or four-year institution, that offers occupational curricula designed primarily to prepare students for immediate employment in an engineering or physical science occupation. In the United States such programs generally lead to an *associate degree* or equivalent certificate or diploma. See also *technical college, technical education*.

Technical secondary school. See *technical high school*.

Technician. A highly skilled semiprofessional worker,

generally a graduate of a *short-cycle* program, who works below the level of a professional but above the level of a skilled worker.

Technikum.   See *felsöfokú technikumok*.

Technische Hochschule.   A technological institution of higher education—often translated as university—having the same status as a university (Federal Republic of Germany, German Democratic Republic).

Technische Universität.   Technological university (Austria, Federal Republic of Germany, German Democratic Republic). See also *Technische Hochschule*.

Technological institution.   An independently organized professional school or unit within a larger educational institution that offers programs primarily in engineering and physical science disciplines. Also called institute of technology or *polytechnic* institute. Course offerings are generally broader and more scientifically oriented than those in a *technical college* or *technical institute*.

Technological university.   A type of university, prevalent in many countries, that specializes in such studies as engineering, mining, mathematics, and physics. See also *Technische Hochschule, Technische Universität*.

Technology.   (1) The systematic study and application of science to the practical and industrial arts; (2) the facts, principles, and knowledge related to man's understanding and control of his physical environment; (3) the solution of practical problems by the use of applied science.

Technology transfer.   The communication and adoption of the latest technological and scientific achievements in one industry, economy, or country into a different industry, economic sector, or nation.

Técnico. A *technican*, qualification for which is granted on completion of a two- to three-year program of technical study in a university or technical institute. Generally the title is qualified by the field of specialization, such as *técnico en administración* or *técnico superior en agronomía* (Spanish-language systems).

Técnico auxiliar. An auxiliary or assistant technician who is a graduate of a secondary technical program (*primero grado de formación profesional*) that prepares students for technical employment but also serves as a stepping stone to the *bachillerato* and postsecondary study (Spain).

Técnico especialista. A specialized *technician*, who has completed secondary-level professional preparation at the intermediate level (*segundo grado de formación profesional*) (Spain).

Tehničke škole. A four-year secondary school offering programs designed to prepare *technicians* for intermediate-level technical positions (Yugoslavia).

Teknikum. Two-year trade schools established by the Education Law of 1946 (Albania). See also *technical secondary school*.

Télé-enseignement. *Distance education* (France).

Telecourse. A college-level course offered via closed-circuit or broadcast television, which may or may not be taken for academic credit toward a degree or certificate. Sometimes supplemented by classroom sessions under the auspices of an instructor and often accompanied by assignments, written homework, and examinations. See also *educational television, Open University*.

Telelecture.
The presentation of a lecture to one or more classes at different locations via telephone lines that may permit two-way communication between the speaker and the audience.

Television.
See *educational television*.

Telewriting.
The use of telephone lines for the transmission of graphics, which are displayed on a television monitor or similar device; together with audio information it permits two-way conversation about visual material between a teacher and students at separate locations.

Tentative admission.
The admission generally granted to a transfer student on the basis of a transcript indicating satisfactory but incomplete work (United States). See also *admission condition*.

Tenure.
The status of a permanent faculty member until retirement age, granted to academic personnel after a specified number of probationary years and by vote of the appropriate tenure-determining body. After achieving such status, a faculty member may thereafter be dismissed only for adequate cause, such as physical or mental disability, financial exigency, or discontinuance of subjects taught by the individual concerned.

Tercéiro ciclo.
The last two years of the seven-year secondary school program providing preparation for the university (Angola).

Term.
A segment, usually half or a third, of an *academic year*. See also *nonresident term, off-campus term, quarter, semester, session*.

Terminal contract.
An agreement between an individual and a university or college that stipulates the time when services of the individual will not be required and remuneration will cease.

Terminal course.
See *terminal education*.

Terminal curriculum.   See *terminal education*.

Terminal education.   Postsecondary courses or programs that are not designed to lead to additional study. See also *terminal-occupational program*.

Terminal-occupational program.   A two- or three-year program preparing a student immediately for an occupation and not leading to additional study.

Terminal pay.   (1) The final installment of remuneration for work that is ending; (2) a financial settlement consisting of extra remuneration, such as three to six months' pay, in recognition of termination of appointment.

Terms examination.   An annual examination held by a college as a qualifying examination for university (or degree) examinations (New Zealand).

Tertiary education.   The third level of education after primary and secondary schooling, comprising postsecondary programs ranging from short-cycle medical, technical, teaching, and nursing programs to first-degree programs in colleges and universities and extending to advanced degree programs leading to master's and doctoral degrees. See also *primary education, secondary education*.

Test.   Any instrument, questionnaire, or device for measuring mental or physical capacity, ability, or achievement. See also *achievement test, aptitude test, diagnostic test, placement test, prognostic test, psychological test, standardized test*.

Test battery.   A group of tests administered to individuals or groups for a particular purpose, such as career counseling.

Test of English as a Foreign Language (TOEFL).   A test measuring competency in English of a person whose native language is not English. Many United States colleges and universities require satisfactory completion of this test as a prerequisite for admission of foreign students from non-English speaking countries.

Testing.
The selection, administration, scoring, and interpretation of tests given to measure achievement, award credit, select applicants for admission, and provide information for placement counseling.

Textbook.
(1) A book that provides basic information in a subject or course of study; (2) the principal recommended written source of information for a course.

Thammayut.
A reform Buddhist sect founded by Mongkut, a Thai king, in the early 1800s. The sect combined classical *Hinayana* and modern ideas and, due to its royal founder, had great influence in Thailand.

Thanawiya.
Arabic: general secondary education examination.

Thematic Apperception Test (TAT).
A psychological test that requires the examinee to interpret series of pictures. Analysis of these interpretations reveals various values and cognitive and personality aspects of the individual being tested.

Theological institution.
An educational institution that offers professional programs for careers in the areas of theology and religious education. Also called a religious school. May be independent or part of a university, *denominational* or *nondenominational*. See also *seminary*.

Theoria.
Aristotle's belief that the best use of leisure is the disinterested search for truth, not for utilitarian or economic motives but purely as an activity in itself.

Thesis.

A written presentation of research or study that is submitted as partial fulfillment of the requirements for an advanced degree. The thesis submitted for the doctor's degree is usually termed a *dissertation*.

Thick sandwich course.

A *sandwich course* that includes one full year of work experience in addition to three years of academic work. The work period may occur as early as the beginning of the second year but more commonly occurs after two years of academic work (United Kingdom). See also *sandwich plan, thin sandwich course*.

Thin sandwich course.

A number of periods of work experience, ranging in time from as few as two to as many as six months, spread throughout the academic experience of a student in a *sandwich course*. (United Kingdom). See also *sandwich plan, thick sandwich course*.

Third-world country.

Any country that is not aligned with either of the two major power blocks: the United States and its West European-Australasian allies, or the Union of Soviet Socialist Republics and the East European socialist countries.

Tiempo completo.

Full-time; refers to the workload of full-time faculty members in many Central and South American countries. *Tiempo completo, tiempo medio* (half-time), and *tiempo parcial* (part-time) all require different time commitments in the various countries. See also *full-time teacher*.

Title.

A designation referring to an individual's occupation. May be distinguished as (a) formal titles, such as Doctor or Reverend, which always precede the name; (b) semiformal titles, such as chairman or professor, which may precede or follow the name; (c) informal occupational titles, such as dean of the faculty, which indicates an educational appointment or successful completion of a program of study and which follow the name; (d) restricted occupational titles, such as Registered Nurse or Certified Public Accountant, which are awarded by the state or its subdivisions or by a chartered occupational society as a license to practice and which follow the name; and (e) professional designations awarded by chartered professional societies, such as Fellow of the American College of Surgeons, which also follow the name. See also *professional title*.

Título profesional. Spanish: occupational title. See also *title*.

Toga. The gown required for graduation at Oxford after 1636 according to the Caroline Code (United Kingdom).

Toga talaris. An appendage to the gown of the masters and bachelors in theology, consisting of an addition behind the elbow that extended gradually to the hem of the gown, worn in Europe in the sixteenth century.

Top management. The senior executive officers responsible for the entire operation of a business or institution. See also *management*.

Total enrollment. The number of students enrolled in all undergraduate, graduate, and certificate programs of an institution on a given date, permitting comparisons from year to year.

Továbbképzö iskolák. Two-year, secondary-level continuation school for industrial or agricultural studies (Hungary).

Town-gown. Of or relating to the relationships between a college or university and the citizens of the local city or town where the institution is located.

Trade and industrial education. Educational programs designed to develop skills, technical knowledge, and competency to enable individuals to undertake occupations in industry or to upgrade and retrain workers employed by industry.

Traditional education.   Informal education provided by societies, generally through the family, prior to or alongside of a formal educational system.

Trailer section.   A course that is repeated in the term following the term in which it is normally offered, used to meet needs of new students in programs that alternate work and study.

Trainee.   A participant in an administrative, technical, or vocational training program designed to develop job skills. See also *cooperative education, sandwich course*.

Training.   Broadly, the teaching in all programs leading to the acquisition of job-related skills. More specifically, the teaching in vocational, administrative, and technical programs where one learns by observation or practice, as opposed to programs that broaden one's general knowledge through reading and experimentation in laboratory work.

Training agreement.   A statement defining the period of work, hours, salary, and other information for student trainees in work-study (*cooperative education*) programs (United States).

Training college.   An institution, such as a teacher training college or a religious college, that offers training to those seeking to enter certain professions.

Training laboratory.   A facility where students may gain experience to enhance their understanding of human relations skills and increase their ability to analyze personal and group behavior.

Training plan.   A definition of what the learner or *trainee* is expected to learn and how and where the learner is to be taught (in classroom, laboratory, or on the job).

Training sponsor. The person who is responsible for providing instruction and on-the-job training for a student *learner*.

Transcript. A document presenting the educational record of a student, showing courses attempted, completed, grades, and degrees awarded, if any. The document is official when signed by the appropriate authority and stamped with the seal of the institution (United States).

Transcript evaluation. The appraisal of the official record of a student from another institution to determine eligibility for admission or advanced placement and to determine whether previously taken courses are acceptable substitutes for those offered by the institution to which the student is transferring (United States).

Transdisciplinarity. The establishment of a common set of axioms for a hitherto unconnected or partially interacting cluster of disciplines. See also *disciplinarity, interdisciplinarity*.

Transdisciplinary approach. The study or analysis of problems that involves courses or use of knowledge of more than one field of study.

Transfer credit. Credit earned in one institution or instructional program that is accepted by the institution or program to which a student is transferring (United States). See also *credit*.

Transfer curriculum. A program offered by two-year or short-cycle colleges that is acceptable to four-year colleges as meeting their degree requirements. Also called parallel curriculum (United States).

Transfer student.   A student, previously enrolled at another college or university, who is accepted as a candidate for a degree, certificate, or diploma, usually with advanced standing based on work completed at the previous institution.

Transient admission.   The brief admission or registration of a student who is enrolled at another institution (United States).

Transient student.   A student who is taking courses at an institution for transfer credit to the institution where he or she is a degree candidate.

Transnational institution.   An institution financially supported by more than one nation and enrolling students from the supporting nations on the same basis.

Transnational organization.   An international, nongovernmental, non-profit organization. See also *international organization*.

Transnational research.   Cooperation among scholars and scientists of two or more nations in the conduct of research. Research may either be so highly specialized that it can be accomplished only by scientists in different nations who have capabilities to carry out the research or it may be of such concern to all nations, such as solving problems of hunger and energy, that it requires international cooperation and communication.

Travel course.   Course based on travel or a planned tour. Reading to prepare for travel and a summary report on educational features are required. One hour of credit is usually given for each week of travel (United States).

Treasurer.   The officer in charge of business and financial affairs of a college or university (United States). Also called *comptroller, bursar*.

Trimester.   A term in the three-term system calendar. See also *calendar, Hilary, Michaelmas, Trinity*.

Trinity.   (1) The first quarter in the four-term calendar adopted by Harvard from the four-term academic calendar used by Oxford and Cambridge; (2) the first term in the three-term calendar adopted by other early United States colleges, such as William and Mary (the Easter term being dropped); (3) in the United Kingdom, the third term in the three-term calendar. See also *Hilary, Easter, Michaelmas*.

Tripos.   The final honours examination given at Cambridge University.

Trivium.   The elementary disciplines of the medieval curriculum consisting of grammar, rhetoric, and logic. See also *liberal arts, quadrivium*.

Tronc industriel commun.   The first introductory year of a four-year vocational secondary program (French-language systems).

Trust, charitable remainder annuity.   A plan whereby money or property is transferred to a trustee, such as a college or university, and is segregated from other funds, permitting the donor to personally design a life income plan that provides for fixed annual dollar payments to the beneficiaries—at best, five percent of the value of the gift property at the time the trust is created.

Trustee.   A member of the board of control or the governing board of a college or university which holds all property in trust. Usually serves for a limited period unless elected to lifetime membership.

Tuition.   The amount specified to be paid by students for instructional services of a college or university. See *tuition fee*.

Tuition fee.   The fee for educational services that the institution assesses to students at each registration. As generally used, synonymous with *tuition* in denoting the amount of money charged by an educational institution for instruction. In some institutions the term *fee* refers to charges that may be assessed to all students for certain items not covered by tuition or assessed to students only under certain circumstances, such as registration for a laboratory course or private music lessons or for late registration. In public institutions the tuition fee is often called the incidental or registration fee. See also *tuition*.

Tuition remission.   The cancellation of tuition, allowing students to receive instruction free of tuition expense.

Tutor.   (1) A member of the teaching staff who instructs and examines students, sometimes while maintaining residence with the same students; (2) an undergraduate or graduate student elected and recommended by a professor to assist other students by means of private conferences; (3) in certain universities, a member of the academic staff of a college appointed to give individual teaching and to direct the work of the students of that college in his special subject. In some cases a tutor may be appointed to act as an adviser to certain students.

Tutorial course.   A course completed by independent work under the direction of a faculty member, in which the student reports on work regularly and takes a written or oral examination. See also *correspondence study, Open University*.

Tutorial system.   A teaching method that relies on the student reading intensively on his own and presenting his knowledge verbally or in essays in periodic meetings with a tutor. The system was developed at Oxford and Cambridge, where class attendance in many courses is optional, and since has been adopted in many newer institutions. It is well suited to the humanities, but it is not as useful in subjects that require laboratory work.

Two-year college.   See *two-year institution*.

Two-year institution.   A college offering the first two years of college-level work leading to an associate degree and usually accepted for transfer credit by four-year colleges. Includes community colleges, junior colleges, two-year technical institutes, and two-year agricultural institutes. Many of the programs of two-year institutions are terminal, in that they do not require additional formal education for the pursuit of a career. Two-year institutions also frequently offer short courses, conferences, and adult education. They often have a special relationship to their communities by offering programs that provide skilled and semiskilled manpower for a variety of local occupations (United States). See also *short-cycle education*.

U

Umetničke academije.   Four-year postsecondary art academies (Yugoslavia).

Umetničke škole.   Four-year secondary schools specializing in the performing arts (Yugoslavia).

Unconditional admission.   The status of an applicant who meets all requirements for admission to the program he or she wishes to study.

Undergraduate.   See *undergraduate student*.

Undergraduate education.
The programs of study and courses that comprise the curricula leading to an associate or bachelor's degree (United States).

Undergraduate school.
See *undergraduate education*.

Undergraduate student.
A student who is pursuing studies leading to the first degree in a four- or five-year program, or leading to a certificate or associate's degree in a vocational or technical program of one to three years.

Undervisnings-assistent.
Faculty rank: part-time teaching assistant (Denmark).

Unexcused absence.
An absence from class or laboratory session without advance permission of the appropriate authority.

Unified studies approach.
The development of curricula to achieve unification and integration of knowledge by removing barriers between related fields of study.

Unifying studies.
See *unified studies approach*.

Union.
(1) A body of students organized to carry out student activities, such as a special society or group organized to hold meetings and debates. It may have its own facilities or separate building. Unions of this type exist in countries such as Great Britain, Canada, Australia, India, and the United States. (2) A faculty or staff organization established for purposes of *collective bargaining*.

Unionism.
The principle or policy of a group of workers organized for the purpose of collective bargaining.

Unit.
See *Carnegie unit, credit hour*.

Unit cost.
Total outlays divided by the total number of units; for example, institutional or de-

partmental student cost is the total institutional or departmental expenses divided by total institutional or departmental full-time equivalent students.

Unit cost study.

The study of cost of units as defined by management to determine what functions are being performed and the relative costs of each.

Unitary university.

A university where teaching and research are conducted on one campus or single center only (Bangladesh, India). See also *affiliating university*.

Unités d'enseignement et de recherche.

Units of a teaching and research, resulting from breakdown of old faculties (of universities) into smaller units under the Orientation Act of 1968 (France).

Universal access.

The admission of all interested students to some form of higher education based on secondary school or high school graduation (United States).

Universal higher education.

The availability of higher education to all, not attendance by all. Represents that stage of societal development where at least 75 percent of the entire population has obtained some postsecondary education.

"Universalización."

A strategy of the Cuban revolution to break down the walls isolating the university from society and to integrate workers and farmers into university study, with students and faculty carrying their skills to fields and factories.

Universidad a distancia.

(1) A Spanish university functioning on the principles of the *Open University*; (2) university programs that bring programmed postsecondary *extramural education* to areas where no educational facilities exist (Colombia).

Universidad nacional.
Spanish: National—that is, public—state-controlled university.

Universitas.
The medieval university, a corporation or guild of students and teachers.

Université du Troisème Age.
University of the Third Age, initiated in 1973 at University of Toulouse in France. This program has become a forerunner of other educational programs for the elderly by offering courses of a practical or intellectual nature geared to the needs of older students regardless of educational background. The basic program consists of two six-week sessions and an intersession during summer and offers a diverse program of social, cultural, and physical activities that complements more traditional sessions of lecture and discussion.

Universities Commission.
A body of selected persons, appointed for a specified period by the Queen in Privy Council to inquire into and report on matters affecting the universities. The commissioners have power to frame ordinances to carry out the conclusions of their report (United Kingdom).

University.
A complex institution that in the United States has a liberal arts undergraduate college, a graduate school, and two or more undergraduate and graduate professional schools awarding professional and doctoral degrees. In universities not following the United States model, instruction is offered in faculties, such as a faculty of medicine or a faculty of sciences. There is no separation into an undergraduate and graduate division, and students generally proceed directly on enrollment into their chosen faculty without first attending a liberal arts curriculum. Research is conducted for the discovery of new knowledge and services are offered to make instructional and re-

search activities available and useful to society. The scope of activities of a university is defined by the institution's charter, which may limit the type of degrees that may be conferred.

University Appointments Boards. An organization that advises students in the choice of careers and opportunities for employment after graduation (United Kingdom).

University branch. See *branch campus*.

University catalog. The official publication of a college or university that lists and describes courses, programs, and requirements for degrees; includes the names and titles of faculty and staff; and outlines the official calendar for the current and the next academic year.

University center. An institution differing from a full university in that it offers only a limited number of disciplines; often it is a locale for programs intended to foster cooperation among universities and industries.

University college. (1) A division or unit of a university offering special courses and programs for beginning or part-time undergraduate students; (2) a university-affiliated college that offers programs in a location distant from the parent institution; students take examinations prepared by the parent institution and receive degrees from the parent institution. See also *affiliated college*.

University community center. A center operated jointly by a college or university and the community in which the institution is located to promote public welfare through educational and civic activities (United States).

University council. In many universities, the governing body of the institution, with powers and duties generally spelled out in the charter. The composition of a university council under the British structure usually includes the chancellor, vice-chancellor, pro-chancellor, treasurer, and deans, and generally varying numbers of elected and appointed members. The powers of the council vary under the different charters but generally include making appointments; making or amending statutes; governing finances; investing, selling, and buying university property; making contracts; and delegating its powers to officers or committees. In South American universities the university council usually includes student members in varying proportions.

University extension.

Courses and programs that are conducted away from the main campus of a college or university. Such courses may be professional, nonprofessional, short courses, workshops, conferences, or correspondence courses. Extension programs are usually organized as a separate division of the institution (known as the extension division) with its own dean or director and with full-time and part-time faculties to conduct courses and programs throughout a state or region. In the United States these programs may lead to degrees or certificates. Extension programs of the colleges of agriculture in the United States are known as cooperative extension programs, with extension faculty and county agents working together to help rural inhabitants improve farming and homemaking techniques.

University Grants Committee (UGC).

The agency responsible for the financing of universities in countries following the British model. In the United Kingdom, the UGC receives from each of the universities estimates of current and noncurrent financial need which are combined and then submitted to Parliament. The funds appropriated to the UGC in lump sum by Parliament are then allotted to each university. The committee of twenty-one members is chosen by the secretary of state for education and science. Thirteen members are active academics, two are from another branch of education, and three are from industry, in addition to the full-time salaried chairman and his two part-time salaried deputies. Appointments are made for five years and may be extended. The original purpose of the UGC was to give financial support to universities from tax monies without political control or interference (United Kingdom).

University-level education.

See *university-level institution*.

University-level institution.

Any postsecondary educational institution offering doctoral programs and with a demonstrated commitment to pure and applied research as well as to teaching. Usually subdivided into *faculties, schools, institutes*, or *research centers*.

University museum.

A museum owned and operated by a university for purposes of instruction and enrichment of educational offerings in such subjects as fine arts, ceramics, history, and geography.

"University of the Air."

A concept first referred to publicly by Harold Wilson in a speech in Glasgow in 1963 when he advocated the use of broadcasting as an integral part of the teaching system. This was the original idea for what later became the *Open University;* however, broadcasting accounts for only one hour of twelve of the student's study time each week in the Open University.

University ordinance.

A regulation that has the force of an Act of Parliament, drawn up by university commissioners or by university authorities themselves. Any ordinance must be formally laid before Parliament and receive the assent of the Crown in council before becoming operative (United Kingdom).

University press.

A university-owned and university-controlled press for the publication of scholarly works of high quality but having limited marketability. Works may be those of institutions' own faculty or of other faculties.

University reform.

A process of planned institutional change of a fairly basic or structural nature.

University relations office.

An office that handles news releases, public information sources, and public relations functions of a university (United States).

University system.

The institutions of various nations or states that offer university-level programs and conduct pure research, as opposed to other types of postsecondary institutions.

University without walls.

Collaborative education based on the conviction that students should be involved in developing their own programs of study and utilizing many different educational resources, both off and on campus. A student and faculty advisor determine the educational objectives and then plan a program in accordance with these objectives. The program may vary in length from one to twenty years and may include a combination of internship, independent study, travel, course work, and programmed learning.

Unrestricted grant.

(1) Financial aid awarded to students without restriction as to institution of study or field of study; (2) grants of funds to defray operating and capital costs without designation as to specific use. See also *grant*.

Unrestricted scholarship.

Financial aid awarded to students without restriction as to institution of study or field of study. See also *scholarship*.

Upanayana.
Hindu ritual or ceremony of initiation and investiture with the sacred thread, marking person as "twice-born"; signifies handing of initiate over to private teacher.

Upanishads.
Intellectual and mystical Hindu interpretations and elaborations of the religious ideals and principles of the four *Vedas*. The Upanishadic period lasted from approximately 800 to 500 B.C.

Upasampada.
Full initiation after a minimum of twelve years of study as a monk or nun into the *Sangha* (Buddhist monastic community).

Updating courses.
The revamping of the content of courses to introduce new knowledge and up-to-date information.

Upper division.
The part of a curriculum following the *sophomore* year in a four- or five-year bachelor's degree program (United States). Contrast *lower division*.

Upper division student.
A student who has completed his second or *sophomore* year in a four-year program (United States).

Upper school.
The fifth and final year of the secondary school; actually at a higher level than secondary education, being equivalent to the first year of university (Province of Ontario, Canada).

Upward Bound.
Special college- or university-based programs for college-bound *disadvantaged students*, started in the 1960s by the United States Office of Education to provide academic assistance during the last two years of high school and to prepare and assist students to apply for college entry (United States).

Urban university.
A university located in an urban setting.

Urheberrecht.
German: Right of the author. See also *copyright*.

Usable instructional space.

All physical space involved in the instructional process, including classrooms, lecture halls, laboratories, and libraries.

al-Ustad.

Arabic: faculty rank: master or professor, the highest rank in early Islamic universities, such as the Nizamiya of Baghdad.

V

Vacation course.

A course offered during the summer or other vacation period to teachers and others wishing to refresh their knowledge or pursue special new subjects. Also called *summer school*.

Validation of degrees.

(1) The establishment and preservation of standards of degrees awarded by an institution; (2) the certification by an appropriate official that a degree has been conferred on a certain individual.

Vanredni profesor.

Faculty rank: *associate professor* (Yugoslavia).

Vedas.

Four collections of sacred Hindu religious hymns and scriptures of the pre-Christian era; the basis of ancient Hindu learning.

Vedic literature.

Literature of Vedas. See also *Vedas*.

Venia docendi.

See *licentia docendi*.

Venia legendi.

Permission to teach granted after examination to scientists who have carried out high-level scientific work (Austria).

Veterans' assistance.

An educational allowance made available to veterans to assist them in defraying costs of approved educational programs. In the United States, the allowance is currently authorized by Public Law 94.502, the Veterans Education and Employment Assistance Act of 1976 (S. 969), which also provides for rehabilitation and training benefits for service-connected disabled veterans and educational benefits for eligible dependents of certain deceased or totally disabled veterans (United States).

Vice-chancellor.

In many nations, the chief administrative officer of a university, who usually holds office until retirement. The title is comparable to *principal, president,* and *rector*.

Vice-president.

Title accorded to the second administrative officer or the head of a major division of a university headed by a president, like vice-president of academic affairs, vice-president of finance, vice-president of development, vice-president of student personnel affairs. See also *administrative officer*.

Vice-provost.

The officer who assists the provost in the administration of academic affairs of an institution, and who acts for the provost in his absence.

Vice-rector.

The officer who assists the rector in handling academic or administrative affairs and who acts for the rector in his absence.

Vihara.

A monastery that offered advanced Buddhist education (college) during the early Christian era and reached its zenith in the seventh and eighth centuries. If several *viharas* existed in the same center, the term used was *mahavihara* or university.

Vinaya-pitaka.

Burmese scripture of pragmatic and society-oriented Buddhist rules of conduct.

Visa.

Authorization issued by consuls allowing persons who are not citizens of a country to enter it. The United States issues two types of visas for international students. An F visa authorizes nonimmigrant student status for a period of one year and is subject to renewal, provided the student's passport is valid and he maintains a full academic load. A J visa authorizes exchange student status and permits stay in the United States for study, research, and teaching for a specified period. A holder of a J visa must return to his own country for two years before applying for an immigrant visa.

Viša škola.

Two-year postsecondary occupational school offering such programs as economics, medical training, teacher training, agriculture, and transportation, generally of a terminal nature (Yugoslavia).

Visitation.

A visit to an institution by representatives of an accrediting agency or evaluation committee (United States).

Visiting professor.

Title given to an outstanding authority in a field of knowledge who is temporarily appointed to give courses or a series of lectures in his special field; often used to attract scholars from other countries. Also called visiting scholar.

Visitor.

A person invited by a university to be a supreme officer and a final court of appeal. Generally an important personage, such as the head of state (Commonwealth Countries). See also *administrative officer*.

Visoke škole.

Four-year postsecondary institutions offering university-level programs leading to a diploma in such areas as technology, teacher training, political science, and music (Yugoslavia).

VISTA (Volunteers in Service to America) program.

A program that supports volunteers who work in locally sponsored projects in the United States; designed to strengthen and supplement efforts to eliminate poverty and poverty-related human, social, and environmental problems in the areas of education, health, community planning, housing, economic development, and social services.

Vocational counseling.   See *vocational guidance*.

Vocational curriculum.   A course or program of study leading to a diploma or associate degree that offers training required for specific skilled and semiskilled occupations.

Vocational education.   Programs designed to prepare individuals for gainful employment as semiskilled or skilled workers and as technicians and semi-professionals in recognized occupations; also prepares individuals to enroll in advanced technical educational programs. Also called occupational or *career education*.

Vocational guidance.   The counseling and advising on occupational programs, to assist students to choose careers, including such materials and activities as testing, films, classroom discussion, and field visits.

Vocational-technical program.   A type of short-cycle program in a variety of technical career areas (United States).

Volkshochschule.   Adult education formalized by the German Adult Education Association offering programs that generally do not lead to degrees. Some of the programs prepare adults for secondary school examinations (Federal Republic of Germany).

Volksschule.   (1) Primary school offering four years of education (Austria); (2) four-year primary school of a type that has ceased to function in most states (Federal Republic of Germany).

Volksschuloberstufe.   Senior division of primary school (Austria).

Voluntary accreditation.   Accreditation by external, independent organizations, which invite institutions into membership on the basis of on-site inspections of courses, programs, administration and academic standards, and degree requirements.

Voluntary association. An unincorporated group associated to promote a common purpose.

Voluntary withdrawal. A termination of attendance in a class, or departure from a school, initiated by the student.

Volunteer. A person who contributes his or her services to an organization for various reasons, such as for fund-raising efforts for a college or university.

W

Warden. In universities following the British system, the head of a college or of a student resident hall or hostel; in some cases the head specifically of a residence for women students (Ireland, Canada).

Warning. See *academic warning, disciplinary warning*.

Wastage. Broadly, that percentage of students who start and do not finish their programs of study. More narrowly, a function of national conceptions of the roles, purposes, and aims of higher education. If the role of education is to prepare trained manpower, wastage occurs when people are trained for fields where there are no jobs. If the role of education is to create a highly literate society, wastage occurs when stringent examination and quotas prevent all but a few citizens from completing an education. Wastage also occurs when teaching methods and materials are inadequate and students' potential for learning is not fulfilled. See also *attrition, student gross wastage, student net wastage*.

West African Examinations Council Certificate (WACE). A secondary school–leaving certificate. One of the certificates accepted for admission to higher education in some West African nations.

Wetenschappelijk medewerker.

Faculty rank: lecturer. Position requiring both teaching and research and divided into three ranks: (1) *mederwerker,* (2) *medewerker l^e klas,* and (3) *hoofmedewerker* (the Netherlands).

Whitsunday.

Third of three academic terms in some United Kingdom universities and certain other universities patterned on the British system. See also *Martinmas* and *Candlemas.*

Withdrawal.

A student's departure from a class or school by transferring, completing school work, dropping out, or by death. If the student notifies the appropriate authorities in advance, his departure is termed an *official withdrawal.* If the student stops attending classes without notifying authorities, so that failing marks are recorded and charged against him, his departure is termed an unofficial withdrawal. See also *involuntary withdrawal, passing withdrawal, voluntary withdrawal.*

Women's education.

(1) The provision of courses and programs for female students either in a separate college, a co-ordinate college affiliated with a college for males, or in a coeducational institution where female students are enrolled with males; (2) a program of studies, usually called *women's studies,* presenting the role of women in society.

Women's studies.

Courses on sex roles, sex inequality, politics of gender assignment, and male-female differences. Also called female studies, gender studies, feminist studies. See also *dimorphics.*

Work experience (exploratory).

The opportunity for students to observe and take part in a variety of job conditions in order to help determine career choices and to ascertain the suitability of an occupation for the student.

Work-experience credit.

Credit awarded for on-the-job experience

related to a field of study, usually limited in amount of credit to a portion of the total educational program. Credits may be *additive* or *nonadditive*.

Work-experience program.

An instructional program that provides on-the-job training, as an integral part of the curriculum, related to a field of study and supervised by a teacher-coordinator and employer. Required in *cooperative education, sandwich courses,* and many other programs.

Work permit.

Permission for a person to work in a country other than his own, often granted by a ministry of labor and manpower or by immigration officials.

Work-study program.

A program funded by the federal government under a 1965 act to assist needy students by providing part-time employment during the academic term (United States). See also *financial aid, work experience program*.

Workers education.

Education and training of trade union members sponsored by unions, sometimes in cooperation with educational institutions.

Workload.

(1) The total work assignment of faculty or instructional staff members, including the class hours and courses assigned to be taught; preparation and clerical work related to classes or courses to be taught; research assignments; college, university, or departmental committee work; advisory work; administrative assignments; and consultations with students. Also called teaching load. (2) The number of courses (or credits) carried by a student during a *term*.

Workshop.

An education program bringing together persons for organized group study, usually with the cooperation of specialized personnel, for a period of several days, with the participants working on problems of special concern to themselves or their organizations or college.

World copyright. See *copyright*.

Y

Yang-wu. The management of Chinese affairs by Western methods. A term used to indicate the officials within the top bureaucracy in China in the mid nineteenth century who advocated the application of Western methods in technology and diplomacy. Although their slogan was "Chinese foundation and Western use," they were concerned only with superficial aspects of Western techniques (Peoples' Republic of China).

Yearbook. A publication with a pictorial and written record of a college or university year prepared and edited by students of a *class* or by a special group and published either privately or under the auspicies of the institution.

Year-round university calendar. An academic calendar that includes eleven or twelve months a year, usually divided into four quarters. See also *academic year, Hilary, Easter, Trinity, Michaelmas.*

Yeshiva. An ancient or contemporary institution of advanced study and research of talmudic and rabbinic law with the authority to ordain graduates for the rabbinate. Rabbinical scholars trace the yeshiva to institutions established by Shem and his grandson Jacob (Genesis 46:28).

Youth agency. A governmental or private organization whose purpose is to deal with problems of adolescents and young adults.

Youth organization. A group of adolescents or young adults organized for various purposes, such as educational, political, recreational, or service activities.

Yüksek lisans.

Higher education qualification granted after one to two years of study following the first degree, *lisans diplomasi* (Turkey).

Yüksek mimar mühendis.

Higher qualification in architectural engineering awarded by technical universities after five years of study (Turkey).

Yüksek mühendis.

Higher engineering qualification awarded by Istanbul Technical University and Karadeniz Technical University after five years of study (Turkey).

Yüksek mühendislik.

An advanced degree in various specialties of engineering that requires from four to six years of study, depending on the institution (Turkey).

Yunku-won.

Research institute offering the bachelor's degree, *haksa* (Democratic Peoples' Republic of Korea).